CHAMPIONS FROM NORMANDY

RAFE DE CRESPIGNY

CHAMPIONS FROM NORMANDY

AN ESSAY ON THE EARLY HISTORY OF
THE CHAMPION DE CRESPIGNY FAMILY
1350-1800 AD

BY

RAFE DE CRESPIGNY

SAINT BARBARY
LILLI PILLI, NEW SOUTH WALES
AUSTRALIA

2017

© Copyright Richard Rafe Champion de Crespigny 2017

A catalogue record for this book is available from the National Library of Australia

For the Members
of a most enterprising and entertaining
Family

Epigraph: A Note on Pronunciation
The "pig" is silent – as in pork:
attributed to Constantine Trent Champion de Crespigny (1882-1952)

Foreword

In December 1988 I prepared *Champions in Normandy; being some remarks on the early history of the Champion de Crespigny family*. Since that time, the internet has made a great deal more material available, and there have been useful publications on French and British history. I have therefore revised and rewritten the earlier work with a slightly different title.

While the book is substantially longer, and extends through the eighteenth century, the essentials of the argument in the previous version remain the same: this is the story of a long-lived but essentially minor family in France, just within the fringes of the gentry, whose lineage can be traced in the male line back to the mid-fourteenth century, who prospered from their Huguenot connection, but acquired their greatest good fortune when they were forced into exile in England.

Richard Rafe Champion de Crespigny

CONTENTS

INTRODUCTION: Surname and Shield, Place and Lineage 1
    The surname and the shield 1
    The sites of Crespigny 6
    On genealogy, lineage and family 10
    Acknowledgements 10

CHAPTER ONE: The Material on the Pedigree 12
    Introductory 12
    The Lancaster Book 13
    The Kelmarsh Book 16
    The Consolations Book 17
    The South Sea Book 18
    The Reveley Book 21
    The original Pedigree Book and other provenance 24
    The Extract from the Register of the Court of Aides 26
    The College of Arms 27
    The Daumont Letters 28
    Summary: the text history of the family records 32

CHAPTER TWO: Calvados and the Duchy of Normandy 36
    Part I: A History of the Champion Family to 1600 36
        Chronology 1000-1600 36
        The geography and early history of Lower Normandy 37
        A note on noblesse, taille *and other terms* 39
        Maheas, Richard, Jean and Michel 1350-1470 40
        The seigneury of La Fleurière 1463-1641 50
    Part II: Tales, Legends and Fictions 58
        William de Crespigny and the King of England 58
        Mollerus-Le Champion and Mad King Charles 60
        Burke, Debrett, and Horace Round 66
        The Champions de Cicé and other reputed cousins 71

CHAPTER THREE: The Seventeenth Century:
        Huguenots and Crespignys 78
    Chronology 1600-1708 78
    The Huguenots and the royal government of France 1540-1629 78
    Richard Champion and the estate of Crespigny 80
    Claude Champion and the Vierville connection 84
    Nobility and Taxation: noblesse *and the* taille 90
    Persecution and the Revocation of the Edict of Nantes 96
    Emigration to England 100
    A Note on the Question of Compensation 106

CHAPTER FOUR: The First Generation in England (*c*.1685-*c*.1750) 109
    Introductory 109
    Chronology 1680-1740 111
    Pierre and his sisters 112
    Thomas, his wife Magdalen, and their family 119
    Gabriel, his wife Elizabeth, and their children 127

CHAPTER FIVE: English Establishment 1730-1805   137
- *Introductory*   137
- *Chronology c.1700-1800*   137
- *Philip and Claude, sons of Thomas*   139
  - Claude Crespigny (1706-1782) of South Sea House   140
  - Philip Crespigny (1704-1765) of Doctors Commons and Champion Lodge   147
- *The children of Philip Crespigny and Anne nee Fonnereau*   157
  - Susanna (1735-1766   157
  - Anne (1739-1782)   157
  - Jane (1742-1829)   161
  - Claude (1734-1818) the first baronet, and his family   162
  - Philip the younger (1738-1803), Member of Parliament   167
- *The children of Philip the younger*   176
- *Epilogue*   178
  - Crespigny in Australia   179

BIBLIOGRAPHY   181

INDEX   189

LIST OF TABLES

Table I: The First Generations 1350-1500	42
Table II: The Champion Family in Normandy 1450-1650	57
Table III: The Family and Kinfolk of Claude Champion de Crespigny *c.*1600-1750	110
Table IV: Putative kinship of Elizabeth Champion de Crespigny and the Glasscock family of Essex	136
Table V: Descendants of Thomas Champion [de] Crespigny *c.*1700-1800	138
Table VI: The Family of Claude Fonnereau *c.*1650-1750	151
Table VII: The Godparents of Philip CdeC's children with Anne nee Fonnereau	156

LIST OF MAPS

Map One: Lower Normandy	xiv
Map Two: The medieval provinces of northern France	xiv
Map Three: Detail from Sheet 95 of Cassini's *Carte Générale de la France*	7
Map Four: Sheet 94 of Cassini's *Carte Générale de la France*	9
Map Five: Detail of Sheet 94 of Cassini's *Carte Générale de la France*	9
Map Six: The region of the Champion family in southern Calvados 1350-1650	36
Map Seven: The area of La Fleurière	50
Map Eight: The territory south of Rennes in Brittany (1720)	72
Map Nine*: The Duchy of Normandy* (1635) by Willem Blaeu	76
Map Ten: Detail from Blaeu's map of Normandy	76
Map Eleven: Regions of Huguenot influence during the sixteenth century	79
Map Twelve: Northern Calvados and the southeast of the Cotentin peninsula	87
Map Thirteen: The Election of Vire in the late seventeenth century	92
Map Fourteen: The southwest of Lake Geneva	115
Map Fifteen: Spain in the early eighteenth century	123
Map Sixteen: The site of Doctors Commons, London (1720)	149
Map Seventeen: Camberwell and Peckham in the early nineteenth century	166
Map Eighteen: The County of Suffolk (1787)	172

LIST OF ILLUSTRATIONS

The shield of Normandy	xiii
The shield of the Champion family	3
A spreader/cross moline	3
Arms of the baronet and "commoner" lineages of the Champion de Crespigny family	4
An image of Saint Crépin	8
The Frontispiece of the *Lancaster Book* with the arms of the baronets	13
From the *Kelmarsh Book*	16
Front pages of the *Consolations Book*: the spread second title page and notes by Philip CdeC on the births of his children	18
Pages from the *South Sea Book* relating to Thomas and Gabriel Champion	20
Pages from the *South Sea Book* and the *Reveley Book* relating to Richard Champion	22
Pages from the *Reveley Book* with an account of the visit to Fleurière in 1843	23
Copies from the original *Daumont Letters*	30
Marriage shields of Richard Champion and Michel Champion	41
The donjon of the castle of Vire	45
Shields of the Champion de Cicé and Champion [de Crespigny] families	48
The landscape of La Fleurière	51
Marriage shields of Hebert Champion and Antoine Champion	55
Marriage shields of Raoul Champion and Jean Champion	55
Louis VI at Brenneville	60
Shields of the Champion de Caimbie, Champion [de Crespigny] and Marmion families	61
The Mollerus-Le Champion statement	63
Shields of the Champion de Cicé, Champion [de Crespigny] and Champion de Chartres families	73
The Huguenot Cross	79
Le Temple des Isles at Proussy in Calvados	81
Shield and coronet of Richard Champion married to Marguerite nee Richard	82
Portrait of Marthe nee du Bourget, mother of Richard Champion	83
Portrait of Richard Champion	83
Memorial to Claude CdeC and Marie nee de Vierville in Marylebone Churchyard, London	85
Crespigny House at Vierville-sur-Mer	86
The chimney-piece and coat of arms at Crespigny House	86
Shields from the marriage of Claude CdeC with Marie nee de Vierville	88
Portraits of Claude CdeC and Marie nee de Vierville [?]	88
Remains of the medieval castle at Vierville-sur-Mer	89
Page from the *Daumont Letters*: the Council of State held on 27 January 1681	98
Shield of Pierre Champion de Crespigny, Director of the French Hospital	108
The Seal of the French Protestant Hospital *La Providence* showing Elijah being fed by Ravens	113
Title page of *Mémoires pour servir a l'histoire du XVIII siècle* by Geronimo de Lamberty	117
Page from a letter from Philip CdeC to his uncle Pierre, 1736	117
Guidon of Cardross's Dragoons 1689-1690	118
Front pages of the *Consolations Book*: the first title page and notes by Thomas CdeC on the births of his children	122

A soldier of the 35th Foot [Donegall's Regiment and later Gorges']	126
The siege of Namur in 1695	128
The Siege of Gibraltar 1704	129
The Battle of Almansa 1707	130
Price of stock in the South Sea Company 1711-1855	141
The *Asiento* contract for the South Sea Company to trade with Spanish colonies in America	142
Trade label of the South Sea Company	141
South Sea House, London, in the early nineteenth century	143
The Dividend Hall of South Sea House 1810	144
Claude Crespigny, Secretary of the South Sea Company	145
Bookplate of Hugh Reveley, and the binding and bookplate of a book owned by Claude Crespigny of South Sea House	146
A Court Sitting at Doctors Commons 1808	148
Portrait of Claude Fonnereau	150
Bookplate of Philip Champion [de] Crespigny married to Anne nee Fonereau	152
Champion Lodge, Camberwell about 1800	153
Portrait of Philip Champion [de] Crespigny (1704-1765)	155
St Giles Church, Camberwell in 1750	157
Portrait of Susanna Sutton nee Crespigny (1735-1766)	158
Portrait of Ann Glover nee Crespigny (1735-1766)	158
HMS Argo	159
Arms of the Vernon family and a bookplate of J G Vernon, with Vernon impaling Champion de Crespigny	160
Trinity Hall, Cambridge, in the eighteenth century	161
Crespigny House, Aldeburgh	162
Heaton's Folly, Peckham, in 1804	163
Meeting of the Society of Royal British Archers 1794	164
Portraits of Claude Champion de Crespigny, first baronet, and his wife Mary nee Clark	165
Portraits of Philip Champion [de] Crespigny (1738-1803) and his second wife Betsy Hodges nee Handley	167
Portrait of Clarissa nee Brooke, third wife of Philip Champion [de] Crespigny with her daughters Clarissa and Maria	169
Portraits of Philip Champion [de] Crespigny (1738-1803) and his fourth wife Dorothy nee Scott	170
The Old Palace of Westminster 1834 and Old Palace Yard at the present day	174
Hintlesham Hall, Suffolk	175
Portland Place, Bath	175
Llangasty Talullyn and Cathedine in the County of Brecknock, Wales	176

THE SHIELD OF NORMANDY

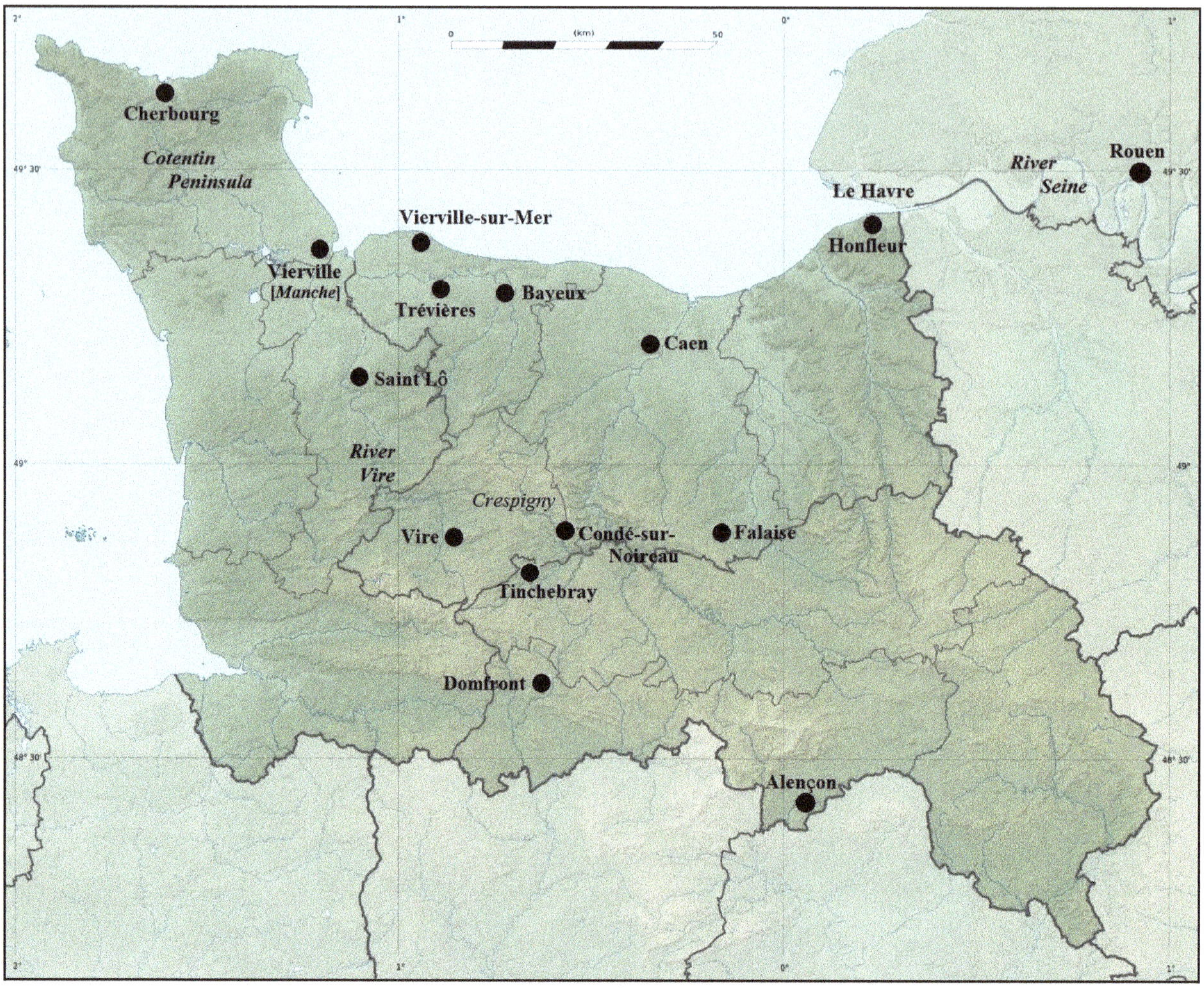

Map One: Lower Normandy

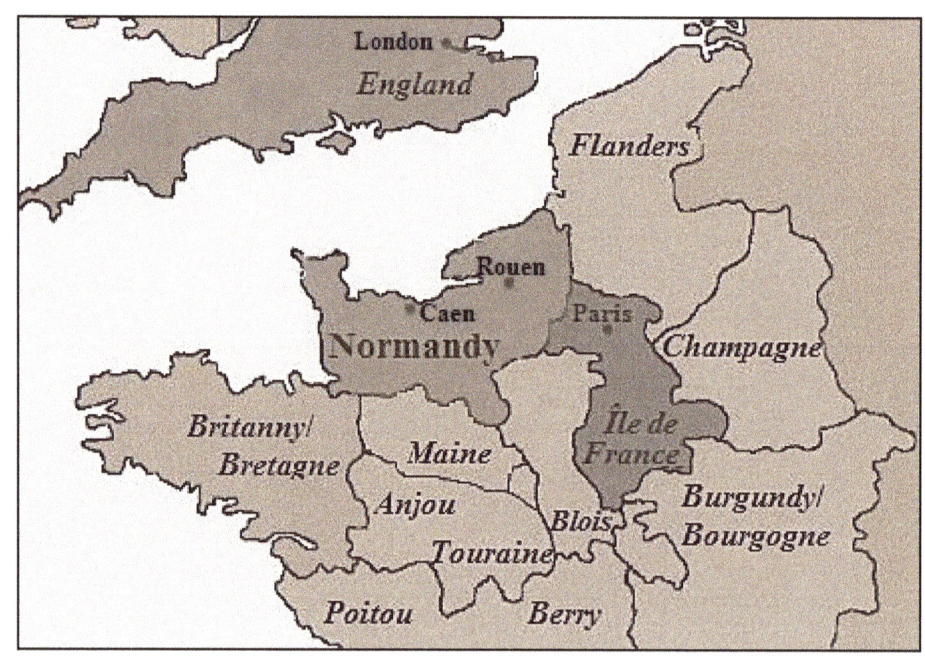

Map Two: The Medieval Provinces of Northern France

INTRODUCTION

Surname and Shield, Place and Lineage

The surname and the shield
The sites of Crespigny
On genealogy, lineage and family
Acknowledgements

The surname and the shield

The present work is concerned with the family now generally known as Champion de Crespigny. The full name dates only to the seventeenth century, but through an unusual set of circumstances it is possible to trace the male line back several hundred years earlier. The documentation, however, is sometimes obscure, and for the early years at least there is confusion between family history and family fiction.

Though the fact is all but obvious, anyone dealing with the history of a family called Champion must recognise that the surname relates to an occupation. During the Middle Ages "champion" described a man hired to take part in trial by combat on behalf of a person who was unable to fight on their own behalf: a woman, a child, a priest or someone otherwise incapacitated. In criminal cases it was expected that accuser and accused would each act on their own behalf, but in civil matters it was accepted that either side might call on the services of a champion.[1]

There must have been many calls for stout fighting men to engage in combat as rather practical attorneys at law.[2] The trade was not so common as that of a blacksmith or a miller but, like Smith or Miller, the surname Champion indicates only that at some relevant time – and possibly for only one generation – an early member of a lineage was noted for his employment in that fashion. And as with Smith and Miller, there is no reason to believe that anyone of the Champion surname is necessarily related to anyone else of that name.

In early centuries, on the other hand, there was one way to distinguish between families, even if they bore the same name: by the insignia they displayed on their shields and banners. At the present day, the study of heraldry is little more than a pastime, but medieval and early modern heralds were important state officials, and paid serious attention to an individual's right to bear arms and to the arms that he claimed. There were well-kept lists of the arms of gentry families, checked at intervals by "Visitations," and it was forbidden for one person to usurp the arms of another.

---

[1] The modern English word "champion" can be traced to old French *champiun*, old Norman French "*campiun*" and Anglo-Norman French *campion*. The *Oxford English Dictionary* relates the origin of the terms to "late Latin *campio, -ōnem* combatant in the *campus* or arena, professed fighter, < Latin *campus* field of athletic or military exercise, place of combat..." *e.g.* the Campus Martius of Rome.

There is an excellent account of the system in Neilson, *Trial by Combat*, with pages 46*ff* dealing with the occupation of a champion, and the development of the surname at 69, remarking that "the name carried with it into private and clerical life some tradition of turbulence.

"Round, "Huguenot House," 117-119, has references to the regular employment of champions by bishops and abbots, to a man hired as a champion for the County of Surrey, and to men named "Champion" who were connected only by their common calling.

For detail on Horace Round and his article concerning the Champion de Crespigny family, see Chapter Two at 70-71. The present discussion cites only a few of the points that he makes.

[2] In his chapter "The Folklore" of *Crisis of Truth* at 78*ff*, Green discusses the system, including an amusing account of a legal engagement with champions held at Northampton in 1330. The custom was already in decay by that time, but Guillim and Mackenzie, *Display of Heraldry*, 229-230, describes a formalised ritual for trial by combat in the sixteenth century, more than three hundred years later; on that occasion, however, one of the parties withdrew his plea and the match was abandoned.

INTRODUCTION

A celebrated case is that of Scrope *v.* Grosvenor. In 1385 it was found that two men in the English army, Richard Scrope and Robert Grosvenor, were bearing the same arms, *azure, a bend or*: a blue shield with a yellow diagonal bar. There was a lengthy court hearing, with hundreds of witnesses, and in 1389 Scrope was found to have the prior claim. On instructions from the king, Grosvenor took a new shield: *azure, a garb or*: blue with a yellow wheatsheaf.

In corollary, even though two men may have the same surname, if they bear different shields they are not related:

Examples may be seen in Fox-Davies, *Armorial Families* I, 249-250, listing gentlemen who shared the Chambers surname but came from different parts of England:[3]

- the shield of George Frederick Chambers of East Bourne in Sussex showed a negro cutting sugar-cane;
- the shield of George Henry Chambers, a new-made knight, showed a sailing ship;
- the shield of George Wilton Chambers of Yorkshire had a chevron and five yellow cinquefoils (a five-pointed leaf, formalised as);
- the shield of John Edmund Frederic Chambers of Nottingham had a pair of squirrels and three yellow cinquefoils.

None of the four lineages are related, and though the third and fourth gentlemen on the list shared the comparatively common insignia of cinquefoils, the shields are otherwise quite different.

Besides this, the *Armorial générale de France*, compiled for King Louis XIV in 1696-1700 by Charles René d'Hozier, lists a large number of families surnamed Champion from several different provinces, all with different shields. [The Champion de Crespigny family had emigrated ten years earlier, so it is not surprising that their arms are not included.]

This principle is applied in the work which follows.

It should be observed that the generic family shields advertised and sold at occasional booths in shopping malls and by such internet websites as "Arms and Badges" [www.armsandbadges.com] "House of Names" [www.theredthread.net], and "4crests" [www.4crests.com], are quite unreliable. The designs may or may not be connected to a particular surname but, as above, a shared surname does not necessarily indicate a common shield.

At the present day there is little control over the display of crests and shields. President Donald Trump of the United States has been criticised for his unauthorised use of the coat of arms of the Davies family, former owners of the Mar-a-Lago estate in Florida which he now owns. He was prevented from using it in Scotland, where Lyon King of Arms exercises legal authority, but there is no such difficulty in the United States, while the High Court of Chivalry in England is essentially in abeyance: during the last two hundred years only one case has been heard – in 1954 – and it is unlikely there will be more.[4] In other countries, including Australia, the use of arms is restrained only by laws of copyright – seldom applicable – and by a proper reluctance to claim insignia to which one is not entitled.

The basic shield of the Champion de Crespigny family is first ascribed to Maheas Champion about 1350. In heraldic language it is blazoned as *argent* [a white shield], *a lion rampant*

---

[3] *Armorial Families* I, 163-164; the arms of Sir Claude Champion de Crespigny, fourth baronet, are at 251; see also below at 4..

[4] On the Trump controversy see, for example, the *New York Times* of 28 May 2017: "The Coat of Arms said 'Integrity.' Now It Says 'Trump,'" by Danny Hakim.
  On the history and jurisdiction of the court, see Squibb, *High Court of Chivalry*, Chapter VII "The Dormant Years 1737-1954." Philip [Champion de] Crespigny (1704-1765) held a sinecure appointment as Proctor to the court: Chapter Five at 153.

sable [black], *armed and langued gules* [red claws and tongue], *in dexter base* [bottom left] *a fer-de-moulin* [or *cross moline*] *pierced sable* [black, with a hole showing through to the white of the shield behind].

The lion *rampant* is a common device, appearing on the royal arms of Scotland, of Bavaria in Germany and on a host of private shields. The *fer-de-moulin*/cross moline, also known as a mill-rind, is slightly less common, but is not exceptional. *Fer de moulin* [literally, "the iron of a mill"] is identified as the wrought piece which supports the upper stone of a corn-mill as it turns, but the shape may frequently be found as a spreader for the wall of a building. Though it is sometimes shown as a form of the Christian cross, it has no specifically religious significance.

A spreader on a wall in the Dordogne, France

More recent times have seen developments and adaptations of this basic family design.

Firstly, following the marriage of Claude Champion de Crespigny with Marie nee de Vierville in 1651, it became customary to quarter the Champion arms with the blue and white bars of Vierville.[5]

Second, at the beginning of the nineteenth century, when Claude Champion de Crespigny was made a baronet in 1805, that lineage became entitled to display the "red hand of Ulster" as a mark of that hereditary rank. In contrast, the descendants of Claude's younger brother Philip, while using the same shield, added a small crescent in the upper left corner: this is a so-called sign of "cadency" indicating the second son of a family, and though it is now largely meaningless – particularly since the end of the male baronet lineage in 1952 – it has continued in use for generations.

Confusingly, moreover, both branches of the modern family have commonly shown the lion not as *rampant* – with one foot down and the other three clawing forward – but *salient* "leaping," with both hind feet down and the two front paws extended together.

---

[5] Chapter Three at 87-88. Illustrations of the shields discussed here appear on the following page.

INTRODUCTION

The *Lancaster Book*, compiled by Sir Claude William the third baronet in the mid-nineteenth century, consistently shows the family lion as *rampant*, and this is followed by Fox-Davies' *Armorial Families*. The *Reveley* and *South Sea* books, however, have the lion *salient*, and this design is supported by bookplates and other sources of the eighteenth century, and notably by the very handsome shield of Pierre CdeC, son of Claude and Marie nee de Vierville, marking his position as a founding Director of the French Hospital in London in 1718.[6]

The two designs are similar, and it is impossible to judge which was the true original. For practical purposes, either form can be used, for it does not appear that any other family combines a lion, *rampant or salient*, with a cross moline.

There is likewise room for variation in the motto and the crest. The full motto in Latin – shared with a number of other families – reads *Mens sibi conscia recti* "A Mind Conscious of Its Own Righteousness," but the shorter form *Mens conscia recti* "A Mind which Knows what is Right" sounds a little less self-congratulatory.[7]

The essential crest is a mailed arm with a bare hand holding a broadsword emerging from a "cap of maintenance," but the arm may be shown as "cubit" length – from just above/below the elbow – or the hand may appear from little more than a metal cuff: the shorter form looks rather better. The cap of maintenance – coloured red with a turn-up of ermine [white with black markings] – represents the lining worn inside the crown of a king or the coronet of a peer. It is not common – most crests are connected to the helmet or based upon a simple band of colour – and as in the examples below it may be placed upon a helmet or used alone.

Left: Arms of Sir Claude Champion de Crespigny, fourth baronet, from Debrett 1904.
Centre: Arms of Sir Claude CdeC from Fox-Davies, Armorial Families, *1905.*
Right: Arms widely used by descendants of Philip CdeC, younger brother of Sir Claude the first baronet.

The "Red Hand of Ulster," mark of baronetcy, may be seen at the centre of both versions of the arms of Sir Claude the fourth baronet. The lions in the left-hand version are salient while the central design has them rampant: both shields are ascribed to the same man.

The small crescent in the top left-hand quarter of the right-hand "commoner" shield is the sign of cadency for a second son.

---

[6] The *Lancaster, Reveley* and *South Sea* books are discussed in Chapter One. On Pierre's appointment as a Director of the Hospital, see Chapter Four at 112-113; his shield is illustrated at 108.

[7] The original phrase comes from the *Aeneid* of Virgil, Book 1, line 604. In that context, however, it is part of a speech by the hero Aeneas, praising Queen Dido of Carthage and asking for her protection. It reads better as flattery of someone else than as a description of oneself.

INTRODUCTION

Inspired by the surname, there has been a widespread family belief that ancestors of the Champions de Crespigny had at some time held appointment as Champions to the Dukes of Normandy. It is a pleasant conceit, but historical evidence and circumstance are against the proposal. There were some high and hereditary officers of the duchy: the post of Chancellor lay with the Tancarville family, that of Butler was held by the Aubigny, and that of Constable was held first by the Montforts and later by the Harcourts; while the important position of Marshal appears to have been granted to individuals. There is, however, no independent record of any official Champion.

From 1066 onwards, moreover, except for the period of Duke Robert's rule between 1087 and his conquest by his brother King Henry I of England in 1106, Normandy was an appanage either of the kingdom of England or (after 1204) of the crown of France. In such circumstances there could be no occasion for the appointment of a ceremonial champion. In theory at least, a Champion might defend the right of a new king against rival claimants or critics at the time of his coronation, for it was neither desirable nor practicable for a monarch to defend his position in person. A sub-feudatory, however, no matter how powerful, held his position by royal authority, not by defiance of others; the service of a champion would be unnecessary and inappropriate at a ceremony of enfeoffment.[8] On any other occasion, a nobleman should be prepared to defend his position by the force of his own arm – or, if he were not capable of doing so, could hire a representative to take the field on his behalf.[9] There are a number references to champions hired by members of the nobility, by royal officials, and even by the kings of England and of France, but these were for particular occasions, the men employed did not possess high rank or dignity, the appointments were not hereditary and there was no association with landed tenure.[10]

In "A Huguenot House," Horace Round has some harsh words on the pretensions of the family using the "aristocratic suffix" *de Crespigny* after their arrival in England. There is, however, good evidence that the addition had been adopted and used in France well before the migration. Most obviously, the *Daumont Letters* are consistently addressed to and from a person named de Crespigny, and there is no doubt that the eponymous Daumont was in fact Pierre Champion de Crespigny, son of Claude.[11]

Though the original surname of the family was Champion, therefore, after the acquisition of Crespigny in the early seventeenth century *Crespigny* or *de Crespigny* was used either to make distinction from other families bearing the shorter and more common form or – as in the case of Daumont/Pierre – as a name in its own right. Over time, the full style Champion de Crespigny became established and was cited when necessary, as in the Certificate granted by the College of Arms to Pierre, Thomas and Gabriel, on the memorial

---

[8] "Huguenot House," 117-120.
[9] To give two examples:
In 1256, when the great nobleman Enguerrand IV of Coucy was charged with murder in 1256 he demanded judgement by his peers and trial by combat. King Louis IX, however, later known as Saint Louis, compelled Coucy to submit to a civil trial. There was great opposition, but Coucy was convicted, and the case made legal history. See Tuchman, *Distant Mirror*, 12-13.

And in a celebrated incident of 1398 Henry of Bolingbroke, Duke of Hereford and future King Henry IV of England, accused Thomas Mowbray the Duke of Norfolk of treason. They were due to make trial by combat on 16 September, but King Richard II intervened and sentenced both men to banishment: *Historians' History of the World* XVIII, 505 [on which work see also Chapter Two at 58] and Shakespeare's *Richard II*, Act I, Scene 3.
[10] Round, "Huguenot House," 117. The first appearance of a royal Champion in England was at the coronation of Richard II in 1377. The office is associated with the lordship of the manor of Scrivelsby in Lincolnshire and is held by the Dymoke family, but the coronation banquet of George IV in 1820 was the last ceremony in which the Champion played a role.
[11] See Chapter One at 28-31, Chapter Three at 97-99, and [Minet], "A Note on Daumont de Crespigny."

INTRODUCTION

to Claude and his wife Marie nee de Vierville at Marylebone,[12] and on some – but not all – legal documents such as wills. Commonly, however, a shorter form was used, and for most of the eighteenth century it was simply Crespigny – subject to erratic spelling on some occasions – while "Champion" may appear as part of the surname or as a given name.

During the nineteenth century the baronet lineage adopted the full form, but other branches were slower to do so. In 1849, when Philip [Robert] CdeC (1817-1889), founder of the family in Australia, was issued with a passport at St Mâlo for his journey to Paris to be married to Charlotte Frances nee Dana, he was identified as Philip C Crespigny, and his signature endorses the style.[13] The full surname appears quite late in Australia: Grayden's *Chronicle* indicates that Philip Robert's son Philip, future General Manager of the Bank of Victoria, began to use it in the 1890s and 1900s, and his obituaries in 1927 refer to him as Philip Champion de Crespigny. The tombstones of Philip's sisters Ada (1848-1927) and Viola (1855-1929) identify them as daughters of (retrospectively renamed) Philip [Robert] Champion de Crespigny.[14]

At the present day, while the surname is largely established in the full form for official purposes such as passports, day-to-day use varies from one member of the family to another, so that fathers and sons, cousins and brothers, may use different styles.

In the course of this work, I naturally refer to members of the Champion family up to the early seventeenth century simply by that surname. Thereafter, as seems appropriate, I reflect the form by which each appear to have styled themselves, allowing for the fact that in quoting or citing documents it is sometimes necessary to reflect the actual [mis-]spelling. For this "modern" period, moreover, in referring to the family or the lineage as a whole, it is often convenient to use the general abbreviation CdeC.

The sites of Crespigny
Perhaps the first point to clarify is that there are two places called Crespigny or something similar, though neither is of any significant size.[15]

Firstly, there is the *lieu-dit* – "[small] place known as" – or *hameau* "hamlet" of Crépigny, a short distance from the village of Saint-Jean-le-Blanc, which is itself some twenty-five kilometres northeast of Vire, just off the D 26 leading to Aunay.[16]

Crépigny is north of Saint-Jean-le-Blanc: to get there you go to the left of the post office and follow the D 106 toward Danvou-la-Ferrière. Three kilometres along is Crépigny

---

[12] Chapter Three at 106 and 85.
[13] The original passport is in my possession. Newspaper reports of the divorce of Charlotte Frances from her first husband John James similarly refer to Philip Robert as Mr Crespigny: *e.g. The Times* of London, 21 March 1849, page 7, cited in "Anne's Family History" *sub voce*.
[14] In a slight anomaly, the birth certificate for Viola, first of the children to be born in Australia, has the full surname; the registration of her younger sister Helen Rose, however, reverted to the simpler form.
[15] The different spelling is accounted for by the reform of French orthography in the late eighteenth century: the letter *s* in the old style indicated that the preceding *e* was accented; the new arrangement showed the accent directly above the letter. The change may be observed in such words as *hôtel*, formerly *hostel* (as in English); while some forms of modern German make comparable use of the letter *e* in to show an umlaut: *e.g.* Muenchen for München.

It will be observed that Map Three and Maps Four with Five below, from the eighteenth century, have other spellings of the place-name: in Map Three it is Crepigni, and in Maps Four and Five it is Crepigny. For two small places some distance apart there was limited interest in consistency.
[16] The general area of this first Crespigny/Crépigny is shown on Map One above. Map Six, at the beginning of Chapter Two, has a detailed road map of the region taken from *Michelin France* 2003.

Crépigny in Calvados, with postcode 14770, may be found on Google Maps, including aerial and street views. Though it is not common, the place-name appears elsewhere in France: there is a village named Crépigny in the Commune of Caillouël-Crépigny of the Department of the Aine, north-eastern France; postcode 02300, and a Bois de Crépigny near Azé in the Department of Saône et Loire.

Sud [Crespigny South], which is a private farm. One kilometre further is Crépigny proper. There is a small cul-de-sac with several houses – some quite old, a couple very new, but none of chateau quality – surrounded by fields of good farmland. The postcode is 14770. It is this territory which was acquired by Richard Champion in the early seventeenth century by virtue of his marriage to Marguerite nee Richard.

Map Three: Detail from Sheet 95 of Cassini's Carte Générale de la France[17] showing Crepigni, north of Saint-Jean-le-Blanc and close to Danvou

The earliest reference I can find for Crespigny in present-day Calvados dates to 1174, when King Henry II of England was also Duke of Normandy and held other great fiefs in western France. His Constable for Normandy, Richard de Humeto, issued a charter in his name granting William de Mesheudin the land of Crespigny.[18] The estate was therefore large and productive enough to form a knight's fee, supporting not only the fief-holder and his family, but also his esquires and other retinue with horses and armour – the base unit of a feudal array.

The name Crespigny – as in the old orthography – is probably related to Saint Crispin. According to legend, Crispin and his brother Crispianus were members of a noble Roman family who fled persecution for their faith. Arriving at Soissons in Gaul, they taught Christianity to the local people but supported themselves by making shoes by night, and

---

[17] The *Carte de la France*, commissioned by Louis XV in 1747, was the first topographical map of the whole kingdom. It was prepared in separate sheets, of which number 95, covering the region of Vire-Avranches, was surveyed between 1754 and 1762, and published 1761-1767.

On the map, Crepigni is shown to the east rather than, more accurately, to the southeast of Danvou, now Danvou la Ferrière; Saint-Jean-le-Blanc is circled to the south.

[18] *Calendar of Documents Preserved in France 918-1206*, Part 3: Calvados; item 552 from Cartulary I, No. 271, Trans. Vol. III, fo. 21, dated 31 May 1174.

This charter and other documents relating to the territory of Crespigny are listed also in the collection compiled by d'Anisy, volume 2 at 71-73, where Crespigny is identified as a parish under the Augustinian Priory [Prieurié] of Plessis-Grimould [now Plessis-Grimault], separate from its neighbour Saint-Jean-le-Blanc.

INTRODUCTION

earned sufficient money from that trade that they were able to give alms to the poor. The imperial governor, however, had them tortured, tied to millstones and thrown into the river. It is claimed that they survived, but were then beheaded by the Emperor Diocletian in 285 or 286 AD. They were later identified as the patrons of shoemakers and leatherworkers, and the date of their martyrdom, believed to have been 25 October, became their saints' day.[19] Since the Second Vatican Council of the early 1960s, Crispin and his brother are no longer recognised with a special day, but they retain their places in the official list of martyrs. They were popular in medieval Europe, and many churches have statues or shrines in their honour.

Image of Saint Crépin/Crispin in a church at Gien on the Loire
The saint is working with leather, and a jacket of that material is shown on the shield below him.

The second part of the place-name, *igny*, is common in the northwest of France: there are four places called simply Igny and many which include it in their name. It may have been derived from the Latin *ignis* "fire," with the extended meaning of a hearth-fire and hence a place of settlement. On this basis, Crespigny first acquired its name as a settlement containing a church, a chapel or some form of a shrine to Saint Crispin.[20]

The second place named Crespigny or a variant is a substantial house at present-day Vierville-sur-Mer, on the coast west of Caen and east of the base of the Cotentin peninsula. Vierville-sur-Mer is also in the Department/*département* of Calvados; the postcode is 14710. In the D-Day landings of June 1944 this area was identified as Omaha Beach.

In 1651, when Claude Champion de Crespigny married Marie, daughter of Pierre de Vierville, the couple went to live at Vierville-sur-Mer, in a house which was probably built for their use and served as the centre of a local estate. Evidently in reflection of the property held further south – and despite the potential for confusion – the new residence was named Crespigny, and can still be seen at Vierville-sur-Mer; it is discussed in Chapter Three.

---

[19] The battle of Agincourt was fought on 25 October 1415; Act IV, Scene 3 of Shakespeare's *Henry V* has the celebrated speech of the king on the eve of that encounter, referring to the "feast of Crispian."
[20] Mont Crespin, just east of Tinchebray, is very likely also named after the saint: see Map Six.

INTRODUCTION

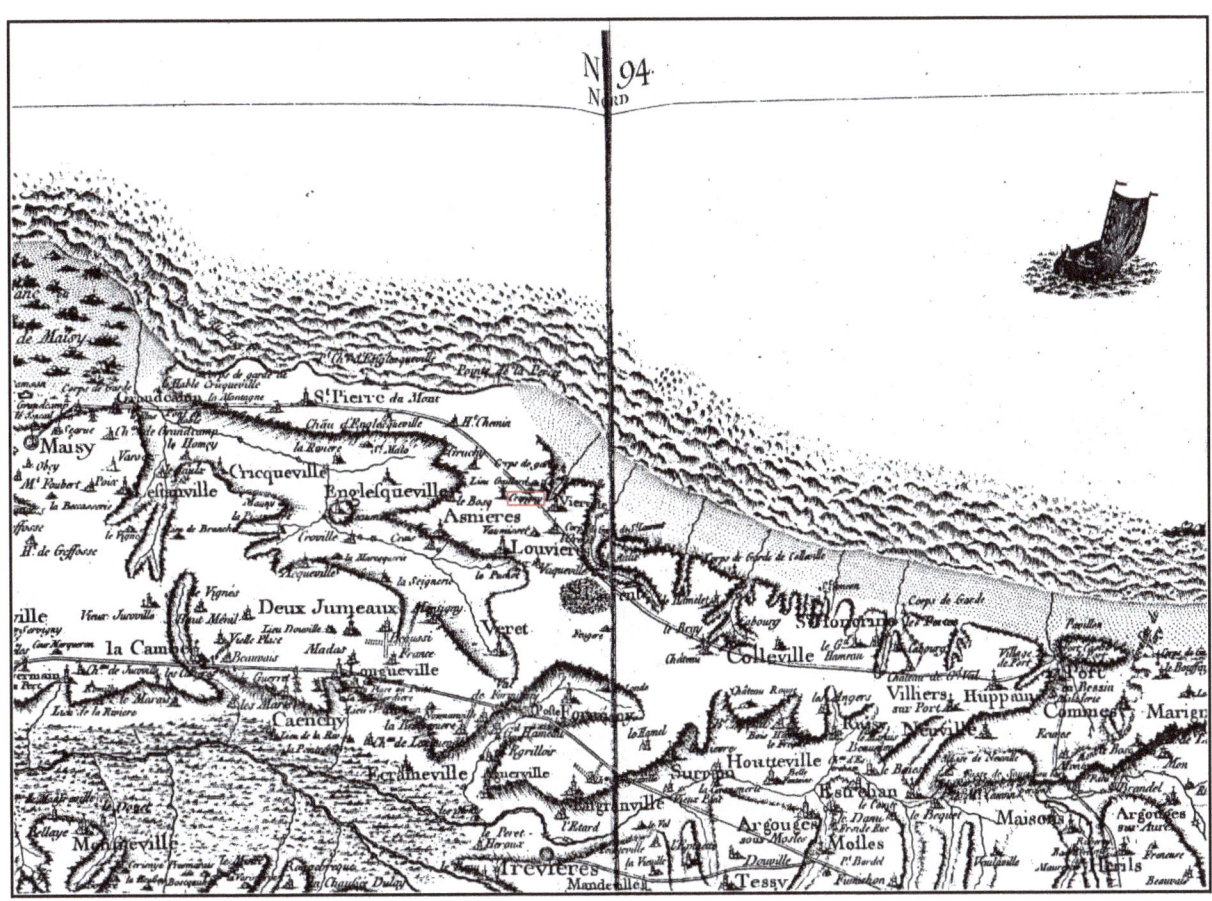

Map Four: Sheet 94 of Cassini's Carte Générale de la France
of the mid-seventeenth century[21] *showing Crepigny to the west of Vierville[-sur-Mer]*

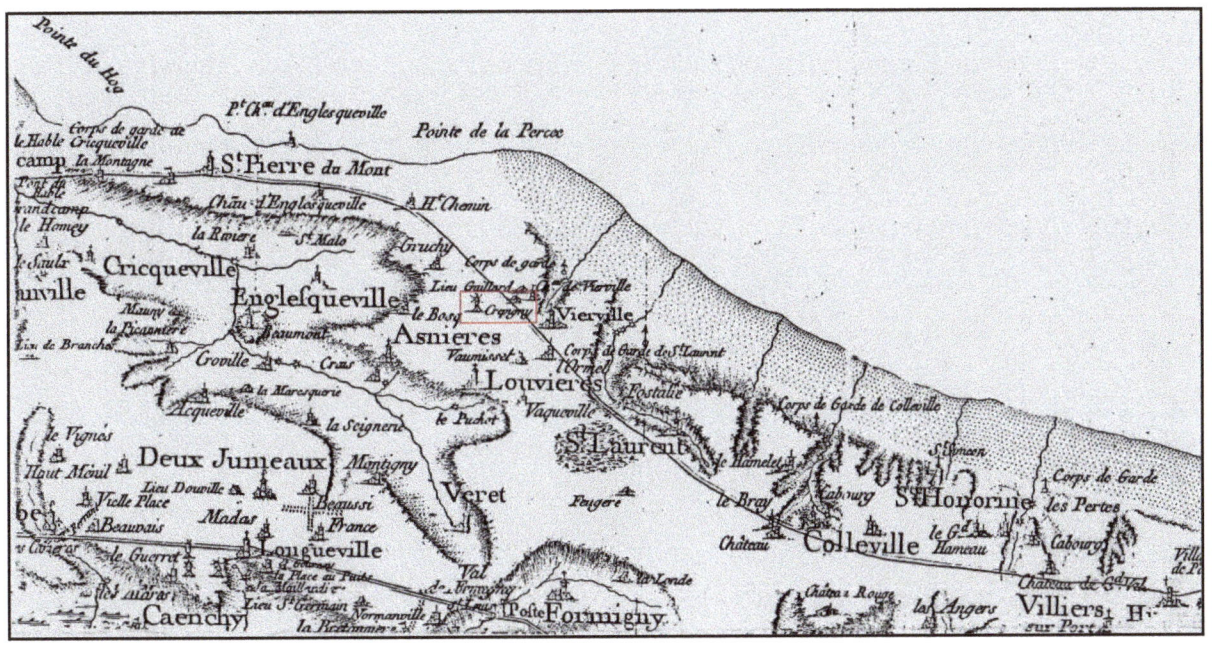

Map Five: Detail of Sheet 94 of Cassini's Carte Générale de la France *as above*

---

[21] On the *Carte de la France*, see note 11 above. Sheet 94, covering the region of Bayeux-Caen, was surveyed between 1754 and 1759 and published in 1760.

9

INTRODUCTION

On genealogy, lineage and family

The present work is concerned with the men and women who held the surname of Champion – and later that of Champion de Crespigny in one combination or another. Inevitably it deals for the most part with the male lineage. Marriages are recorded, but until the seventeenth century there is little known of the wives' family background or of their extended kinship.

While the history of a surname may be interesting, therefore, heredity, kinship and inheritance depend upon more than the male lineage; and in that regard this study is limited. The fortunes of the family have frequently been associated with marriages: during early generations several estates were acquired through dowry, contract or settlement; in the seventeenth century both Crespigny and the property at Vierville came from wives' families, and the success of the family in England after the forced emigration was markedly assisted by their marital connections and their distaff kinsmen.

Despite the limitations of male-based genealogy, therefore, one trait links the generations of Champions de Crespigny: they marry well.

Acknowledgements

I am most grateful to the late Miss Valencia Lancaster of Kelmarsh Hall, Northamptonshire, and to Stephen Champion de Crespigny. Both provided me with essential information, including copies of documents, published and private, together with Stephen's own detailed notes. It is to Stephen, moreover, that the family owes the major charts of descent, first prepared in the early 1960s and since developed and updated.

The late Bernie Grayden was good enough to take an active interest in the family's history, and did a great deal of research to produce *The Champion de Crespigny Chronicle*, a valuable resource particularly for the history of the family in Australia but with a great deal of information on earlier generations.

Most recently my daughter Anne Young has been maintaining a website, Anne's Family History: https://ayfamilyhistory.com, which is now archived by the National Library in Canberra. Her interests are broader than the Champion de Crespigny family, and she deals for the most part with comparatively modern times, but the entries are detailed and carefully studied, and she has been of constant and most valuable assistance in the preparation of this work.

Rafe de Crespigny
St Barbary, Lilli Pilli
New South Wales
December 2017

Chapter One

The Material on the Pedigree

Introductory
The Lancaster Book
The Kelmarsh Book
The Consolations Book
The South Sea Book
The Reveley Book
The original Pedigree Book and other provenance
The Extract from the Register of the Court of Aides
The College of Arms
The Daumont Letters
Summary: the text history of the family records

Introductory
As discussed in the Introduction, there is no reason to believe that any person with the surname Champion is necessarily related to any other person of that name. The present work is concerned with the family now broadly known as Champion de Crespigny. The full surname first appeared in the seventeenth century, but by an unusual set of circumstances it is possible to trace the male lineage several hundred years earlier.

The original documents which permit this research have been lost, but their content survives in well-attested secondary sources. This chapter considers those texts and other information available on the position of the family in France, from the earliest records to the time of migration to England at the end of the seventeenth century.

There are a variety of manuscripts in the possession of members of the family, notably in England, and I have most of them in photocopy form, chiefly provided through the generosity of Stephen Champion de Crespigny. In some instances I have seen the originals, in others I must rely entirely upon the copies, and on occasion I have to deal with transcriptions and even translations of items which I have had no opportunity to study adequately at first hand. Some arguments and conclusions are therefore very tentative.

Naturally enough, in considering the history of these early texts and manuscripts, I take account of the people who possessed them in more recent times, and some useful clues may be found from internal evidence dealing with events of the eighteenth and nineteenth centuries. I emphasise, however, that I am concerned chiefly with the history of the family in France before the end of the seventeenth century, and of the first generations in England during the eighteenth century. There is no attempt here to write a detailed history of the family during the nineteenth and twentieth centuries.

At the outset, however, it must be made clear that this work relies for the most part upon material held in England. I use and cite some general histories of France and a few French web-sites, but there is not a great deal of specific information in such sources.

Similarly, it is not possible or practicable to make good use of material such as tombs or inscriptions in France. Such information can be most valuable in England, particularly when a family has remained in one locality and has maintained a burial site or memorials in a parish church or graveyard: though abbeys and monasteries were ruined when Henry VIII proclaimed his independent Church of England, churches and cathedrals were left largely intact. In France, however, the Wars of Religion in the sixteenth century and the French Revolution at the end of the eighteenth century did far greater damage. Apart from destruction of buildings, it was a feature of Puritan, Protestant or anti-religious iconoclasm

CHAPTER ONE

that monuments such as tombs, gravestones and inscriptions, whether in public sites or in private chapels, were seen as signs of mortal vanity and were commonly destroyed or defaced.

So although the Champion family were Roman Catholic until the early seventeenth century, and in England one might hope for connection with an established church, this option must be discounted in France. It is impossible to ascertain or to guess where the family might have left inscriptions, and though some surviving records are being placed on the internet, many have been lost.[1] In particular, a great deal of Huguenot material in France was destroyed when their temples were abolished in the 1680s, and the best evidence may be found among the *témoignages* presented by migrant refugees as they arrived in England.[2]

We are left, therefore, with documentary and archival material, and it is these which I make chief use of in the discussion which follows.

The Lancaster Book

I have in my possession photocopies of several pages of a book which my father, Richard Geoffrey CdeC, acquired through the courtesy of Miss Cecily Valencia Lancaster, granddaughter of the late Sir Claude Champion de Crespigny, fourth baronet, in 1952. The title page reads:

> ***Extraction***
> ***et***
> ***descente de Noblesse antienne***
> ***de Maheas Champion Chevalier de***
> ***basse Normandie dans la Royaume***
> ***de France***
> ***le quel vivoit AD 1350***
>
> ─────────
>
> *Entered at the Heralds Coll:*
> *AD 1695*
> *by Pierre Champion de Crespigny Esc^{wr}*
> *eldest son*
> *of*
> *Claude Champion de Crespigny, Sieur de Crespigny*
> *and Marie de Vierville his wife*
> *who quitted France at the Revocation of the Edict of Nantes AD 1685*
>
> ─────────
>
> *In an action tried between the inhabitants of the Parish*
> *of Vierville and the above Claude held at Rouen before the King's Attor:*
> *ney Gen^{nl} Aug^{nst} 9^{nth} 1674 He proved his right to be enrolled as a* <u>Noble</u>.

A frontispiece to the book has a fine display of the family coat of arms, including the "red hand of Ulster" badge, symbol of the baronetcy.

The collection is in two parts. The first eight pages have a main text in good "copper-plate" hand, and list the male members of the family from Maheas Champion "died 1350" to Claude the first baronet, Philip his younger brother, and their three sisters Susanna, Anne and Jane. For all except this last generation there are illustrated shields of the family, without crest or

---

[1] One list from French records is "All Saone-et-Loire, France Births, 1546-1905" on ancestry.com.au. There is as yet no such collection for the Calvados, however, and the information would relate to Catholics, not/ to Huguenots: they can be of small value for the Champion family after their conversion to Protestantism in the seventeenth century: Chapter Three at 80 and 83.

[2] On *témoignages*, see Chapter Three at 103.

MATERIAL ON THE PEDIGREE

The frontispiece of the Lancaster Book
*with an elegant display of the CdeC arms.
The crest is borne on a knight's helmet, and the shield bears the "Red Hand of Ulster,"
badge of a baronet*

other appurtenances, but incorporating as appropriate the arms of each wife's family. The last shield to be shown is that of Philip, the father of Claude, Philip and their three sisters, which has Champion de Crespigny-Vierville impaling Fonnereau, the family of his wife Anne.[3]

In places among these first eight pages there are additional notes, one set written in a smaller, somewhat scrawled hand; one in a second copperplate hand.

The second section, two pages long, is written in the same scrawled hand as the notes in the first part, and is signed at the end "C.W.C. de Crespigny, Wivenhoe Hall, Essex, June 29 [18]60." This was Sir Claude William the third baronet (1818-1868).[4]

The two-page text is copied from the fly-leaves of a book *Les Consolations de l'Âme fidèle*, which had been owned by Thomas Champion [de] Crespigny (1664-1712) and his son Philip (1704-1765) and in which they recorded the births, deaths and marriages of the family from 1698 to 1742. I discuss the *Consolations Book* below.

A note by Sir Claude William at the end of his transcription adds:

> The book from which the above extracts were taken was given to me on January 29th 1860 by Mr Fuller Maitland of Stanstead, Bishops Stortford, J.P. of the co[unty] of Essex and I suppose was sold by Mr Herbert de Crespigny with the valuable library which was at Champion Lodge and which (*horrendum dictu* ["terrible to tell"]) was with all the family heirlooms bequeathed to him by Sir W.C. de Crespigny Bt.[5]

Since this note is in the same handwriting as one set of the annotations in the first eight pages, we know that Claude William the third baronet was responsible for them; and that provides a *terminus post quem*.

The second set of notes, in the "second copperplate" handwriting, is identified at the top of the sixth page, where there is a copy of the memorial inscription in Marylebone to Claude the immigrant (1620-1695) and his wife Marie nee de Vierville (1628-1708). On either side of this there are four drawings, three of seals and one of the mantelpiece decoration in the house at Vierville-sur-Mer in Normandy formerly called Crespigny. There are notes to these drawings both in Claude William's hand and also in the "second copperplate". One of the drawings of seals is signed in the "second copperplate" hand, "E.N.C.deC pinxit". This is surely Eyre Nicholas CdeC (1822-1895), son of the Reverend Heaton and first cousin to Claude William, being four years younger.[6]

The date of compilation of the first section is confirmed, and the compilers identified, by a very small inscription immediately below the motto scroll of the baronet arms which serves

---

[3] The Fonnereau connection is discussed with more detail in Chapter Five at 150-152.

[4] Sir William the second baronet, identified here as "Sir W.C. de Crespigny," was the grandfather of Sir Claude William the third baronet. Sir William had five sons, of whom the first four served in the Royal Navy. The eldest, Claude, was a Flag-Captain but died at Palermo in Sicily in 1813; the second, William Other, died on service in 1816 – neither were married.

Augustus James the third son was distinguished for saving the lives of several seamen in danger of drowning. He too became a Captain but died off Port Royal, Jamaica in 1825. In 1817 he had married Caroline the daughter of Sir William Smijth, Bart; they had three sons, the eldest being Claude William.

The fourth son of Sir William the second baronet was Heaton, who also served in the Royal Navy but later took Holy Orders; his eldest son was Eyre Nicholas CdeC below. The fifth son of Sir William was Herbert Joseph, who married Augustus James' widow Caroline nee Smijth and became step-father to Claude William as below.

[5] On the dispersal of the library by Herbert Joseph CdeC, see the *Consolations Book* below at 18 and Chapter Five at 165.

The phrase *horrendum dictu* appears in Virgil's *Aeneid* at line 454 of Book Four and line 565 of Book Eight.

[6] After graduating in medicine at Heidelberg in Germany in 1842, Eyre Nicholas was in England until he took up a position with the Indian medical service in 1845. He became known for his drawings of plants, both Indian and English.

as a frontispiece. On my photocopy the words are indecipherable, but Stephen CdeC, using a magnifying glass on the original, advises that the line reads:

Pix C.W.CdeC, H.CdeC, E.CdeC 1846

Pix must be an abbreviation for *pinxit* ["drawn" or "designed"]; C.W.CdeC refers to Claude William; E.CdeC would be Eyre Nicholas; and H.CdeC is most probably Henry Other (1819-1883), younger brother of Claude William.[7]

Stephen advises also that a bookplate of Sir Claude William is placed inside the front cover of the book, and the fly leaf is inscribed with the signature "C.C. de Crespigny 1846" – this is no doubt Claude William.

Besides the eight pages of main text, plus two pages of notes from the *Consolations Book*, plus title page plus the frontispiece with the coat of arms, one further page contains a sketch map of the Calvados region of Normandy, showing the sites of two places named Crespigny, one near Aunay and the other near Vierville. This appears to be from the hand of Claude William, and we know from the last pages of the *Reveley Book*, discussed below, that in 1843 he and his younger brother Frederick (1822-1887) made a tour of that region in Normandy. They visited the house called Crespigny at Vierville and studied the great mantelpiece, and a note in the second copperplate hand says that the arms on the mantelpiece were "sketched on spot by Sir C and F CdeC AD 1840." An additional note in Claude William's scrawled hand adds that the interior of the shield had been erased during the French Revolution.[8]

From internal and other evidence, therefore, the *Lancaster Book* in its present form was compiled in stages between 1830 and 1860. Though the title page describes the book as the lineage of the family presented at the College of Arms in 1695, this is not the original work which was entered nor is it a direct copy: all but a very few words are in English, and the document presented in the late seventeenth century must have been in French. In addition, the main text of the book is carried through in similar format to the latter part of the eighteenth century, particularly including the shields of Thomas and of Philip.

There exist, moreover, two other books, the *South Sea Book* and the *Reveley Book*, which support the presumption of the existence of an original *Pedigree Book* of the family, compiled in French and extending only to the three brothers Pierre/Peter, Thomas and Gabriel, sons of Claude and Marie de Vierville. On these see below, and also the sections on the *Pedigree Book* and on the decision of the Court of Aides.

So the present *Lancaster Book* is a combination of three periods of work:
1. pages one to three and the first part of page four translate an early French compilation, tracing the descent from Maheas Champion in the fourteenth century to Richard and Claude in the latter part of the seventeenth century;
2. there is then a continuation covering the period from the migration in the late seventeenth century up to about 1830, primarily concerned with the descent of the baronet family, and including the present title page and the coat of arms frontispiece;
3. between 1840 and 1860 Claude William and Eyre Nicholas added further notes, while Claude William also copied information from the flyleaf of *Les Consolations de l'Âme fidèle* giving details of the family of Thomas; he also compiled the map based upon his travels in the early 1840s.

Stephen has advised me that the *Lancaster Book* contains additional pages. The genealogy in copperplate continues to page 31, where the marriage is recorded of Sir Claude William to

---

[7] The letter *H* in the last set of initials could be read as an *A*, in which case it would presumably refer to Albert (1824-1873), younger brother of Eyre Nicholas and cousin to Sir Claude William. This is less likely.

[8] Though the date 1840 is written in Claude William's own hand, the *Reveley Book* tells us that he went to Normandy in 1843. On Crespigny House at Vierville-sur-Mer, see further in Chapter Three at 86-87.

CHAPTER ONE

Marie the daughter of Sir John Tyson Tyrrell in 1843. Then a page has been torn out, and the book continues with some handwritten notes commencing with the birth of Sir Claude the fourth baronet (1847-1935). The missing page probably contained notes concerning Sir Claude William, but according to Valencia Lancaster, grand-daughter of Sir Claude, he destroyed it because he hated his father. There is other evidence that the two were not on good terms.

The Kelmarsh Book
In June 1986, when I visited Miss Lancaster at Kelmarsh Hall in Northamptonshire, I saw briefly a manuscript, hand-written in copperplate, with a few amendments in pencil. This *Kelmarsh Book* is a copy of the *Lancaster Book*, in similar but not identical format: whereas the *Lancaster Book* has different scripts, the *Kelmarsh Book* is uniform, in good copperplate.[9]

I later received a photocopy of the upper part of the *Kelmarsh Book* version of the page of the *Lancaster Book* relating to the memorial inscription of Claude and Marie de Vierville, with facsimiles of seals and a sketch of the decoration over the fireplace at the Crespigny house in Vierville-sur-Mer. These may also have been drawn by Eyre Nicholas CdeC.

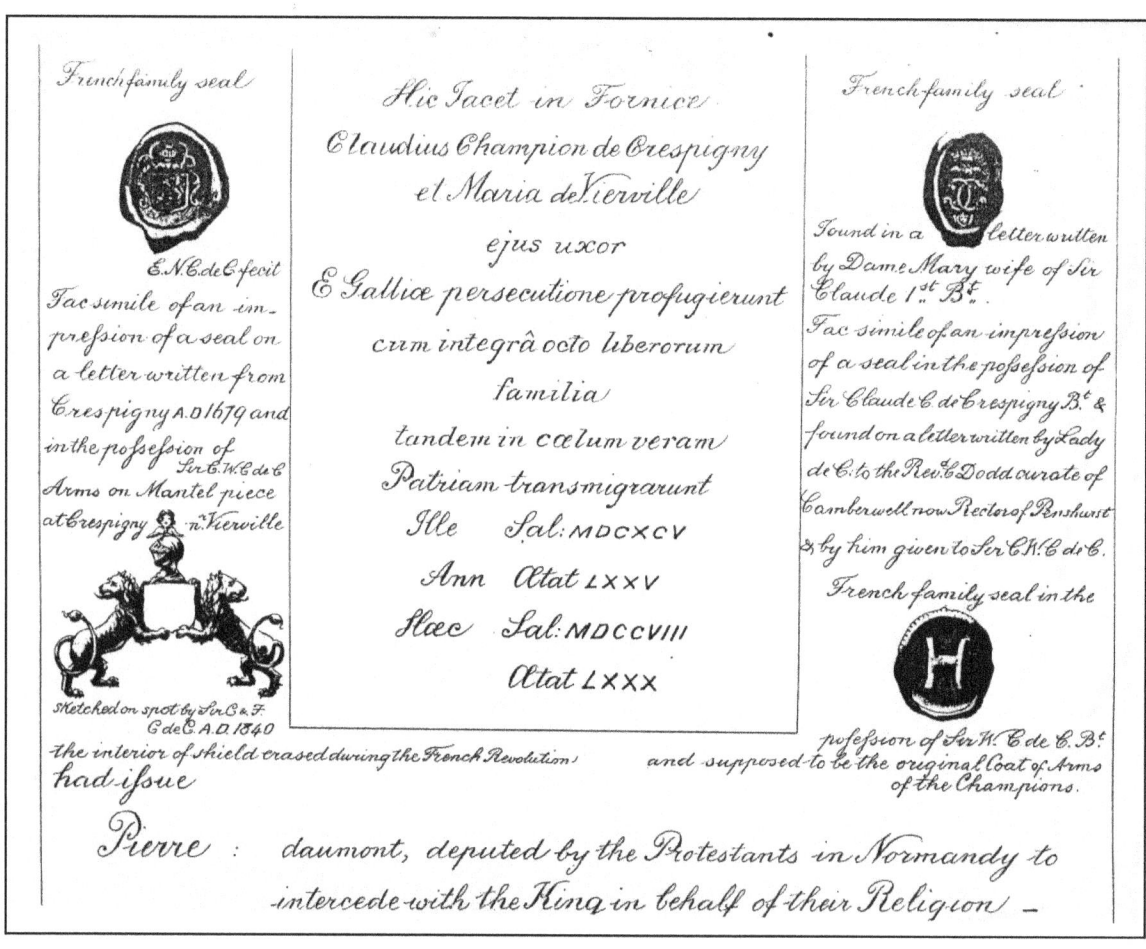

Photocopy from the Kelmarsh Book

While the wording is identical, the illustrations in the *Kelmarsh Book* are clearer. The picture of the mantelpiece in the *Lancaster Book*, at least in my old photocopy of it, is poor. The design shows a blank shield surmounted by a helmet facing dexter (to the viewer's left) and supported by two animals with heads turned away from the shield. In the photocopy of the

---

[9] In a letter of 8 August 1986, Stephen CdeC confirms that this *Kelmarsh Book* is a copy of the *Lancaster Book*.

Lancaster Book the animals are very blurred, and I long believed them to be foxes; the *Kelmarsh Book*, however, shows them as lions, matching the lion on the shield. In addition, while the crest on top of the helmet is no more than a blob in the photocopy, the *Kelmarsh Book* has the head of a cherub: a child's face supported on two folded wings.[10]

The Consolations Book
I have a photocopy of the original fly-leaves and title page of the old book referred to above by the title *Les Consolations de l'Âme fidèle*. The text of the accounts of the births and other details are as transcribed into the *Lancaster Book*, preceded by an additional inscription by Sir Claude William:

> Claude William Champion de Crespigny, given to him by Mr Fuller Maitland Esqre of Stanstead, Essex –
> the births are in the hand writing of Thomas (2nd son of Claude Champion Sieur de Crespigny) and his eldest son Philip Champion de Crespigny of Champion Lodge Camberwell, father of Sir Claude 1st Bart.
>
> Wivenhoe Hall – Essex, Jany. 29 1860

There are two title pages, the first with a picture of a skeleton with a scythe leading an elderly man through/to a graveyard. The second – shown immediately below – has the more cheerful vignette of a man sitting under a tree with birds bringing him food – the picture is labelled *Exspectando*, and surely refers to the legend of Elijah fed by ravens: 1 Kings 17:4-6.[11]

The second title page has slightly more information than the first. A translation from the French could read as follows:

> *The Consolations of the Faithful Soul against the Terrors of Death,*
> *with the dispositions and preparations necessary for a good ending.*
> *Ninth edition of those reviewed and corrected by the author.*
> *By Charles Drelincourt*
> *Pastor of the Reformed Religion,*
> *compiled at Charenton*
> *[published] at Amsterdam*
> *by Jean de Ravenstein, book merchant and printer of the city*
> *M.DC.LX/1660*

Charles Drelincourt (1595-1669) was a celebrated pastor of the Reformed Church and a prolific writer, and his book is a guide to Christian life, with emphasis on the death to come. It may have been in the family since its initial publication in 1660, but Thomas' first entry tells of the birth and baptism of Guillaume/William Champion at Bruges in December 1698 and it is possible that he bought the book at that time precisely for his first-born son.

Thomas died in 1712, and after the death of William in 1721 and that of his widowed mother Magdalen nee Granger in 1730, the book passed to the elder surviving son Philip, who added details of his own marriage and children.

The entries made by Thomas are in French, but Philip's, beginning with Thomas' death and mentioning his military service, are in English. The last in the series mentions the birth and baptism of Philip's daughter Jane – later to marry Henry Reveley as below – at his house Champion Lodge in Camberwell on Tuesday 12 October 1742.

---

[10] During a visit to Vierville in 1983, Stephen CdeC and his son Alexander photographed the chimney-piece: Chapter Three at 86. Though nothing could be identified of the shield or the crest, the supporters indeed appear to be lions.

[11] The first title page appears as an illustration in Chapter Four at 122. The full list of Thomas's childen is in Chapter Four at 121-122; the list of Philip's children is given by Table VII in Chapter Five at 156.

The image of Elijah and the ravens was used as the seal of the French Hospital *La Providence* when it was founded at London in 1718: Chapter Four at 113.

CHAPTER ONE

Though its records were no longer maintained, the book was kept in the library at Champion Lodge in Camberwell, which had been purchased by Philip in 1755 and became the residence of his son Claude the first baronet. In 1831, however, following the death of Claude's son the second baronet Sir William (1765-1829) the library and family papers were sold by his brother Herbert, much to the distress of the third baronet Claude William, Herbert's nephew and stepson.[12] Thirty years later the *Consolations Book* was found and returned by Mr Fuller Maitland, and it remained thereafter with the family.

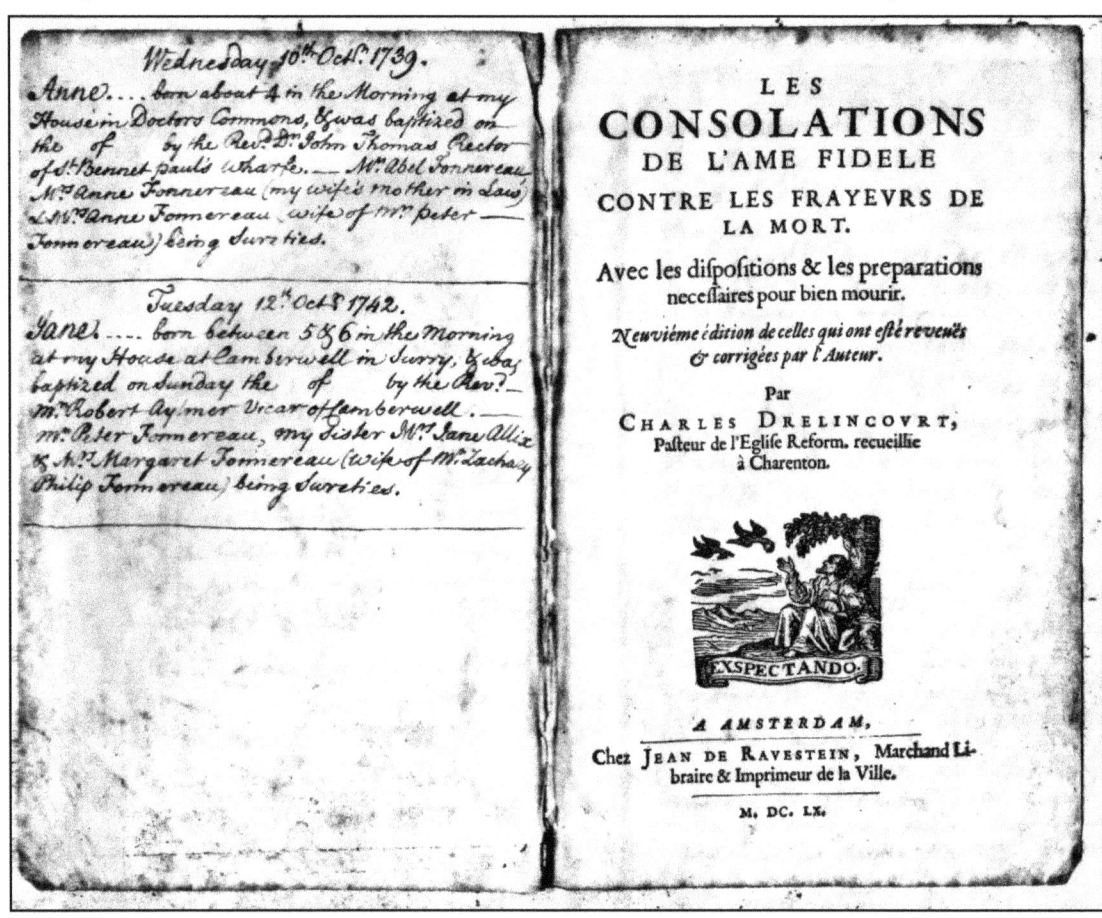

Spread of the second title page of the Consolations Book
with illustration of the prophet Elijah and the ravens and details of the contents
The facing page has notes written by Philip CdeC, son of Thomas, recording the births of his daughter Anne in 1739 and of his youngest child Jane at Champion Lodge in 1742.
[*The first title page is shown in Chapter Four at 122. See also Chapter Four at 156-157.*]

The South Sea Book
In June 1986, when I visited Kelmarsh Hall, Miss Lancaster showed me a small red leather-bound book of the family pedigree. The front cover bears the Champion arms of a lion and cross moline, the back has an insignia of intertwined Cs, and inside, on the marbled endpaper, is the bookplate of Claude Crespigny of the South Sea House, who lived 1706-1782. The first page has the handwritten annotation:

---

[12] Following the death of his father Augustus James CdeC in 1826, Sir Claude William's mother, Caroline nee Smijth, had married her brother-in-law Herbert CdeC: note 3 above.

Born in 1818, Claude William was eight years old when his father died, and eleven when he inherited the title after the death of his grandfather Sir William the second baronet. From the note inserted in the *Lancaster Book*, he had strong feelings about the loss of the family records, and relations with his mother and stepfather/uncle must have been strained.

Given to GChdeC by Major [Sely?] 1883
and by him to Sir Claude Champion de Crespigny.

This Sir Claude is the fourth baronet. GChdeC is probably George Blick CdeC (1815-1893), second son of Charles Fox CdeC, who was a son of Philip the younger brother of the first baronet; George Blick was thus a distant cousin of Sir Claude.

The book is handwritten in French. The title page may be translated as:

Genealogy of Peter [Pierre], Thomas and Gabriel Champion
Squires and Lords of Crespigny, brothers,
descended from Messire Maheas Champion, Knight,
who was living in the year 1350
and who bore [the arms of]
argent [silver], a lion [rampant] sable [black],
with claws and tongue gules [red],and a mill-rind also sable
as shown following

The body of the text has one entry to the page, beginning with Maheas Champion, who married the Demoiselle Busnel, and of their marriage had issue Richard Champion. At the base of each page is a shield with the simple arms of Champion together with, on occasion, another shield of the arms attributed to the wife's family for each generation. Unlike the *Lancaster Book*, the arms are not presented impaled, but on two separate shields.

The book has thirteen openings, with genealogy from Maheas to Pierre, Thomas and Gabriel Champion, the sons of Claude and Marie nee Vierville. The main text of all entries except these last three have considerable detail; Pierre and Thomas are cited only by name at the head of their respective pages, with the single Champion shield below, but Gabriel's entry mentions his marriage to Elizabeth nee Glasscock, and the Glasscock shield is shown with the Champion insignia at the base of the page.

The main text concludes with a copy of the English-language Certificate from the College of Arms accepting the Noble and Ancient descent of the family. Dated 4 May 1697 and signed by Piers Mauduit, Windsor Herald of Arms, and by Johan Gybbon, Bluemantle Pursuivant, it refers to the decision of the Court of Aides in 1674 and to perusal of an old book of the pedigree of the family.

The handwriting of the main text of the book is of good quality and quite ornate. On the two-page opening for Thomas Champion, however, there is an addition, also in French but in somewhat scrawled handwriting. This gives the year of Thomas' birth and mentions his marriage to Magdelaine nee Granger and his commissions as Captain in two regiments. It then lists his surviving children: William described as being of St James, Westminster; Jane who had married Gilbert Allix; and Philip CdeC, described as being of Doctors' Commons, who had married Anne nee Fonnereau and had children by her named Claude, Philip, Anne and Jane.[13] On the last page of the book, the same scrawled handwriting tells how Claude Champion married Mary Clark, was enfeoffed as a baronet in 1805, and had a son Guillaume [William]. The writing is in French, but it is miswritten or misspelt in several places, with corrections and alterations.

Finally, on the last half-page, following the Certificate, an even more scrawled hand, writing in English, records the marriage of Claude's son William, second baronet, to the Right Honourable Lady Sarah Windsor, daughter of the Earl of Plymouth. The date is not given [it took place in 1786] and, more curiously, an empty space was left for the personal names of the Earl of Plymouth and was never filled in – the owner of the scrawled English hand evidently knew little of that family. [The father of the bride was Other Lewis Windsor, fourth earl, and Other became a family name of the baronet lineage.]

---

[13] Details of Thomas' marriage, his military career, and his children are in Chapters Four and Five.

Chapter One

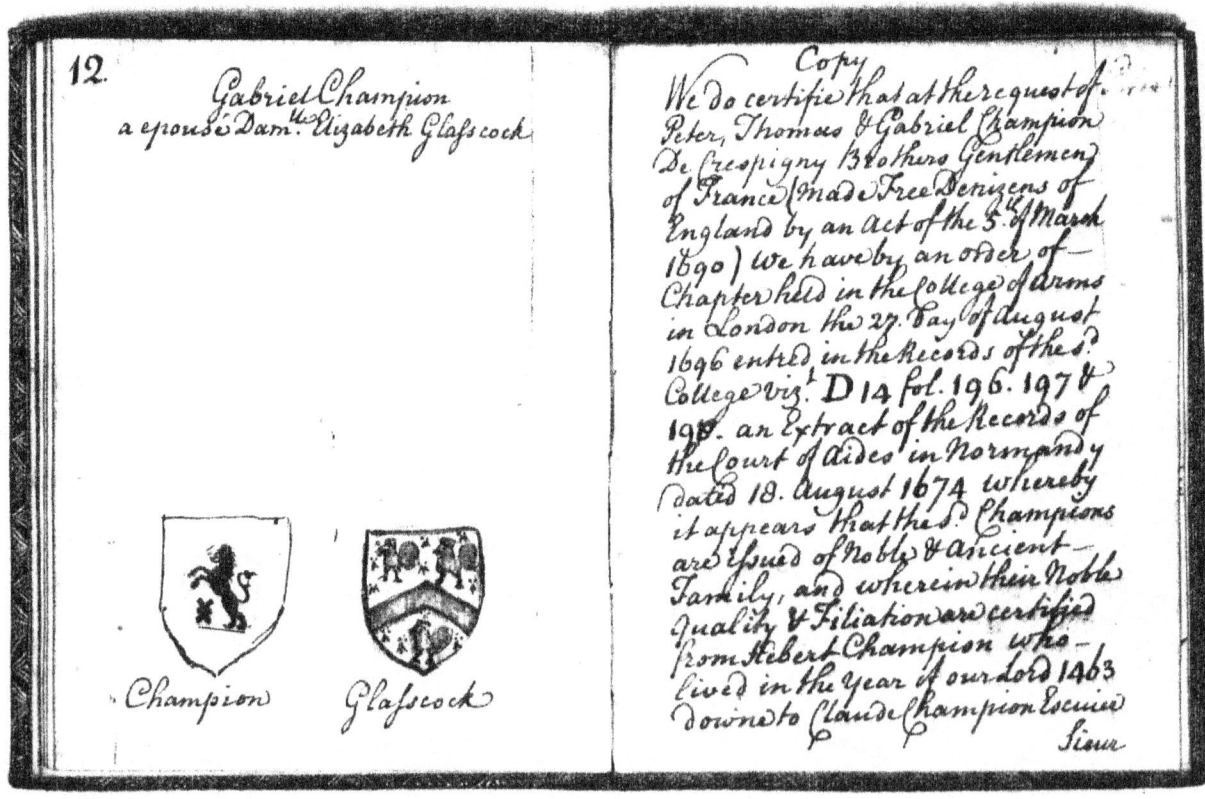

Pages from the South Sea Book *relating to Thomas and Gabriel Champion*

While the record of Gabriel's marriage to Elizabeth Glasscock matches the body of the text, and the Glasscock shield is included, the account of Thomas' marriage and children is by a different hand. On both sheets, moreover, it may be seen that the lion and cross moline on the Champion shields have been cut from another document and then pasted in: see page 21 immediately below.

Besides these three texts, the shields at the base of each page may represent a set of additions: though the writing of the surname under each shield (*e.g.* "Champion" or "De La Rivière") is in similar style to the ornate script at the head of the page, it is not quite identical. Stephen CdeC points out that the Champion insignia in each case has been added by cutting out and pasting the relevant portion from the bookplate of Claude Crespigny (or that of another person taken from the same block: we know that Claude gave his book-plate block to his nephew Claude, the future first baronet).[14] The cut-and-paste, however, is amateurish, and the drawing of the distaff shields is of poor quality. The artwork is by no means so good as in the *Lancaster Book*, nor is it worthy of the ornate handwriting which it is designed to illustrate.

So there were at least three and probably four people involved in the work: one producing the ornate handwriting in French; one the shields with their captions; another the scrawled handwriting in English; and another the scrawled handwriting in French. The latest date for the English hand is 1786, but the latest date for the scrawled French hand is 1805. It is not possible to identify the two writers, but Claude Crespigny of South Sea House was not one of them, for he died in 1782.

The book as we have it was thus compiled in stages:
1. the original genealogy, written in ornate handwriting in French;
2. the addition of shields, apparently taken from the bookplates of Claude Crespigny of South Sea House or those of the first baronet, at an uncertain date.
3. the scrawled French handwriting, no earlier than 1805;
4. the scrawled English handwriting, some time after the scrawled French.

In its original form it was either a direct copy or closely connected to the *Pedigree Book*.

Though Claude of South Sea House owned the book, it may have been compiled earlier: on this question, see *The Pedigree Book* below. In a codicil to his will, written in September 1782 shortly before his death, Claude left ten guineas to his godson Hugh Reveley "to help fit up his chambers when he goes to college" and also "my library of books wherever they are."[15] The same codicil, however, appointed Hugh's father Henry Reveley, husband of Claude's niece Jane, to act as an executor with Claude's nephews Claude the future baronet and Philip. Since the Reveley family already had a version of the *Pedigree Book* – on this, see below – it is likely that the executors agreed to pass this copy to the elder nephew Claude, and it later suffered the addition of the shields and the two sets of notes.

The *South Sea Book* remained in the baronet library until its dispersal by Herbert about 1830. It was recovered some fifty years later and returned to the family collection.

The Reveley Book

Jane, youngest daughter of Philip and Anne nee Fonnereau, and sister of Sir Claude the first baronet, was born in 1742 and married Henry Reveley in 1771. The Reveley family, later Jelf-Reveley, were landed gentry of Merionethshire in Wales. Jane evidently brought to that family another book of the Champion pedigree, which was added to by her descendants. I have not seen this book myself, but Stephen CdeC has given me a photocopy.[16]

In general format, the *Reveley Book* is identical to the *South Sea Book*: the title page is word-for-word the same, the wording is the same, and the arrangement of the pages, with text for each generation at the top half and shield or shields at the bottom, is identical. The handwriting, however, is slightly different, being in a lighter ornamented style, and captions

---

[14] Stephen CdeC, "Bookplates and Family Trees," 93.
[15] The will was proven on 15 October 1782.
[16] In a letter of 29 October 1988 Stephen CdeC advised me that he was lent the book to photocopy in the early 1960s by Mrs Bennett nee Reveley, sister of the then owner Algernon Reveley who died in 1974. In 1980 the book was in the possession of Mrs Gauntlet, niece of Mrs Bennett and the late Mr Reveley, who was living at the Reveley House at Bryn-y-Gwyn, Dolgelly, Merionethshire.

CHAPTER ONE

for the shields appear have been written by the same person as wrote the main text. The shields are not well drawn, but are better than those of the *South Sea Book*, and the Champion insignia is not identical from one page to the next – it has been drawn and is not based upon a pasted print.

The pages of the South Sea Book *(on the left) and the* Reveley Book *(right) dealing with Richard Champion. The copies have been adjusted in size to match one another. It may be seen that while the style is very similar, the two sheets are not written by the same hand.*
The French text reads:

Le dit Richard Champion Escui^r, fils du dit Maheas, epousa Dam^{lle} Mensant fille de Hector Mensant – Escuier Sieur de Lesentière en la paroisse de Bron en Bretagne, et par Lettres du Roi le dit Mensant prit le surnom D'Oüssé, et de ce Mariage sont issus Jean et Michel Champion Escuiers. Le dit Jean alla faire sa residence en Bretagne, et de lui sont sortis les Sieurs de Chartres, de Sisey et autres Champions de Bretagne.

This may be rendered into English as:

The said Richard Champion, Esquire, son of the said Maheas, married Mademoiselle the daughter of Hector Mensant, Esquire, Lord of Lesentière in the parish of Bron in Brittany,[17] and by [by the authority of] letters from the king the said [Hector] Mensant took the surname D'Oüssé, and from this marriage are issued Jean and Michel Champion, Esquires. The said Jean went to take up residence in Brittany, and from him are descended the lords of Chartres, of Cicé [as Sisey] and other Champions of Brittany.

The passage is discussed in Chapter Two.

The *Reveley Book* has a larger format: the pages measure about 19x11.5 cm, while those of the *South Sea Book* are 11.5x9 cm. And the *Reveley Book* is considerably longer: the first

---

[17] In fact, as discussed in Chapter Two at 72, the place-name Bron is miswritten for Bruz. It is notable that both texts make the same error, possibly through misreading the original in the *Pedigree Book*. They are followed by the *Lancaster Book*, which has the adopted surname as D'Oüessé, with an extra *e*.

fourteen pages after the title page have the same information as the *South Sea Book*, being the lineage to Pierre, Thomas and Gabriel the three sons of Claude and Marie de Vierville, followed by a copy of the statement from the College of Arms. There follow another thirty-two pages in a different hand, giving an account of the family, with anecdotes and quotations, up to and including the time of the third baronet Claude William CdeC (1818-1868). There is particular reference to the Reveley connection and to members of that family up to Hugh Reveley (1772-1851), son of Henry and Jane nee CdeC. The *Reveley Book* tells how Sir Claude William travelled to Jamaica to visit the place where his father was buried, and it also contains a journal with a description of Claude William's travels in Normandy in 1843, looking for family sites with his brother Frederick. Besides this lengthy extension, notes in the same hand are added to some earlier pages.

Stephen CdeC suggests very plausibly that the later additions were made by Henry John Reveley (1812-1889), probably in the late 1840s. A grandson of Jane nee CdeC, Henry John was a second cousin of Claude William and the most likely person to have been interested in the family and aware of the expedition to Normandy.

The original texts of the *Reveley Book* and the *South Sea Book* are taken from the same source, most probably from the *Pedigree Book* discussed below.

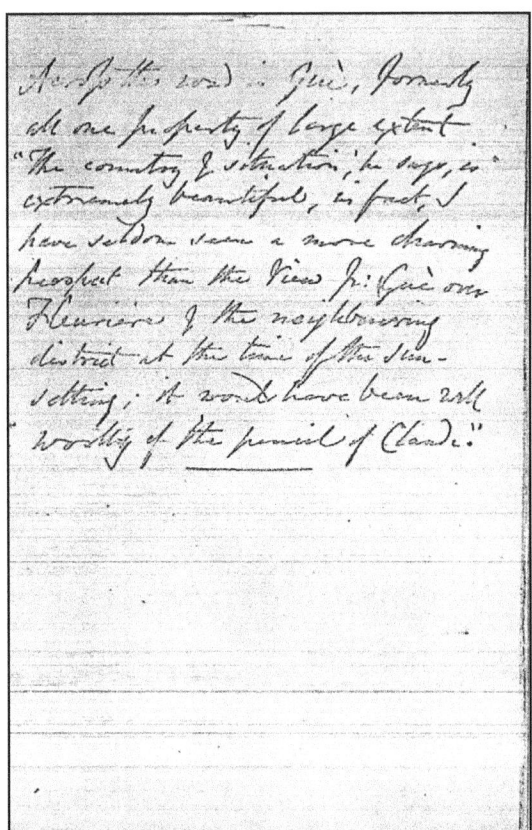

Two pages from the Reveley Book, *with part of an account of the visit to Fleurière made by Sir Claude William CdeC and his brother Frederick in 1843.*

At the centre of the first page is mention of a pavilion with a fine serpentine staircase, lately demolished, and at the bottom of that page it is noted that there is a small hamlet nearby called Championière, with one or two families of that name.

The second page refers to the property at Gué, and describes the sunset view over Fleurière as a subject worthy of the celebrated seventeenth-century landscape painter Claude Lorrain.

CHAPTER ONE

The original Pedigree Book and other provenance
Late in the seventeenth century and early in the eighteenth, there was a *Pedigree Book* of the family.

The most obvious evidence is the document from the College of Arms of 1697, cited in the *Lancaster*, *South Sea* and *Reveley* books, which observes that

> ...we do also certify that we have seen and perused an old Book of the pedigree of the said Champion from Maheas Champion Chevalier who lived in the year of our Lord 1350 down to the said Claude Champion their father....

The impression is that the book perused by the College of Arms included reference to Claude CdeC, but not necessarily to his sons Peter/Pierre, Thomas and Gabriel.

As to the question of the provenance and authority of this French-language *Pedigree Book*, we know that there were at least four cases brought against the Champion family claim to the rank of nobility, granting exemption from the *taille* tax: in 1591; in 1622; in 1667; and in 1674, when they were at last successful. For any such case, the claimants must have been required to present a document of lineage, and a passage from the *Recherche/Enquiry* of Intendant Chamillart in 1667 indicates that that royal official acknowledged the descent from Michel Champion of the fifteenth century. It was not the descent but the claim to nobility which was rejected, for the Intendant determined that it was Michel's brother Jean who had been ennobled, not Michel himself.[18]

So a document of the Champion lineage must have been needed for each occasion. The first draft would have been prepared in 1591 or earlier, and it was brought up to date until at least 1674, when the last case was heard and won in the Court of Aides just before the family left Normandy. The document, in the form of a *Pedigree Book*, was then brought with the family to England and shown to the College of Arms in 1695, together with the record of the Court of Aides. While the judgement of the Court of Aides was translated and preserved by the College of Arms, they found it necessary only to "peruse" the *Pedigree Book*, which would then have been returned to the family.

If we consider the original text of the *Reveley Book*, and its close relation the *South Sea Book*, then it appears likely that they are copies from the original *Pedigree Book*. Both are in French, and the main texts have no account of the genealogy beyond Peter, Thomas and Gabriel. Assuming they were made at the end of the seventeenth century, it was appropriate for them to include the three brothers who had put the case to the College of Arms, and equally sensible that they should not go further.

In this regard, the dating of the main text of the *Reveley* and *South Sea* books is noteworthy. We have noted that entries for the three brothers are very limited: while Gabriel's entry mentions his marriage to Elizabeth nee Glasscock, Pierre and Thomas are cited only by name. [The *South Sea Book* does have an account of Thomas' marriage and of his children and grand-children, but the writing differs from the main text and was clearly added later.]

While Pierre never married, Thomas wed Magdelaine/Magdalen nee Granger in 1696.[19] Gabriel, however, though born in 1666 and the youngest of the brothers, had married Elizabeth nee Glasscock by 1687.[20] This would explain why the marriage of Gabriel, but not the marriage of Thomas, was recorded in the *Reveley* and *South Sea* books. If the main text of those books followed the *Pedigree Book* as presented to the College of Arms about 1695,

---

[18] In his article in "A Huguenot House," Horace Round presents an attack on the family legends, and at 111-112 he cites the decision by Chamillart of 1667 with its references to the findings of 1591 and 1622. As below, however, the decision of Intendant Chamillart was the subject of the family's successful appeal to the Court of Aides in 1674. On Chamillart's *Recherche de Noblesse en la Généralité de Caen* "Enquiry into those of noble status in the *Généralité* of Caen," and the case as a whole, see Chapter Three at 91-93.

[19] Further details of Thomas are in Chapter Four.

[20] Further details of Gabriel are in Chapter Four, and his marriage is discussed particularly at 127-128.

then a marriage of 1687 could have been included but a marriage of 1696 would have been just too late.[21] Since neither text gives dates for births, deaths or marriages, one can draw no conclusion from the fact that the date of death of Claude in 1695 is not recorded.

I believe, therefore, that the *Reveley* and *South Sea* books are copies of the original *Pedigree Book* as shown to the College of Arms in the mid-1690s, and that they were prepared for the two younger brothers Thomas and Gabriel. Pierre, as eldest brother, would have kept the original and the *Reveley Book* was Thomas' copy, later transferred to his son Philip. Gabriel presumably had also a copy, and since his children had no descendants it may have passed to Gabriel's nephew and Thomas' younger son Claude of South Sea House.

On this basis, my reconstruction of the origins and later history of these texts goes as follows:
1. The original **Pedigree Book** – written in French, possibly accompanied by an English translation – was held by Pierre the eldest brother. Thomas and Gabriel had copies made soon after the College of Arms had issued its Certificate.

    When Pierre died unmarried in 1739, the *Pedigree Book* passed to his nephew Philip (1704-1765), eldest surviving son of Thomas and senior member of the next generation. It later went to Philip's elder son Claude (1734-1818) the first baronet.

    In 1829, however, the whole library was bequeathed by Sir William the second baronet to his youngest son Herbert, who sold almost everything, including the *Pedigree Book* which was never recovered.
2. When Thomas died in 1712, his son Philip inherited his copy of the *Pedigree Book*. After he received the original from his uncle Pierre in 1739, however, the copy became superfluous, so it was available for transfer to his youngest daughter Jane; when she married in 1771 this became the **Reveley Book**.[22]
3. Gabriel and his family moved to Ireland, and Gabriel died at Dublin in 1722, leaving a son Charles and a daughter Elizabeth. Charles, however, died unmarried in 1733, also in Ireland, and though Elizabeth survived him she too never married.

    It is possible that Gabriel's copy was then transferred to Thomas' younger son Claude of South Sea House, cousin of Charles and Elizabeth – we know that Elizabeth had some indirect contact with Claude following her brother's death[23] – though it is also possible that Claude had his own version prepared independently. In any event, after Claude's death in 1782 his **South Sea Book** went likewise to his nephew Claude, son of his elder brother Philip and the future first baronet, where it was held in the baronet library but suffered embellishments.

    Though the original *Pedigree Book* disappeared completely after the library was dispersed, the *South Sea Book* was recovered in 1883, when it was given by a friend to George Blick CdeC and passed by him to Sir Claude the fourth baronet; it has since remained in the possession of the family.

After all that, the **Lancaster Book** was compiled in the mid-1840s by Sir Claude William the third baronet, who was seeking to restore some part of the records which had been lost when the family library was dispersed by his uncle Herbert fifteen years earlier. Claude William was assisted by his brother Henry and his cousin Eyre Nicholas CdeC, the latter being largely responsible for the heraldic and other illustrations. The basic information probably came from

---

[21] The *Lancaster Book* states that the initial approach to the College was made in 1695, but the Certificate issued on 4 May 1697 refers to a meeting of the Chapter of the College of Arms held on 27 August 1696. The process was not swift.

[22] Jane had two elder sisters, Susanna and Anne, both of whom married; Susanna had a child which died in infancy, however, and Anne left no children: Chapter Five at 157-161. There is no way to tell whether the *Reveley Book* came directly to Jane or whether it had at some time been held by Susanna and/or Anne.

[23] Chapter Four at 135.

CHAPTER ONE

the *Reveley Book*, for this was the only compilation based upon the *Pedigree Book* which was available at the time, and Claude William's second cousin Henry John Reveley was in close connection. Sir Claude William also carried out investigations, research and writing on his own account. He evidently had access to documents held at the College of Arms, notably the ***Extract from the Register of the Court of Aides*** as below, which he used to add to the basic *Pedigree Book* information about Richard and Claude CdeC, and he also visited family sites in France. He later added information from the ***Consolations Book***, recovered in 1860, and a fair copy of the work became the ***Kelmarsh Book***.

The Extract from the Register of the Court of Aides
The *South Sea*, *Reveley*, *Lancaster* and *Kelmarsh* books all contain the text of the original Certificate from the College of Arms dated 4 May 1697:

> We do certify that at the request of Peter, Thomas and Gabriel Champion de Crespigny, brothers gentlemen of France made free denizens of England by an Act of the 5th of March 1690; we have by an Order of Chapter held in the College of Arms in London August 27th AD 1696 entered in the records of the said College *viz.* D 14 folio 196.197.198 an *Extract of the Records of the Court of Aides* in Normandy dated 15th of August 1674[24] whereby it appears that the said Champions are issued of a noble and antient family and wherein their noble quality and filiation are justified from Hebert Champion who lived in the year of our Lord 1463 down to Claude Champion Escuier Sieur de Crespigny father to the said Peter, Thomas & Gabriel Champion...

In 1963, when Stephen CdeC made enquiry at the College of Arms about the family pedigree, he was shown two documents: one being the old records, "which were the same as the Pedigree book belonging to Valencia Lancaster [*i.e.* the *Lancaster Book*], as far as the arms were concerned." The other was some pages of old legal French, signed at the bottom by P[ierre] Ch.de Crespigny in 1697.

In September 1964 the College of Arms gave Stephen CdeC a translation of these pages, entitled *Extract from the Registers of the Court of Benevolences in Normandy*.[25] This *Extract* must be the document presented by the Champion brothers to the College of Arms in London at the time of their application for registration in 1695, and the 1697 endorsement by Pierre was his certification for their records. I have a photocopy of the translation.

The Court of Aides, sitting at Rouen in association with the *Chambre des comptes*, the office for royal finances, was the highest authority on matters of taxation for the whole province of Normandy, and the *Extract* represents the last formality of the case between Claude Champion and the Citizens of the Parish of Vierville and their tax collectors. The judgement of the Court had been in favour of Claude Champion in 1674, but the parish and tax officers appealed, and the Court issued a final confirmation of the earlier judgement, which was then accepted.

So while the *Extract* is dated to August 1675, it is based upon a decision made on 9 August 1674. The legal technicalities of appeal and counter-appeal are confusing, but there is no question that the *Extract* confirms the existence of a judgement by the Court, and in the process of rejecting the appeal it rehearses in detail the evidence which had been presented.

The exact date of the judgement of 1674 has been confused by the various copiers of the Certificate: the *Reveley Book* and the *South Sea Book* give it as 18 August, and the text of the *Lancaster Book* has 15 August, though the title page has 9 August. The *Extract* itself refers to

---

[24] The copy of the Certificate in the *Lancaster Book* has this date as 1694; it should, of course, be 1674. The *South Sea* and *Reveley* books have it as 1674.

[25] "Court of Benevolences" here renders the French *Cour des Aides;*" *aides* was a euphemistic term for taxes paid to the royal government of France: Chapter Three at 90-93. I prefer to follow the Certificate from the College of Arms, rendering the title as Court of Aides, and I refer to the document hereafter as the *Extract*.

a basic judgement of 9 August 1674, but there were a number of other hearings and decisions, notably on 18 May 1674, when Claude Champion made his first appeal, and a supplementary judgement of 18 December 1674. The last dates involved are 13 August 1675, when the order for execution of the decision was signed on behalf of the Court, and 23 August 1675, when the attorney for Claude Champion served a copy on his opposite number representing the tax officers.

I discuss the nature and significance of this tax case in Chapter Three. For the history of the Champion family, however, the *Extract* is remarkable, not so much for the claim to ancient nobility, but rather for the documents which were introduced to support it.

In order that Claude Champion could prove he was of noble descent and entitled to the privileges of that rank, it was necessary for him to show that he and his ancestors had each been recognised as *Escuier*/Esquire, or given other noble attributes, from one generation to another without interruption. In order to do this, he presented an account of his family lineage:

> Writing furnished by the said Champion in the form of a Pedigree of his origin and descent from ancient nobility [this was surely the *Pedigree Book*];

and also a series of attested legal documents, starting from the original purchase of the property at La Fleurière by Hebert Champion in 1463:

> Contract of Sale drawn up in the presence of the Notaries of the Viscounty of Mortain on the 4th of May, 1463, made between Jean l'Anglais and Hebert Champion, styled Esquire, of the Estate of La Fleurière;

the point of this item being not so much to prove the purchase of the estate, but rather to show that an officially notarised document of that time described Hebert as "Esquire" and hence as a man of noble rank.

As a result of this requirement for proof, the *Extract* preserves a list of documents, all of which must have existed in 1674, providing a random picture of various activities of the family over more than two centuries. Many items are banal, but they are evidence of the existence of individual men and women, often with information on births, deaths or marriages, and they supplement the material in the *Reveley* and *South Sea* books and much of the *Lancaster Book*.

The College of Arms
We have already noted the correspondence and contact of Stephen CdeC with the College of Arms in 1963. A letter from York Herald of 12 June 1963 states that "your own line is taken down in our records to Philip Champion de Crespigny:" this is Philip the younger brother of Claude the first baronet, from whom all males of CdeC surname are now descended. At that time, besides obtaining the translation of the *Extract*, Stephen also saw the College records of the family matching the *Lancaster Book*].

College records trace the baronet lineage to 1944, but it was of course registered in stages, and in correspondence with Stephen in 1987 and 1988 Dr Conrad Swan, York Herald, identified them as follows:

- First are recorded eleven generations from Maheas Champion, living in 1350, to the brothers Pierre, Thomas and Gabriel, sons of Claude and Marie nee de Vierville, entered on 4 May 1697.[26] This is the original registration and the basis for the Certificate.
- Second is an extension of two generations and connection recorded with the Fonnereau family in March 1730/31.[27] This was no doubt entered as a result of, and in reference to, the marriage of Philip (1704-1765), son of Thomas and grandson of Claude and Marie

---
[26] 2.D14.197 (1966/198).
[27] 3.D14.146.

CHAPTER ONE

nee de Vierville, to Anne nee Fonnereau, which had taken place in February of that year. The Fonnereau family was wealthy and important, and this marriage did a great deal to establish the fortunes of the CdeCs in England.
- Third, there is an unfinished (*i.e.* unconfirmed and unsigned) pedigree entered about 1760/61.[28] It is likely this was intended to establish an independent record of descent, without reliance on the Fonnereau connection. It may have been initiated either by Philip or by his brother Claude of South Sea House.
- Fourth are four descents relating to the baronet family, in 1805, 1841, 1878 and 1944.[29]
    1805 was the year the baronetcy was granted to the first Sir Claude (1734-1818), eldest son of Philip and Anne nee Fonnereau, and the descent included his brother Philip (1738-1803), from whom all present CdeCs descend;
    1841 was in the time of Sir Claude William the third baronet and is very likely associated with the compilation of the *Lancaster Book*;
    1878 was in the time of Sir Claude the fourth baronet, establishing his own descent and inheritance from his father, whom he had succeeded ten years earlier. The College of Arms also has a collection of notes and rough drafts, likewise dated 1878, relating to a claim of "Seize Quartiers."[30]
    1944, last of the series, was in the time of Sir Henry (1882-1946), nephew of Sir Claude and the sixth baronet.

Besides these Stephen has proved and registered his own descent to 1969.[31]

Should any member of the Australian branch wish to record connection with the lineage in England, Stephen's is the closest line of descent: his great-grandfather George Blick CdeC (1815-1893) was the second son of Charles [James] Fox CdeC (1785-1875); Philip Robert CdeC (1817-1889), who came to Australia in 1851, was the third son of Charles Fox and the younger brother of George Blick.

The Daumont Letters

Volume 14 of the *Proceedings* of the Huguenot Society, published in London in 1931, contains "A Note on Daumont de Crespigny." The author is anonymous, but he was certainly William Minet, a regular contributor to the *Proceedings*.[32]

---

[28] 5.D14.140.

[29] Barts.3.6; Barts.5.203; Barts.7.132; Barts.13.162.

In addition, a connection with the Bowyer family was recorded in 1817 [Norfolk VIII/24 (1840)]. This must be associated with the marriage of Augustus James (1791-1826), third son of Sir William (1765-1829) the second baronet, who married Caroline, daughter of Sir William Smijth, in 1817. At that time Augustus James was heir to the baronetcy, his elder brothers Claude and William having died unmarried: note 4 above. Augustus James died in 1826, and it was his and Caroline's eldest son, Claude William (1818-1868), who became the third baronet.

A Bowyer baronetcy of Buckinghamshire had been established in 1660, and another Bowyer baronetcy of Berkshire was established in 1794. The Smijth baronetcy, of Essex, had been established in 1661. The Smijth family was connected to the Bowyers, and in 1839 the 10th baronet of the Smijth lineage took the name of Bowyer-Smijth, and quartered the arms of the Bowyer lineage: *Debrett, Baronetage* 1904, 69-70 and 567-568.

Since the marriage of Augustus James to Caroline nee Smijth in 1817 was the occasion for an addition to the genealogy recorded at the College of Arms, it is somewhat surprising that Caroline later allowed her second husband Herbert CdeC, brother of Augustus James, to deal so summarily with the collection of family papers; the more so as her son Claude William the third baronet was seriously interested in the history and resented the dispersal: 14 above.

[30] M.G.18/292. (Scott-Gatty coll). Seize Quartiers, "Sixteen Quarterings," means the claimant can show that each of his [sixteen] great-great grandparents was of gentry class with the right to bear arms – it is extremely unusual. Sir Claude hoped to enhance the record of his lineage, but his entry in *Debrett, Baronetage* 1885, at 152 has no mention of the achievement, so his claim was evidently unsuccessful.

[31] Norfolk 44.25.

The Note discusses the problem of identifying a man of this name among the Huguenot immigrants: he was said to have been a leader of the Trévières congregation, in competition with that of Vaucelles near Bayeux, shortly before the Revocation of the Edict of Nantes.

Among other items of evidence, the Note mentions a collection entitled *Lettres Françoises*, copied into a volume of vellum paper in a handwriting "more than copperplate," and accompanied by the baronet coat of arms.[33] The first letter is dated 1673, the remaining eight to 1679 and 1680. The first seven letters are in French, five of them with an English translation appended; the last two are in English; all, however, were part of a correspondence between Paris and Normandy, so the originals must have been in French. This small collection had been deposited with the family pedigree compiled by Henry Wagner and kept at the French Hospital "La Providence" in London.[34]

The Note states that the watermark in the sheet of paper used for the baronet coat of arms can be ascribed to 1840. Since the rest of the volume was on vellum, it could not be dated by similar evidence.

A far more substantial set of the *Daumont Letters* is held in the library at Kelmarsh Hall. It comprises two leather-bound volumes, one with the original text in French, the other its translation into English. I have a typescript copy of all the English translation, commissioned by Stephen CdeC in 1978 and sent to me in 1986, together with photocopied samples of the copperplate handwriting, of a flyleaf note made by Claude William the third baronet, of the Introduction which he composed for the collection, and also photocopies of some of the original letters, handwritten in French. The first of these letters, written by Je[an] Cartault at Trévières to M de Crespigny lodging in Paris, is dated 14 February 1679 – misread as 1673.[35] The final correspondence was in February 1682, and some additional papers confirm the success of the Trévières cause.

Sir Claude William's flyleaf note states that the original collection of letters was sold from the library of Champion Lodge in Camberwell after the death of his grandfather Sir William the second baronet in 1829. They were discovered at a public sale by a friend of the family, who presented them in 1841, and Sir Claude William had them translated and transcribed into copperplate handwriting by a Mr Pettit of Islington, who completed the work in January 1842. Claude William then composed his Introduction.

Though neither the author of the Note on Daumont, nor the very competent genealogist Henry Wagner, could identify anyone styled Daumont in the CdeC lineage, Sir Claude William argues in his Preface to the *Letters* that Daumont was a secondary name of Pierre/Peter Champion de Crespigny (1653-1739), eldest son of Claude and Marie nee de Vierville. Among the items of evidence:

- a letter of 7 January 1680 to M de Crespigny at Paris from a correspondent named Lamotte Blagny [typescript page 9] refers to seeing M de Crespigny (presumably the addressee's father Claude) and Mlle de Vierville (presumably his mother).[36]

---

[32] A letter of 27 November 1931 from C[harles] E[dmund] Lart to "Mr Minet" refers specifically to "your note on Daumont de Crespigny." Lart suggests that Daumont belonged to a different family, but the present discussion makes it clear that he is mistaken and that Daumont was a name used by Pierre CdeC.
The letter is in the Library of the Huguenot Society, and has been photocopied by Stephen CdeC.

[33] In present-day French the title would be *Lettres Françaises*, but it appears consistently as *Françoises*, a standard form in the seventeenth and eighteenth centuries. For obvious reasons, I refer to them as the *Daumont Letters*.

[34] Henry Wagner FSA [Fellow of the Society of Antiquaries of London], a founder of the Huguenot Society of London, compiled over nine hundred pedigrees of Huguenot families. They were deposited in the Society's Library and are now in the National Archives.

[35] On the traditional dating to 1673, see note 38 below.

[36] As in note 47 to Chapter Three at 99, M LaMotte Blagny was probably Jacob Philippe de Bechevel de la Motte de Blagny, who was later a close associate of the exiled CdeC family in London.

CHAPTER ONE

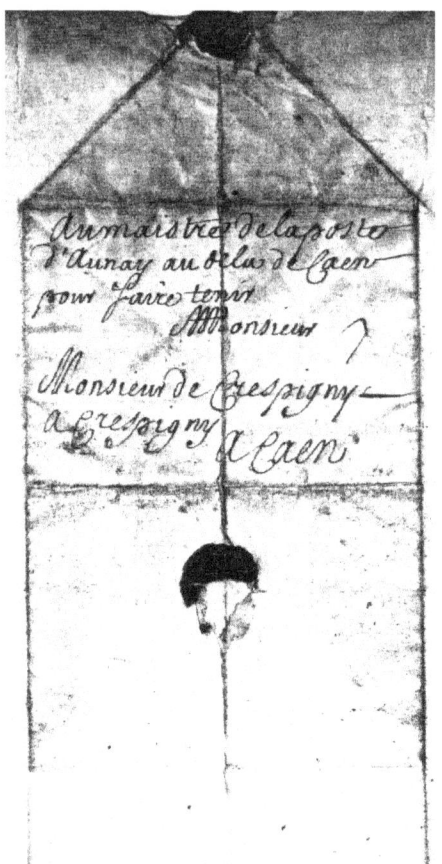

Copies from the original Daumont Letters

Left: Envelope addressed to Monsieur de Crespigny at Crespigny. The lines at the top request the post-master at Aunay in the region of Caen to hold it for him; the Crespigny referred to is the estate near Saint-Jean-le-Blanc, not the house at Vierville-sur-Mer.

Right: Letter of thanks sent by Pierre/Daumont [Champion de] Crespigny to Monseigneur Pellot, First President at Rouen. Pellot had written to members of the Royal Council in January 1680, supporting the claim of Trévières, where he was lord of the manor. [The English translation of Pellot's letter is at page 11 of the typescript copy of the Daumont Letters.*]*

The letter of thanks is dated 28 January 1681, the day after the Council made its decision in favour of Trévières, and is signed by "your humble and most obedient servant Crespigny, Deputy of those of the [Reformed] Religion at Trévières." [The English translation is at page 81 of the typescript copy of the Letters*].*

Though it is an original document of the seventeenth century, this cannot be the letter itself, for that went President Pellot. It is a file copy kept for reference.

- a letter of 15 December 1680, signed "Daumont" is sealed with the family seal of the lion salient with a cross moline [typescript page 66 with a note by Stephen CdeC];
- a letter of 4 February 1682 [typescript page 94], written by de Crespigny from Crespigny, refers to the recent death of his grandmother Mme de Vierville, that is his

---

The title Mademoiselle at this time could refer to a married woman: a letter of 23 January 1680 from de Crespigny in Paris is addressed to Mlle Cartault, almost certainly the wife of the pastor of Trévières. A similar blurring between Miss and Mrs can be found in seventeenth-century England – the modern distinction developed later. [It may be noted also that whereas modern French abbreviates *Monsieur* as *M*, seventeenth century texts write *Mr*.]

30

mother's mother, from smallpox,[37] and mentions also "our people" at Vierville; it is clear that the family still held the estate of Crespigny near Saint-Jean-le-Blanc as well as that of Vierville.

- Sir Claude William also claims to have identified the signature of "Daumont" with that of Pierre/Peter on various letters and on documents at the College of Arms.

In the late 1670s and early 1680s, when the letters were written, Pierre would have been in his late twenties, not an inappropriate age for such advocacy,[38] and he was later a leader of the Huguenot community in England, among other things being a member of the Committee of French Churches in London and a founding Director of *La Providence* Hospital.

Further strong and convincing evidence comes from a combination of the *Consolations Book* and the will of Pierre CdeC. The *Consolations Book* records the birth of Claude Champion, later to be of South Sea House, at London on 5 April 1706, and his baptism on the following day. His godfather (*parrain*) was Mr Daumont, and he is the only godfather mentioned. Then, in the will of Pierre CdeC, made in London in 1738, two years before his death, Pierre left six hundred pounds sterling to his nephew and godson (*filleul*) Claude CdeC. It is clear that Pierre CdeC and Mr Daumont the godfather of Claude CdeC were the same person.

So Daumont had been a secondary name of Pierre when the family lived in France, it was used for a time in England (as on the occasion of his nephew's christening), but was then simply dropped. One can only speculate whether the name was truly personal, or had some reference to a piece of landed property; and why, indeed, after using it regularly in correspondence during the 1670s and 1680s, Pierre should have abandoned it in England, not even mentioning it in the pedigree registered with the College of Arms.

As to the *Daumont Letters* themselves, the typescript is over a hundred pages long, and there are many more letters than the nine referred to in the Note on Daumont. Minet can have seen only a partial transcription, though the format he describes is extremely close to that of the collection at Kelmarsh. The letters listed by Minet can be identified in the Kelmarsh collection, being the first six and the eighth, ninth and tenth. It is not so much a question of some items having been separated, but rather that someone began a further copy of the main collection, including the introductory coat of arms, but the work was never completed.

The full content of the *Daumont Letters* is of interest for the sake of the case itself, and for incidental family information as above. I consider them in greater detail when discussing the history of the family in France in the seventeenth century. At this point, however, it may be enough to say that the letters appear genuine, and that they were written by and to Daumont [being Pierre, eldest son of Claude CdeC and Marie de Vierville], for the most part in the years 1679 to 1682.[39]

---

[37] The *Lancaster Book* says that Marguerite nee Richard died at St Lô on 23 January 1682 at the age of 90. This appears to be a mistaken entry, however, based upon the reference in the *Daumont Letters* [at pages 94 and 95 of the typescript] to the death of Mme de Vierville. In two letters written on 4 February 1682, de Crespigny refers to his mother, that is Marie nee de Vierville, being sick with smallpox, and to his concern because of the recent death of his grandmother, Mme de Vierville, who had lately died of that disease.

In context, the elder Mme de Vierville must be Judith nee Gascoin, wife of Pierre de Vierville and mother of Marie the mother of Pierre/Daumont de Crespigny. Marguerite nee Richard, wife of Richard and mother of Claude, could have been referred to as Mme CdeC or possibly as Mme Richard, but never as Mme de Vierville: her only connection with that family came through the marriage of her son.

[38] The first letter, addressed to Mr de Crespigny in Paris, is dated to February 1673. The second is dated April 1679, and the others follow in order into 1682. The 1673 date is something of an anomaly, as a six-year gap is unaccounted for, while Pierre/Daumont de Crespigny would have been only twenty years old at that time. It is difficult to believe such a young man would have been involved in the case, and I suggest that 1673 has been miswritten for 1679 – in some scripts 9 can be confused with 3.

[39] The *Letters*, and the case they were concerned with, are considered in Chapter Three at 98-100.

CHAPTER ONE

Summary: the text history of the family records

From analysis of the books and texts discussed above, I offer a tentative historiography:

The earliest account of the family was the *Pedigree Book*, begun in some form as early as the late sixteenth century, when the family was required in 1591 to justify its exemption from payment of the *taille* tax.

The documents presented in support of the case at that time went at least as far back as the agreement for purchase of the property at La Fleurière by Hebert Champion in 1453, some hundred and fifty years earlier. It is not certain what material there may have been regarding Hebert's father, grandfather and great-grand-father Michel, Richard and Maheas.

In 1674 and 1675, Claude and his son Pierre finally won and settled the case about the family liability to the *taille*, and this was recorded in a document issued by the Court of Aides, the chief taxation tribunal for Normandy. In the *Extract from the Register of the Court of Aides*, the court itemised the material which had been presented by the family and upon which it had based its decision. Apart from their legal significance, the documents provide incidental items of information on births, deaths and marriages within the lineage from the purchase of La Fleurière in 1453 to the time of the judgement in 1674.

In 1695, after the migration of the family to England, Pierre, Thomas and Gabriel, the three sons of Claude and Marie nee de Vierville, presented the *Pedigree Book* and the *Extract* to the College of Arms, and on 4 May 1697 the College issued a Certificate acknowledging the lineage as recorded in those documents. The *Pedigree Book* was returned to the brothers – and Thomas and Gabriel had copies made – but the College made and kept a copy of the *Extract*.

At the time of the registration with the College of Arms, Thomas CdeC, second son of Claude and Marie nee de Vierville, who was serving with the British Army in the Netherlands, used a copy of the work entitled *Les Consolations de l'Âme fidèle* as the equivalent of a family bible to record the births of his children. After Thomas died in 1712, the record in the *Consolations Book* was continued by his son Philip, the last entry being the birth in 1742 of Philip's daughter Jane, who would marry Henry Reveley.

Thomas's copy from the *Pedigree Book* also came to Philip; it was later passed to Jane and became, with additions, the *Reveley Book*.

Gabriel the third brother died in Ireland in 1722, and neither his daughter Elizabeth nor his son Charles married or had children. Some time after Gabriel's death, possibly when Charles died in 1733, or perhaps after Elizabeth died later, Gabriel's copy may have been transferred to their cousin Claude, son of Thomas and younger brother of Philip: this became the *South Sea Book*. It is possible, however, that Gabriel's copy disappeared and Claude had a copy of the *Pedigree Book* made independently.

Following the death of Pierre, eldest son of Claude CdeC and Marie nee de Vierville in 1739, the male lineage of the family was isolated to Philip and Claude the sons of Thomas. Major family records, including the *Pedigree Book* and the *Consolations Book*, were in the possession of Philip, and after his death in 1765 they went to his elder son Claude, who was made a baronet in 1805. When Philip's brother Claude of South Sea House died unmarried in 1782 his *South Sea Book* also joined the main collection.

At the beginning of the nineteenth century, therefore, the baronet library at Champion Lodge in Camberwell held the *Pedigree Book*, the *Consolations Book*, and the *South Sea Book*. Some of Pierre's papers had also been transferred to his nephew Philip and then to the future Sir Claude; among them was the collection of *Daumont Letters* written by and to Pierre during the court case between the Reformed Church congregations of Trévières and Vaucelles from 1679 to 1682.

The collection remained intact until the death of Sir William, second baronet and son of Sir Claude, in 1829. The title of baronet went to Sir William's grandson, Claude William, who was the son of Sir William's third son Augustus James. In his will, however, Sir William left his library to his youngest son Herbert, who would marry Augustus James' widow Caroline nee Smijth. Within little more than a year Herbert had sold off the collection, including the family records.

In contrast to his uncle and stepfather Herbert, Claude William was extremely interested in family history, and from about 1840 he made a serious attempt to pick up the pieces, while in 1843 he went with his brother Frederick to explore the ancient family territory in Normandy.

In 1841 Claude William also up-dated the genealogy recorded with the College of Arms, which had last been amended in 1805 at the time of the award of the baronetcy, and during that process we may assume that he obtained access to the records of the College, particularly including the *Extract from the Register of the Court of Aides*.

With information from the College, and probably also with assistance from his Reveley cousins – for his excursion to Normandy was recorded in the *Reveley Book* – Claude William arranged a reconstruction of the lost *Pedigree Book*. This is now the *Lancaster Book*, written in copperplate, mostly in English, accompanied by shields and other illustrations, with additional notes and drawings by Claude William and his cousin Eyre Nicholas CdeC. A good copy was later made of this *Lancaster Book*, and that became the *Kelmarsh Book*.

Also in 1841, Claude William recovered the originals of the *Daumont Letters* and had them transcribed into a fine copperplate hand by Mr Pettit of Islington. The originals and transcription remained thereafter in the family collection. Fragments of another transcription, possibly also Pettit's work, came later into the hands of Mr Minet of the Huguenot Society, who compiled his Note on Daumont in the early 1930s; those items were then deposited in the Huguenot Society Library, which was later combined with the collection of the French Hospital *La Providence*; the whole is now held in the National Archives in London.

The *Lancaster Book* was largely completed in the 1840s, but in 1860 the *Consolations Book*, which had disappeared after the sale of the library, was recovered and restored to the family through the good offices of Mr Maitland. Claude William kept the book itself, but he also copied the late seventeenth and early eighteenth century information about Thomas, Philip and their families, preserved in the fly-leaves, as an appendix to his reconstructed compilation the *Lancaster Book*.

In 1883, after the death of Sir Claude William and the succession of his son Claude the fourth baronet, the *South Sea Book* was also recovered through a friend of George Blick CdeC, and was presented to Sir Claude.

By the end of the nineteenth century, therefore, the collection of family papers which had been dispersed when Herbert CdeC sold off the library had been largely recovered. The great loss was the main *Pedigree Book*, together, of course, with other documents of which we have no record. There is no way to tell what deeds and letters may have been preserved from France but disappeared in 1830. It is unlikely that anything more will be found.

By and large, however, though it must be recognised that the *Lancaster Book* is a compilation of the mid-nineteenth century, while other items go back only to the late seventeenth or early eighteenth century, we can be reasonably confident of the information they provide concerning the history of the family in France. In particular, the *Extract from the Register of the Court of Aides*, preserved in the archives of the College of Arms, appears authoritative, and extends, albeit at second-hand, the documentation of the family as far back as the middle of the fifteenth century.

This is not to say that everything is accurate, nor that the record is complete. We are dealing with material from several different sources, subject to the chances of transcription and translation from French into English. Some items of information cannot be supported by any earlier record now available: they may have been once; or they may be no more than

CHAPTER ONE

legend or invention. What we can accept, however, is that the tradition represented by the *Lancaster Book*, and the earlier sources as we have them, is valid material for the history of the Champions in Normandy.

CHAPTER TWO

Calvados and the Duchy of Normandy

Part I: A History of the Champion Family to 1600
    Chronology 1000-1600
    The geography and early history of Lower Normandy
    A note on noblesse, taille *and other terms*
    Maheas, Richard, Jean and Michel 1350-1470
    The seigneury of La Fleurière 1463-1641
Part II: Tales, Legends and Fictions
    William de Crespigny and the King of England
    Mollerus-Le Champion and Mad King Charles
    Burke, Debrett, and Horace Round
    The Champions de Cicé and other reputed cousins

Part I: A History of the Family to 1600

Chronology 1000 to 1600[*]

1035	Death of Robert I, Duke of Normandy, succeeded by his son William
1066	Duke William conquers England
1106	King Henry I of England, son of the Conqueror, defeats and captures his elder brother Duke Robert II of Normandy at Tinchebray
1119	skirmish at Brenneville/Brémule: *William de Crespigny knocks the English King Henry from his horse*
1204	King Philip Augustus of France seizes Normandy from King John of England
1220	*Ricard le Champion is Viscount de Vire*
1346	commencement of the Hundred Years War; the English plunder Normandy and then defeat the French at the Battle of Crécy
1348-49	the Black Death in Normandy
*c.*1350	Maheas Champion comes to Normandy
1356	The English defeat the French at the Battle of Poitiers; regular English raiding against Normandy
1368	Vire is captured by brigands
c. 1370	Maheas Champion marries a daughter of Jean Busnel; birth of Richard Champion
1370-80	Bertrand du Guesclin, Constable of France for King Charles V, restores the French position against the English
c. 1380	Maheas Champion is Viscount of Vire
1392	madness of King Charles VI of France; the royal government is contested by rival princes
c. 1400	Richard Champion marries a daughter of Hector Mensant; he succeeds his father Maheas as Viscount of Vire
c. 1405	births of Jean and Michel Champion, sons of Richard
1415	King Henry V of England defeats the French at Agincourt
1417	Henry V commences the conquest of Normandy and establishes the Lancastrian kingdom in France; members of the Champion family migrate to Brittany, *where Jean Champion establishes the lineage of the Champions de Cicé*

---

[*] Items in blue are general historical facts; items in normal font relate specifically to the Champion family; items in *italics* relate to the family history but are either false or confused.

    All dates for family events marked ***c.*** [*circa* = approximate] must be considered uncertain; they are discussed in more detail below.

Chapter Two

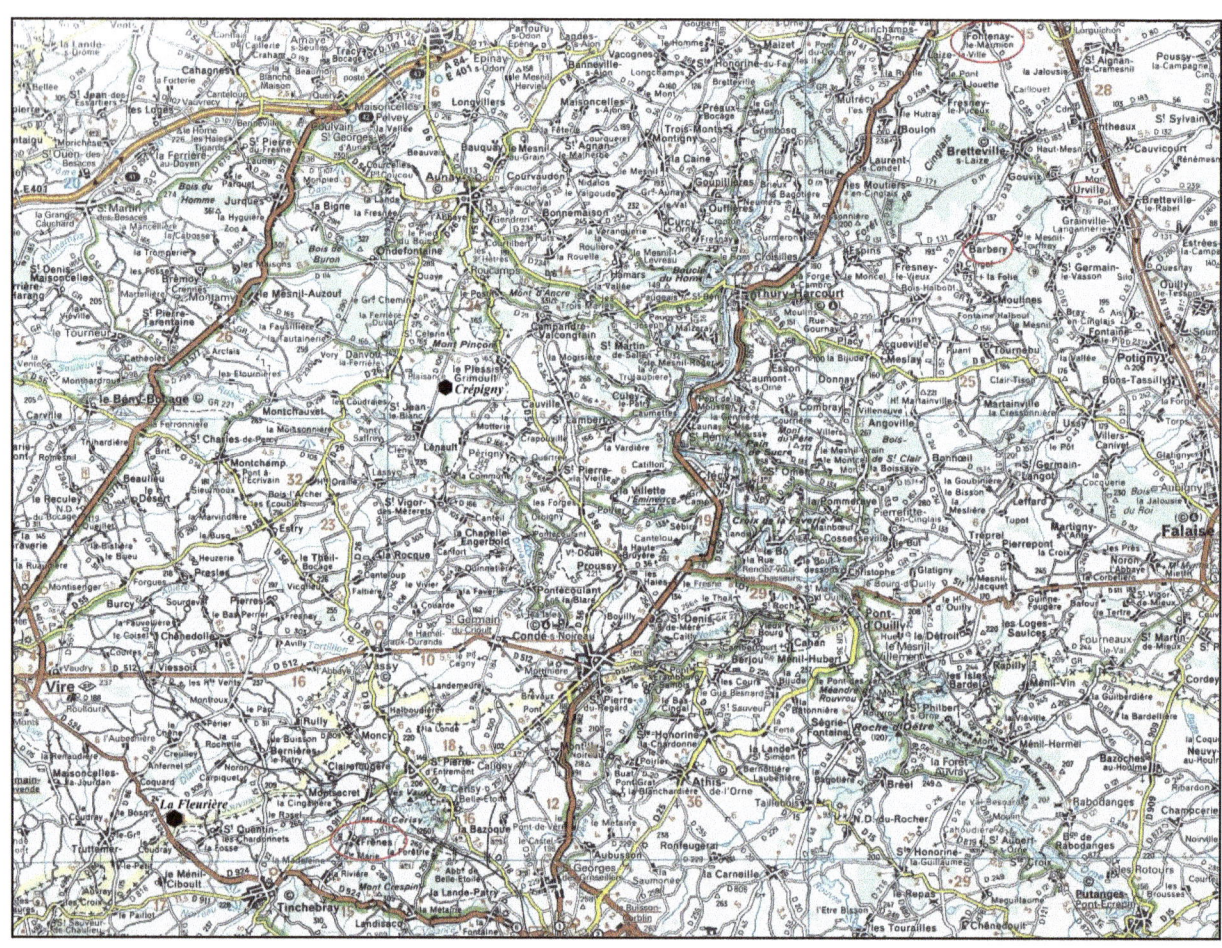

Map Six: The region of the Champion family in southern Calvados 1350-1650
Detail from Michelin France *2003 sheet 37.*
The sites of La Fleuriere and Crespigny are added. Fontenay-le-Marmion, Urville and Barbery are circled in the northwest; Frênes in the southwest. Falaise may be seen in the west and Vire in the east.

1418	*Henry V grants the manors of Urvyle and Fonteneys, formerly held by Bertrand Champyon, to his knight Robert Shottesbroke*
1420	The Treaty of Troyes brings a peace settlement: Henry of England is named heir to the throne of France
1422	deaths of Henry V of England and of Charles VI of France
c. 1425	Michel Champion returns to Normandy; he marries Jeanne nee de la Rivière; birth of Hebert Champion
1429	Joan of Arc raises the siege of Orleans and has Charles VII of France crowned at Reims; revival of French fortunes
1449-50	French reconquest of Normandy and reunification of the kingdom
1463	Hebert Champion, son of Michel, purchases La Fleurière from Jean l'Anglais
1470	Jean Champion, elder brother of Michel, is granted noble rank in Brittany
c. 1475	Hebert Champion marries Jeanne nee Abot; birth of Nicolas Champion
c. 1480	birth of Antoine Champion, son of Hebert and Jeanne nee Abot
c. 1507	death of Hebert Champion
c. 1510	Antoine Champion marries Catherine nee Marye, birth of their sons Nicolas and Raoul
1517	Martin Luther publishes his *Ninety-Five Theses* at Wittenberg in Germany[1]
c. 1540	death of Jean Champion, father of Raoul
1541	John Calvin establishes a Puritan regime in Geneva; his doctrines spread widely France
c. 1545	Raoul Champion marries Jeanne nee la Forestier; they acquire estates at Saint-Opportune and Magny from her family; birth of Jean Champion, son of Raoul
1555	The Peace of Augsburg in Germany establishes the principle of *Cuius regio, eius religio*: subjects are to follow the faith of their ruler
1555	The Amboise Conspiracy: a group of Huguenot nobles attempt to seize power over the government of the young Francis II
1562	The Massacre at Vassy, regarded as the beginning of the French Wars of Religion
c. 1570	death of Raoul Champion
1572	The Saint Bartholomew's Day Massacre of Huguenots in Paris
1573	death of Nicolas Champion, a priest
c. 1580	Jean Champion marries Marthe nee du Bourget; subsequent births of their sons Richard and Jacques Champion and of their daughter Marie
1587?	birth of Richard Champion
1587-89	War of the Three Henrys: King Henri III; Henri de Bourbon, King of Navarre and future Henri IV; and Henri, Duke de Guise, head of the Catholic League
1588	victory of Henri of Navarre at Coutras; assassination of Henri, Duke de Guise
1589	assassination of Henri III; he is succeeded by Henri of Navarre, now Henri IV
1591	The Court of Aides at Rouen finds that the Champion family is not entitled to the status of *noblesse* and is therefore liable to the *taille* tax
1593	Henri IV converts to Catholicism
1598	The Edict of Nantes marks the end of the Wars of Religion, but creates Huguenot enclaves within the kingdom of France

The geography and early history of Lower Normandy
The area of Champion family history, from the mid-fourteenth century and the putative Maheas Champion, up to the time of the Revocation of the Edict of Nantes and the emigration to England at the end of the seventeenth century, is remarkably limited. Indeed, until the last generation, when Claude Champion de Crespigny married Marie de Vierville in

---

[1] Events relating to Protestantism and Huguenots are discussed in Chapter Three following.

CHAPTER TWO

1651, almost every place named in the *Lancaster Book* may be found within thirty kilometres of one another, from Vire in the west to Condé-sur-Noireau in the east, and from Aunay in the north to Tinchebray in the south. This region lies among the Norman Hills, *Collines de Normandie*, of which Mont Pinçon is a notable peak, and it is now part of the Department/ *département* of Calvados. The town/*commune* of Vire is the headquarters of a sub-prefecture/*sous-préfecture*; it was badly damaged in the Second World War, but there are remains of a castle from the twelfth century, and its geographical position has always kept it a place of at least local significance.

One reason for the importance of Vire is its site on the river of that name. Rising in higher ground a little to the south of the town, the river flows generally northwards, past Saint Lô to the plain of Bessin and then to the sea in a large estuary, which receives other rivers, on the eastern side of the base of the Cotentin peninsula. Two towns named Vierville lie close to the sea on either side of the estuary: Vierville in the west is a commune in the Department of Manche; Vierville-sur-Mer, on the open coastline to the east, is a commune in the Department of Calvados – both places no doubt take their name from that of the river, and both have significance in the history of the Champion de Crespigny family.

The Vire is not a major stream, but its valley serves as a route of approach from the northern coast into the hill country and south towards the Loire, while Vire itself lies on an east-west communication route: the Sée River and some lesser streams run down to the Bay of Mont Saint Michel on the west, and there is comparatively open country eastwards to Falaise and further on to Paris. A modern railway follows that line, and in medieval and early modern times there was military and other movement between Vire and Evreux, south of Rouen, by way of Falaise. In 1944 Vire was a centre of a German position under attack from British forces advancing south through Saint Lô and an American approach from the region of Granville and Avranches in the west.[2]

This region south of the Cotentin peninsula and the Bay of the Seine, and particularly the department of Calvados based upon Caen, is traditionally known as *Basse-Normandie*, Lower Normandy, as distinguished from Upper Normandy [*Haute-Normandie*], which covers the valley of the Seine dominated by the city of Rouen. In many respects the two are separate and different: Lower Normandy is hill country, with access to the sea on the north and west, while Upper Normandy is more open, with winding but navigable reaches of the Seine leading inland from Le Havre [the site of ancient Harfleur] and Honfleur past Rouen towards Paris. The region about Rouen, and particularly the border territory known as the Vexin further upstream, was critically contested by the Dukes of Normandy [or Kings of England] and the Kings of France during the first centuries of the second millennium AD.

The unified province of Normandy was recognised by the French king in the time of Rollo, or Robert, during the early tenth century, and for the next hundred years its ruler was known variously as marquis and count. The title of Duke was first taken by Robert I, known as *le Diable* "the Devil", father of William the Conqueror.

William succeeded his father as Duke of Normandy when Robert died in 1035. Though his parents had never married and he was sometimes called a bastard, his mother was a recognised concubine and Robert had formally designated him as his heir. As Duke of Normandy William was a feudatory of the King of France for that territory, and even after he became King of England in 1066 he continued to hold Normandy as a fief. For a short time after William's death in 1087 the duchy of Normandy and the kingdom of England were

---

[2] The hamlet of Crépigny, south of Mont Pinçon, appears on a map of that campaign in Wilmot, *Struggle for Europe*, at 468. The *bocage* hedgerows of the area, however, meant that a direct advance eastwards through Vire was slow and difficult, and German defeat in the Falaise pocket was achieved by a pincer movement south from Caen and north from Alençon.

separated, but in 1106 Henry I of England defeated his elder brother Duke Robert II at the battle of Tinchebray, southeast of Vire, and the duchy was joined again to the English crown; some traditions see Tinchebray as an English revenge for the battle of Hastings

This situation continued through the twelfth century, during which the Angevin empire, formed by the marriage of King Henry II of England with his Queen Eleanor of Aquitaine, produced a dynastic power extending from England through Normandy, Anjou and Maine to the southwest of France. Though their territory was greater than that of the kings based on Paris, Henry and his son Richard I of England still owed allegiance for Normandy and their other French possessions to those formal feudal overlords.

In 1204, however, King Philip Augustus of France seized Normandy and his other lands on the continent from the unfortunate King John, youngest son of Henry II, and the cession of Normandy was confirmed by Henry III of England, son of John, at the Treaty of Paris in 1259. From that time the duchy of Normandy was associated directly with the French crown, and was ruled by bailiffs responsible to the king. Though it was recognised as a separate region, as for example by a Charter to the Normans in 1315, the independent fief was never re-established. As one work has it, Philip Augustus' position in relation to the duchy of Normandy was not that of a conqueror, but rather that of a property owner who has dispossessed an annoying tenant, and he did not style himself duke: as King of France he had always held ultimate power in theory, and the royal title of itself was sufficient for all acts of authority.[3]

Administratively, after 1204 Rouen was recognised as the capital of the whole province, and until the French Revolution and the establishment of the department system both the Parlement of Normandy and the Court of Aides for the province were at Rouen. In Lower Normandy, the chief city was Caen, which became the headquarters of an Intendant in the seventeenth and eighteenth centuries, but the region was subject to higher authority at Rouen.

In the thirteenth century the duchy was divided into *bailliages*/bailiwicks and by 1280 it had also been organised into viscounties, the unit next below the bailiwick: the viscounty of Vire, together with those of Caen, Falaise and Bayeux, was in the bailiwick of Caen.

The title Duke of Normandy was restored for a short time during the fourteenth century, but the province remained an appanage of the French throne and was held only on limited tenure: as heir to the kingdom of France, the future King John II was Duke of Normandy until his accession in 1350. The title might have filled the same role as that of Prince of Wales under the English crown, but in 1349 the county of Dauphiné in south-east France was sold to King Philip II on condition that the heir to the throne would hold that title.[4] Philip's eldest son the Dauphin Charles, later King Charles V, was concurrently Duke of Normandy from 1350 to his accession in 1365, but thereafter the title was awarded only intermittently.

A note on noblesse, taille *and other terms*

Since the greater part of the material relating to the early history of the Champions de Crespigny is concerned with the family's claim to noble rank, it is appropriate to begin by a summary of the question and of the terms which are used. Many points are repeated later in this work, but this note is offered a preliminary to more detailed discussion.

The core of the matter is that the status of *noblesse* "nobility" gave exemption from the *taille* tax – a form of scutage: those ranked as noble were expected to provide military service to the king, while *roturiers* "commoners" had no such duty but paid tax instead. In medieval times the military service had been a real obligation, but from the sixteenth and seventeenth

---

[3] Strayer, *Administration*, 6.
[4] Though the territory of Dauphiné is not close to the sea, a dolphin [Fr: *dauphin*] was the insignia of the ruler, who further styled himself *Dauphin*. The dolphin still appears on the badge of the modern administrative région *Provence-Alpes-Côte d'Azur* [PACA], which controls the southeast of France.

centuries the requirement was largely abandoned, so exemption from the *taille* became no more than a perquisite and privilege of noble rank.

From this point of view, any claim to such status was liable to investigation from two directions: on the one hand, the royal government was concerned to ensure that the king's subjects were not evading their fiscal responsibilities; while members of the local community were reluctant to see one of their number gaining exemption, for they could then suffer an extra burden of taxation.

It is to one of these investigations and its resolution that we owe the survival of the family records. In 1667 the Intendant Guy Chamillart compiled his *Recherche de Noblesse en la Généralité de Caen* "Enquiry into those of Noble Status in the *Généralité* of Caen [*i.e.* Lower Normandy],"[5] and found that the Champions de Crespigny were not entitled to that rank and privilege. Over the next several years the family appealed the case to higher authority, the Court of Aides situated at Rouen, capital of the whole province, and in 1674 the court found in their favour and overturned Chamillart's decision. It is the evidence produced and approved in the course of this action that forms the basis of the family records we have now. This whole matter, including Chamillart's observations, is cited frequently below, and a detailed discussion of the case is offered in Chapter Three.

It must be noted, however, that while the term *noblesse* is often rendered as "nobility," those entitled to describe themselves as "noble" were not all hereditary peers as in the old English House of Lords. The term identifies members of a broad gentry class, which certainly included the hereditary nobility but might extend also to gentlemen without specific title but with some landed property. Some estates were held on such feudal terms, but not all men who possessed land were obliged or entitled to provide military service, and many landowners were regarded as commoners and subject to regular taxation.

In this regard, while a member of the *noblesse* may be described as *Sieur* or *Escuier*, neither are hereditary feudal ranks and neither title is a sure indicator of noble status. *Escuier*/"esquire" is essentially a courtesy form, and *Sieur* means no more than the English "lord of the manor:" those who held them were surely gentlemen, but they were not necessarily members of the *noblesse*.

Like much of the administration of the *ancient regime* in pre-Revolutionary France, the system was confused, frequently arbitrary and always open to challenge and question.

Maheas, Richard, Jean and Michel 1350-1470
Evidently based upon the original *Pedigree Book*, the position described by the *South Sea*, *Reveley* and *Lancaster* books is as follows:[6]
Maheas Champion was living in 1350 (title page) and may have died in that year (main text).
>He married the daughter of Jean Busnel, Sieur and Baron of Frénes/Frênes; Frênes is a little to the northeast of Tinchebray, some fifteen kilometres southeast of Vire.[7]

The name is unusual, and the record may have been corrupted over such a distance of time with uncertain documentation.[8] There are a few examples of Maheas as a surname, chiefly in France, but it is extremely rare as a personal name. The best suggestion for its origin appears to be that it is a form of Mathias "Matthew" which has been used in parts of Brittany.

---

[5] The system of provincial government in France was amended in the mid-sixteenth century, and *bailliages*/bailiwicks were largely replaced by *généralités*, with the greater part of Lower Normandy under the Généralité of Caen. From the early seventeenth century Intendants were appointed to each *généralité*, with wide-ranging legal, police and financial authority.

[6] The original texts of the *South Sea* and *Reveley* books are shown in Chapter One at 22. My conclusions on the relationship of those collections with the *Pedigree Book* are given in Chapter One at 25.

[7] Following old orthography [note 16 to the Introduction at 6], the *Reveley* and *South Sea* books have the place-name as Fresnes. The *Lancaster Book* gives it an acute accent, the modern name has a circumflex.

[8] The name occasionally appears as Maheus, but this is, if possible, even more uncommon.

Richard, the only recorded son of Maheas, married the daughter of Hector Mensant, later granted the surname d'Oüssé, who was Sieur of Lensentière in the parish of Bruz [miswritten as "Bron"].[9] We are also told that Richard Champion was Viscount of Vire in consequence of his father having obtained the "*domain du Roi*."

Jean, eldest son of Richard, took up his residence in Brittany and became the ancestor of the Champion families in that duchy, including the Champions de Chartres and the Champions de Cicé. As in discussion below, however, there is room for doubt whether this Jean Champion was indeed a member of this lineage.[10]

Michel (rendered in the *Lancaster Book* by the anglicised Michael), younger son of Richard, married Jeanne the daughter of the Sieur de la Rivière; he is described simply as a Squire *Escuier*, and we are told that he "died in Normandy."

Shield of Richard Champion married to Mlle Mensant[11]   *Shield of Michel Champion married to Jeanne de la Rivière*

The point which needs consideration at this stage is the date 1470 for the ennoblement of Jean Champion, son of Richard, elder brother of Michel and uncle of Hebert the purchaser of La Fleurière in 1463. If he was alive to receive such honour, then it is unlikely that Jean was born any earlier than 1400.

Hebert, on the other hand, must have been a man of some maturity to have been able to buy La Fleurière; he possibly acquired the property after his marriage and with the assistance of his mother's family, for Michel his father does not appear to have been a man of substantial means. Hebert was presumably born some time before 1440; and Michel would have been born about 1410.[12]

From this analysis, Jean and Michel, the two sons of Richard Champion, were born in the early 1400s. It is possible, but unlikely, that Richard sired them when he was in his forties; he could well have had children when he was in his twenties, and we may compromise with the idea that Jean and Michel were born when Richard was in his thirties. So Richard was probably born about 1370.

If that is so, then Maheas his father must have been alive about that time, and by any analysis it is hard to see how a man who died in 1350 could have a grandson still alive in

---

[9] On the miswriting of "Bron" for Bruz, see 72 below. The *Lancaster Book* has Hector Mensant's adoptive surname as D'Oüessé, with an extra *e*.

[10] See Part II at 71-75.

[11] The "marriage shields" here and following are scanned from black-and-white reconstructions presented in the *Lancaster Book*. It may be noted that all the lions are shown rampant, not salient, and the illustrations do not show the piercing of the cross moline; this latter I have amended.

[12] The *Extract* refers not only to Hebert's purchase of La Fleurière in 1463, but also to legal documents associated with his death about 1508. On this, see the next section.

CHAPTER TWO

1470. Such a gap is theoretically possible, but one must bear in mind that many people in the Middle Ages were married before the age of twenty, while a man of fifty was considered old: if Maheas died in 1350, then his son Richard and his grandson Jean were men of exceptional longevity and – in Richard's case – of exceptionally late and delayed fertility.

I suggest, therefore, that 1350 is not the date of Maheas' death, but that it was a year in which he was alive. It is possible it was the year in which he was born, or it may have been the time that he arrived in Normandy and established himself in that region of France.

My proposed dates for the first generations of the family are thus tabulated below – noting that dates are highly generalised, and may have varied by ten years either way (except of course for the "established" dates of 1463 and 1470), while with the exception of Hebert (on whom see below), we have no information about the years of death. Though it is based upon only two fixed dates, however, and the uncertain reference to Maheas in 1350, the table offers a possible interpretation of family chronology in the early and uncertain period from the middle of the fourteenth century to the second half of the fifteenth century.

Table I: The First Generations 1350-1500

Maheas Champion
born *c.*1330   arrived Normandy *c.*1350?
marries 1360 the daughter of Jean Busnel
dies 1380

Richard Champion
[son of Maheas]
born *c.*1360
marries *c.*1390 the daughter of Hector Mensant
dies *c.*1420

Jean Champion
[son of Richard]
born *c.*1400   leaves for Brittany *c.*1415
ennobled 1470
dies *c.*1475

Michel Champion
[son of Richard]
born *c.*1400   in Normandy *c.*1425
marries *c.*1430 Jeanne de la Rivière
dies *c.*1460

Hebert Champion
[son of Michel]
born *c.*1430
marries *c.*1460 Jeanne Abot
purchases La Fleurière 1463
dies *c.*1508

other sons of Michel: Pierre, Rioul, Gabriel: *known only by their names*

This, of course, was just the time of the Hundred Years War between the English and the French, and the presumptions I have made about the vital dates of the individual members of the family may now be applied to a broader background.[13]

The late 1340s were extremely difficult times for the region of Lower Normandy. One of the first campaigns of the Hundred Years War was the invasion of France by King Edward III of England, landing on the Cotentin peninsula in 1346 and then marching along the coast road through Caen towards Paris and ultimately to victory at Crécy, south of Boulogne. In following years, notably 1348 and 1349, Normandy was affected by the plague of the Black Death, and a second French defeat at Poitiers in 1356, including the capture of King John by Edward III's son Edward the Black Prince, brought renewed activity and English incursions from the Cotentin peninsula.

---

[13] For the general history of this period, I use Perroy, *The Hundred Years War*, Tuchman, *Distant Mirror*, and the major compilation by Sumption – four large volumes with more to come. The basic facts are well known, and can be confirmed in any standard account.

The region of the peninsula and the territory directly to its south, including Vire, was part of the fief of Charles the Bad, King of Navarre and Count of Evreux, the latter title being more important at this time.[14] He attempted to set up a semi-independent state, but in 1365 he was forced to submit to King Charles V of France, the far more competent successor to King John.

At the same time, besides the national or quasi-official campaigns of kings and high nobility, Normandy was ravaged by bands of wandering troops, some English, some claiming to support Charles of Navarre, but many simple brigands. During the mid-1350s Vire was at the centre of raiding and was surrounded by troublesome strongholds, and in 1368 the city was captured by the English wing of the Great Company and had to be ransomed by the French crown.[15] This, however, was one of the last such bandit successes, and over the next several years the armies of Charles V and his great commander Bertrand du Guesclin gradually regained territory, avoiding pitched battles such as Crécy and Poitiers while engaging in small-scale raids and captures. Despite his surrender, Charles of Navarre continued to cause trouble, and in 1378 his long history of treachery and double-dealing was punished by the royal seizure of Evreux and the Cotentin. This was one of the last campaigns of that phase of the war, and for the next forty years the country remained – at least notionally, for disturbance continued – in the hands of the King of France.

Charles V died in 1380, however, and the reign of his son Charles VI saw the kingdom divided between rival princes of the royal house. They first gained influence as uncles of the young king, who came to the throne at the age of eleven, but in 1392 Charles suffered his first attack of insanity – probably paranoid schizophrenia – and in following years he became quite incapable of carrying on government.

In 1415, moreover, Henry V of England renewed the war and gained his great victory at Agincourt. Two years later, taking advantage of that success, of the continued disruption of French government and of his own alliance with Jean "sans Peur" [the Fearless], Duke of Burgundy, he invaded and occupied Normandy. The province became the heart of "Lancastrian France," with its capital at Rouen and a secondary administrative centre at Caen.

Of this period, Perroy emphasises that control was maintained primarily by English garrisons without great support among the people, and adds that

> Almost all the local nobility had remained faithful to the Dauphin and preferred exile to servitude. Their fiefs were confiscated *en bloc* and given to English captains...a feudal class of conquerors...[16]

The Treaty of Troyes in 1420 marked the high point of English success. By its terms the Dauphin Charles, future Charles VII, was declared illegitimate and formally disinherited, while Henry of England married Katherine the daughter of Charles VI and was named heir to the throne of France. Since the conflict had begun when the French insisted that Salic Law forbade inheritance through a woman, the agreement was of questionable authority, but it did produce a form of settlement, and peace on any terms was widely welcomed.[17]

---

[14] Navarre, a small kingdom in the Pyrenees astride the frontier between France and Spain, was at this time an appanage of the French royal house. When Joan, daughter of Louis X of France, married the Count of Evreux, Louis granted it to his son-in-law. Charles the Bad was the issue of that union and was frequently in conflict or in an active state of war with his Valois cousins the kings of France.

[15] See Sumption, *Trial by Fire*, 286-287 and 566-567, and on the capture in 1368 de Fréville, "Grandes compagnies." On the latter occasion, by quite a common ruse, some fifty men made their way into the town with weapons concealed in their clothing, then killed the gatekeepers and let their fellows in.

[16] *Hundred Years War*, 250.

[17] Charles IV, last surviving son of Philip IV, died in 1328, and his cousin Philip VI, son of the brother of Philip IV, was chosen to succeed him. Isabelle the daughter of Philip IV, however, had married Edward II of England and was the mother of Edward III. So Edward III claimed the throne of France through right of

CHAPTER TWO

Two years later in 1422, however, quite against expectations, Henry died at the age of thirty-six, before his father-in-law whose death followed a few weeks later. Henry's infant son Henry VI was proclaimed king of both England and France, with his uncle John of Lancaster, Duke of Bedford, regent for his French possessions; but the Dauphin Charles found opportunity to defy the agreement of Troyes and claim the throne for himself.

There followed a period of disordered stalemate, with the River Loire serving as a frontier between the territory loyal to the Dauphin in the south and that of the Anglo-Burgundians to the north and east. In 1429, however, as the inspiration of Joan of Arc raised the siege of Orleans and brought Charles to be crowned at Reims, there was a revival of French energy. Joan was captured and then burned at Rouen in 1431, and the English position was maintained for several more years, but it depended very largely upon divisions among the French, and in 1435 Charles VII managed a reconciliation with Duke Philip of Burgundy.

Faced by reunited French power, English military resources were limited, reinforcements could not be maintained, and there was no local support for the alien regime. After a period of truce, Normandy was reconquered in a twelve-month campaign through 1449 and 1450. In Lower Normandy, Saint Lô and the Cotentin peninsula were taken in October and November of 1449, and the decisive battle was fought at Formigny, on the coast west of Bayeux, when an English relief force was thoroughly defeated in April 1450. The three major English fortresses Falaise, Domfront (both in the area of Vire) and Cherbourg (at the tip of the Contentin peninsula) were captured in late July and early August.

Thereafter Normandy was once more a province under the French crown.

If we consider the early genealogy of the Champion family, as postulated above, against this background of the Hundred Years War, some further points may be suggested:
First, it seems likely that Maheas was active from about 1350 to perhaps 1380.

In the entry for Maheas in the *Lancaster Book* Sir Claude William CdeC noted that:
> In the Bibliothèque du Roi [Royal Library] at Paris there is an account of the family of Champion from which it appears they initially came from Holland and their arms were simply the *fer de moulin*. Probably they impaled the lion rampant at the marriage of M[aheus] Champion with the heiress of the Baron de Frênes, whose arms might have been the said lion rampant.

And on page five of the *Lancaster Book*, among the drawings of seals mentioned earlier is one showing the plain *fer de moulin*/cross moline, which is described as a "French family seal in the possession of Sir [C.]W.C.de C Bt, and supposed to be the original coat of arms of the Champions."

These heraldic suggestions, however, may be too imaginative. It is unlikely that a plain cross moline would have been carried at that time by a man of comparatively recent gentility – in general, the simpler the shield the more ancient the ancestry. It is possible, however, that the cross served as a badge for a member of the family – not as the entire charge on the shield – and was used for that purpose on a seal.

Otherwise the sources have no information on Maheas' origins. It is certainly possible, however, that he was a recent arrival from outside Normandy. The period immediately after the Black Death, which may have killed a third or even a half of the population, saw many survivors moving into areas which had lost people and now offered surplus lands and new opportunities. The kings of France had an interest in Flanders, present-day Belgium, which was formally subject to their suzerainty,[18] but we should note, as above, that the name

---

his mother, but the French court refused him, arguing that so-called Salic Law did not allow inheritance through a woman.

[18] As at 46 below, Richard d'Amphernet, a leading figure in the region of Vire, was with the French army at Bruges in 1386.

Maheas is best known in Brittany, and there were family connections there later. While Maheas need not have come from so far afield as Flanders, however, it was certainly a time when a man who had lived through the plague might travel to seek his fortune. His marriage to the daughter and heiress of a local baron would then have established his position in the region.

The *Lancaster Book*, moreover, says that Maheas' son Richard became Viscount of Vire "in consequence of his father having obtained the 'domain du Roi'." The expression *domain du Roi* in this context does not appear to make sense, the whole sentence appears only half-rendered from some original French, and – strangely – it does not appear in the *Reveley Book* or the *South Sea Book*, which appear to be close copies of the original *Pedigree Book*.[19] Assuming the phrase has some authority, however, my proposal would be to translate it fully, using the phrase *du Roi*, which would often be understood as "of the king" in the possible, albeit slightly less common, meaning of "from the king." The sentence would then be saying that Richard obtained the position of Viscount of Vire because his father Maheas before him had held that domain from [a grant of] the King of France.

If we accept that Maheas received his position in this way, then it should have happened about 1378, when Charles the Bad, King of Navarre but in local terms the Count of Evreux, was dispossessed by King Charles V. "King" in this context certainly refers to King Charles of France, not to the distant and subordinate title of Navarre.

The story, then, would be that Maheas had settled in Lower Normandy and made a good local marriage. When the crisis broke in 1378, Maheas supported the new regime of King Charles and was appointed Viscount of Vire with command of that local garrison.

Remains of the Donjon of the castle of Vire, dated to the eleventh or twelfth century

It is also possible that Maheas had come to Normandy with the royal army of France, that he was appointed Viscount of Vire as an outsider, and that he married about 1380 (rather than 1370 as suggested earlier). Richard would then have been born about 1380, and could easily have had two sons born in the first decade of the 1400s. In such case the date of 1350 may relate to Maheas' birth rather than to his arrival in Normandy, and he may have lived until 1400 or later.

---

[19] On this argument, see Chapter One, particularly 24-25.

CHAPTER TWO

In any event, it is my hypothesis that Maheas Champion, a "new man" in the region, was appointed Viscount of Vire by the King of France after the conquest of 1378, and that he was able to pass that position to his son Richard.

One must note, however, that a viscount in Normandy was a servant of the crown, not a hereditary feudal lord: both the appointment and its transmission were at the discretion of the sovereign. Elsewhere in France viscounts (originally the delegates of counts), were able to make themselves effective territorial rulers in their own right, but Abbott observes that the position of a viscount in Normandy was never more than that of an administrator: there was no recognised, independent and heritable tenure of territory.[20]

There is, however, a further problem: the history sketched above is based entirely upon records of the Champion [de Crespigny] family, with little independent evidence to support it; and while local records from that early period are rare, they are sufficient to throw doubt on the tradition.

First and most important, the d'Amphernet family was dominant in the region of Vire.[21] Jehan I d'Amphernet, Seigneur de Montchauvet in the late thirteenth century, founded the chapel of St Michael [now Notre-Dame de Pitié] in the church of Notre-Dame at Vire, and this remained a family site until its destruction during the French Revolution. Jehan's son Richard was a knight at the battle of Crécy in 1346, and it is claimed that he later fortified the town of Vire at his own expense, holding it against the English and engaging in sorties. As Chamberlain to King Charles V, he presented reports on the situation in Normandy to the royal court.

Richard d'Amphernet died at Vire in 1368, but his son Guillaume/William likewise became Chamberlain to King Charles VI, held command in Vire, and was a comrade in arms of Bertrand du Guesclin. As *Grand Bailli* [Chief Bailiff] of Cotentin during the 1380s, he was authorised to fortify Tinchebray and other places in the vicinity of Vire – Vire being associated with Cotentin at this time rather than with Caen – and he was with a substantial French army at Bruges in present-day Belgium in 1386. He died in 1390, without children, but the d'Amphernet lineage was continued by descendants of his brother Jehan II.

If this account of the d'Amphernet family is correct, then the role of Maheas and Richard Champion is less important than CdeC sources would indicate. They must surely have been subordinate to the d'Amphernet family, and though they may have held title as viscounts of Vire they were presumably acting in the position while Richard and/or Guillaume d'Amphernet held higher office as royal chamberlains or as chief of the larger bailiwick.

A second, albeit marginal point, is that there is a good deal of information about the seizure and short-lived occupation of Vire by the English Great Company in 1368. It is discussed in the article by de Fréville, who quotes several documents relating to the event, including the names of defenders such as the *chatelaine* Raoul d'Auquetonville; but no-one with the Champion surname is mentioned in any capacity.[22]

Even if we accept the statement that Maheas and Richard Champion held appointment at Vire, therefore, they would have been lieutenants for members of a more distinguished local family, and they were officials rather than men of feudal status. In time, since the position

---

[20] Abbot, *Provinces, Pays and Seigneuries*, 12, and also Strayer, *Administration*, 9.
[21] http://maison.omahony.free.fr/AmphernetN.htm is the basis for the account which follows. It is possible that family enthusiasm has exaggerated the authority of its representatives – in much the same way as that of the Champions de Crespigny – but the d'Amphernet family remained in the region into modern times, and there is quasi-independent evidence to support the history, including a chateau at Bréville-les-Monts close to Caen and continuing references to members of the family. The credibility of the source appears superior to that of the CdeC's.
[22] "Grandes compagnies," especially at 275-277. See also above at 43.

was transmitted from father to son at least once, it might have developed into a true fief, possibly still subordinate to the d'Amphernets, but other matters now intervened.

These matters – as discussed above – were consequences of the English occupation of Normandy after Henry V's victory at Agincourt in 1415. Maheas was surely dead by the early 1400s, and possibly Richard too, but the conquest would explain why a member of the family might go to Brittany. Anyone who had held office under the French crown would find it sensible to leave, for although the duchy of Brittany was confused and contested, it was never fully controlled by the English. We are told that Jean Champion became established there and was formally granted status as a member of the *noblesse*.

The award of nobility, cited by Chamillart and quoted by Round, is supported also by the *Nobiliaire et armorial de Bretagne* of Potier de Courcy, which states more precisely that Jean Champion, first ancestor of the Champions de Cicé, came originally from Condé-sur-Vire in Normandy and that he was *anobli aux francs-fiefs* in 1470.[23]

The system of *francs-fiefs*, literally "free fiefs," had been developed by King Louis XI.[24] His father Charles VII had driven the English first from Normandy and then from Aquitaine in the southwest, and the surrender of Bordeaux in 1453 marked the effective end of the Hundred Years War. When Louis succeeded to the throne in 1461, however, he still had to deal with a country where regions such as Normandy had been many years under foreign control and where archives had been destroyed in the years of disorder.

Faced with such confusion, Louis ordered that – regardless whether they were of commoner origin – men with estates formerly held by military service should now be deemed as noble and exempted from the *taille* tax.[25] So the government gained the allegiance of major land-holders in the newly-recovered territories; and Jean Champion, who had acquired the fief of Cicé, gained noble rank.

The royal ordinance of 1470 also made provision for members of ancient noble families who had either been unable to provide the service required – frequently, of course, because they had been in enemy-occupied territory – or were unable to prove their former status because the documents had been lost. The fact that Jean received his rank through his estate of Cicé, therefore, does not necessarily indicate that he and his family had been regarded as commoners in the past; this, however, was of no great assistance to Jean's putative younger brother Michel.

Despite the claim of family tradition, however, and even the endorsement of Chamillart, there is room for doubt whether Jean Champion de Cicé and Michel Champion in Normandy were actually related.

The problem arises from differences in heraldry. The arms of the Champions de Cicé are *azure, three escutcheons argent charged with three bendlets gules*: that is, a blue shield with three small silver/white shields, each with three diagonal bands in red. This, of course, has no resemblance to the white shield with a black lion and a cross moline traditionally ascribed to the Champions, future holders of Crespigny, and it is almost impossible to believe that two related families could bear such radically different insignia.[26]

It is difficult to resolve this conundrum, but the best answer I can suggest is that if Jean Champion was a member of the family – and he certainly came from the right area at an appropriate time – then he may have married into an established Breton family holding the fief of Cicé and adopted the arms of that family. His younger brother Michel, less well

---

[23] *Nobiliaire et armorial* I, 218. Condé-sur-Vire is some twenty-five kilometres northeast of Vire on the road to Saint Lô. As the name indicates, it lies on the river of that name: above at 38.
[24] A brief account of the system is provided by Reulos, "Anobli aux francs fiefs."
[25] On the *taille*, see 39-40 above and Chapter Three at 90-93.
[26] See the discussion in the Introduction at 2.

CHAPTER TWO

connected, may then have claimed relationship as a means to enhance his own position in Normandy. In any event, the connection with the Champions de Cicé was still recognised four hundred years later, so the legend was a powerful one.[27]

Champion de Cicé   *Champion* [de Crespigny]

The *Lancaster Book* describes Michel simply as an *Escuier* with no specific estate, but adds that he married the daughter of the Sieur de la Rivière and that he died in Normandy. I suggest the force of the last comment is that Michel, unlike his brother Jean, returned to the region of his father and grandfather. There are naturally a number of places called La Rivière "the River," but a village of that name lies east of Tinchebray and south of Frênes, and this may be the place referred to.

There is no way to know when Michel went back to Normandy. It may have been only after the French reconquest in 1450, but it was probably earlier. Given that Michel's son Hebert was old enough to purchase the estate of La Fleurière in 1463, he should have been born about 1430, and if we can indeed assume that the family name of Michel's wife and Hebert's mother was connected to a place in Normandy, then Michel should have married her during the 1420s and he was presumably in Normandy at the time.[28]

In fact, the Treaty of Troyes in 1420 was followed by some years of comparative peace – fighting continued between the English and the Dauphin's supporters, but less intensely than before – and Michel, born in the first years of the century and now in his twenties, may have decided to return to the former homeland.

The family history makes no claim that Michel held any special position, and though his father-in-law may have owned land there is no reason to believe Jeanne obtained anything from her family beyond the usual dowry. The vicissitudes of defeat and exile had removed the connection between the Champions and the viscounty of Vire, and they may well have been in reduced circumstances. Though the names of four sons, Hebert, Pierre, Rioul and Gabriel, are recorded, nothing is said of any except the first. As Chamillart observed, while Jean was ennobled Michel was not, and his status had probably fallen below that of the recognised gentry.

On this question, Perroy's article on "Social Mobility" makes some important points:
- First, in the middle ages the status of gentry or *noblesse* (and for present purposes I use the terms as interchangeable) depended upon the capacity of the individual concerned to bear arms on behalf of his lord. In order to do this he (and by definition it had to be a

---

[27] The connection to the Champions de Cicé and other families of that surname in Brittany is discussed further in Part II at 71-75.

[28] It is also possible that Michel never left Normandy. He and his brother Jean, however, were probably no older than their middle teens at the time of the English conquest in 1417. They would both have needed support, and for one boy to stay and the other to go to Brittany would have required a real division within the family.

man) was required to possess and maintain the equipment of a knight; and he needed the skill at arms which could only be acquired by training.

Such equipment and training required money: a full suit of armour and the horse to carry it were extremely expensive, and weapon-training required the freedom from other duties that an ordinary peasant could never find. So the feudal relationship between land-holding and military service was not just a matter of birth and title: in a primitive economy land-holding was the one notable means by which an armoured warrior could be maintained.

- The second point is that the status of a knightly lineage was by no means fixed. It was perfectly possible, and indeed likely, that a family or an individual could decline in wealth and property so far as to become unable to maintain the expenses of military service, and would then descend into the ranks of *roturiers*, the non-gentry. The divisions of society were comparatively fluid: a prosperous peasant – or, very often, the trusted servant of a high baron or a church estate – could rise to membership of the gentry, and on his way up he would overtake or pass the representative of a declining lineage who could no longer afford to maintain that position. Perroy's observations and calculation of family fortunes in the county of Forez (now the Department of the Loire) indicate that, for one reason or another, half of those recorded as gentry at any one time would have disappeared from that rank over the following hundred years.[29] Sometimes this occurred through poverty, sometimes because the male line had died out – and the custom of putting younger sons into the Church was quite as effective a means of ending a lineage as any misfortune of war or pestilence.

- This is a third point from Perroy: not only was a family of marginal gentry at risk through loss of fortune and descent into poverty, but any lineage was quite likely to die out – and a long succession of "regular" inheritance from father to mature-age son was an exception rather than the rule. Of the kings of England from the early eleventh century to the thirteenth, only two, William the Conqueror and Henry II, were succeeded on the throne by sons grown to maturity (and in neither case were they the eldest sons). For the kings of France, from the late tenth century to the early fourteenth century, succession had followed from father to mature-age son, but this has been fairly described by Perroy as "a stroke of luck unique in history."[30] The accident did a great deal to confirm the authority of the French crown and, by reverse, when the direct male line of heirs failed in the first half of the fourteenth century it became a major factor in the claim to France by Edward III and the beginning of the Hundred Years War.

Perroy concludes that membership of the gentry rested not so much upon a legal grant from any higher authority, but rather upon local recognition and social acceptance:

> The accepted view, even among the gentry, was that nobility was exclusively a matter of birth..... Yet, in fact, the noble class was freely open to newcomers, through the acquisition of rural lordships, the holding of fiefs, matrimonial alliances with the gentry, the trade of war. None of these conditions made a gentleman *ipso facto*. They were influential in bringing about the consent of the local gentry.[31]

From this it becomes easier to understand how an elder brother, Jean Champion, who remained in Brittany, can have been recognised as noble and become the ancestor of a noble lineage, while the younger brother Michel, returning to Normandy, held lower status. In the middle fifteenth century we are observing a lineage, from Maheas through Richard to Jean and Michel, which had held gentry status through matrimonial alliances and the trade of war,

---

[29] "Social Mobility," 31.
[30] *Hundred Years War*, 71.
[31] "Social Mobility", 36.

briefly reinforced by notice from the king, but which was now, in Michel's case, in danger of moving down again.

The seigneury of La Fleurière 1463-1641
La Fleurière, which may be translated simply as "The flowery field", is shown on the map in the *Lancaster Book* and is described there as being "in the Parish of Saint-Quentin near Tinchebrais." The site and the village of Saint-Quentin-les-Chardonnets is some four kilometres northwest of Tinchebray, just off the D924 to Vire. There is a small blue place-sign reading "La Fleurière" on the right hand side of the D924, and a slip road, the D924E, leads to the hamlet. Frênes, the home of Maheas' father-in-law Jean Busnel, lies a short distance to the east. There are now only fields and a few modern houses; nothing of any size or age,[32] but for the Champions descended from Michel, grandson of Maheas, the acquisition of La Fleurière in 1463 by Michel's son Hebert is of great importance.

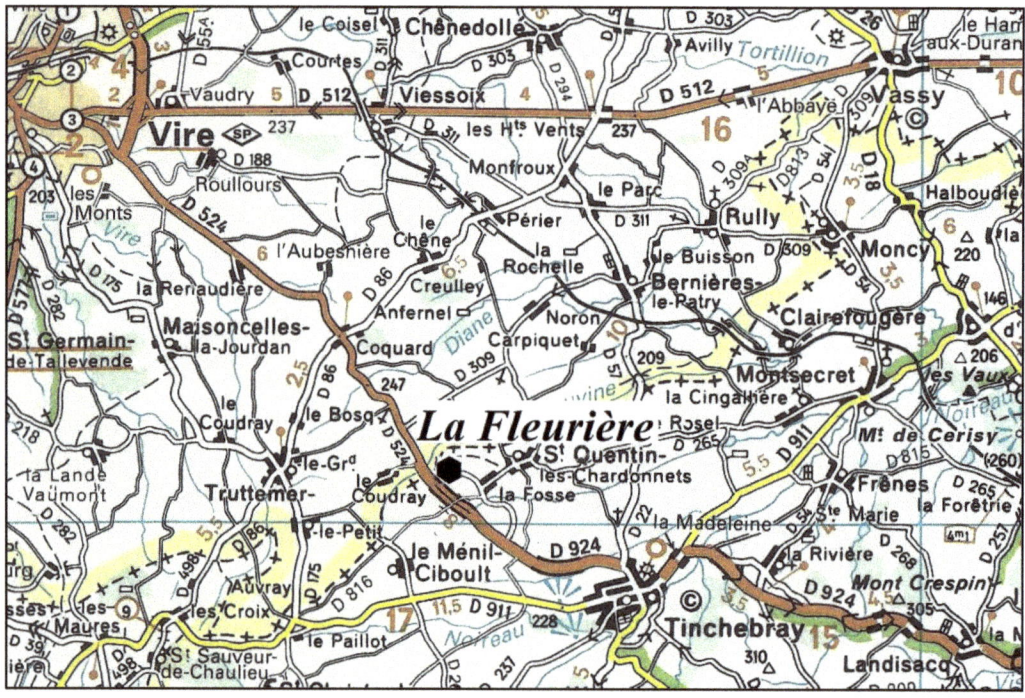

Map Seven: The area of La Fleurière; detail from Michelin France *2003 sheet 37*

Hebert purchased the estate from Jean l'Anglais [John the Englishman]. "L'Anglais" may have been a description rather than a true surname, and it is certainly possible that the previous owner of La Fleurière had been involved with the English occupation and was now, a few years after the reconquest by the French king, selling up and leaving. There is no account of where Hebert obtained the means to purchase La Fleurière – it may have come from his wife's dowry – but the Champions would hold the estate for almost two hundred years until it was sold in 1641.

---

[32] The *Reveley Book*, recording the journey of exploration of family sites in Normandy made by Sir Claude William, third baronet, and his brother Frederick in 1843, notes that they were told "a Pavilion supposed to have existed two centuries had lately been removed, which contained a very handsome staircase in form of a serpent, which led to the top." There was a place nearby called Championière, presumably named for the Champions, and the parish of Saint-Quentin still contained one or two families of that name. They must have been very distant cousins, with a connection earlier than Richard Champion and thus before 1600.

Stephen CdeC has observed that at the back of a small nineteenth or twentieth century house there are some old farm buildings, one of which may be part of a more ancient dwelling house.

La Fleuriere in the Department of Orne, postcode 61800, is too small to appear on a Michelin map, but it may be found on Google Maps.

The *Extract from the Register of the Court of Aides*, citing the original deed of purchase, gives the date as 4 May 1463, and it is followed by the *Lancaster Book*. This quoted document was the earliest recognised by the Court, and in many respects it marks the beginning of the history, as opposed to the prehistory, of the family.

One may see this principle most obviously in the Certificate of the College of Arms granted to Peter, Thomas and Gabriel Champion de Crespigny in 1697. The Certificate notes that the Court of Aides at Rouen in 1674 had "justified" their noble quality and filiation from Hebert, living in 1463, while the Heralds remark that "we have seen and perused" the old book of the pedigree from Maheas: neither the Court of Aides nor the College of Arms actually endorse the early claim to descent from Maheas through Richard and Michel to Hebert.

Indeed the acquisition of La Fleurière is the first record of a member of the family holding land in his own right. As viscounts of Vire, Maheas and Richard had been government officials: they may have possessed landed property, and Maheas in particular may have held something in right of his wife, who is said to have been an heiress of the Busnel family. There is no account of any specific territory, however, and it seems certain that any such property was lost at the time of the English occupation; Michel is not said to have possessed an estate. So the purchase by Hebert is the first evidence of the establishment of the Champions as local proprietors.

The landscape of La Fleurière between Tinchebray and Vire

Though they may appear almost random, it is possible to make some sense of the various accounts and authorities for the lineage before Hebert. We may consider the items in order:
1. In 1673 the Intendant Chamillart, citing earlier decisions, found that Richard and Claude Champion were not members of the *noblesse* because, among other reasons, they were descended from Michel, not from Jean, and only Jean had been granted the rank. Those

decisions were based upon the distinction between a noble lineage and a non-noble cadet branch, and for that purpose they went back one generation beyond Hebert to his father and uncle.

2. For the subsequent appeal to the Court of Aides, however, it was only necessary for the family to trace their lineage back as far as Hebert. If they could show that Hebert was of noble rank, and that the family had been in possession of landed property and maintained its status for more than two hundred years, then earlier members of the lineage could be assumed to have held that position; and this indeed had been largely acknowledged by Chamillart. There was no need to explore or "justify" any earlier generations.

3. And then the *South Sea*, *Reveley* and *Lancaster* books claim descent from Maheas and Richard, two further generations back. This again is reasonable: if Maheas and Richard had both been men of standing, they were of interest to Hebert who was their great-grandson and grandson. The establishment of the family at La Fleurière may have provided occasion to make a record of the immediate ancestors, and since Jean was alive until 1470, and possibly Hebert's father Michel too, some account of Maheas and Richard would have been available.

Round has remarked:

> If this descent [from Maheas] could be proved, it is strange that the Cour des Aides should only have carried back the pedigree to Herbert.....[33]

My argument from the above, however, is that the Court of Aides had no need to carry the pedigree back, so it is not strange that they failed to do so.

The *Extract from the Registers of the Court of Aides* provides further information on the period after Hebert's purchase, as additional documents were presented to the Court and are duly listed:

- on 22 November 1483 Hebert received the transfer of some income from Philippe Champion, of whom nothing more is known;
- in 1488 and 1489 four deeds of unspecified content were executed at Tinchebray, all of them describing Hebert Champion as Esquire and of noble rank;
- on 2 January 1491 Hebert is mentioned in a judgement of the Assizes of Tinchebray;
- and in 1500 and 1501 Hebert was involved in a taxation case with ramifications into the neighbouring bailiwick of Cotentin and its viscounty of Mortain.

Finally in regard to Hebert, between 4 March 1508 and 22 April 1511 there were a series of documents drawn up by the notaries at Tinchebray to settle the inheritance of Hebert Champion between his three sons **Antoine**, **Martin** and **Jean**. It would appear that Hebert died either late in 1507 or early in 1508.

Also on 4 March 1508, Antoine Champion, son of Hebert, acknowledged before the notaries of Tinchebray the marriage contract of Guillaume Vaillant with Demoiselle Magdelaine Champion his sister – and thus the daughter of Hebert. Such acknowledgement of a previous contract was part of the procedure for distributing property after Hebert's death: besides whatever dowry was paid at the time of the wedding, an agreement had granted an additional share of the property when the bride's father died.[34]

---

[33] "Huguenot House," 111. Round uses the anglicised form of the given name as "Herbert." One might have expected the name in French to have an accent: "Hébert." All family sources, however, agree on Hebert.

[34] The acknowledgement before notaries of a marriage contract was not made at the time of the marriage and the formation of the contract, but as the result of some later change, normally a death: see, for example, Shorter, *Making of the Modern Family*, 41. In this case Magdelaine's father Hebert had died and her husband Guillaume Vaillant was calling in the commitment.

In similar fashion, though the *Lancaster Book* has the date of marriage of Magdelaine (written as Madelaine) as 4 March 1508, I do not believe that interpretation is correct: the marriage had taken place and the contract made some years earlier; the contract was now being enforced.

The *Extract* continues in similar fashion, citing legal documents concerning Hebert's descendants. The sole purpose of these citations was to prove that ancestors of the family had been consistently described as Esquires and/or of noble/gentry status, and since they were selected just for that reason, many items are of limited information or interest. I summarise only those which may be useful for genealogical or more practical historical purposes.

- Following the inheritance from his father Hebert, three further documents relate to Antoine Champion; in one dated 1527 Guillaume Abot, no doubt a brother or cousin of his mother Jeanne nee Abot, transferred thirty-four *livres* of rent to him by a deed recorded at the town of Mortain. As the last document is dated 1539, Antoine may have died about 1540.
- **Raoul** [also as Roul or Raul] Champion, son of Antoine, is first mentioned in 1541, as author of a writ served against a certain Nicolas Fourey for the assizes at Tinchebray, and he also appears in judgements and deeds made at Mortain and at Vire. On 10 March 1550 the marriage contract for Raoul Champion with Jeanne la Forestier was acknowledged before notaries,[35] and the contract included a schedule of the estates possessed by Raoul Champion and his brother **Nicolas**; the properties themselves, unfortunately, are not listed in the *Extract*.[36]
- In 1555 a contract was drawn up between **Giles** and **Jean** Champion on the one part and Nicolas and Raoul, sons of Antoine, on the other. Giles and Jean were presumably cousins, probably the sons of Antoine's younger brother Martin.[37]
- In 1564 Jeanne nee la Forestier gave a power of attorney to her husband Raoul and their son **Jean** so they might acquire the estate of Guillaume le Forestier, who appears to have been her brother and is described in the *Lancaster Book* as Lord of Saint-Opportune and Magny.[38]
- In the following year Jeanne obtained in Falaise a judgement against the widow of Sebastien le Forestier; she may have been Jeanne's natural mother or – perhaps more likely – her stepmother. Raoul Champion is also referred to in a series of deeds and contracts between 1565 and 1569: he presumably died soon after the latter date.
- Jean Champion, son of Raoul and grandson of Antoine, appears again in a deed of 14 December 1573, by which the priests of the parish of Saint-Quentin gave him a receipt of payment on account for the obsequies and memorial service for his late uncle the priest Nicolas Champion. As we have seen, La Fleurière was situated in the parish of Saint-Quentin.

---

[35] As above, the acknowledgement before notaries of a marriage contract was made, not at the time of the marriage and the formation of the contract, but when some later change triggered the application of the terms of the agreement. In this case, Raoul had married some time before 1550, and this formality probably related to the death of his father-in-law and a claim made by him against that estate.

[36] In this and other deeds Nicolas is given first mention, so he was presumably the elder brother. He was, however, a priest, and we may assume that Raoul had effective control of the greater part of the family property. It is a little surprising for the eldest brother of a landed family to become a priest, but it may be that Nicolas had an elder brother who died after he had taken the vows – secular property then passed to Raoul.

[37] Jean Champion, third son of Hebert, is described as a priest. It is possible, but less likely, that Giles and Jean were descended from Pierre, Rioul or Gabriel, sons of Michel and younger brothers of Hebert: above at 42 and Table I.

[38] Neither the *Extract* nor the *Reveley* and *South Sea* books contain any reference to these titles, and it is difficult to see where the information came from. No place named Saint-Opportune appears anywhere in the modern Michelin, but there were several called Magny in this region of Lower Normandy: the closest to La Fleurière is Magny-le-Desert, some thirty kilometres to the southeast, but there is also a Magny-la-Campagne near Falaise, a little further in the northeast. Since it appears immediately below that a family court case was heard at Falaise, it is perhaps more likely that the Forestier family was based at Magny-la-Campagne.

CHAPTER TWO

A number of other documents show Jean Champion engaged in various transactions, debts and judgements, frequently supported by his son Richard: in 1627, for example, there is reference to "several Estates" which had been pledged under a disputed judgement at Tinchebray; and 1629 Jean Champion granted his son Richard an extension of time in some matter of the dowry of Marthe nee du Bourget, wife of Jean and mother of Richard. Curiously, there is no mention of the marriage of Jean and Marthe, but we must assume that it took place during the 1580s, followed by the births of three children: **Richard**, **Jacques** [see below] and daughter **Marie**.[39]

Jean Champion evidently died in February 1632, for he was interred in the parish of Saint-Quentin on the 22nd of that month. The marriage contract of Pierre Thomas with Jean's daughter Marie was acknowledged before the notaries of Saint-Jean-le-Blanc on 1 March 1633 as part of the settlement of the deceased estate; the contract had been made on 8 April 1625.

The name of **Richard** Champion, son of Jean, had already appeared in documents in association with his father, and in 1617 he dealt on his own account with the prosecution of a certain Richard Cornu at Le Tourneur.[40] In 1623 Jean Champion granted a power of attorney, drawn up before the notaries at Tinchebray, to Richard, described as "his only Son," authorising him to institute proceedings against a certain Etienne Hardy [the French surname presumably being Hardi] for manslaughter of the late Jacques Champion, son of Jean and brother of Richard. No details of the case are preserved, but the reference to Richard as Jean's only son presumably meant he was the only one still alive.

For the future of the family, the most important event took place in December 1617. On the 6th of that month the contract of Richard Champion – styled noble and described as the son of Jean and of his wife Marthe nee du Bourget – for marriage with Marguerite nee Richard, was drawn up before the notaries of Vassy. And the Registers of Marriages and Baptisms of the Protestant church at Condé[-sur-Noireau] recorded that Richard Champion and Marguerite nee Richard were married on 13 December.[41] Their son Claude was baptised two and a half years later, on 17 May 1620.[42]

On 10 June 1624 Richard Champion's wife Marguerite nee Richard, with the other co-heirs of her father Adrian Richard, chose portions and shares from the estate which he had left at his death. It was presumably at that time Richard and his wife came into full possession of the lands of Crespigny in the parish of Saint-Jean-le-Blanc.

---

[39] As below, Richard Champion married Marguerite nee Richard in 1617. The couple were probably in their mid-twenties when they married.

The website of family portraits at Kelmarsh Hall, Northamptonshire, gives Richard's year of birth as 1587. This is possible, but I do not know upon what authority the statement is based.

A portrait of Marthe nee du Bourget, now at Kelmarsh Hall, is illustrated in Chapter Three at 83.

[40] The commune of Le Tourneur is northeast of Vire, some distance from the family property at La Fleurière but only a few kilometres west of Saint-Jean-le-Blanc and Crépigny. There are no details of the case.

[41] Vassy lies east of Vire on the D512, almost due north of Tinchebray and some twelve kilometres northeast of La Fleurière. It must be distinguished from Vassy [also known as Wassy] in the department of Haute-Marne, which was the scene of a religious conflict and massacre in 1562: 37 above.

Condé-sur-Noireau is ten kilometres east of Vassy, also on the D512. There are other places named Condé in Normandy but they are much further away: *cf.* Condé-sur-Vire at 47 above.

The *Lancaster Book*, followed by Ball, "History," gives the date of the marriage as 6 December. The *Extract from the Register of the Court of Aides*, however, makes it clear that 6 December was the day on which the marriage contract was signed, and the wedding took place a week later: see immediately below.

[42] Though the Court of Aides referred disdainfully to the "so-called Reformed/Protestant Religion," as part of the evidence for the family claim to nobility it was prepared to accept the entry dated 13 December 1617 in the Register of Marriage from the Huguenot temple at Condé for Richard Champion, "styled noble," and Marguerite nee Richard, and the subsequent entry in the Register of Baptism for Claude dated 17 May 1620.

CALVADOS AND THE DUCHY

I consider other matters relating to Richard and his son Claude in Chapter Three. So far, however, based upon the documents cited from the *Extract*, and the account in the *South Sea* and *Reveley* books, the lineage of the family at La Fleurière may be reconstructed as follows:

Hebert Champion married Jeanne, daughter of Jean Abot Esquire, Squire of Melly;[43]
    he was probably born about 1440; he died in 1507 or 1508.

The eldest son of Hebert Champion and Jeanne nee Abot was Antoine Champion;
    of their other children: there was a son Martin of whom nothing is said;[44]
    another son Jean became a priest;
    and a daughter Magdelaine/Magdalene married Guillaume Vaillant Esquire.

Shield of Hebert Champion married to Jeanne Abot

Shield of Antoine Champion married to Catherine Marye

Antoine Champion, eldest son of Hebert, married Catherine nee Marye;
    Antoine was probably born about 1480 and died about 1540.

Of their sons, Nicolas became a priest and died about 1573;

Shield of Raoul Champion married to Jeanne le Forestier

Shield of Jean Champion married to Marthe du Bourget

Raoul Champion, son of Antoine and younger brother of Nicolas, married Jeanne nee la Forestier and gained estates from her family, very likely at Saint-Opportune and Magny;
    Raoul was probably born about 1510 and died about 1570.

---

[43] Melley may be identified as the commune of Mellé in the department of Ille-et-Vilaine in north-eastern Brittany. Sixty kilometres from Vire, it lies close to half way on the route to Rennes. Mortain is a major local centre, and pages 52 and 53 above mention several legal matters dealt with there.

[44] As above at 53, however, it appears Martin may have had sons named Giles and Jean.

CHAPTER TWO

Jean Champion, only child of Raoul, married Marthe du Bourget;
> of their children:
>> the second son Jacques was killed/murdered about 1623;
>> their daughter Marie married Pierre Thomas in 1633;
> Jean was probably born about 1545; he died at La Fleurière on 22 February 1632.

Richard Champion, elder son of Jean and Marthe nee de Bouget, married Marguerite, daughter of Adrian Richard, on 13 December 1617;
> Richard was born about 1590; he died, presumably at Crespigny, on 11 November 1669;
> Marguerite was born in 1601 and died at Saint Lô on 23 January 1682, age 80 years.

Claude, only son of Richard Champion and Marguerite nee Richard, was born on 17 May 1620.

In 1641, with his son Claude, Richard sold the estate of La Fleurière to Henri du Gué.[45]

The property had been held by the family for 178 years, through five generations from Hebert to Richard inclusive. The lineage was fortunate to have had male heirs from one generation to another, while the men were comparatively long-lived and had children quite late in life; the average for the five generations from 1463 to 1641 is over thirty-five years.

Apart from Jacques' murder or manslaughter, there is no great excitement in the history, and in particular it should be observed that, although there were Huguenot communities in Calvados, it was not until the marriage of Richard Champion in 1617 that there is any sign of connection to the Reformed Religion. On the contrary, the Champions remained Catholics during all this period and, as was common among good families of the faith, two sons in successive generations became priests: Jean the son of Hebert and Nicolas son of Antoine.

I deal with the Huguenot question in the next chapter. We may observe here, however, that at the beginning of the seventeenth century the family was reasonably well established among the minor gentry of their neighbourhood. There was an estate, though not a particularly large one; the marriages of each generation had gained property or rent, at least in the form of dowry; and the alliance of Raoul with Jeanne la Forestier was certainly advantageous. Even before the marriage of Richard Champion with Marguerite daughter of Adrian Richard, the Champions were comfortable.

The records contain no account of any military or political distinction, and no mention of any member receiving office or honour from the crown, but the social position maintained over the better part of two centuries is worthy of note. There was question on the family's true entitlement to status among the *noblesse*, a privilege first challenged in 1591, but I discuss that matter below.[46] In any event, as Round remarks, not many families in England can show descent from the fifteenth century:[47] the Wars of the Roses and the suspicions of the Tudors eliminated several tall poppies among the aristocracy, and many lesser families disappeared from records, in England as in France, through loss of the male line or simply through poverty and obscurity. In terms of Perroy's "Social Mobility," it was a considerable achievement to maintain lineage and property for so long.[48]

---

[45] As above, for purposes of the documents recorded in the *Extract* there was no need to provide more details about the purchaser of the estate than just his name. The map in the *Lancaster Book* shows a village called Le Gué [The Ford] close to La Fleurière: it is likely that Henri du Gué was a neighbour of the Champions.

[46] Chapter Three at 90-96.

[47] "Huguenot House," 109.

[48] On Perroy, see above at 49.

A major threat, of course, was the endemic warfare and disorder during the period of the Hundred Years War. At the battle of Agincourt, for example, French casualties were so heavy that "Entire families were wiped out in the male line, fathers and sons, brothers and cousins:" Sumption, *Cursed Kings*, 460. And while the capture of a town or fortress was regularly accompanied by the slaughter of its defenders and the pillage and killing of its civilian population, custom permitted also that "those who give aid and

By the beginning of the seventeenth century, therefore, the Champions of La Fleurière were still at that site. If asked what they had done, the reply might be, like Talleyrand's after the French Revolution, that they had survived. It is no small boast.

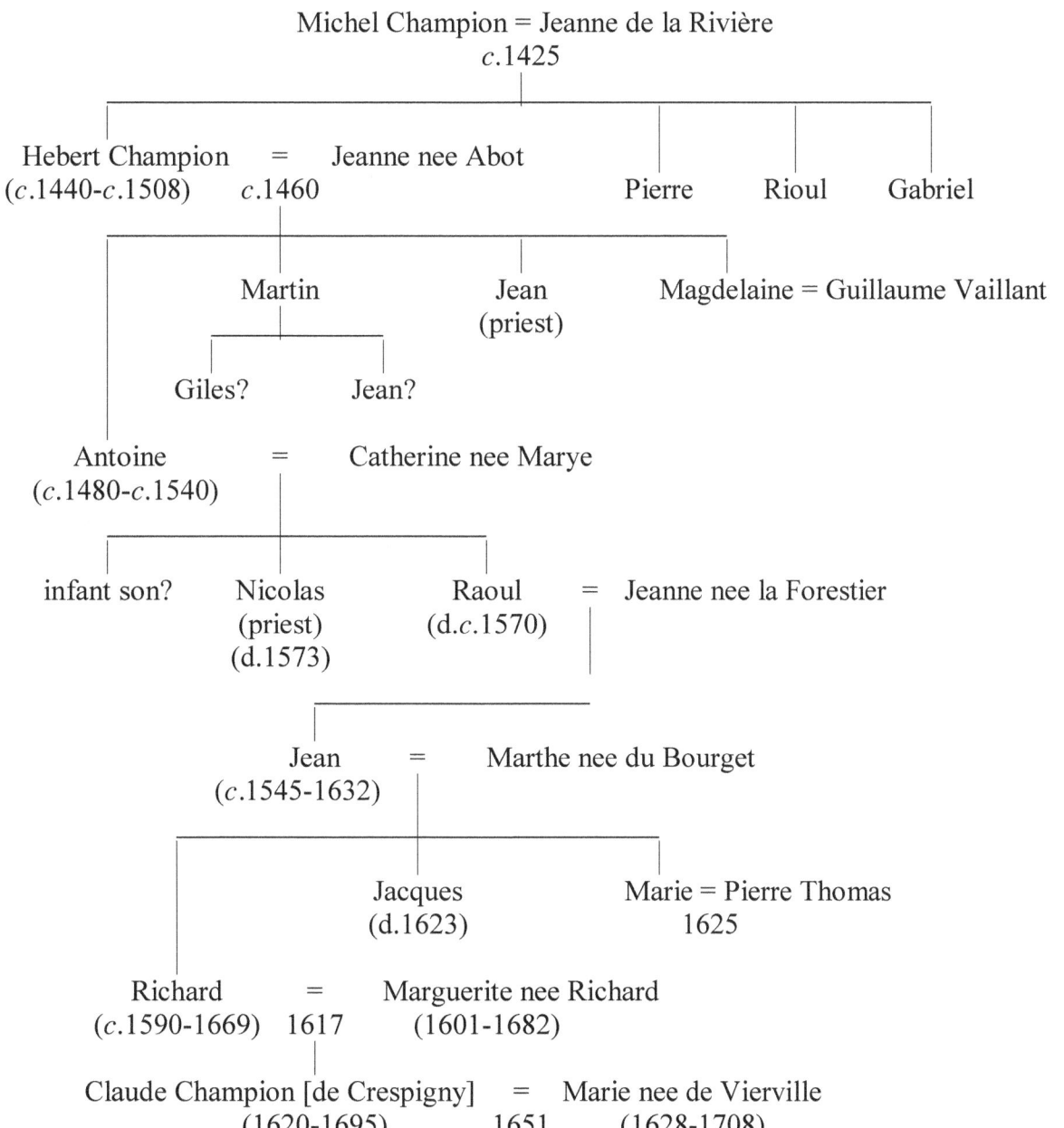

TABLE II: THE CHAMPION FAMILY AT LA FLEURIERE
purchased 1463, sold 1641

countenance to war may be despoiled in the same way as soldiers," so even peasants working in their fields were considered fair game: *e.g.* Keen, *Laws of War*, 191.

There was also high mortality from plague, not only the widespread Black Death of the mid-fourteenth century, but from frequent recurrences in individual localities: Le Roy Ladurie, *Carnival at Romans*, considers a small town in the Dauphiné, where an outbreak in 1586 killed half the inhabitants. At page 21 he remarks that the list of names of those who died provides "a thorough and valid poll (with 51 per cent responding!) ..." In times such as those, there were many ways that a life and a lineage could be cut short.

CHAPTER TWO

Part II: Tales, Legends and Fictions
So far in this chapter I have sought to relate the history of the Champion [de Crespigny] family on the basis of reasonably secure historical documentation. Not surprisingly, however, there are a number of tales and stories which have been variously accepted by members of the family and some putative kinsmen. There is the matter of William de Crespigny in the skirmish at Brenneville/Brémule; there are the very broad claims of the Mollerus family; there is the legend of prehistory presented by Burke and Debrett, owing a good deal to the enthusiasm of Sir Claude the fourth baronet; and there is the long-distance relationship with the Champions de Cicé and others of that name in Brittany. These may all be considered as family fictions, but they deserve to be considered and to be checked against some historical background and relevant facts.

William de Crespigny and the King of England
In 1908 *The Times* of London published *The Historians' History of the World*, edited by Henry Smith Williams LlD and subtitled *A comprehensive narrative of the rise and development of nations as recorded by the great writers of all ages*. It is very Euro-centred – of its twenty-five volumes, the single volume XXIV covers Turkey, Minor Eastern States, China and Japan; India is a British colony, and Africa is mentioned only as the subject of Western empires – but it is nonetheless a fair survey of the state of knowledge of European history at the beginning of the twentieth century.

Volume XI of the *History* deals with *France 843-1715*, and pages 31 to 32 have an account of the battle of Brenneville, which took place on 20 August 1119.

The king of France at that time was Louis VI, known as "le Gros:" the soubriquet is often rendered as "the Fat," but he was more competent and enterprising than that would imply, and it can be understood simply as "the Large;" he was a big, strong man.

King Henry I of England, youngest son of William the Conqueror, had succeeded to the throne after the death of his brother William Rufus in 1100, and in 1106 he defeated and captured his eldest brother Robert Curthose at the battle of Tinchebray and took the duchy as well. Normandy was regarded as the more valuable possession, but it was notionally held as a fief of the king of France, and Robert's son William Clito joined the following of Louis VI, who was prepared to support the deposed duke in hope of confirming suzerainty over his territory.

Brenneville, more commonly known as Brémule, is a plain near Les Andelys in the Vexin, the borderland between Normandy and the royal territory of Isle de France in the valley of the Seine. Louis and Henry encountered one another there unexpectedly; Louis had some four hundred mounted knights and Henry had five hundred armoured men, just one hundred of them mounted, with some light infantry on foot. The *History* goes on to say that

> William de Crespigny, a Norman knight on Clito's side, charged first with eighty men-at-arms, penetrated as far as King Henry himself, and smote him such a blow on the head as, but for his cap of mail, must have split his skull; but Crespigny was instantly thrown from his horse and made prisoner with most of his followers.

The rest of the royal force joined the attack, but were driven back and King Louis, seeing that he was in danger of capture, abandoned the field. His banner and more than a hundred of his men were taken by the enemy.

The encounter was little more than a skirmish, but it had political effect, for the swift defeat was embarrassing to Louis and stories were told that he lost his way in the confusion of retreat and had to be guided to safety by a peasant he met in the woods. In the negotiations which followed he was obliged to abandon his support of William Clito and his father Robert and to recognise Henry as ruler of Normandy.

The engagement is described in a number of contemporary or near-contemporary sources:
- the *Ecclesiastical History* [*Historia Ecclesiastica*] of the Benedictine monk Ordericus Vitalis (1075-1143?)[49] – this is the source quoted by the *Historians' History* for the enterprise of William de Crespigny;
- the *Hyde Chronicle*, compiled at the abbey of that name near Winchester in England;[50]
- the Peterborough text of the *Anglo-Saxon Chronicle*;[51]
- The *History of the English People* [*Historia Anglorum*] by Henry of Huntingdon (*c*.1088-*c*.1157), Archdeacon of the diocese of Lincoln.[52]

The modern scholar Matthew Strickland has a detailed study of the incident in his article "Henry I and the Battle of the Two Kings."

The various chronicles add different details. Orderic observes that the Anglo-Normans killed the horses of William Crispin and his comrades – which Chibnall suggests would explain why so many of them were captured so easily and quickly – and goes on to say that

> William Crispin, however, who had been surrounded with his men as I have described, caught sight of the king. Tearing through the ranks towards the man he hated above all others, he struck a fierce blow at his head with his sword, but the collar of the noble prince's hauberk protected his head from injury.

William was then taken prisoner by one of Henry's following and barely escaped with his life.

The *Hyde Chronicle* says that William landed two blows to the king's helmet, and Henry of Huntingdon also says that he hit the king twice, and although the helmet protected him it was forced down onto his forehead and cut it so that it bled. Henry, however, struck back and forced William from his horse.

Orderic Vitalis claims that only three of the nine hundred knights engaged on either side were killed, explaining that this was because of their heavy armour, while they also spared one another "out of fear of God and fellowship in arms." As many of the combatants were kinsmen and neighbours, moreover, they were not anxious to develop feuds, and there was in any case more profit in capture than in killing. Such consideration, however, did not apply to common footsoldiers, who were often slaughtered in large numbers.

And there is a rather strange reverse story, attributed to French chroniclers and the basis for an account in the popular nineteenth-century *Histoire de France* by L-Sam Colart. This claims it was King Louis who was attacked, but that he dealt firmly with his assailant:

> Louis VI gave proof of his courage in the fight of Brenneville, hurling himself into the midst of the enemy.
>
> An English soldier seized the bridle of his horse and shouted, "The king is taken!"
>
> "Don't you know?" replied Louis with complete aplomb, "No-one takes the king, not even in a game of chess!" And with a single blow of his mace he laid the man dead at his feet.

---

[49] *The Ecclesiastical History of Orderic Vitalis*, edited and translated by Chibnall, VI, 238-241. Though born in England, Orderic spent most of his life at the Abbey of St Evroul in Normandy.

[50] *Chronica monasterii de Hida juxta Wintoniam*, in *Liber monasterii de Hyda* edited by Edward Edwards, 318.

[51] Whitelock *et al.* [eds], *The Anglo-Saxon Chronicle*, *sub* 1119.

Compilation of the *Chronicle* was begun at the time of Alfred the Great in the late ninth century, and copies were later distributed and individually up-dated. Five of the six principal versions of the *Chronicle* which survive end their history before or soon after the Conquest in 1066, but so-called manuscript E, partially based on an original text from Canterbury but continued in Peterborough, goes as far as 1155: Bagley, *Historical Interpretation*, 18.

[52] Forester [ed], *Chronicle of Henry of Huntingdon*, 247-248. The work has also been edited by Thomas Arnold and translated by Diana Greenway.

The incident was considered worthy of an illustration, and copies are available on the internet, but the story appears to be a conflation of the assault on the English king, devised to save some face for the French.

Louis VI at Brenneville
Plate 39 from Colart's Histoire de France

After all this, it is disappointing to find that the man identified by *The Historians' History* was not actually surnamed "de Crespigny." The Latin text of Ordericus Vitalis refers to him as "Guillelmus Crispinus," rendered by Chibnall simply as "William Crispin," and William Crispin appears in number of other incidents of the time: he had been captured at the battle of Tinchebray in 1106 – thirteen years earlier – and though he was subsequently pardoned by King Henry he remained a firm and active supporter of Louis VI and – from what Orderic says, a bitter and personal enemy of the English monarch.

There is no way to tell how William acquired the soubriquet Crispin: he may have been born on the saint's day, or even have come from a place named after Saint Crispin – including the small hamlet of Crespigny in the Calvados. The core problem, however, is that anyone named William de Crespigny was, by definition, no close ancestor of the family later named Champion de Crespigny. There is no record of the Champion family before Maheas the Viscount of Vire in the mid-fourteenth century; there is no reason to believe that Maheas was in any way related to William Crispin over two hundred years earlier; and the Champion family did not acquire the estate of Crespigny until the 1620s, following the marriage in 1617 of Richard Champion to Marguerite nee Richard, heiress of her father.

The whole story is a good example of how legend may confuse family history. A recent version claims that a member of the family knocked Edward the Black Prince off his horse – this feat being presumably achieved by Maheas either at the battle of Crécy in 1346 or at Poitiers in 1356. It's a nice idea, and one can see where it comes from, but it just didn't happen like that.

Mollerus-Le Champion and Mad King Charles
I have in my possession some photocopied sheets from a printed book, reproduced from the collection of Miss Valencia Lancaster at Kelmarsh Hall and passed to me by Stephen CdeC. They concern the "Family of Le Champion-Marmion, Formerly Vicomtes de Fonteneys-Le-Marmion et de Vire et Everche, etc." Stephen CdeC has added some notes based upon various nineteenth-century editions of *Burke's Peerage* and the 1863 edition of *Burke's Landed Gentry*, and has compiled a genealogical tree from the information.

The material relates to the claimed ancestry of Lieutenant-Colonel Henry von Mollerus le Champion, also known as Henry Le Champion-Möller, whose father Charles Champion le Champion-Mollerus had served in the Waterloo campaign of 1815 as an officer in the 18th Hussars. Further documents describe how the Moller family claimed descent from a Senator Joachim von Mollerus, who received grants of nobility from King Henry VIII of England in 1538 and from the Holy Roman Emperor Charles V in 1541. They also assert that an ancestor of the Senator, Johan von Moller, had been ennobled in 1440 by Christoph von Bayern, king of Sweden, Denmark and Norway, and a descendant, Henricus von Mollerus, was similarly honoured by King Christian V of Denmark in 1674.

From the point of view of the Champion family, however, the notable point is that the Moller/Champion lineage (as I refer to it hereafter) claims to be descended from Maheas Champion, described as the first Viscount of Vire, through Richard his son and then through Oliver/Olivier Champion, the eldest of three sons of Richard. The second son was Jean/John, who became the ancestor of the Champions of Cicé, and the third was Michel/Michael, who was the father of Hebert and ancestor of the Champions de Crespigny. From Oliver, a lineage is traced to Jacques Le Champion, a Huguenot who held title as sixteenth Viscount of Vire until his emigration to Dublin in 1688. Jacques' grand-daughter Elizabeth married Andrew George Moller [or Möller] of Butterston[e], in Perthshire, Scotland. Charles Champion their son "assumed his mother's name by royal licence" and – since "Champion" was also his given name – produced a very strange combination.[53]

Besides this, the Moller/Champion lineage claims the distinction of a crusading ancestor and a connection with the great Marmion family, whose members played leading roles in England from the Norman Conquest of 1066 until the end of the thirteenth century. Horace Round, however, has given his views on the CdeC claim in that line, and I do not believe that his criticism and dismissal of attributions before the time of Maheas in the mid-fourteenth century can be effectively challenged.[54]

With regard to the lineage from Oliver the eldest son of Richard, we must note that there is no CdeC family record which mentions these cousins, and there is strong argument from heraldry against any close relationship.

Champion de Caimbie   *Champion [de Crespigny]*   *Marmion*

Burke blazons the shield of Oliver's family as *azure, au sautoir d'or, cantonné de quatre fleur-de-lys d'argent*: that is, blue with a gold/yellow saltire [St Andrew's cross] surrounded

---

[53] A royal licence, granted on recommendation of the College of Arms, permits a change of surname and the transfer of the right to arms to a person not in legitimate male line of descent. It does not appear, however, that Charles Champion le Champion-Mollerus made use of any form of the Champion arms, real or imagined.

[54] See 71 below.

CHAPTER TWO

by four silver/white fleurs-de-lys at the top, the bottom, the left and the right. The Moller/Champion sheets assert that these were the arms of the French Marmions d'Urvyle, which were evidently used in preference to those of the Champions, The connection to the Marmion family is quite unproven, however, and the arms are in fact those of another family, the Champions de Caimbie, who held estates near Saint Malô on the northern coast of Brittany.[55] The main lineage of the Marmion family, which had estates both in France and in England, had quite a different shield: *vairée argent and azure, a fess gules*: a blue-and-white patterned field with a red bar across the centre.[56]

The uncertain connection to the Champions de Cicé through Jean the elder brother of Michel/Michael has been raised and considered above, and I discuss the question further below.[57]

As to the descent as Viscount of Vire in a senior line through Oliver as the eldest son of Richard, the printed sheets and Burke offer no more than a list of names, unaccompanied by any supporting evidence; and we have observed above that a viscounty in Normandy was an appointed office, not a hereditary fief.[58]

One document cited by the Moller/Champion sheets, dated to 7 October 1668, refers to Pierre le Champion, "*Vicomte de Vire, Seigneur de Belle-esze*," descended from Ricard le Champion, "*Vicomte de Vire en l'an 1220*;" and the main text refers also to "another Ricard … Vicomte de Vire in 1350." There are problems with this and with many such statements:

- Ricard le Champion appears to have been Viscount of Vire some 150 years before Maheas held that office; it is said that he was also Governor of Mont-Saint-Michel in 1203, but that is no more relevant or helpful. As Champion is and was a fairly common occupation and surname, there is no reason to believe the Ricard of 1220 and Maheas of 1350 were related.
- The Ricard said to have been Viscount of Vire in 1350 would have been holding the office at the same time as Maheas. The contradiction could be resolved if Maheas died in 1350 and Ricard/Richard his son succeeded him, but I have argued that it is unlikely Maheas died so early.
- I can find no reference to a place named Belle-esze in Brittany or anywhere else.
- Besides the fact that a viscounty in Normandy was a royal appointment and could not be inherited automatically, if the family had settled in Brittany and severed connection with Normandy it would have been neither practicable nor possible for men living in Brittany to have maintained an office and position in Vire.

In the fourth edition of his *Genealogical and Heraldic History of the Landed Gentry*, published in 1862-63, Burke also quotes this document – the text varies slightly but the date and signature are the same – but with descent from Ricard le Champion, "*Vicomte De Vire, en l'an 1350*."[59] In a section on the *Family of Le Champion de Vire*, moreover, included in the broader treatment of the Moller/Möller family, Burke repeats the account of the descent from Oliver as founder of the senior lineage, and refers to the baronet Champions de Crespigny as merely "supposed to be the head of the Huguenot branch in the male line." In effect, the Moller/Champion family – in whatever combination the name appears – claims seniority over the Champions de Crespigny.

---

[55] These, and other Champion families, including the Champions de Cicé, are discussed in Section 4 below.

[56] "Vair" refers to a blue-grey squirrel, whose fur – both the inside and the outside – was used for the lining of clothes. This is formalised in heraldry as an alternating pattern of blue with white.

In the fairy-tale of Cinderella, it is probable that the essential slipper was originally made of fur (French: *vair*), and at some stage this was mistakenly or deliberately confused with glass (French: *verre*).

[57] Above at 41 and 47-48; below at 71-74.

[58] Above at 46.

[59] The family of Le Champion-Moller of Butterstone is treated on pages 1020-22 of volume 2, with a hand-written umlaut on the surname Moller: *viz*. Möller. The Le Champion de Vire discussion is at 1021-22.

Family of Le Champion-Marmion,
Formerly Vicomtes de Fonteneys-Le-Marmion et de Vire et Everche, etc.

By KING CHARLES VI. OF FRANCE,
Surnamed "THE MAD."
(TRANSLATED FROM THE LATIN.)

Latin DEED, dated at Falaise, 1st January, 1418, depriving BERTRAND LE CHAMPION-MARMION, last Viscount and Baron de FONTENEYS and d'URVYLE, Vicomte de VIRE, etc., of the office of Champion, and of the title and estates of Fonteneys le Marmion and Urvyle, in favour of ROBERT SHOTTISBROKE, the King's favourite.

The King Greeting, etc. Know that of our special grace we have granted and conceded to our beloved Armour Bearer, ROBERT SHOTTISBROKE, all those manors, lands, and fortified dwellings, etc., etc., which were possessed by BERTRAND LE CHAMPION, Armour Bearer, with the manors of Urvyle and of Founteneys (le Marmion), which were held by WILLELMA (LE CHAMPION) mother of the aforesaid BERTRAND, with all other lands, manors, rents, and possessions held by the said BERTRAND and WILLELMA DE FONTENEYS under our dukedom of NORMANDY, the said manors, lands, tenements, rents, and possessions to be held and possessed by the aforesaid and before described ROBERT SHOTTISBROKE, and by the male heirs begotten of his body, together with all the liberties, rents, services, franchises, privileges, wards, reliefs, escheats, courts, military covenants, lands, meadows, pastures, parks, warrens, chaces, waifs, strays, fish-ponds, lakes, mills, offices, marshes, ecclesiastical benefices whatsoever, with all other reversions, profits, and advantages, manors and lands of the aforesaid BERTRAND and WILLELMA, held by them of us and of our heirs by homage and oath of fealty, and by rendering and presenting to us and to our heirs, at the feast of St. George, a flag with the arms of St. George, at our camp of Caen, every year for ever. **Provided always** that the said ROBERT SHOTTISBROKE and his heirs, or his deputies in his absence from our camp at Caen, shall, with his kindred and men-at-arms, well and properly arrayed for war in full armour at their own cost, await our pleasure as often as there is necessary occasion, a reasonable summons thereto being issued on the part of ourselves and our heirs. **In witness whereof**, etc., etc.,

Given at our royal town of Falaise, on this 1st day of January, A.D. 1418.

(See deed in possession of Lt. Colonel H. Mollerus-Le Champion.)

FAMILY OF LE CHAMPION-MARMION.

AFTER its deprivation of Fonteneys and Urvyle, on 1st January, 1418 (*vide supra*), this family settled on its Breton estates of Belle-esze and Guembie (Cambis), and is described by Chamillart, in 1666, as "Noblesse tres ancienne de la province de Bretagne." Ce nom qui dut designer primitivement un officier de la cour faisant la service de Champion des ducs de NORMANDIE, GEORGES LE CHAMPION, Champion au duc, Vicomte de FONTENEYS, nommé dans un acte de donation faite à l'Abbaye de St. Georges vers l'an 1050," etc., etc. This GEORGES LE CHAMPION was common ancestor of the French and English MARMIONS. The family held the hereditary office of Champion to the Dukes of NORMANDY, up to 1205, and to the Kings of France, as Dukes of NORMANDY, up to 1st January, 1418. In its several branches it held the title of Count, Viscount, and Baron, viz., Viscount and Baron de FONTENEYS, by "tenure," and long before the Conquest; Baron MARMION of Tamworth, Lutterward, and Scrivelsby; Baron MARMION, of Wittrington, and of Berwick, in Surrey; Baron d'URVYLE, Vicomte de VIRE, Seigneurs de BELLE-ESZE, et QUEMBIE, de MOULINS, de MAY, de LOUVIGNY, de LEOTANE, de VIRE, de KOYU, de LESQUEN; Comtes and Vicomtes de ST. HUBIEN, etc., with many other titles and lordships in Normandy and Brittany. ROBERT, the second Baron MARMION of Tamworth and Scrivelsby (killed in 1143), founded the Abbey of St. Barberie, in 1140. His son ROBERT, the third Baron, followed RICHARD CŒUR DE LION to Poicton, and in 1180 was assisted by Baron MARMION of Berwick, in Surrey. and by his near relative (proche parent) WILLIAM LE CHAMPION, Baron d'URVYLE, in the endowment of the said Abbey (deed still extant). On the acquisition of Normandy by France, in 1205, the URVYLE branch succeeded to Fonteneys, and held the same, as above shown, up to 1st January, 1418. RICARD LE CHAMPION was Governor of Mont St. Michel, in 1203, and Vicomte de VIRE; another RICARD was Vicomte de VIRE in 1350. The family intermarried with the great Norman and Breton families of le TESSON, de BEAUCHAMP, de VASSY, du MESNIL, le ROUS, de LAUNAY, etc. ROBERT LE CHAMPION DE FONTENEYS gave lands to St. BARBERIE (deed still extant), and sailed from Aigues-Mortes with St. LOUIS, as a crusader, in 1248. His descendant, BERTRAND, last Vicomte de FONTENEYS, and last owner of Fonteneys and Urvyle, on being deprived of this property and title and office by CHARLES VI. (see deed), settled in 1418 on his Breton estates, but retained the title of Vicomte de VIRE, and took the oaths of fealty to the Duke of BRITTANY, at Brehand-Moncontour. His son, ROBERT of Guembie, in 1480, proved his descent and arms (Az: au Sautoir d'or, Cantonné de 4 fleurs de lys d'arg.) from ROLAND LE CHAMPION of Fonteneys, who mounted guard at St. Arnoul, in Iveline, on the 26th November, 1356, and who was fifth in descent from ROBERT the Crusader. The official entries of the payments of the Breton fees of nobility are dated 1427, 1470, 1st April, 1489, 1583. The last was on 7th October, 1668, by the sons of PIERRE LE CHAMPION, Vicomte de VIRE, Seigneur de BELLE-ESZE et GUEMBIE (Cambis) under the following Deed, viz.:—

Declaration. BARTHELEMY LE CHAMPION (D.S.P.), HYACINTHE-ALLAIN (D.S.P.), PIERRE et son fils Jaques, enfants de PIERRE LE CHAMPION, Vicomte de VIRE, Seigneur de BELLE-ESZE, et de HELEINE LE MATAYER, leur mère et tutrice, declarés nobles d'extraction, descendus de RICARD LE CHAMPION, Vicomte de VIRE,* en l'an 1220, et maintenus en la qualité de Chevalier, par arrêt, 7th October, 1668.

M. DES CARTES, Pro.

(Deed in possession of Lt. Col. v. Mollerus-le Champion.)

---

* RICARD LE CHAMPION DE FONTENEYS was Govenor of Mont St. Michel and Vicomte de VIRE, where he had a garrison in 1203.

JAQUES, son of PIERRE LE CHAMPION (named in the above "Declaration" or official proof of descent from RICARD LE CHAMPION DE FONTENEYS) emigrated as a Huguenot, in 1688, to the United Kingdom, as attested by his signature to the burial register of his children, ELIZABET and PIERRE both buried on the 19th December, 1710. He left some curious family MSS., and his portrait, with that of his son, is preserved. He married MARY, daughter of DUDLEY LOFTUS DAVIES, Esq., M.P., and had one son JAQUES LOFTUS, married to his cousin ELLINOR (portrait) daughter of DUDLEY, a son of the above D. L. DAVIES, M.P. His only surviving child ELIZABETH LE CHAMPION (portrait) married ANDREAS V. MOLLERUS, son of OLAUS, and grandson of Archdeacon FRANCIS V. MOLLERUS † (brother of the celebrated author, JOANNES V. MOLLERUS, of Flensburgh). Her surviving son was the late C. C. LE CHAMPION-MOLLERUS, Esq., late 18th Hussars, who with his sons assumed his mother's name by royal licence.‡

Arms of the English MARMIONS: Vairee Arg. a Fesse Gules. French, in 1240 (d' URVYLE): Az: au sautoir d'Or, Cantonne de Quatre Fleur de Lys d'Arg. Devise: Au plus vaillant le prix. French, in 1130, l'Ecu de Vair (de Fonteneys).

THE CASTLE OF FONTENEYS-LE-MARMION.

This ancient fortress, in Calvados, near Caen, conferred the office of Champion, and the titles of Viscount and Baron, long before the Conquest, on its possessors the LE CHAMPION-MARMIONS. "Founteneys qualifie Baronnie et Vicomté, et a laquelle était en outre attaché l'office militaire de Champion hereditaire de nos ducs de NORMANDIE" (*Chamillart*, in 1666). Its ruins are thus described, viz.:—"The interior entrance and mantel-pieces are richly sculptured in marble and stone, part of the 16th and part of the 15th centuries, but a portion is very much more ancient."

---

† The history of the family of v. MOLLERUS, from A.D. 1074, is in Latin (see *Cimbria Literata*, Brit. Mus.)

‡ C. C. LE CHAMPION-MOLLER (MOLLERUS), Esq., who served in the Waterloo campaign in the 18th Hussars, had male issue by MARY HICCOKE, daughter of G. THOMAS, of Wappenham, Esq.:—

1. CHARLES CHAMPAGNI LE CHAMPION, in Holy Orders, married LOUISA, daughter of General F. STRATON, and of ANNE, daughter of General and Lady LOUISA ORDE (daughter of the first Earl RODEN). No surviving male issue.
2. GEORGE HENRY LE CHAMPION, Rector of Wolves-Newton, D.S.P.
3. JOHN OLAUS LE CHAMPION, Major 50th Regiment, killed at Sebastopol, married MARY, daughter of Major DRYSDALE; issue—
    (1) JOHN OLAUS LE CHAMPION, Lt. Col. Yorkshire Regiment.
    (2) BERNHARD DRYSDALE LE CHAMPION, Major 18th Hussars.
4. HENRY V. MOLLERUS-LE CHAMPION, Lieut.-Colonel Royal M. Fusiliers, married EMILY, daughter of FREDK. FRYER, Esq., (by EMILY, daughter of J. RICHARDES, Esq., M.P.); issue—
    (1) LOFTUS DE LAUNAY MOLLERUS-LE CHAMPION.
5. FREDERICK LE CHAMPION, Lieutenant 98th Regiment, lost his life in the Sikh War. D.S.P.
6. ARTHUR MARQUHARD LE CHAMPION, Captain 40th Regiment, married CATHERINE, daughter of Colonel T. GERRARD, late 17th Lancers; issue—
    (1) CHARLES.   (2) LETITIA.

The Mollerus-Le Champion Statement

The account of the Moller/Champion lineage in the printed sheets, however, is riddled with confusion, contradiction and falsehood; and though the quasi-endorsement by Burke is slightly more coherent, it is no more convincing. It is interesting that this entry for Le Champion-Moller appears in no earlier edition of *Landed Gentry*, and – still more striking – it is not found in the fifth edition, published in 1871. Instead, however, in 1868 a short version of the Mollerus claim was inserted into the entry for the [Champion] de Crespigny baronetcy in the 30th edition of Burke's *Peerage and Baronetage*.[60]

The Moller/Champion sheets, however, also contain what is alleged to be the translation of a Latin deed, issued at Falaise on 1 January 1418 by the mad King Charles VI of France. This document, "depriving Bertrand le Champion-Marmion, last Viscount and Baron de Fontenys and d'Urvyle, Vicomte de Vire, etc., of the office of Champion, and of the title and estates of Fonteneys-le-Marmion and Urvyle, in favour of Robert Shottisbroke, the King's favourite," is said to be at that time in the possession of Lieutenant-Colonel H Mollerus-Le Champion. The preface describes Bertrand le Champion-Marmion as a son of Oliver and the fourth Viscount of Vire, while a later part of the sheet says that he retired to estates in Brittany, where the family remained, still keeping title as Viscount of Vire – as discussed above, that would have been a very doubtful claim.

The properties concerned were transferred to Robert Shottisbroke on condition he paid fealty at Caen each year on the day of the feast of St George, and that he bring "kindred and men at arms, well and properly arrayed for war in full armour at their own cost," whenever the king might summon them. The conditions are repeated in Burke's publications.

This is a regular feudal arrangement: Robert Shottesbroke is granted land on condition he show fealty to the monarch and – most important – that he is prepared to provide a contingent of well-armed soldiers when required. The deed is real: it was reprinted in 1835 in *Rotuli Normanniae*, being rolls held in the Public Records Office containing letters and grants of the English kings concerning the duchy of Normandy, some of which relate to the period 1417-1418.[61] Dated at Falaise on 1 January 1418, it does indeed deprive Bertrand Champion of the manors of Urvyle and of Fonteneys in favour of Robert Shottesbroke. While the translation in the Moller/Champion sheet is largely correct, however, the interpretation in the preface is grossly mistaken.

A first major error is that the deed was not issued by King Charles VI of France, mad or otherwise, but by King Henry V of England. In an earlier discussion of this item I suggested that the document "purports to have been signed by a king who was incapable of governing, at a place where he probably wasn't."[62] Now that I have been able to study the original on the internet, it is clear that though my core suspicions were justified, the deed was signed by a most competent king, Henry of England, who was indeed at Falaise. Having captured Caen in September 1417, he laid siege to Falaise in December. He was not actually in the town on 1 January 1418, but the defenders had agreed to surrender on the very next day.[63]

Second, the preface claims that Bertrand le Champion-Marmion was deprived not only of his possessions in Normandy, but also of the office of Champion. The deed, however, does

---

[60] The changes to the *Peerage and Baronetage* entries are discussed in the following section at 66-69.

A revised fourth edition of the *Landed Gentry*, with Supplement and Corrigenda, was also published in 1868. Unfortunately, I have not been able to sight that volume and check whether the Mollerus/Champion entry was affected.

[61] The editor of this and several other collections was Sir Thomas Duffus Hardy (1804-1878). The document is at page 244. It is written with many abbreviations, but a full version is available in the *Mémoires* of the *Société des antiquaires de Normandie*. Both collections are in Google Books.

The Moller/Champion sheet says that the deed is in the possession of Henry Mollerus-Le Champion, but as the original is in the royal archives this cannot be correct: he presumably had a copy.

[62] *Champions in Normandy* [1988], 43.

[63] Sumption, *Cursed Kings*, 551; Barker, *Conquest*, 18.

not say that: it gives his surname as Champyon [Champion], but makes no mention of any office. Furthermore, both Bertrand Champion and Robert Shottesbroke are described as *armigeri*, which the translation renders as "Armour Bearer," with some implication of special status. The term *armigeri*, however, indicates no more than a man entitled to bear arms, a knight or squire. Similarly, the term *dilecto* – here translated as "beloved" – is not a sign of special favour; it is a standard expression used by a monarch for a loyal subject.

Born into a landed family in Berkshire, Robert Shottesbroke served Henry IV, Henry V and Henry VI. Member of Parliament in the 1420s and 1430s, he held royal commissions in his native county and took part in diplomatic and trading negotiations overseas. He also translated a celebrated devotional text, the *Somme le Roi* by Lorens d'Orléans, from French into English under the title *Aventure and Grace*. A noted royal retainer, he is mentioned in several contemporary documents, but none refer to him holding appointment as a champion.[64]

The deed cited by the Moller/Champion papers describes a new arrangement, part of the English seizure of Normandy, transferring feudal land from a Frenchman to an Englishman. Not surprisingly, there were a great number of such confiscations.[65]

Urville lies some fifteen kilometres northwest of Falaise, and Fontenay-le-Marmion is further north again. The English army would have moved to the attack on Falaise by that route, along the line of the present-day N158 from Caen, which had been taken in September amid scenes of slaughter that would encourage any loyalist to flee. It is very likely that Bertrand Champion had already escaped to Brittany, and King Henry was now granting the abandoned property to one of his own men. It is clear from the reference to St George and the flag that this was not a grant made by a French regime, for St George was the patron saint of England, and his emblem, a red cross on white, was the insignia of the English army. Henry V was publicising his conquest of the province and emphasising a display of loyalty on the feast-day of the national saint. Indeed Robert Shottesbroke was knighted on 23 April – St George's Day – of that year 1418, and other followers of the king no doubt received similar rewards and attended the court at Caen in similar array: it would have made an impressive assembly to confirm the conquest.

Burke's *Landed Gentry* of 1863 states that Jacques Le Champion, *soi-disant* sixteenth Viscount of Vire,[66] "left some curious MS" when he died in Dublin. If the sheets discussed above reflects their contents, then the manuscripts are indeed curious.

---

[64] See Wilson, Edward, "Sir Robert Shottesbrook (1400-1471): translator," in *Notes and Queries* 28.4 (August 1981), 303-304, citing Josiah C Wedgwood and Anne D Holt, *History of Parliament: Biographies of the Members of the Commons House 1439-1509*, (London 1936), 766-767, and J Ferguson, *English Diplomacy 1422-1461*, Oxford UP 1972, index; also http://www.historyofparliamentonline.org/volume/1386-1421/member/shotesbrooke-john [L S Woodger], which relates to Robert's elder brother John but contains information about Robert, and the chronology at girders.net prepared by I S Rogers.

It is generally agreed that Robert died in the early 1470s, probably in 1474, but his date of birth is given variously from 1388 to 1400, and the later date is supported by Wilson, Wedgwood and Holt. In *The Cambridge Companion to Medieval English Literature 1100-1500*, edited by Larry Scanlon (Cambridge UP 2009) at 30-31, however, Richard Firth Green suggests that he was a member of a literary circle about Thomas, Baron Berkeley, and Woodger in historyofparliamentonline refers to him as "a royal retainer of all three Lancastrian monarchs." If born in 1400, Shottesbroke would have been extremely precocious to have made his mark as a servant of Henry IV, who died in 1413, or to have been noticed by Lord Berkeley, who died in 1417, and he would have been very young to be granted the manors of Urvyle and Fontenay in 1418. A date about 1390 appears more probable.

Not surprisingly, the Shottesbroke surname appears in various spellings.

[65] The scale of the dispossession may be seen in the *Extrait du registre des dons, confiscation, maintenues, et autres actes faits dans le duché de Normandie pendant les années 1418, 1419 et 1420, par Henri V, roi d'Angleterre*, compiled by Charles Vautier and published at Paris in 1818 [Google Books]. The unfortunate Bertrand Champion is not mentioned, but it is still a very long list.

[66] The attribute *soi-disant* ["self-styled"] reflects the changes brought by the French Revolution. Titles of nobility were formally abolished, but many continued to use them, and *soi-disant* was an unkind way to

CHAPTER TWO

Burke, Debrett, and Horace Round

Oscar Wilde described the *Peerage*, that is the compendia of inherited titles compiled by Burke and Debrett, as "the best thing in fiction the English have ever done,"[67] and in the latter part of the nineteenth century citations for the Champion de Crespigny family made an impressive contribution to that record. Something was owed to the Moller/Champion legend discussed above, but a good deal was developed independently. It is impossible to assess the relationship between the editors and the representatives of the family, and hence how much of the material was presented by one side and/or accepted by the other, but it is clear that Sir Claude the fourth baronet was heavily involved.

As we have seen in the history above, the first ancestor of the family recorded in the *Lancaster Book* and its parallel sources the *Reveley Book* and *South Sea Book* is Maheas Champion, who was living in Normandy in 1350. It is not certain whether he was a native of the duchy or a recent immigrant, and there is no good information about his family or his forebears. Appropriately enough, the early introductions to the back-history of the baronet family present a simple statement. The twelfth edition of *Burke's Peerage and Baronetage*, for example, published in 1850, and the twenty-first edition of 1859, both read:[68]

> This family is of ancient and noble French descent, the proofs of which are registered in the College of Arms.

This is followed by a summary account from Maheas through his son Richard and their descendants, according quite well with documentary evidence, though it is claimed that Maheas died in 1350 and I do not believe that is correct.[69].

In the twenty-seventh edition of 1865, however, there is an interpolation from the Moller/Champion tradition, so that the first paragraph reads [with the addition in italics]:

> This family is of ancient and noble French descent: *one branch, that of Champion de Vire, was established in Ireland by the* CHEVALIER JACQUES-CHAMPION DE VIRE, *and his lineal descendant is* CHARLES-CHAMPION CHAMPION–MÖLLER, *Esq., late of the 18th Hussars, who, with his issue, has been authorised by royal licence to take the additional surname of* CHAMPION. *The proofs of the descent of the Champion family* ~~, the proofs of which~~ are registered in the College of Arms.

In effect, the Champion/Moller legend has been placed – like a cuckoo in the nest – into the entry for the CdeC baronetcy, with which it has only the slightest relationship.

This additional wording was maintained for several editions, but was dropped in the mid-1870s, and for some time thereafter the genealogy began with the plain statement of ancient nobility and then went directly to Maheas Champion.

In 1895, however, the fifty-seventh edition of *Peerage and Baronetage* presented a new and most detailed introduction. Full of false facts, it is a culmination of family mythology:[70]

> **Lineage---**Chamillart in 1666 describes the extinct Comtes de Cicé – related to the Champions de Crespigny of Vierville, near Fonteneys – as taking their name from their office.[71] Jordan and Thomas de Fonteneys served in the first crusade [*c*.1100], and

---

indicate that the person describing himself in such a way had no proper authority to do so. *Cf. ci-devant* at 74 below.

67 In Act III of *A Woman of No Importance*.
68 While I have checked those texts which are available from Google Books, I am most grateful to Stephen CdeC for his initial observations, and for notes and copies of this collection of anomalies.
69 Above at 42.
70 As before, I add some paragraphing for clarity, together with some interpolations in square brackets []. The core Moller/Champion material is in italics.
71 There are several problems with this apparently straightforward statement:
- In "Huguenot House" at 114-115, Horace Round remarks that he has a copy of Chamillart's work in front of him, and this statement does not appear in it: below at 71 and see Chapter Three at 90 *ff*.

Robert of Urvyle et Moulins in that under St. Louis at Aigues Mortes [the Sixth Crusade of 1248][72] (see DE MAGNY's *Memoirs of the Marquisses de Fonteneys*, "dit Marmion," a junior existing branch).

Ricard of Urvyle was Vicomte of Vire, a royal domaine and castle, in 1220, and another Ricard in 1350.

In the 13th century the Urvyle branch succeeded to Fonteneys le Marmion, but Bertrand le Champyon was deprived of his office and of Urvyle and Fonteneys by CHARLES VI, in favour of Robert Shottisbroke, with the original tenure, viz., attendance on summons in full armour with kindred, etc., at the feast of St George, to present to the KING at Caen a flag with the arms of St George for ever (Latin deed dated Falaise, 1 Jan 1418). Bertrand swore fealty to the Duke of Brittany in 1427 for his estates of Cambis and Belleeze,[73] and retained his title of Vicomte of Vire.

Of this family, Ricard, Guillaume, and Raoul proved nobility in 1334, Jean in 1470, others in 1501, 1599, 1635, 1640, and Robert was patron of St Barberie at the end of the 16th century (Laroche, MSS.).[74]

On 7 Oct. 1668, Jacques, son of Pierre, Vicomte de Vire of Cambis, by his wife Madelaine de Launay, proved descent from Richard d'Urvyle, Vicomte of Vire in 1220, and by his wife, Marie, dau. of Dudley Loftus Davies, M.P., had a son, Jacques Loftus, whose only surviving child, Ellise, m. Andreas, grandson of Archdeacon Fras. Oläus v. Mollerus, of a family ennobled in 1440 and again by Charles V. and Henry VIII, both German and English grants attesting to its great antiquity. Ellise's son and grandsons, field officers of cavalry and infantry, served at Waterloo, Inkerman, &c. Lieut.-Col. Olaus le Champion Moller (formerly Mollerus) now represents the last owners of Fonteneys in the female line; the male representative of the Marmions of Urvyle et Fonteneys le Marmion being Sir C. le Champion de Crespigny.

Burke then provides a summary lineage as far as Maheas:

GUILLAUME, Baron d'Urvyle, in 1181 assisted his near relative, Lord Marmion of Tamworth, Scrivelsvy [*sic*],[75] and Fonteneys, in endowing the Abbey of St. Barberie, founded by Robert, Lord Marmion, in 1140. He left three sons,

1. Robert of Moulins, who gave lands to St Barberie in 1223, and joined St Louis at Aigues Mortes as a crusader.[76]

- As discussed in the Introduction at 1, the surname Champion does not come from possession of an official position, but from occupation as a hired combatant, notably in cases of trial by combat.
- Vierville, northwest of Bayeux, is fifty kilometres from Fonteneys-le-Marmion, south of Caen – not very close. And the Champion [de Crespigny] family had no connection to Vierville until the mid-seventeenth century: Chapter Three at 84 *ff*.
- The kinship of the Champions de Cicé in Brittany to the Champion [de Crespigny] family of Normandy is doubtful and certainly very distant: see the following section.

[72] King Louis IX of France, later canonised as Saint Louis, embarked from Aigues Mortes at the mouth of the Rhone in August 1248; the expedition is known as the Sixth Crusade. His army attacked Egypt, for it was the most prosperous province of the Muslim world and there was hope that if it was taken it could be exchanged for Jerusalem. After initial success, however, Louis was defeated and captured at Mansourah on the delta of the Nile in April 1250. He was ransomed and returned to France, but later embarked on another expedition, the seventh crusade; this was diverted against Tunis in North Africa. Louis died on that campaign in August 1270.

[73] As above at 62, I can find no place named Belleeze or anything like it, and Cambis is equally unknown, though there was an Admiral de Cambis in the late eighteenth century. Cambis is probably miswritten for Caimbie: there was a family named Champion de Caimbie: 61-62 above and 73 below.

[74] There is no saint named Barberie; the founding of the Abbey of St Marie at Barbery is discussed below at 71. "Laroche, MSS" is not a meaningful citation.

[75] As below at 70, the relevant estate is named Scrivelsby. It is now held by the Dymoke family, hereditary King's Champions of England.

[76] On the crusades of King Louis, see note 71 above.

CHAPTER TWO

> 2. Ricard, 2nd son, was Vicomte of Vire in 1220. His son,
>   Jean, of Urvyle et Bretvyle, was living in 1289. He had four sons,
>   (1) Robert Bertrand, of Urvyle, Bretvyle, and Fonteneys, founded the fair of St Hermies at Fonteneys le Marmion in 1333,[77] and his son, Roland, *m*. Ellene de Fonteneys, mounted guard at St Arnoul in Iveline, 26 Nov 1357. The son of Roland, viz., Jean, was father of Bertrand, last Vicomte de Fonteneys, who was deprived of Fonteneys le Marmion and Urvyle on 1 Jan 1418. Male line becoming extinct in the 18th century on death of Jaques Loftus le Champion.
>   (2) Oliver, *d.s.p.*
>   (3) Maheas.
>   (4) Roger, supposed to be an ancestor of Le Champion d'Alenson, and of the Marquis de Fonteneys, of Varnhanue.

The third son of Guillaume, Baron d'Urvyle, is not identified, and the genealogy from Maheas continues on much the same lines as the *Lancaster Book*; Maheas, however, is said to have died in 1350; my own assessment is that he lived until about 1380.[78]

It is interesting to note that the pedigree reflects the Mollerus/Champion claim discussed in Part I above, including reference to Jacques Loftus le Champion as last in the male line of descent from the Vicomtes of Fonteneys, deprived of those lands in 1418. Sir C le [*sic*] Champion de Crespigny is now identified as "male representative of the Marmions of Urvyle et Fonteneys le Marmion." Here is a neat riposte to the Moller pretensions – though the whole debate is founded on most uncertain ground.[79]

The development of this impressive but erratic and false account of the family before the time of Maheas is surely related to the interest of Sir Claude Champion de Crespigny, the fourth baronet. Born in 1847, he succeeded his father Sir Claude William in 1868.

Sir Claude was a remarkable sportsman in the nineteenth-century meaning of the term. Physically strong and remarkably courageous, he was a pioneer of ballooning, an enthusiastic horse-rider, both on the flat and in steeple-chasing, and an energetic hunter of big game: the hall of Champion Lodge near Maldon in Essex was decorated with a vast collection of animal heads from all over the world.[80] A strong believer in duelling, Sir Claude was also a bully: he was several times involved in common assault, including an attack on members of the Salvation Army, and he instigated a riot with hired thugs at the general election of 1881. He was also very extravagant: he went bankrupt on two occasions at the expense of his relatives and the tradesmen of Maldon, and he beat up one officer who attempted to serve him with the appropriate papers.[81]

Though he had quarrelled ferociously with his father, Sir Claude was vastly proud of his lineage – he claimed *seize-quartiers*: that each of his sixteen great-great-grandparents were

---

[77] There is no saint named Hermies. St *Hermes*, however, was martyred in 120 and later canonised: his day is 28 August.

[78] Above at 61.

[79] See further at 71 below.

[80] Sir Claude's obituary in the *Daily Telegraph* of 27 June 1935 suggests that an incomplete count of his broken bones must include "two legs fractured while ballooning, three arms smashed while hunting, three ribs cracked in steeplechasing, one rib broken in a cab accident, a finger broken by a horse, and two fingers broken by himself – on a man." A life member of the Ballooning Society, in 1883 he received its gold medal for a crossing of the Channel; he once completed a steeple-chase course on a horse and buggy; and at the age of 78 he stood on the shoulders of another man as they dived from a height of ten metres.

[81] Local history has a slightly different perspective of Sir Claude as an occasionally troublesome neighbour: David Hughes, *The Maldonians: voices of Maldon 1872-1914*, Folk Corporation, Maldon 1996. The distinguished author G K Chesterton also appears to have disapproved: see "The Strange Crime of John Boulnois" in *The Wisdom of Father Brown*. And see also David Long, *English Country House Eccentrics*, The History Press, Stroud 2012, 64-65.

from families entitled to bear arms; but was unsuccessful – and it appears he found the recognised descent from Maheas Champion inadequate. His *Memoirs* presented an improved version.

The first edition of Sir Claude's *Memoirs* was published in 1896. Edited by George Dewar, with a preface and notes by the Duke of Beaufort, the book sold well, reaching a third edition in the following year. In 1910 Sir Claude published *Forty Years of a Sportsman's Life*, with a second edition in 1925. Though much of the material was taken from his *Memoirs*, however, the exaggerated genealogy of the Introduction was now omitted.

George Dewar was known for his writing on wild life and trout fishing rather than for his skill as an historian,[82] and we may assume his Introduction followed the wishes and opinions of Sir Claude. It presents an enhanced but confused history of the family, including the connection to the Marmion family and the estate of Urvyle, the dispossession of Bertrand attributed to Charles VI of France, together with the requirement for appearance at Caen with a troop of armed men and the flag of St George. This reflected Burke's revised account, and that publication in turn gave a veneer of authority to the new genealogy.

The parallel and rival publication by Debrett, *Peerage, Baronetage, Knightage and Companionage* "personally revised by the nobility," was more restrained than Burke. The 1885 edition said only:

> This is a Norman family. Meheus [Maheas] Champion was Lord of Crespigny about 1350. The eighth in descent from him was Claude Champion de Crespigny, whose second son, Thomas, was an officer in the British army. Sir Claude, D.C.L, 1st baronet, entertained George IV. at Champion Lodge; he was for more than fifty years Receiver-General of the Droits of the Admiralty. The 2nd baronet, Sir William, sat as M.P. for Southampton.

Apart from the mistaken connection of Maheas to Crespigny and the exaggeration of Sir Claude's length of office as Receiver-General, this is simple and correct.

No doubt influenced by the 1895 edition of Burke, the 1904 edition of Debrett was more expansive:

> Members of this Norman family fought in the 1st Crusade and in that under St Louis, and were Champions to the Dukes of Normandy and Brittany, and the lands of Fonteney, Fleurière and Crespigny, which latter place Claude Champion-de Crespigny, Vicomte de Vire, and his wife, La Comtesse de Vierville, quitted at the Revocation of the Edict of Nantes, were owned by them. Claude Champion-de Crespigny was at that time an officer of high rank in the French Army, and subsequently obtained a Col[onel]'s commission in the British army.

Debrett, however, never matched the excesses and complications of Burke.

The desire for distant and distinguished ancestry was common in the late Victorian and Edwardian periods, and the claim of Sir Claude was one of many. As editor of *The Ancestor*, a journal published in twelve issues from April 1902, the very competent scholar Oswald Barron (1868-1939) sought to stem the tide with some historical facts and research based upon the medieval records which were available, and he attacked and disproved a number of myths and legends. A good story, however, no matter how mistaken, is often more attractive than simple fact. Burke and Debrett continued largely unaffected, but *The Ancestor* ceased publication in January 1905.[83]

---

[82] George Albemarle Bertle Dewar was later the author of such works as *Life and Sport in Hampshire*, *The Book of the Dry Fly* and, after the First World War, *The Great Munition Feat 1914-1918* and a biography of Field Marshal Haig. It is possible that he made a more substantial contribution to Sir Claude's *Memoirs* than just the Introduction; in his Preface to *Forty Years of a Sportsman's Life* Sir Claude acknowledges the assistance of Mr Harold Simpson, who probably played a similar role.

[83] Copies of *The Ancestor* are available on the internet through archive.org.

CHAPTER TWO

Apart from its scholarly articles, *The Ancestor* had a regular section "What is Believed," which sought to deal with incidental errors in other publications. In the third volume Barron wrote a short item about a newspaper report on the Royal Champion: the article had claimed that the office dated back to the Dukes of Normandy, and that Robert de Marmion, Lord of Fontenay, served as Champion for William the Conqueror when he was crowned king of England.

A Marmion family [not *de* Marmion] had been enfeoffed with the territory of Fontenay-le-Marmion near Caen and later with Tamworth and Scrivelsby in England, but the male lineage died out in 1291. There was a tradition that the Marmions had been Champions to the dukes of Normandy and that their right had been transferred to England after the Conquest. Until the coronation of Richard II in 1377, however, there had been no role for a King's Champion. The office was then contested by two claimants, each descended from the Marmions in a female line: Baldwin de Freville, Baron of Tamworth; and Sir John Dymoke of Scrivelsby. A court of enquiry was established and, finding that the feudal tenancy of the Dymoke family required a special service, declared in favour of Sir John. The nominal office of King's Champion is still held by his descendants.

Leaving aside the question of the royal Champion, Sir Claude and his advisers accepted the Marmion claim to the position of ducal Champion in Normandy and then, based upon the surname Champion, laid claim to the Marmion connection. As discussed in the Introduction, however, the duchy of Normandy had no hereditary office of Champion, and Barron was appropriately dismissive: "One could hardly conceive anything wilder than this."[84]

The note in *The Ancestor* might be taken as a shot across the bows of the family legend, but the full attack had to wait another thirty years.

One of the contributors to *The Ancestor* was John Horace Round (1854-1928), whose scholarship was comparable and perhaps even superior to that of Barron. A graduate in history from Oxford and an Honorary Doctor of Laws of Edinburgh, Round was an expert in British peerage history and law, and an official adviser on peerage cases and on ceremonial. Though born in Sussex, he settled in Essex, the same region as Sir Claude, and his work on the history of that county, including its Domesday records, was prolific and of extremely high standard. He was also an energetic polemicist, he enjoyed a scholarly quarrel, and he was very seldom wrong.

When Round died he left a number of unpublished papers, several of which were published posthumously by his friend William Page, under the title *Family Origins and Other Studies*. One of them, "A Huguenot House," deals with the Champion de Crespigny lineage described by Burke.[85]

The discussion is in two parts. In the first, Round points out that although Burke claims the family was certified as of "noble quality and filiation," and even quotes the inspector Chamillart, Chamillart had in fact found them to be commoners. This matter is discussed in Chapter Four, dealing with the family in the seventeenth century, where I argue the case rather differently. We may note in passing, however, that Round casts doubt on the full surname of Champion de Crespigny, asserting that the noble suffix *de* appeared only after the migration to England; in this he is mistaken.[86]

---

[84] *The Ancestor* III (Oct 1902), 120-121. There was a good deal of interest in the trappings of the coronation at this time: Edward VII succeeded to the throne on the death of his mother Queen Victoria in 1901, but he was crowned only in August of the following year, and this was the first such ceremony for more than sixty years.

On the question of the putative champion for the Duke of Normandy, and the absence of any such official, see the Introduction at 4-5.

[85] *Family Origins*, 109-120.

[86] See the Introduction at 5-6.

The second part of Round's article deals with the alleged earlier history of the family, before Maheas, and here his analysis can only be described as devastating. Where Burke cites Chamillart as saying that "the extinct Comtes de Cicé – related to the Champions de Crespigny of Vierville, near Fonteneys – [took] their name from their office," Round remarks that he has the work of Chamillart in front of him and no such statement appears in it.

In similar fashion, Round goes on to observe that even if "Jordan and Thomas de Fonteneys served in the first crusade, and Robert of Urville and Moulins in that under St Louis at Aigues Mortes," such doubtful facts have no necessary connection with the Marmion or Champion families, while Richard of Urvyle, putative Vicomte of Vire in 1220, has evidently been confused with Richard de Fontenai, a senior official in Normandy several years earlier. "But he is not known to have been a member of the Marmion family and Fontenay is a not uncommon place-name in Normandy."[87]

Furthermore, while it is true that Robert Marmion endowed the Abbey of St Marie at Barbery in 1181, the deed contains no reference to the involvement of Guillaume, Baron d'Urvyle.[88] And although it is claimed that "the Urvyle branch succeeded to Fonteneys [sic] le Marmion," the historical successor to Fontenay was in fact the Bertram family, who obtained the fief through marriage;[89] the Urvyle lineage was not involved. As to the suggestion that Guillaume/William the Baron d'Urvyle, said to be living in 1181, could have been the great-grandfather of Maheas Champion who lived almost two hundred years later: "The wild nature of this chronology is obvious."

The village of Barbery, where there are still some remains of an abbey, is shown on Map Six at the head of this chapter. Though it is quite close to Urville and to Fontenay-le-Marmion, it is thirty kilometres from Saint-Jean-le-Blanc and the hamlet of Crespigny, and even further from Vire and La Fleurière, which was the region of the early Champion family. There is no record of any connection between the Champion family and the abbey at Barbery.

In sum, there is no doubt that Round was fully justified in his scathing remarks on the claim that the Champions were related to the great family of Marmion, and all accounts of crusading ancestors, noble kinfolk and religious benefactions are unproven and imaginary.[90] It is impossible to make any useful statement about the Champion family before Maheas, that is before the middle of the fourteenth century, and there is no justification for the claim to any such notable ancestry.

The Champions de Cicé and other reputed cousins
We have noted above the reference in Burke to the Champions de Cicé as being related to the Champion de Crespigny lineage.[91] Its basis may be found in the statement in the *South Sea* and *Reveley* books concerning Richard the son of Maheas; the relevant sheets are illustrated,

---

[87] "Huguenot House," 115-116.
[88] The endowment is noted by Stapleton, "Observations" II, c.

Round also criticises the reference to the abbey of "St Barbery," pointing out correctly that there is no such saint. Since there was an Abbey of St Marie at Barbery, however, the elision is understandable, and the ancient error has provided an intriguing name for at least two houses in Australia.

[89] Stapleton, "Observations" II, cvii and ccx-ccxi.
[90] As Round observes in "Huguenot House" at 114, the Marmion claim probably owes a great deal to Sir Walter Scott's poem of that name, which was published in 1808 and became widely popular. The eponymous Lord Marmion is said to have been killed at the battle of Flodden in 1513, but the character is entirely fictitious.

As we have seen, the Marmion connection appears in the Mollerus/Champion documents discussed in the previous section, in the editor's Introduction to the *Memoirs* of Sir Claude Champion de Crespigny, and in the lineage presented by Burke as above. It is a fine example of the romantic rambling antiquarianism, unsupported by any real evidence, which Round did his utmost to discredit.

[91] Above at 66.

transcribed and translated in Chapter One.[92] I here repeat my rendering of the passage, which was later accepted and followed by the *Lancaster Book*:

> The said Richard Champion, Esquire, son of the said Maheas, married Mademoiselle the daughter of Hector Mensant, Esquire, Lord of Lesentiére in the parish of Bron [*i.e* Bruz] in Brittany, and by [by the authority of] letters from the king the said [Hector] Mensant took the surname D'Oüssé, and from this marriage are issued Jean and Michel Champion, Esquires. The said Jean went to take up residence in Brittany, and from him are descended the lords of Chartres, of Cicé ["*Sisey*" in the original French] and other Champions of Brittany.

The first thing to note is that "Bron" has been miswritten for Bruz. A commune named Bron is now a suburb of Lyon in eastern France, but this cannot be relevant. The commune of Bruz, however, in the present-day Department of Ille et Vilaine, ten kilometres south of Rennes in Brittany, contains a hamlet now known as Le Cicé [postcode 35170], while the neighbouring commune to the east is Chartres-de-Bretagne [35066]. All these places can be found on Google Maps.

Map Eight: Detail of the territory south of Rennes from the Tabula ducatus britanniae gallis *"Map of the French Duchy of Brittany" published in 1720 by Johann Baptist Homann of Nuremburg.*

Cicé is shown [as Cice] due south of Rennes and just north of Bruz [as Bruts]. Chartres de Bretagne is not shown, but would have appeared close to the N *of Noyal.*

Like the original Crespigny near Saint-Jean-le-Blanc, Cicé was a knight's estate and gave its name to the holder of the fief, but it is now just a few houses on the left bank of the Vilaine River; the Domaine de Cicé-Blossac is a high-quality golf course.

There is no sign now of Lesentiére, Oüssé, or any places of similar name.

The *Nobiliaire et armorial de Bretagne* compiled by Pol Louis Potier de Courcy lists the Champion families of that duchy, with a description of their arms and an account of those who held significant office. He distinguishes three lineages:[93]

---

[92] See at 22.
[93] *Nobiliaire et armorial* I, 218. See also the *Armorial des familles de Bretagne* in Wikipédia [the French version of Wikipedia].

- Champion de Cicé in the parish of Brutz [=Bruz]: enfeoffed as barons in 1598, the family also acquired held estates in several other parishes.

    Potier de Courcy remarks that Jean, founder of the family, came originally from Condé-sur-Vire in Normandy and was recognised as noble in 1470.[94] Besides a number of secular appointments, the family produced several high-ranking clergymen, including abbots, bishops, archbishops and one apostolic vicar at the Catholic mission in Xiamen/Amoy in China.

    Presumably in some part as consequence of so many celibate priests, the male lineage of the Champions de Cicé died out in the early nineteenth century. Before this, however, the Champion de Crespigny baronets in England were able to receive their distant cousin the Archbishop of Aix; the account in the *Lancaster Book* is not quite accurate and is discussed below.

    The arms of the Champions de Cicé were *azure, three escutcheons argent, each charged with three bendlets gules*: a blue shield with three small silver/white shields, each with three red diagonal bands in red. The contrast with the shield of the Champions de Crespigny has already been discussed and is considered again below.

- The Champions de Caimbie *etc*, also known as *le Champion*, held estates in the parishes of Bréhant, Pleurtuit and other regions, all on the northern coast of the Breton peninsula: Pleurtuit is south of Saint Malo and Bréhant, now Bréhand, is further east near Lamballe. Though the family could claim a crusading ancestor, companion to Saint Louis on the Sixth Crusade of 1248,[95] it was otherwise less distinguished. This was the lineage whose shield – blue with a yellow St Andrew's cross and four white fleurs-de-lys – the Mollerus/Champion family claimed on the grounds that it had been borne by the Marmions.[96] It is also likely that the surname "le Champion" was adopted from this source, but there is no good authority for either claim.

Champion de Cicé   *Champion [de Crespigny]*   *Champion de Chartres*

- The Champions de Chartres, who took their name from a parish south of Rennes and close to Bruz and to Cicé, were also lords of Laz near Quimper, a considerable distance to the west along the southern coast of the peninsula. They too held some offices during the sixteenth century; their arms were *azure, three greyhound heads argent, collared gules*: a blue shield with three greyhound heads, each with a red collar.[97]

---

[94] On the significance of the expression *anobli aux francs-fiefs*, and its relevance to the Champion [de Crespigny] family, see above at 47; also Chapter Three at 91 quoting Chamillart's *Recherche* on Jean Champion.

[95] On the crusade, see note 71 above.

[96] Above at 61-62.

[97] French: *D'azur à trois têtes de lévrier d'argent, accolées de gueules*.

CHAPTER TWO

We have noted that the Champion de Caimbie shield is quite different to that of the Marmion family.[98] It is also apparent that though the Champions de Cicé and those of Chartres were neighbours, their shields too were different – and none bear any resemblance to that of the Champions [de Crespigny]. It is true that the shields of both Cicé and Chartres have blue backgrounds with three charges in red and white, so it is possible those two families were related – with the Champions de Chartres showing a particular fondness for dogs.

We have also noted that CdeC family sources – the *South Sea* and *Reveley* books, followed by the *Lancaster Book* – have Jean Champion, son of Richard and elder brother of Michel, as first ancestor of the Champions de Cicé, and that the *Nobiliaire et armorial de Bretagne* likewise describes him as a man from Condé-sur-Vire in Normandy. Condé-sur-Vire lies some twenty-five kilometres northwest of the town of Vire, close to Saint Lô, and it is certainly a possible place of origin for the son and grandson of Richard and Maheas Champion. The difference in the shields is difficult to account for, though I have suggested above that when Jean Champion established himself in Brittany he may have decided to adopt the arms formerly born by the previous holders of the estate of Cicé, who were by this time extinct in the male line.[99]

The first page of the main copperplate text of the *Lancaster Book* tells how the ancient but long-distant kinship was recognised and renewed. The account, however, is slightly confused.

According to the *Lancaster Book*, the *ci-devant* Archbishop of Aix, a member of the family of the Champions de Cicé, came to England with the Duke of Bourbon (later Louis XVIII) after the Revolution of 1789 and stayed with Sir William CdeC the second baronet (succeeded 1818, died 1829) at Champion Lodge. He is said to have been still living in 1830.

Detail from the first page of the Lancaster Book
The entry forms part of the genealogy showing the two sons of Richard Champion (c.1360?-c.1420?). The lineage through the younger brother Michael/Michel [marked by an asterisk *] continues on the following page. See above at 40-42.

The style *ci-devant* ["formerly so-called"] indicates a position held before the French Revolution, but the only member of the Champion de Cicé family to whom this item could refer is Jérôme-Marie, who was born in 1735. Archbishop of Bordeaux in 1789, he was elected to the Estates-General called by Louis XVI on the eve of the French Revolution, and played an equivocal role in the proceedings which followed. Fleeing from France in 1791, he came to England in 1795 in very reduced circumstances. In 1802 he returned to France as Archbishop of Aix-en-Provence, and he died in that office in 1810.[100]

---

[98] Above at 61.
[99] Above at 34-35.
[100] Hanson, *Historical Dictionary of the French Revolution*, 63; *Dictionnaire de biographie française* 8, 338-339.

So Jérôme-Marie Champion de Cicé was *ci-devant* Archbishop of Bordeaux – not of Aix – and while he did spend ten years in England during the 1790s in some association with the future Louis XVIII, his appointment to Aix was made by the post-Revolutionary government of Napoleon, First Consul from 1799 and Emperor of the French from 1804.

The CdeC baronetcy, moreover, was not awarded until several years after the archbishop had left, for Sir Claude the first baronet was granted the title only in 1805. His son William, who succeeded him in 1818, was born in 1765 and could certainly have hosted their kinsman, but it is more likely that Jérôme-Marie Champion de Cicé was a guest of Claude the future first baronet, who was close to him in age and was living at Champion Lodge in Camberwell at the relevant time; the property had been purchased by Philip CdeC in 1755 and inherited by Claude in 1765.[101] One may assume that the exile stayed at Champion Lodge during the second half of the 1790s or the early 1800s, presumably as a guest of Claude CdeC the future baronet but no doubt meeting his son and heir William. The statement that he was living in 1830 is either miswritten or reflects a lack of good information – Aix is a long way away.

---

[101] Chapter Five at 162.

Map Nine: The Duchy of Normandy (1635) by Willem Blaeu

Map Ten: Detail [marked in red] from Map Nine

Tinchebray is at the base; Vassey [Vassy] and Condé[-sur Noireau] are above; Aulnay, north of Crespigny, is at the top. The map is slightly disoriented, for while Vire, Vassy and Condé are close to the same latitude, Vire is here shown further to the south, east of Tinchebray.

CHAPTER THREE

The Seventeenth Century: Huguenots and Crespignys

Chronology 1600-1708
The Huguenots and the royal government of France 1540-1629
Richard Champion and the estate of Crespigny
Claude Champion and the Vierville connection
Nobility and Taxation: noblesse *and the* taille
Persecution and the Revocation of the Edict of Nantes
Emigration to England
A Note on the Question of Compensation

Chronology 1600-1708*

1610	assassination of Henri IV, succeeded by his son Louis XIII
1617	Richard Champion marries Marguerite nee Richard and converts to Protestantism
1620	birth of Claude Champion [later surnamed as Champion de Crespigny]
	Louis XIII begins to attack the Huguenot separatists in the southwest
1622	The Court of Aides confirms the finding of 1591, that the Champion family is not entitled to the status of *noblesse* and is liable to the *taille* tax; Richard Champion is said to have accepted the verdict
1623	Richard Champion receives acknowledgement from the Citizens of the Parish of Saint-Jean-le-Blanc that he is of noble rank,
c. 1623	Jacques Champion is killed by Etienne Hardi
1624	death of Adrian Richard; his daughter Marguerite and her husband Richard Champion come into possession of the estate of Crespigny; Richard Champion is again recognised as a man of noble rank
1628	the year-long siege of La Rochelle ends with the surrender of the Huguenot stronghold and the elimination of their independent political power
1631	Richard Champion is again certified as being of noble rank, and is identified as an Officer of the local Chapter of Nobles
1632	death of Jean Champion; Richard Champion is again identified as an Officer of the local Chapter of Nobles
1633	Marie, daughter of Jean Champion, marries Pierre Thomas
1634	Richard Champion is again certified as being of noble rank
1635	Richard Champion is acknowledged for his service to the royal cause
	French forces take an active role in the war in Germany and the Netherlands
1639	Richard Champion is again acknowledged for his service to the royal cause at the time of a local rebellion
c. 1640	*Richard Champion is said to have been created Baron and Viscount of Hurien*
1641	Richard and his son Claude sell the estate of La Fleurière to Henri du Gué
1651	Claude Champion [de Crespigny] marries Marie nee de Vierville; the couple take up residence at Vierville-sur-Mer
1653	birth of Claude and Marie's son Pierre [also known as Daumont]
1654	birth of Claude and Marie's daughter Marguerite
1655	birth of Claude and Marie's daughter Marie

---

* Items in blue are established historical facts; items in normal font relate to the Champion [de Crespigny] family; items in *italics* relate to the family history but are confused, doubtful or false.
   All dates for family events marked *c.* [*circa* = approximate] must be considered uncertain; they are discussed in more detail in the relevant part of this work.

CHAPTER THREE

1656	birth of Claude and Marie's daughter Susanne
1661	Louis XIV begins a campaign of oppression against the Huguenots
1664	birth of Claude and Marie's son Thomas
1666	birth of Claude and Marie's son Gabriel
1667	birth of Claude and Marie's daughter Renée
	the Intendant Guy Chamillart publishes his *Recherche de Noblesse*, finding the Champion family to have usurped that status
1668	birth of Claude and Marie's daughter Jeanne
1669	death of Richard Champion
	death of Pierre de Vierville, father of Marie; Claude and Marie share in his inheritance
1674	the Court of Aides at Rouen approves the appeal of Claude Champion against the findings of Intendant Chamillart and accepts the family claim to *noblesse*
1676	Thomas CdeC, age twelve, is sent to England
1678	Gabriel CdeC, age twelve, is sent to England
*c.*1679-81	Pierre/Daumont CdeC represents the congregation at Trévières in opposition to their co-religionists at Vaucelles before the Royal Council at Paris
1681	the beginning of intense official persecution of Huguenots, marked by *dragonnades*
1685	Louis XIV proclaims the Revocation of the Edict of Nantes
1687	Claude CdeC and his family make their *reconnaissances* at the French Church of the Savoy in London
1688	William of Orange and his wife Mary seize the British throne from the Catholic King James II
1690	the children of Claude and Marie CdeC are granted denization
1695	death of Claude CdeC
1697	The College of Arms certifies the noble descent of the family
1699	Gabriel is naturalised as an English citizen
1705	Pierre and Thomas are naturalised as English citizens
1708	death of Marie CdeC nee de Vierville.

The Huguenots and the royal government of France 1540-1629
As we have observed at the end of Chapter Two, the marriage of Richard Champion to Marguerite nee Richard in 1617 is the first occasion the family had any recorded contact with Huguenot religion; they had been Catholics through all the sixteenth century, and two were ordained as priests. One result of the marriage was the acquisition of the estate of Crespigny as part of Marguerite's inheritance from her father Adrian Richard; the other was a commitment to the Reformed tradition of Protestantism, which brought the family not only to a new system of belief and worship but also to a changing climate of politics. To appreciate the significance of the change, we must consider the early history of the Huguenots in France.

Centuries of Christianity had seen a multitude of rival theories about the true nature of the religion – all of which were dismissed and persecuted as heresies – with frequent protests against the authority of the Catholic church headed by the Pope in Rome. Martin Luther's demand for reform, based upon his *Ninety-Five Theses* published at Wittenberg in 1517, was the beginning of the great division of the Western church.

In Germany, Luther's teachings obtained support among territorial princes opposed to the authority of the Holy Roman Empire ruled by the house of Hapsburg, but many people took the new doctrines to extremes, and the empire was ravaged both by peasant revolts and by the war of Lutheran rulers against the imperial government. In 1555 the Peace of Augsburg provided a basic settlement on the principle *Cuius regio, eius religio* ["Whose realm, his religion"]: the ruler could choose to be Catholic or Lutheran, and his subjects were obliged to follow his lead or leave the state. This was by no means the end of conflict, and the Thirty Years War from 1618 to 1648 would devastate Germany, but it did create an ideal of religious uniformity within each polity.

Lutheranism in France was largely restricted to regions of the east close to Germany, but the puritanical regime of John Calvin, established in Geneva from the early 1540s, became widely influential. The Reformed Church was popular among craftsmen and merchants in many large towns and, despite some persecution, by the 1660s there were more than two thousand "temples" – the term they used for their places of worship. The number of adherents may have reached two million, perhaps ten percent of the population, mainly in the south and southwest of France. Further north, the great city of Paris was resolutely Catholic but there was a local presence in the countryside of Calvados.

The Huguenot Cross
Badge of the Reformed Church

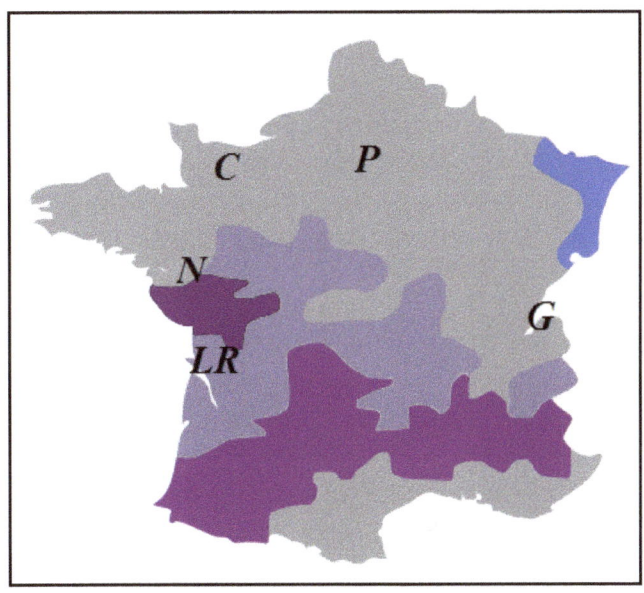

Map Eleven: Regions of major Huguenot influence during the sixteenth century[1]
Deep and pale purple indicate degrees of influence; blue shows Lutheranism
C: Calvados; P: Paris; N: Nantes; LR: La Rochelle; G: Geneva

The origin of the name Huguenot is confused and obscure, varying between possible references to real or legendary men named Hugo/Hughes, and corruption of German or Dutch terms for members of a confederacy – Wikipedia discusses the etymology in some detail. Huguenots were noted for their strong organisation – inspired by the model of Calvin at Geneva – and for their aggressive proselytising, including the destruction of graven images such as the statues of saints and sacred reliquaries. The reaction from Catholics was predictable, with frequent disturbance and riots among the common people, while a political faction of Huguenots was formed at the court of King François/Francis II; its leaders included Louis de Bourbon, Prince of Condé and a member of the royal house, with other men of rank opposed to the influence of the Catholic Guise family.[2]

In the Amboise conspiracy of 1560 a group of Huguenot nobility attempted to take control of the government; the coup failed, and hundreds were executed. Two years later, the Massacre at Vassy – when Protestants and others were killed by retainers of the Guise –

---

[1] The map is adapted from that of Ernio48, published on Wikipedia in September 2016.
[2] There are more than twenty places in France with the name Condé. The fief of Louis de Bourbon was Condé-en-Brie in the Department of the Aisne; he had no connection to Condé-sur-Noireau in Calvados.

CHAPTER THREE

marked the beginning of open conflict.[3] As Francis was succeeded by his brothers Charles IX and Henri III, the Queen-Dowager Catherine de Medici, widow of Henri II, became regent for her sons and attempted to restore some peace to the kingdom. In 1672, however, the Saint Bartholomew's Day Massacre of Huguenots in Paris brought a complete break-down of trust and warfare became endemic, with atrocities on both sides, while Huguenot privateers along the western and northern coasts attacked Catholic vessels, including the treasure ships of Spain.

The final stage of the conflict, known as the War of the Three Henrys, followed the death of Duke Francis of Anjou, younger brother of Henri III; in consequence the Huguenot leader Henri de Bourbon, King of Navarre, became heir to the throne. Henri Duke of Guise, leader of the Catholic League with support from Philip II of Spain, compelled the royal government to disinherit Henri of Navarre and declare war against him, but a major victory at Coutras in 1588 gave Henri of Navarre the opportunity to establish a reconciliation with the king, and Henri III had Henri of Guise murdered at Blois. In the following year Henri III was assassinated by a Catholic monk, and Henri of Navarre succeeded him as Henri IV.

Though he gained several victories against the Catholic League and its Spanish allies, Henri IV could not take Paris, and he was faced by firm hostility from the majority of his Catholic subjects. In 1593 he formally converted to Rome and in 1598, now firmly established as ruler, he proclaimed the Edict of Nantes to set the basic terms of a settlement between the religions.

The Edict is commonly identified as a proclamation of religious tolerance, but it was in fact more of a truce between two warring parties. The first clause provided for the ending of all memory of deeds committed by one side against the other, bringing a hoped-for end to any search for vengeance. Roman Catholicism was confirmed as the official religion, with all its former rights, but members of the Reformed Church were entitled to live anywhere in the kingdom without harassment. On the other hand – and this would be important later – they were permitted to carry out the public functions of their religion, including worship, discipline and the education of children, only in places where it had been established by 1597. Elsewhere, notably at the royal court and in Paris, such activity was forbidden.

At the same time, Huguenots were granted some fifty "places of security," including Montauban, Montpellier and Nimes in the south, the port-city of La Rochelle on the Atlantic coast and Saumur on the Loire, where they were entitled to defend themselves and where Catholics were forbidden to worship. In effect, this created a separate state within the French kingdom, and though the initial grant was made for just eight years, it was renewed by Henri IV in 1606 and again during the first years of the reign of his son Louis XIII.

Following the death of Henri IV in 1610, however, the royal government became increasingly concerned with the situation. There were other problems, notably civil war with the Catholic nobility and dispute with Marie de Medici, Louis' mother who acted as regent, but when Louis came of age in 1614 he embarked upon a deliberate program to break the independent power of the Protestants. A royal edict of 1617, demanding the restoration of Catholicism in the southern territory of Béarn, which had long been Protestant, was a direct attack on the privileges and status of the Reformed Church, and it was met with rioting, disorder and war culminating in the siege of La Rochelle. The British attempted to bring assistance to their co-religionists by sea, but they were unsuccessful, and after a siege lasting more than a year, with heavy mortality from starvation, the city surrendered in October 1628. In the following year the Edict of Alès removed all political and military privileges from the Huguenots: the rights of worship awarded by the Edict of Nantes were confirmed, but Protestants no longer held special status in any region of France.

---

[3] The Vassy concerned is not in Calvados, but was present-day Wassy in Haute-Marne.

Richard Champion and the estate of Crespigny
On 13 December 1617 Richard Champion, eldest son of Jean Champion and his wife Marthe nee du Bourget, married Marguerite, daughter of Adrian Richard Esquire, Squire of Crespigny in the Parish of Saint-Jean-le-Blanc near Aunay, Lower Normandy. The wedding was held according to the rites of the Reformed [Protestant] Church at Condé-sur-Noireau, the marriage contract having been drawn up the week before at the neighbouring town of Vassy. It seems certain that Adrian Richard was a Huguenot, and that his permission for the marriage of his daughter was given on condition his future son-in-law adopt the creed of his family.

Le Temple des Isles *at Proussy in Calvados*
On the present-day D184 between Condé-sur-Noireau and Pontelicour, this was a centre for Huguenot worship in the region. Constructed in 1630, the temple was demolished by royal decree in 1680.[4] Richard Champion and Marguerite nee Richard cannot have been married in this building, but they may well have attended services here later.

In April and June 1624, presumably following the death of Adrian Richard, Marguerite took part in negotiations for the disposition of his property, and it is likely that it was at this time Richard Champion gained possession of Crespigny near Saint-Jean-le-Blanc through right of his wife.

As we have seen, the *Extract from the Register of the Court of Aides* notes the record of the wedding in 1617, and observes that Richard Champion the bridegroom was styled "noble." The *Extract* remarks further that in March and November of 1623, evidently as preparation for his entry into possession of the property at Crespigny, Richard Champion received acknowledgement of his rank from the Citizens of the Parish of Saint-Jean-le-Blanc, and the recognition was repeated in September 1624, following the death of his father-in-law and the consequent inheritance of his wife. Richard Champion was again certified as being of noble rank by the citizens of Saint-Jean-le-Blanc in 1631, 1632 and 1634, and on the first two of those occasions he is described as an Officer of the Chapter of Nobles in the parish. It appears that he and Marguerite had made their home at Crespigny by 1624, while Richard's father Jean remained at La Fleurière. On several occasions during this period both father and son are described as Esquires of La Fleurière: Richard as early as the time of his marriage contract in 1617, while his father Jean held the same title in deeds dated as late as 1628, 1629 and 1632.

Some years later, however, in 1667 an investigation by Guy Chamillart, Intendant of Lower Normandy, noted that in 1591 and 1622 the Court of Aides for the province had decided that the Champion family had failed to justify their claim to *noblesse*. On the latter occasion, moreover, Richard Champion acknowledged his lack of such entitlement and was specifically prohibited from making any such claim in future.

Both sets of statements appear equally well documented and valid: Chamillart is citing previous negative decisions of the Court of Aides; but the accounts of local endorsement are

---
[4] Source: Delafontenelle, *Eglises protestants du bocage normand*, cited by http: temples.free.fr.

CHAPTER THREE

cited in the judgement of the same Court in 1674. I discuss the contradiction, and attempt a reconciliation, in dealing with the whole question of *noblesse* and the *taille* tax below.[5]

Following the death of his father Jean in 1632, Richard obtained the property of La Fleurière as well as that of Crespigny, and the *Extract* cites a series of documents which indicate his recognition as a person of standing in the local community. On 24 April 1635 the Count de Maulèvrier, Captain of a Company of Light Cavalry, attested his service to the royal cause,[6] and the same encomium was repeated on 12 October 1639 by the Captain of Infantry of the Barons and Retainers in the jurisdiction of the Bailiff of Caen. In addition and probably also in 1635, the Count Charles de Goyon de Matignon, *lieutenant-général*/Lieutenant-Governor of Normandy, sent an Authority to the Esquire of La Fleurière (evidently Richard Champion) or, in his absence, to his son the Esquire of Crespigny (presumably Claude).[7]

The documents of 1635 probably relate to the entry of the government into full involvement against Spanish, imperial and Hapsburg interests in Germany. The conflict which would be known as the Thirty Years War had broken out there in 1618, but Louis XIII and his minister Cardinal Richelieu had only now decided that it was advantageous to take an obvious military role, and the first engagement took place in May of that year. The commendation of 1639, on the other hand, may best be associated with a local disturbance: in July of that year a peasant group called the *Va-nu-pieds* "Barefooters" rebelled against the imposition of new taxation. The rising began at Avranches, on the coast near Brittany, extending rapidly through Mortain, Domfront and Vire to affect all Lower Normandy, including Caen and Bayeux, and spread even as far as Rouen. The rebellion was defeated by November, but it had been a serious distraction from French involvement in the foreign war.[8]

Shield and coronet of Richard Champion married to Marguerite nee Richard

---

[5] On Intendant Chamillart and his *Recherche de Noblesse en la Généralité de Caen*, see below at 90-93.

[6] The typescript translation of the *Extract* has the name as Manleurier; the *Lancaster Book* writes it as Manleurière; the correct reading is probably Maulèvrier. Maulèvrier is a small place southeast of Nantes.

The *Lancaster Book* dates this first document to 1625, but I follow the *Extract*, 8. If the year was 1625, the commendation probably recognised his loyalty at a time of tension when the king was at war with his Huguenot subjects at La Rochelle: 80 above and 83 below.

[7] Count Charles de Goyon de Matignon (1564-1648) held military command at this time as *lieutenant-général* of Lower Normandy.

The date of the document is given by the *Extract* at 9 as 22 May 1655, but this cannot be right. We have seen in Chapter Two at 56 that La Fleurière was sold to Henri du Gué in 1641, and de Matignon died in 1648. My suggestion is that 1655 is miswritten for 1635. If this is correct, it appears that the error was in the original French text, not in its later translation and transcription, for the *Extract* regularly cites documents by their date and this entry follows immediately after the reference to the sale of La Fleurière.

[8] Tapié, *France in the Age of Louis XIII and Richelieu*, 399.

Some sources claim that Claude CdeC held high rank in the French army and later became a colonel in the British; the question is discussed below at 105. We may note that he was eighteen years old in 1635 and the war in Germany continued until 1648; this would have been an appropriate time for a period of military service.

Besides the events referred to by the *Extract*, the *Lancaster Book* claims that Richard Champion was created Baron and Viscount of Hurien. Neither the *Reveley* nor the *South Sea Book* mention the title, and there is no additional evidence. The only place named Hurien is in the Department of Lozère in the south of France, but this cannot be relevant, while the Larousse dictionary has no entry for the word *hurien*. The *Extract* makes no reference to the title; and it is difficult to imagine where the *Lancaster Book* can have found justification for such a claim. I discuss the matter further below.[9]

The *Lancaster Book* shows the shield of Richard surmounted by a coronet. The effect is spoilt, however, by the fact that the half of the shield where the arms of his wife's father should appear is blank; we must assume Adrian Richard was not a gentleman of coat armour.

Marthe nee du Bourget, wife of Jean Champion, and her son Richard Champion (1587-1669)
Now at Kelmarsh Hall, Northamptonshire, the pictures are reproduced at https://artuk.org/*discover/ artworks/ search/venue:kelmarsh-hall-4095. There is no secure provenance, and they are described – surely wrongly – as "British (English) School," but the traditional attribution is firm, and the portraits may have been brought from France. If they are genuine, Marthe's would date from 1600 or earlier.*

We have noted that the marriage of Richard Champion to Marguerite nee Richard is the first record of any connection between the Champion family and the Protestant religion, and Richard almost certainly undertook his conversion at the insistence of his future wife's family. Henri IV of France, who had been leader of Huguenot resistance to the Catholic League before he came to the throne, later converted to Catholicism as a means to reconcile the common people to his new regime; he remarked as he did so that "*Paris vaut bien une messe*: Paris is well worth a Mass." One may suggest that Richard Champion, on a far lower scale of operation and moving in the opposite direction, felt Crespigny was worth a sermon.

There is no indication that Richard Champion's own family were concerned by the change, they remained on good and close terms, and the conversion was primarily a matter of domestic arrangements and property. Such a move, however, had political implications.

Calvados was a centre of Reform religion, and there were established communities at Caen, Vire and Domfront and in the countryside including Condé-sur-Noireau and Tinchebray.[10] The region had been spared the worst excesses of the Wars of Religion during the sixteenth century, but the 1620s saw Huguenot anxiety over royal policy, with incidents at Vire, at

---
[9] At 95.
[10] Delafontenelle, *Protestant du Bocage normand* summary at http://erbn.delafontenelle.net/.

CHAPTER THREE

Frênes and at Condé-sur-Noireau, frequently involving official interference with Protestant temples. In response to both the general and the particular alarm, and despite prohibitions, Normans were represented at national assemblies of Huguenots based on La Rochelle and opposed to the king.

In an attempt to divide this opposition, and to isolate the potential and actual rebels at La Rochelle, the authorities in Normandy were instructed to demand oaths of fealty to the king from all leading Protestants, and to require them to surrender any arms in their possession.[11] Many ministers left the country to avoid such an undertaking, but most laymen accepted the imposition, and Richard Champion gave his oath in June 1621. Since he had just joined the ranks of the Huguenots, and held estates and interests in the very centre of a region of local disturbance, it was essential for him to confirm that the change of religion had no effect upon his loyalty as a royal subject.

Following the fall of La Rochelle in 1628 the royal government brought the south under control, so that pressure was eased, and France was soon engaged in the war in Germany. Commencing in 1618 and concluded in 1648, the Thirty Years War was concerned both with religious enmities and with the struggle of the northern states to free themselves from imperial control. Though Louis XIII was Catholic, and his chief minister Richelieu was a Cardinal, they took the opportunity to attack the Hapsburg monarchs who controlled both the Holy Roman Empire and the kingdom of Spain, and in 1635 they formally joined the Protestant cause. In such circumstances their Huguenot subjects were better reconciled to the royal authority and their loyalty was more secure.

In later years the commendations of Richard Champion, notably that of 1639, recognised his support in time of stress. Despite – or even because of – his Huguenot connections, Richard appears a somewhat establishment figure, who did well by his marriage and was prepared to develop the fortunes of the family within the system which obtained at the time.

Claude Champion and the Vierville connection
No doubt repeating the text of the now lost *Pedigree Book*, the *Reveley* and *South Sea* books provide no more than a brief account of Claude, on the same lines as their previous entries:
> *Le dit Claude Champion Escuier, fils du dit Richard, epousa Dam[oise]lle Marie de Vierville, et de leur marriage sont issu, Pierre, Thomas et Gabriel Champion Escuiers Sieurs De Crespigny*
>
> The said Claude Champion Esquire, son of the said Richard, married Mademoiselle Marie de Vierville, and from their marriage came Pierre, Thomas and Gabriel, Esquires and Lords of Crespigny.[12]

As founder of the family in England, however, Claude has a generous entry in the *Lancaster* and *Kelmarsh* books:

> **Claude Champion** *Escuier*, Sieur de Crespigny in the Parish of Saint-Jean-le-Blanc near Aulnay, and of Crespigny in the Parish of Vierville-sur-Mer near Bayeux, both in the bailiwick of Caen;
>
> born at Crespigny [near Saint-Jean-le-Blanc] and baptised in the Reformed Religion at Condé[-sur-Noireau] 17 May 1620;
>
> married at Bayeux 9 June 1651 to Marie, daughter and co-heir of Pierre de Vierville, Esquire of the Château de Vierville; she was afterwards Countess of Vierville in her own right – she died 21 June 1708.

---

[11] Gailland, *Essai sur l'Histoire du protestantisme*, Chapter 4, 28-35, contains an account of the activity in Normandy at this time, including the concerns of both sides, the enforced collection of arms, and a short-lived local rebellion in 1621 which was raised by a local agent of the Rochellais.

[12] On the *Reveley* and *South Sea* books as early copies of the original *Pedigree Book*, and the *Lancaster Book* as a later reconstruction, see Chapter One at 25-26.

He was an officer of high rank in the French service, but at the Revocation of the Edict of Nantes AD 1685 he quitted France with the whole of his family. Being allied by marriage to the family of Pierrepont, he was received with open arms by that noble family.[13]

His rank and principles gained him immediate protection from the state, he was honoured with a Colonel's commission in the British Army. He died 10 April 1695, age seventy-five, and was buried (at St Marie la bonne) with his wife, where there is the following inscription to their memory...

There follows a half-page of illustrations, including the Latin text of the couple's memorial:

Hic jacet in fornice Claudius Champion de Crespigny et Maria de Vierville ejus uxor
E Galliae persecutione profugierunt cum integrâ octo liberorum familiâ
tandem in cælum veram patriam transmigrarunt
Ille: Ann. Sal: MDCXCV; Ætat LXXV
Haec: Ann Sal:MDCCVIII; Ætat LXXX

Which may be translated:

In this vault lie Claude Champion de Crespigny and Marie de Vierville his wife
who, on account of persecution, fled from France with all eight members of their family
and have at last reached their true home in the heavens:
He in the Year of Salvation 1695, at the age of seventy-five;
She in the Year of Salvation 1708, at the age of eighty.[14]

At the beginning of the twentieth century the stone was still in the churchyard of St Marylebone but much of the inscription was illegible. A new memorial was set up, with an inscription in English but with the year of Claude's death wrongly as 1697 instead of 1695:[15]

The Burial Place of Claude Champion de Crespigny
a refugee from France, Died April 10, 1697
Also of Marie de Vierville his wife, Died June 21, 1708

Born some two and a half years after his parents' marriage, Claude appears to have been their only child. He was thirty-one when he married Marie de Vierville, elder daughter of her father Pierre with no brothers, and she was eight years his junior.[16]

---

[13] On the Pierrepont connection, see below at 101.

[14] The equivalent half-page from the *Kelmarsh Book* is reproduced in Chapter One at 16; the layout is very slightly different to that of the *Lancaster Book*.

[15] Manchée, W H, "Marylebone and its Huguenot Associations," 75.

[16] The genealogical tree prepared by Ibbetson and presented as a supplement to the paper of Miss Huet traces rather vaguely a cousinly connection with Vierville or Wierville families to Switzerland and America. It

CHAPTER THREE

It is probable that Claude and Marie went to live at Vierville-sur-Mer soon after their marriage. Their house was named Crespigny, from the property still held by Claude's father Richard. A large building, typical of the period, it was very likely constructed for the new couple.

Crespigny House at Vierville-sur-Mer in 2007[17]
Recent renovations include the addition of two dormer windows in the roof. The double window below the dormer on the left belongs to the large upstairs room with the grand fireplace as below.
Holes along the right-hand wall formed a pigeon-house – a privilege of the local lord.

The chimney-piece of Crespigny House at Vierville-sur-Mer
Left: photograph by Stephen CdeC 1983   Right: The coat of arms with supporters in 1843[18]

---

has many gaps, however, and the cadet branch appears to have been separated no later than the mid-sixteenth century, a hundred years before Claude CdeC married Marie. That branch of the Viervilles was evidently also Huguenot, for its people emigrated to Westphalia in Germany at the Revocation of the Edict of Nantes.

[17] The photograph is taken from the internet at http://vierville.free.fr/644-Crespigny.htm, part of the official site of the Commune of Vierville-sur-Mar. It has a detailed survey of *L'ancien manoir de Crespigny* based upon volume 1 of *Notes historiques sur le Bessin* compiled by the Société historique of Trévières.

[18] This illustration is taken from the *Kelmarsh Book*, and is labelled as "sketched on spot by Sir C[laude

On the main upper floor, reached by a fine stone staircase, there is a grand salon with a massive fire-place, so heavy that it is supported by corbelling into the wall of the room below. The face of the chimney-piece had a blank shield with the crest of an angel's head and two lions *regardant* [looking backward] as supporters. When Sir Claude William was there in 1843, the design was still visible and he was able to make a sketch, noting that the charge on the shield had been erased at the time of the French Revolution. When Stephen CdeC visited the site in 1983 he was given access to the interior of the house and was able to study the construction of the chimney-piece. The paint-work was by this time very faded: there were traces of the lion supporters, but nothing more.[19]

Map Twelve: Northern Calvados and the southeast of the Cotentin peninsula
showing Vierville-sur-Mer with the site of Crespigny House to the west marked CH; also identifying Trévières and Vaucelles near Bayeux in Calvados, and Vierville, Creville and Réville in the Department of Manche.
Detail from Michelin France *2003 sheet 15*

The Vierville marriage has been commemorated ever since on the family shield, for Marie had no brothers and was a "heraldic heiress." Regardless of any physical inheritance of property, a heraldic heiress can transfer her family arms to her husband and children; when there are sisters, each is "co-heir" and has the same right.

The husband of a heraldic heiress may place his wife's father's arms on an "escutcheon of pretence" in the centre of his shield; after her death their children can quarter the arms of the

---

William] and F[rederick] CdeC A.D. 1840." The date should probably be 1843, and the *Kelmarsh Book* copy from the *Lancaster Book* may also have been drawn by Eyre Nicholas CdeC: Chapter One at 16.

[19] In 2008 Robert James CdeC visited the site with his wife Melanie and son George, but the interior was no longer accessible. Describing the new work, he remarked that "the bad news is that I doubt we are ever going to see the fireplace again up close, as it has become a locked up area and part of a renovated home. The good news is that I think the fireplace will now be properly protected."

CHAPTER THREE

two families, with the paternal insignia in the first quarter [top left; being top right from the point of view of the wearer]. Heraldic heiresses are not unusual, and the quarterings which a family displays are largely a matter of choice, but the Vierville connection was distinctive and important for the Champions de Crespigny. Since that marriage the family has regularly combined the lion and cross moline of the Champions with the blue bars of Vierville.

Left: The shield of Claude Champion de Crespigny married to Marie nee de Vierville:
Champion with the arms of Vierville "in pretence."
Right: The shield of the family after the death of Marie nee de Vierville in 1708: Champion quartering Vierville

Though Marie de Vierville is described as Countess, this was a personal title, and the honour could not be transferred to her husband Claude. It is even questionable whether it was valid, for though the Court of Aides at Rouen would later accept the Champion family's claim to noble rank, the *Extract* from the formal report has no reference to any title held by either Marie or her father Pierre.[20]

Claude Champion de Crespigny (1620-1695) and Marie nee de Vierville (1628-1708)
Like those ascribed to Marie nee du Bourget and Richard Champion (above at 83), these portraits, now at Kelmarsh Hall, Northamptonshire, are reproduced at https://artuk.org/discover/artworks/search/venue: kelmarsh-hall-4095. There is no secure provenance, and they are described as "British (English) School," but one may nonetheless choose to accept the traditional attribution.

---

[20] *Extract from the Register of the Court of Aides*, 9, and see below at 94-95.

Disconcertingly, moreover, and despite the indication in the *Lancaster* and *Kelmarsh* books, Claude and Marie never resided in the chateau at Vierville-sur-Mer.

Vierville-sur-Mer was not the original homeland of the Vierville family, who took their name from Vierville in the Department of Manche: the village lies at the base of the Cotentin peninsula, just across the broad inlet and marsh which separate the peninsula from the northern coast of Calvados. From there the Viervilles acquired lands and built a castle at Vierville-sur-Mer, but it was heavily damaged in the Hundred Years War. The family were driven away, and though they returned after the French triumph of the 1450s the original fortress had been largely destroyed. All that remained was part of the surrounding wall and a tower with a fine peaked roof. The roof was destroyed during the D-Day landings of June 1944, but the tower and some of the medieval wall can still be seen.

The ruined castle was never rebuilt, and in 1523 the property was sold to the Bailleul family, passing then by inheritance and by marriage. In 1670 the heiress Marie-Thèrése Canivet married Gilles de Marguerye, squire of Colleville-sur-Mer a few kilometres to the east, and a new building, basis of the present-day chateau, was constructed at the end of the seventeenth century. Neither the Viervilles nor the Champions ever owned or occupied it. They probably looked somewhat askance at their new future neighbours – particularly since the Marguerye family was firmly Roman Catholic[21] – but they had very likely gone into exile before the work was completed.[22]

The present-day chateau is large and imposing. Apart from the damage to the medieval tower, it was left largely intact by the bombardment and subsequent fighting of 1944: it was spared deliberately, for it then served as headquarters for the supply port of Omaha Beach.

Remains of the wall of the medieval castle at Vierville-sur-Mer
The present-day chateau is in the middle distance on the left; in front is the medieval tower whose peaked roof was destroyed in the bombardment of 1944; the road on the right is the D514 leading past Crespigny House.

Though La Fleurière had been sold in 1641,[23] the estate of Crespigny by Saint-Jean-le-Blanc remained in the family's possession, and was duly inherited by Claude after his father's death in 1669. It is referred to in the *Daumont Letters*, and Pierre/Daumont, eldest son of Claude and Marie nee de Vierville, used the surname de Crespigny. He was certainly committed to

---

[21] According to local tradition, at the time of the French Revolution the medieval tower served as a hiding place – a "priest's hole" – for the Abbé Edgeworth, former confessor to the deposed King Louis XVI.

[22] The history and description of the castle and of the chateau, with the accompanying photograph, are taken from http://vierville.free.fr/641-Chateau.htm, in the official website of the Commune of Vierville-sur-Mer.

There is an attractive church close to the chateau at Vierville, but since the Champion and Vierville families were Huguenot, we must assume that none of them attended services there.

[23] Chapter Two at 56.

CHAPTER THREE

the church at Trévières near Vierville, but he spent time at the Crespigny estate and may have acted as manager there.[24]

So Claude and Marie owned at least two properties, some hundred kilometres apart, and may have held other estates. Though they lived in a manor house rather than a chateau, they were certainly doing well. A source in the French National Archives states that the property which was confiscated when Claude left for England brought an annual income of 1089 livres – a considerable amount of money.[25]

At home in Normandy there were two problems: the first was a tax case, which was dealt with successfully in 1674 and is discussed below; but the second was the Huguenot connection, and that was insoluble. Richard and Claude had both shown loyalty to the crown, but Claude and Marie appear to have been sincere and strict in their adherence to the Reformed Religion which was increasingly disapproved by King Louis XIV. As persecution increased through the late 1670s and early 1680s, the family may have been to some extent insulated – many measures were directed primarily at town-dwellers and artisans – but Louis' formal Revocation of his grandfather's Edict of Nantes left no room for manoeuvre. Rather than convert, the family abandoned their property and fled to England.

Nobility and Taxation: noblesse *and the* taille

After the discussion of the family history above, we may consider the long series of court-cases concerning the Champions' right to membership of the *noblesse*, the "nobility" or "gentry", particularly the questions raised by Horace Round.

We have earlier noted John Horace Round as a most competent historian of medieval England, with a strong interest in genealogy and a constant concern to correct the excesses of family legends. In his article "A Huguenot House," published in 1930 in the posthumous collection *Family Origins and Other Studies*, he made a fierce attack on the CdeC lineage presented in Burke and Debrett.[26] His strongest comments were reserved for the idealised ancestry before Maheas in the fourteenth century, but he expressed doubt whether the family was actually called Champion de Crespigny, using the aristocratic indicator *de*, before the arrival in England; on this question he was mistaken.[27] He also criticised aspects of the later genealogy, and notably the claim to *noblesse*; again, though he demolished many pretensions, not all his arguments are fully correct.

Considering the claim to *noblesse*, Round observes that
> ...it is somewhat startling to find that, though the Champions are alleged to have been certified, in 1674, as of 'noble quality and filiation,' an official record of no more than seven years' earlier proves that the first immigrant [Claude] and his father were found to be usurpers of nobility and were actually fined as such.

He then quotes the French text from the *Recherche de Noblesse en la Généralité de Caen*, compiled in 1667 by the Intendant Guy Chamillart.[28] My rendering is:
> Richard Champion and Claude, his son, the first of the parish of Saint-Jean-le-Blanc in the *élection* [tax district] of Vire, the second of the parish of Vierville in the *élection* of

---

[24] The *Daumont Letters* at 94-95 preserve the translation of a letter of 4 February 1682 addressed to M. de Brais at Rouen, with the heading "de Crespigny" just before the date. In context, the phrase must be understood as "from Crespigny:" it cannot be a reference to the writer himself, for the typescript, as for all other letters, has the citation of the signature "De Crespigny" at the bottom..

[25] Quoted by Gailland, *Histoire du protestantisme*, 239, citing series TT.4 of the French National Archives/ *Archives Nationales*. This is unfortunately a very large collection and not readily accessible.

[26] Chapter Two at 70-71.

[27] Introduction at 5 and see note 24 above and 98-99 below.

[28] "Enquiry into those of Noble Status in the *Généralité* of Caen:" see also Chapter Two at 40. Round at 111-112 cites page 776 of the 1887 edition of Chamillart's *Recherche* by du Buisson de Courson. This text has the given name of Antoine's son as Raul; for consistency with Chapter Two, I amend it to Raoul.

Bayeux, are each sentenced, on 20 September [or October, date uncertain] to a fine of 300 *livres*.....

They are descended from Michel Champion, who was the brother of Jean; it was Jean, not Michel, who was granted in 1470 the status of *noblesse*:[29] by a judgement of the Court of Aides in 1622, confirming an earlier judgement of 1591, the descendants of Michel have been liable [to pay the *taille* tax].

Rolls of persons liable to the *taille* were presented at those cases of 1591 and 1622, and the widows and children of Antoine and of Raoul were included on those tax-rolls [as liable]; Antoine and Raoul being the grandfather and great-grandfather of the defendants [Richard and Claude his son].

Furthermore, on 8 April 1622 (miswritten as 1652) Richard Champion himself, the present defendant, admitted before the Electors at Vire that he had been subject to the *taille* tax, and for these reasons he was prohibited, under threat of being fined, from making any future claim to be of noble quality.

As Round points out, the question had financial significance. Members of the *noblesse* were not required to pay the *taille*, which was levied only against *roturiers*, or commoners: "The Crown and its officers, therefore, had to be ever on their guard against the usurpation of *noblesse* and of the valuable privilege it conferred."[30] Chamillart's *Recherche*/Enquiry was designed for just that purpose: to check all claims to membership of the *noblesse* and their consequent exemption from the *taille*.

To fully understand the text which Round quotes and which I translate above, it is necessary to consider the nature of French tax administration in the seventeenth century.

Firstly, members of the *noblesse* were indeed exempted from the *taille*. The origins of the tax are uncertain, but it was probably intended originally as compensation paid by commoners for the fact that they could not take part as knights in time of feudal levy; some early references, however, appear to regard it as no more than a direct tax levied by the king and/or by local lords on commoners under their sway, without any necessary or expressed association with feudal military service. In any event, in 1439 the *taille* was established as a permanent annual tax to be paid by commoners. Affecting either real or personal property, it was a major source of revenue, and though incidence varied from one part of the kingdom to another, Normandy was assessed very heavily.

Administration of the tax was carried out through *généralités*, each headed by an Intendant. The *Généralité* of Caen dealt with Lower Normandy, and that of Rouen with Upper Normandy. Below the *généralités* were a number of *élections*, so-called because their chief officers, the *élus* ["Electors"] had at one time been elected by the people – but they had long become officers appointed by and directly responsible to the crown. Within the *élections*, tax was collected by parishes, whose collectors, locally chosen, assessed each individual and collected the required amount.

In practice, the tax was largely collected by quota applied to a region, based upon estimates to be fulfilled rather than, as accepted in the modern West, upon a detailed and hopefully realistic assessment of each individual's capacity to pay. As a result, if one person in a parish evaded his responsibilities, the shortfall was borne by his neighbours.

As we have observed, there is substantial disagreement between the reported decision of the Court of Aides in 1622 and the statements from the local community of Saint-Jean-le-Blanc compiled over the next several years. And since they are cited in the judgement of 1674 as recorded in the *Extract from the Register of the Court of Aides*, these later statements can be considered to have the same authority as those cited by Chamillart.

---

[29] On the nature of Jean's grant and the general family history at this time, see Chapter Two at 73.
[30] "Huguenot House", 112.

CHAPTER THREE

I believe the best way to resolve the contradiction is to suggest that the property at La Fleurière was comparatively small and could not be used to justify a claim to higher rank; so the attempt in 1591 was rejected. In 1622, before he had come into the estate of Crespigny, Richard Champion's position was still inadequate. Despite the fact that he had been forbidden to repeat his claim, in subsequent years – and probably after considerable politicking – members of the local community were persuaded to endorse his higher rank. The Champions were clearly acquiring wealth and influence, and since they were newcomers to the territory their exemption from the *taille* placed no extra burden upon their neighbours: whether or not they were entitled to a coat of arms, it is probable that the Richard family had likewise been excused from the tax, at least in the parish of Saint-Jean-le-Blanc. The repeated affirmations – and the office in the Chapter of Nobles – were designed to bolster the family status against just such a future contingency as Chamillart's investigation, and this proved to be a valuable and ultimately successful stratagem.

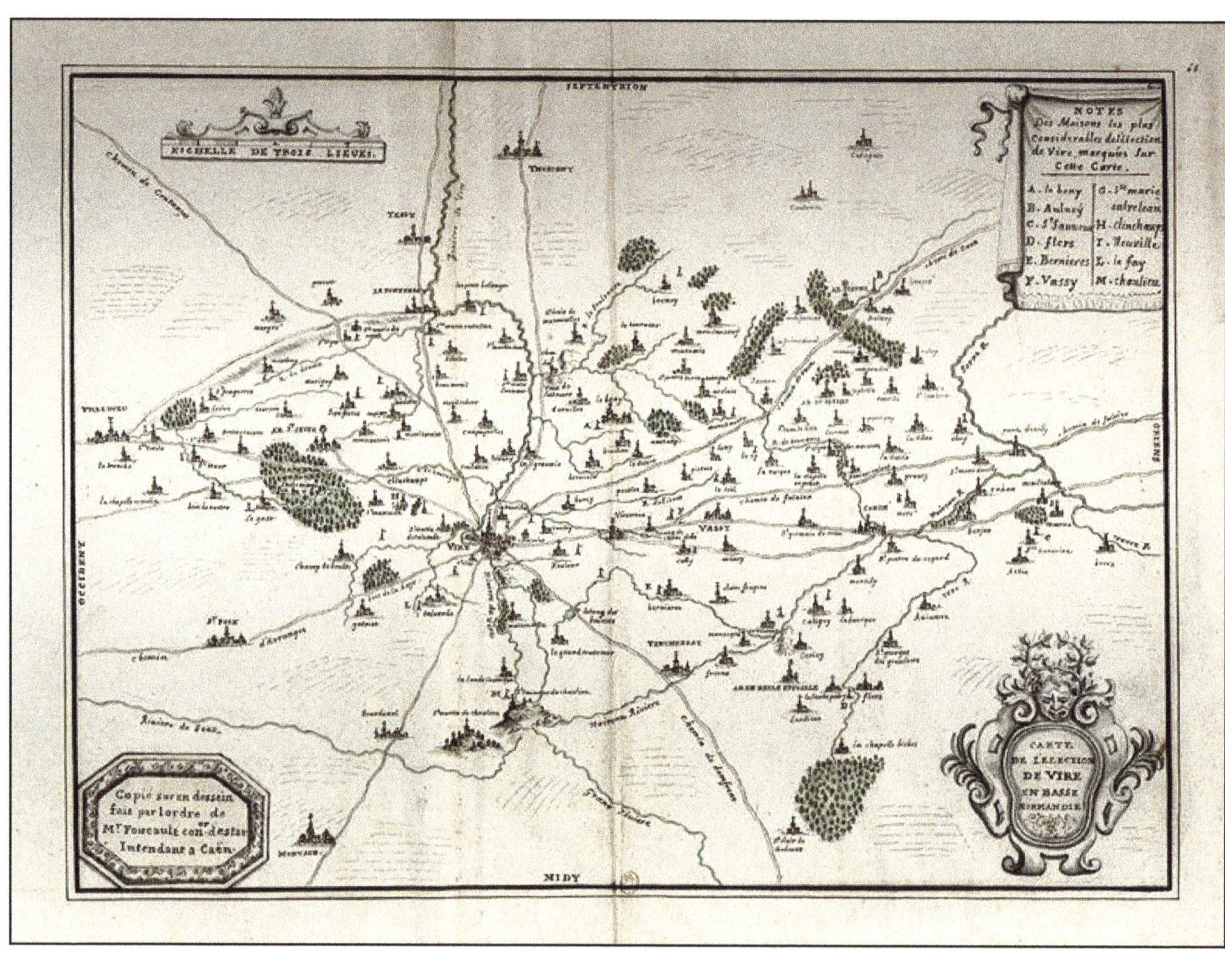

Map Thirteen: The Election *of Vire in the late seventeenth century*
Copied from an original ordered by Nicolas-Joseph Foucault (1643-1721), Intendant of the Généralité *of Caen during the 1690s.*
Reproduction is not clear, but Vire *is the large town on the left-hand sheet and* Vassy *and* Condé*[-sur Noireau] can be discerned on the right, just south of the* Chemin de Falaise*;* Tinchebray *lies to the south of* Vassy *on the* Chemin de Domfront.
The alignment of the left-hand sheet is slightly skewed to the west: Tessy*[-sur-Vire] is shown just west of due north of* Vire*, and* Torigny *[now Torigni-sur-Vire] just to the east of due north [*Septemtrion*]; in fact, both lie to the northwest in the direction of Saint Lô. Similarly, the* Chemin de Coutances *is shown running almost directly northwest; Coutances is slightly further south than that would indicate.*

Richard died in 1669, soon after Chamillart's report, and so he is not cited as an appellant to the Court of Aides in 1674. The case was then described as an action between Claude

Champion and his neighbours in the parish of Vierville-sur-Mer, for those people were concerned that Claude should share their responsibilities. Claude was successful, and the family was found to be members of the *noblesse* and thus exempt from tax.

Round's argument against the Champions' claim to noble rank is based entirely on the *Recherche* of 1666-1667. Since he gives no weight to the decision of the Court of Aides in 1674 he accordingly doubts the validity of the Certificate from the College of Arms. In summary, he observes:

> After this decisive proof that, in 1667, the family were judicially found to be liable, as *roturiers*, to payment of the *taille*, and therefore, not to be entitled to use such arms as the *noblesse*, it is strange to read the alleged finding, in 1674, of the 'Cour des Aides.'[31]

On the other hand, since the *taille* provided a substantial part of the royal revenue, it is fair to assume that the *Recherche* was specifically designed to call the maximum number of claims into question and to compel those claims to be tested in court. Round is right to point out the tax significance of *noblesse* – but it is somewhat naive of him to believe that a tax officer will give an immediately favourable response when it is in government interest that he should not do so.

I note, moreover, that the officers of the College in England were prepared to accept the evidence presented to them in the form of the original French *Extract from the Register of the Court of Aides*. If we accept that the document is genuine – and it certainly appears detailed and convincing in translation – then Round's "decisive proof" is unsustainable: Chamillart's finding at Caen in 1667 was subordinated to, and annulled by, the decision of the Court of Aides at Rouen in 1674.

There remains, of course, the question of why the Court of Aides, which had twice rejected the family's claims, should have changed its mind. The question cannot be easily answered. It is possible that Richard's title as a baron, acquired after the loss of the case in 1622, together with his repeated confirmation by the parishioners of Saint-Jean-le-Blanc and his further endorsement as a loyal subject of the crown, had changed the situation. It may be that the transfer from the *élection* of Vire to that of Bayeux, coupled with the increased prosperity of the family and Claude's connection to the Vierville and Pierrepont clans, strengthened the claim. In any event, the evidence and arguments submitted were now viewed more favourably; judgement had perhaps always been close, and the scales now tipped the other way.

It is still necessary, however, to explain what the term *noblesse* actually implied in the France of the *ancien régime* before the French Revolution, and perhaps the most important point to make is that the renderings "nobility" or "noble" are exaggerations.

As a starting-point we may take the discussion of "Foreign Titles" in the Introduction to the 1904 edition of *Debrett's Peerage, Baronetage, Knightage and Companionage*:[32]

> ...their relative value has to be judged by the fact whether their possessors belong to the *nobiles majores* or *nobiles minores* ...of their respective countries.
>
> Foreign authorities generally assume that titular distinction accompanied by an hereditary seat in the Diet or Parliament constitutes high nobility, and in France and Germany this is co-extensive with the ducal titles only. In England, however, the *nobiles majores* (or high nobility) are co-extensive with the whole peerage (dukes, marquesses, earls, viscounts and barons), such having an hereditary seat in the Upper House. It, therefore, follows that only those families of the high nobility abroad, such as the herzogs and a few landgraves in Germany, and in France the dukes and two or three of the feudatory comtes can claim our peerage (dukes to barons) as equals in titular distinction,

---

[31] "Huguenot House," 113.
[32] *Debrett* (1904), xxxi.

Chapter Three

while the marquises in France and the margraves and grafs of the empire in Germany - if the latter are chiefs of their families - are equal to our rank of baronet, the next rank (but without parliamentary seat) in England below the peerage; further, the *nobiles minores* of Germany and France, varying between in France the rank of comte to that of baron or plain ecuyer gentilhomme, and in Germany the grafs of the new Empire down to, and including, the freiherrs (by courtesy) and the herr vons, rank according to the antiquity of their families with the families in England who are also of the *nobiles minores* (knights, esquires and gentlemen).

This is superbly Anglocentric: the whole of the English peerage is by and large superior to any on the continent, while the English gentleman is equal to all but the highest ranks of foreign nobility – and one may note the rather condescending reference to the "new Empire" of the *parvenu* Kaiser in Germany.[33] There is nonetheless truth in the argument that the *noblesse* of France should be compared to the broad field of "noblemen and gentlemen" in England, rather than to the more limited group who were members of the House of Lords.

Until the recent development of life peers, and further reforms of the late twentieth century – including restrictions on hereditary peers from 1999 – all members of the English peerage with rank of baron or above were entitled to a seat in the House of Lords [in Scotland, from the time of union in 1707 it was necessary for a person not only to hold such a title but also to be elected by his peers]. In France of the *ancien régime*, the situation was made more fluid by the fact that the nearest equivalent of the national Parliament, the *États-Généraux* or Estates-General, did not meet from 1614 in the time of Louis XIII until 1789 under Louis XVI on the eve of the Revolution. Since the matter had no immediate concern, there was no regular system to determine who was entitled to sit or to be elected.[34]

The Estates-General comprised three assemblies: the clergy, the nobility and the Third Estate, representing the common people – for the most part burghers of municipalities. After considerable study and debate during 1788 and 1789, arrangements were made for the election of delegates in each region of the country, and representatives of the orders of clergy and of nobles were chosen by ballot at local assemblies. Membership of the order of nobility was checked in each region but, except for the very highest ranks, membership of the order did not guarantee a position as delegate to the Estates-General.[35]

As a result of this very occasional system, for much of early modern French history the critical question was simply whether the person was of noble/gentry lineage or was classed as a commoner: was he liable to the *taille*? The rank he might hold or claim within the broad class of *noblesse* was of far less importance.[36]

There remain three matters of confusion related to the Champion family claim to that status.
- Firstly, there is the statement in Chamillart's *Recherche* that in both 1591 and in 1622 the Court of Aides had found that Michel Champion of the fifteenth century had not been granted noble rank, and that his descendants also lacked that privilege.

---

[33] In fact, Queen Victoria's own title as Empress [of India] dated only from 1876, five years later than the Kaiser's.

[34] On the controversies which accompanied the summoning of the Estates General in 1789, to a large extent because there was no reliable record of precedent from the last assembly almost two centuries earlier, see for example, Stewart, *Documentary History of the French Revolution*, 25-29.

[35] Stewart, *Documentary History*, 40-41, quoting and translating the Regulation for Execution of the Letters of Convocation, 24 January 1789, clauses 42 and 47.

[36] One may consider, for example, the case of Mme du Barry, the lady who became the mistress of Louis XV. In the mid-eighteenth century Jean-Baptiste du Barry, who was personally a man of appalling morals but was formally a gentleman of landed family from the Toulouse region dating back to about 1400, was variously described as *Comte* and *Marquis* even in police documents, while his mistress Jeanne nee Bécu – future companion of the king – was awarded the equivalent title: de Castries, *La du Barry*, 29 and 30.

- Second, in each of those cases the Court had noted that "the widows and children of Antoine and of Raoul were included on those tax-rolls [as liable to the *taille*];" though Raoul was the son of Antoine, this would appear to indicate that Antoine and Raoul were not included on the rolls and were thus exempted from liability.
- And thirdly, there is the claim in the *Lancaster Book* that Richard Champion was Baron and Viscount of Hurien – a place which is not recorded in any regular gazetteer or atlas – while there is no suggestion that Richard's title descended to his son.

To deal with the last question first: it is possible that the titles of viscount and/or baron were purchased by Richard Champion for his own lifetime, in part as an expression of loyalty and recognition to and from the king, and in part as a means to avoid taxation. And Hurien – like Crespigny – may have been too small to be included in any broad-scale map.[37]

During the sixteenth and seventeenth centuries, first with the wars of religion, and then with the growth of royal ambition under the government of Richelieu and of Louis XIV, there had developed a policy of selling privileges. Most obvious was the sale of offices, but tax exemptions and noble titles were also sold.

In practice, the "sale" of an office represented receipt by the government of a lump-sum payment in advance, which was then paid back to the purchaser at an annual rate: in other words, a man put down a sum of money to buy an office, and in following years the government paid him a salary – it was a device to raise money quickly by mortgaging the future. In similar fashion, from the latter part of the sixteenth century there had been sales of exemption from the *taille*, and since titles of nobility gave exemption from the *taille*, it was logical they should also be sold. In 1576 there were a thousand noble titles created in Normandy alone, and the system of "letters of nobility" became a profitable trade for the crown.[38]

Such titles acquired by purchase were limited in value: they could be withdrawn by government fiat and they could not be transferred to sons or other relatives.[39] It is possible, therefore, that Richard Champion bought himself a title of nobility and by that means, if no other, acquired exemption from the *taille*. It is also possible that this short-lived nobility may have assisted the claim of Richard's son Claude before the Court of Aides in 1674.

And it may well be that the same process had taken place in the generations before Richard Champion. If Antoine had paid for a personal immunity from the *taille*, when he died his immunity died with him and his widow and his son Raoul became liable to the tax. Then Raoul in turn purchased immunity, and the same thing happened when he died. At some time, therefore, Antoine and Raoul had bought themselves off the *taille*, either by simple purchase of exemption or, as Richard did later, by paying for a title, whose name in their cases has not been preserved. The basic liability, however, remained, and this was proof in Chamillart's eyes that the family itself was not noble by lineage and had no general right to exemption.

So it could be argued that the *Recherche* was correct in 1667 and that the Court of Aides decided against the weight of precedent in 1674. Its previous decisions, as cited by Chamillart, cast doubt upon its last one, and it is remarkable that the *Extract* makes no reference to the barony or viscounty of Hurien, allegedly held by Richard Champion: if it had been valid or relevant to the case it would surely have been mentioned, and the fact that it was not makes the whole situation suspicious.

---

[37] See also page 83 above.
[38] Clamageran, *Histoire de l'impôt*, 243.
[39] Vieuille, *Nouveau traité des élections*, 553. One must assume that, despite limitations and possible revocation, purchase of office, title, or other forms of exemption did provide some value for money. It may also be noted that governments were quite capable of forcing such purchases upon wealthy citizens: the early baronetcies of seventeenth century England cost money – but a fine of equivalent value was levied on those who refused an invitation to buy.

CHAPTER THREE

Which returns us to the original suggestion. From the time of the purchase of La Fleurière, the Champions had maintained themselves in the rank of squirearchy, on the edges of nobility and gentry but still inherently of commoner status. By the sixteenth century, however, in the time of Antoine and Raoul, they had become sufficiently prosperous – and vulnerable – that it was wise to purchase exemptions from the *taille*, and Raoul's son Richard even bought a title. In the eyes of royal officials, however, this was no more than a trafficking in privilege and did not grant true noble status. That should only be acquired either by great lineage or by special grant of the crown "for good cause," not just for money.

In one case after another, the family had sought to obtain that higher recognition, and in the time of Claude, who possessed personal wealth, a military career and had married a noble heiress,[40] the claim was at last successful, and the Champions de Crespigny "proved" their right to be enrolled among the *noblesse*. It was a near-run thing, it doesn't change the fact that recent family status had been one of respectable middle-class landed prosperity, and it certainly doesn't matter in the slightest now – but it makes a nice conclusion to the story of the Champion family in Normandy.

In all this discussion, it is easy to lose sight of one important fact. Just because the family was so close to the border of nobility and gentry, and because the financial rewards of escaping the *taille* were so considerable, generation after generation of the Champion lineage had pursued the case at law. In doing so, they accumulated quantities of documents, which were eventually cited by the Court of Aides in 1674 and whose existence is attested by the *Extract*. It is by this means, and only by this means, that the names of members of the lineage have been preserved from the fourteenth and fifteenth centuries.

In consequence, despite the harassment of tax collectors which the Champions faced from one generation to another through the sixteenth and seventeenth centuries, their present-day descendants may be grateful for the written history which those law cases required and those investigations produced. Had the Champions been fully established on one side of the line or the other, the cases would never have been brought and the records would never have been collected. As it is, we have the remarkable situation of a petty provincial gentry family, with no great fame or achievement, which can prove its genealogy from medieval times. As Round observed, a proven pedigree in the male line from the fifteenth century is quite uncommon, and despite his other criticisms he did not contest that claim.[41]

Persecution and the Revocation of the Edict of Nantes
Though the Revocation of the Edict of Nantes by Louis XIV is considered to be the critical document in the outlawing of the Protestant "Reformed" or "Huguenot" church and community in France, it was in fact a final stage of persecution and represented the apparent triumph of a policy of repression which had always been latent, but which had been followed with enthusiasm for several years before.[42]

---

[40] It is not my intention to discuss the status of the Vierville family here, nor do I have sufficient evidence to do so, but some points may be made:

Though we may believe that the family was ranked among the *noblesse*, we have seen how titles could vary, and the description of the Viervilles as *comtes*/counts may be rather a matter of courtesy than a strict statement of their feudatory rank. The traditional county of that region was Bessin, based upon Bayeux, and it does not appear that the Viervilles had any authority in that wider territory: Abbott, *Provinces, Pays and Seigneuries*, 227.

On the other hand, the heraldry of the Viervilles, plain white bars on a blue ground, is simple enough to indicate a very early use of arms, and though they no longer maintained a castle or chateau at Vierville-sur-Mer the family had a long history there and in Vierville itself.

[41] "Huguenot House," 109. For Round's attack on the more exaggerated claims, see Chapter Two at 70-71.

[42] The Revocation was proclaimed by the Edict of Fontainbleau on 18 October 1685; some scholars have the date as 22 October, but the weight of opinion is with 18 October.

The privileges granted to Huguenots by the Edict of their former leader Henri IV in 1598 soon caused trouble to the royal government of France, for in many respects they had been authorised to maintain themselves as an almost independent force among the citizenry. We have noted how Louis XIII, son of Henri IV, embarked on a program to bring these people under control, a program which culminated in the siege and reduction of the city of La Rochelle in 1628. Other Huguenot strongholds were likewise eliminated, and while the Edict of Alès in 1629 confirmed the civil and religious rights of the Protestants, it abolished their political and military privileges.[43]

The situation remained comparatively stable for the next forty years, and it was in this time the Champions and the Viervilles were flourishing. In 1661, however, as he began his personal reign free of regency control, Louis XIV determined on a policy seeking the wholesale conversion of Huguenots and the elimination of their special status.

It must be recognised that for almost ninety years, from the proclamation of the Edict of Nantes in 1598 to its Revocation in 1685, France was the only country in Europe which gave essentially equal rights to two versions of Christianity. There was some public prejudice against Huguenots, but the small states of Germany maintained the rule of a single religion under each individual ruler, Spain was notorious for the Inquisition, and the Netherlands, England and Scotland, firmly Protestant, placed heavy restrictions upon their Catholic subjects. By the 1660s, however, while the Counter-Reformation had revived the energy of the Roman church, senior ministers in France were concerned with national unity, Louis's mistress and favourite, Madame de Maintenon, was a devoted Catholic; and Louis was insistent upon his royal authority.

There were a number of ways by which the conditions of the Edict of Nantes could be slighted, and some of the process had already begun. The highest offices of the state and the army were officially open to Huguenots, but they seldom gained such appointments.[44] Similarly, while Protestant schools were guaranteed, some subjects could not be taught in them. And of immediate interest to the Champion family, though Protestant churches or "temples" had been confirmed by the Edict of Nantes in all places where worship had taken place in the two years before 1598, this clause was interpreted with increasing stringency, so that numbers of congregations were dispersed on the grounds that they had been formed more recently.

It was under this last circumstance that the *Daumont Letters*, or *Lettres Françoises*, were composed. As discussed in Chapter One, the letters were evidently written to and by Pierre Champion de Crespigny, eldest son of Claude CdeC, at that time known as Daumont de Crespigny, and the essential correspondence took place between 1679 and 1682.[45]

The case concerned a dispute between the congregation and church at Trévières, west of Bayeux, and that which had been maintained at Vaucelles, close to Bayeux itself. It was

---

[43] Above at 80.

[44] Marshal Turenne, one of the greatest military commanders of the early years of Louis XIV, had been a Huguenot but converted to Catholicism in 1668.

Friedrich Hermann von Schönberg was a successful commander under Turenne and rose to be a Marshal, but he was forced into exile on account of his Protestant faith after the Revocation. Joining William of Orange in his seizure of power in England in 1688, he was enfeoffed as Duke of Schomberg and commanded the English army at the Battle of the Boyne in 1690, which destroyed the attempt of the deposed King James II to regain his throne; he died in that engagement.

[45] The historiography of the *Daumont Letters* is discussed in Chapter One at 28-31. The first of the series is dated to 1673, when Pierre/Daumont was just twenty years old and would have been very young for such responsibility. As I observe in note 38 to Chapter One, however, the next letter is dated to 1679, and the core of the correspondence and Pierre's activity took place between 1679 and 1682, when he was in his late twenties. I suspect that 1673 has been miswritten for 1679.

CHAPTER THREE

decided by the government that one of the two was in excess of the provisions of the Edict of Nantes. The decision as to which was to be abolished was left to the royal Council of State.

Through the course of the dispute, it appears that Pierre CdeC was deputed to act on behalf of the Trévières congregation, and he did so with considerable energy. Trévières now lies a short distance south of the N13, some twenty kilometres from Bayeux and about ten kilometres south of Vierville. On the direct road between the property at Vierville and the more distant region of Crespigny, it was evidently the local parish for the family.

In formal terms, the congregation at Trévières claimed that their church had been established before the one at Vaucelles, and indeed that the Vaucelles church was a *faubourg* – a suburb or colony – of the original foundation at Trévières. It appears that the Council was at first inclined to favour Vaucelles, presumably, among other factors, because it was close to the large and influential city of Bayeux, while Trévières was and is no more than a village. The letters contain frequent references to attempts at influence, patronage to obtain some councillor's ear, and the possibility of bribery.

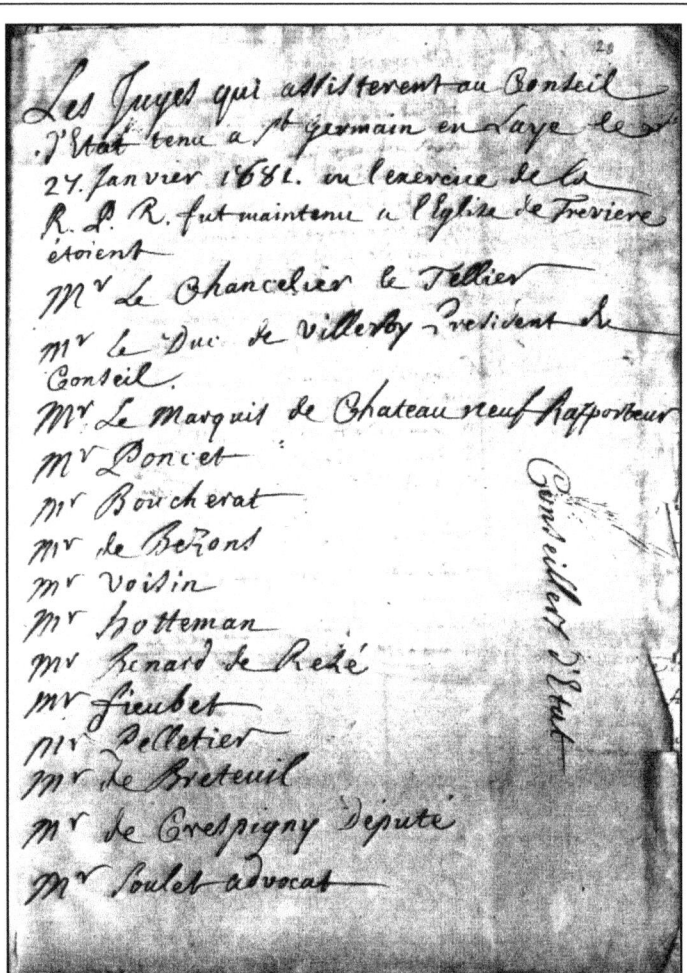

Page from the original collection of the Daumont Letters
"The Judges who attended [the meeting of] the Council of State, held at Saint Germain-en-Laye on 27 January 1681, when the exercise of the 'So-Called Reformed Religion [RPR: Religion Prétendue Réformée] was confirmed for the church at Trévières."

The name of the Deputy from Trévières, M[onsieu]r [Pierre/Daumont Champion] de Crespigny appears at the end, followed by that of his legal representative, Advocate Soulet.

The matter was eventually resolved on 27 January 1681, when the Council, meeting at Saint-Germain-en-Laye, a royal chateau north of Versailles, determined in favour of the Trévières.

In the statement of settlement, M de Crespigny is referred to as "Deputy" – agent for the congregation at Trévières – and M Soulet, a practitioner of law at Paris, served as Advocate – legal respresentative before the Council.[46]

The correspondence contains passing references to matters concerning the family, most of which we have analysed. On the affair itself, however, we may note two particular points:

- First, though he was only in his mid-twenties, Pierre/Daumont CdeC was trusted by his fellows in the congregation at Trévières, and he brought his commission to a successful conclusion. He and his family were leading figures in this small world.[47]
- Second, the long-drawn case must have cost everyone a great deal of money. It is surely remarkable that the royal Council, headed by its president the Duke of Villeroy and attended by Chancellor le Tellier and ten other officers of state, should spend time debating the claims of two heretic congregations. For their part, the rival communities had to pay their representatives' living expenses in Paris and at Rouen, and also the legal costs. Several letters refer to these problems, and there is an awkward group at the end concerning the delays in paying M Soulet's fees. Soulet eventually got his money almost a year later, and in his letter of thanks he remarked to Pierre:

> All my regret is for the great trouble and the many useless journeys you have taken on account of so inconsiderable an affair...

One may feel that an incidental part of the royal policy in fostering these disputes was to make it inconvenient and expensive to be a Huguenot – and in this it surely succeeded.

It was nonetheless a serious matter, particularly for those Reformed Churches which were deprived of their franchise. We are told that in 1680 alone the local temples of Vire, Condé and Frênes, among others, were physically destroyed, public Huguenot worship was forbidden and their pastors were dismissed.

Perhaps the saddest feature is that the congregations had no option but to accept this legalistic persecution in the manner by which it was laid down. In modern Western terms, the idea that two religious communities should be compelled to compete against one another, under the judgement of a Council which had no interest or sympathy for their beliefs, is grossly wrong. But the attitude of the Huguenots themselves is perhaps best summed up by Pierre's comment when the case was won:

> It is true that our joy must be very imperfect, since the same decree that preserves our Church, condemns that of Vaucelles [at Bayeux] to be abolished.
>
> But that one of the two must fall, was a fatal necessity, and an inevitable misfortune; and it is by far better, both for our private interest, as well as the public good, that the church of Trévières should be preserved, since by its situation it is well adapted for collecting the scattered flocks of the neighbouring Churches.[48]

After all that struggle, however, and quite against his expectations, both congregations continued to operate; though they did so in circumstances of increasing difficulty and in the face of continuous legal oppression. In 1683 Jean Cartault the minister at Trévières, and

---

[46] The *Lancaster Book* and other family sources describe Pierre as "deputed by the Protestants in Normandy to intercede with the King on behalf of their religion," but that statement is too broad and positive. He was actually negotiating with the royal government on behalf of his own congregation at Trévières and against that of Vaucelles. His concerns were quite parochial, and he certainly had no authority from the broader Protestant community of Normandy.

[47] One of the more energetic correspondents at this time is a certain LaMotte Blagny, evidently a close connection of the family, not unwilling to offer exhortations and firm criticism on occasion. Years later, in 1704 at London, M de la Motte Blagny acted as godfather at the christening of Philip, sixth child and second son of Thomas CdeC; and Jacob Philippe de Bechevel de la Motte de Blagny, together with Philip CdeC, was one of the original directors of the French Hospital, incorporated by Royal Charter in 1718: Brown, *French Hospital*, Murdoch and Vigne, *French Hospital*, 12, and Wagner, "Montresor Pedigree."

[48] Letter of 29 January 1681 to Mr de la Motte [de Blagny]: *Daumont Letters*, 75

CHAPTER THREE

Samuel Basnage the pastor at Vaucelles, were obliged to plead guilty and were heavily fined for a number of offences, including failure to swear loyalty to the crown, conducting services other than at their own dwelling-places, and carrying out baptisms outside the [Catholic] church.

Regardless of Pierre's efforts, therefore and his hope that matters might be maintained to some extent under a rule of law, no matter how unjustly conceived, the royal policy of restriction and oppression continued unabated. Indeed the very year of Trévières' apparent triumph saw the first of the *dragonnades*, forced billeting of troops upon Protestant families.

The program began in Poitou, the region about Poitiers, but spread rapidly across the country. Formally, it was the duty of civilian subjects to allow garrison or travelling soldiers to lodge with them – but the *dragonnade* took gross advantage of this principle. Officers in charge of such detachments were instructed to select Huguenot homes exclusively, and the troopers were given every encouragement to behave badly. They damaged the houses, ruined furniture and personal possessions, attacked the men and abused the women. In effect, the French army was used as an occupying and punitive force against a section of its citizens.

Conversion offered the obvious means of escape from such oppression, and *dragonnades* made at least the appearance of reconciliation to Catholicism, and abjuration of the Protestant faith, extremely popular. Combined with more legal petty persecutions, such as a refusal to permit Huguenots to hold government offices, restrictions upon schools, and notably upon craftsmen and apprenticeships, it swiftly became clear that neither protection nor mercy could be expected of the king, and that there was no limit which he and the enthusiastic Catholics were not prepared to pass.[49]

When Louis XIV revoked the Edict of Nantes on 18 October 1685, he claimed to do so because there were no more Huguenots in his kingdom, so there was no further need for their special protection and privilege. This was of course quite untrue, for a substantial minority of Protestants remained in France. The audacity of the claim, however, was a reflection not only of the effects of the program by which members of the Reformed Church had been driven either to conversion or into exile, but also of the king's determination to maintain this oppression.

Emigration to England
The forced conflicts between rival temples were vexatious, and the *dragonnades* were vicious, but those were only two of the policies designed by the royal government to make life unpleasant and dangerous for Huguenots and to encourage their conversions. In many respects, the attacks on young people were more dangerous in the longer term: not only were Huguenot schools restricted in what they might teach, but a decree of 1681 stated that children aged seven or over in Protestant families could be taken for conversion against their parents' will; and the full Revocation in 1685 made this program compulsory.[50]

Claude and Marie had eight children, four born in the 1650s and another group some years later. The eldest was Pierre/Daumont, born in 1653, followed by his sisters Marguerite (1654), Marie (1655) and Susanne (1656).[51] All these came of age in the early or mid-1670s, and by 1680 Pierre had taken his leading role at Paris on behalf of the Trévières congregation.

There was an eight-year pause after Susanne's birth before the arrival of her younger brother Thomas in 1664, followed by Gabriel in 1666, and then the sisters Renée in 1667 and

---

[49] See, for example, Gwynn, *Huguenot Heritage*, 6-8 and 21-23.
[50] Gwynn, *Huguenot Heritage*, 22-23.
[51] Chapter Four has more detailed accounts of the children of Claude and Marie. Susanne's name also appears as Suzanne or Sussanna.

Jeanne in 1668.[52] In the developing circumstances of the 1670s under-age children were becoming vulnerable, and it evidently seemed sensible for Claude and Marie to send their two younger sons to England. The *Lancaster Book* says that Thomas left France in 1676 when he was twelve years old, and Gabriel may have followed him two years later, at the same age.[53] Besides any concern for their education, the threat of forced conversion of children, sometimes even by kidnapping, was already apparent, and twelve-year-old boys must have seemed vulnerable.[54] There was a family legend that some children, presumably Thomas and Gabriel, escaped from France across the Channel concealed in baskets; the story has doubtful authority but reflects the situation.[55] There was no military conflict between England and France at that time, the distance was not particularly great, and there was frequent trade – both official and informal – between the two countries.

There is a reasonable question as to who would have looked after these youthful exiles, and it may have been the Pierrepont family. Judith de Vierville, younger sister of Claude CdeC's wife Marie, had married Antoine de Pierrepont in 1663, and they had five children: Antoine and Pierre, probably born between 1664 and 1666; Judith who was baptised in 1669; Jacques who was baptised in 1670; and Etienne/Stephen.[56] The two older boys were the same age as Thomas and Gabriel CdeC, and when Judith was baptised her godparents included her grandmother Judith de Vierville nee Gascoin, and her uncle by marriage Claude CdeC.[57] It is clear that the families were close.

It is not certain when the Pierrepont family journeyed to England, but the *Lancaster Book* tells how they received Claude and Marie CdeC " with open arms" when they came to England in the 1680s.[58] They had evidently left some time earlier, were already established in their new country, and would have been available to support the two young evacuees.

For their part, on the other hand, though Claude and Marie had sent two sons overseas it does not appear that the family were yet in fear of the worst, and they may have expected that Thomas and Gabriel would be able to return safely after a few years schooling. After all, as late as 1679 Pierre was negotiating in good faith with royal officials about the status of the temple and congregation at Trévières, and nothing in the Council's decision of 1681 foreshadowed that the successful party would be destroyed so soon. On the contrary, the Extract from the Registers of the Council of State includes a statement by King Louis himself, counter-signed by Chancellor Michel le Tellier, which read in part:[59]

> We have confirmed, and do confirm the Ministers, Elders, and Inhabitants of the town of Trevières professing the Religion called Reformed, as well in the right of henceforth continuing the Public Exercise of their said Religion in the said place, as in the Possession of their Temple, which they have enjoyed unto the time present. And this by

---

[52] The French name Jeanne is commonly rendered as Joan [*cf.* Joan of Arc], but Jeanne the daughter of Claude and Marie CdeC normally used the English Jane; her example would later be followed by her niece Jeanne, daughter of her brother Thomas and born in 1700.

[53] The *Lancaster Book* mentions only Thomas. Gabriel is asserted by Marks, "Camberwell," 2, and it is indeed likely that the family continued the policy.

[54] Though it was an extreme case, the royal favourite Madame de Maintenon was prepared to use a *letter de cachet* – authority for arbitrary arrest – as a means to seize possession of the children of her Huguenot relatives and arrange their conversion: Haldane, *Madame de Maintenon*, 142-145.

[55] *Playfair's Baronetage* VII, 98-99, says that the parents disguised themselves as fishermen and carried the children onto a boat in baskets; a version of the tale is repeated by Smiles, *History of the Huguenots*, 318.

[56] The will of Etienne de Pierrepont, anglicised as Stephen, was proved at London in 1746. It includes reference to his sister Judith and it was witnessed by Philip and Claude Champion de Crespigny, sons of Thomas – on these two cousins, see Table III and Chapter Five. His date of birth is unknown, but it is most likely that he was the youngest of five children.

[57] Wagner, "Montresor Pedigree," 299.

[58] Ball, "Huguenot Family," 25,

[59] *Daumont Letters*, 84.

CHAPTER THREE

the Decree of out Council of State hereto attached, under the Counter-Seal of our Court of Chancery this day given, We being present.

Four years later, when Louis abandoned this undertaking and revoked the Edict of Nantes, Chancellor le Tellier, known for hostility to Protestants, was a leading proponent of the change.

At the time of the Revocation in October 1685, Claude CdeC was sixty-five years old and his wife Marie was fifty-seven. It cannot have been easy for them to leave their home and their estates – though we must assume they suffered increasing hostility from official agencies and Catholic neighbours – but departure was not straightforward. Though Protestant ministers were forced into exile, laymen were forbidden to leave the country and there were severe penalties for making the attempt – including the possibility of servitude in the galleys of the royal navy.[60] On the other hand, there was no good way for them to remain in the longer term. Their Protestant faith was well known and they were leaders of the local community – marked particularly by Pierre's activity at Paris. So it was impossible to take a low profile and hope to escape attention, and it was clear that persecution and pressure would only intensify.

In theory, they could have made a formal abjuration of their creed and donned the mask of good Catholics. This is what the king and his government wanted, and many Huguenots acceded to their wish, even if some were able to maintain their true beliefs and practices in secret. But the family position made that unthinkable: how could they accept such humiliation? how could they abandon their friends and fellows in the old congregation? and how could they maintain themselves in any society once they had taken such a step?

We must accept, moreover, that these people held their religion firmly and were convinced that they were bound to do so. In the almost post-Christian world of the present day such a conviction may be hard to contemplate, but one can suspect that the family motto meant something to them which was real and true: *Mens conscia recti* – "A Mind Conscious of the Right" – took Claude, Marie and their children to exile and poverty in England.

It is estimated that some forty or fifty thousand Huguenots migrated from France to England during the 1680s.[61] They were variously welcomed, not always well, for many offered competition to English interests, particularly in the trades, and there was a nationalistic and insular distaste for foreigners. In general, however, these refugees met less resentment than others, for they demanded less from their hosts. A French Protestant congregation was already established in London, with an effective system of support for the poor, and the system expanded to assist the newcomers. The British government provided some money for pensions, though not a great deal, but the community as a whole was hard-working and prepared to be self-sufficient. With friendly societies, many based upon the regions of France from which they had come, with alms-houses – *maisons de charité* – and a soup kitchen at Spitalfields, Huguenots made few demands upon local resources for the poor, and the French Hospital *La Providence*, established by Royal Charter in 1718, was a noted foundation.[62]

Politically, moreover, events in France had an effect on public opinion, for Louis' persecution of Protestants enhanced and justified the opposition to the Catholicising policy of James II in England, culminating in the Glorious Revolution of 1688 which drove him from the throne. As William of Orange came from the Netherlands to take his place, several of his

---

[60] Gwynn, *Huguenot Heritage*, 91-93, has an account of the difficulties and dangers of escape.

[61] Gwynn, *Huguenot Heritage*, 23-24 with Map 1. Fifty to sixty thousand are believed to have gone to the Netherlands, twenty thousand to Switzerland, and a similar number to Brandenburg-Prussia in Germany. Ten thousand went to Ireland and another ten thousand to America. Gwynn's article on "England's 'First Refugees'" is a valuable survey of that migration.

[62] See, for example, Gwynn, *Huguenot Heritage*, 107-109, Escott, "Profiles of Relief," and Brown, *French Hospital*; also Chapter Four at 112-113.

senior officers were Huguenots, and Huguenot regiments played a decisive role at the victory of the Boyne in Ireland in 1690, when James' one serious attempt to return was defeated.[63]

The majority of the refugees established themselves both as members of the French community in England and also as British subjects. There were three stages to the process: reception by a church in England, grant of denization or permanent residence by the British government, and formal naturalisation. Each of the latter two required an Act of Parliament, and those seeking naturalization had to present a certificate confirming that they had received the sacraments according to the rites of the Church of England.[64]

The preferred means for individuals to join a new congregation was by *témoignage* – "witness" or "testimony" – being a document of endorsement from the pastor of the former communion. As temples in France were suppressed after the Revocation, these became increasingly difficult to obtain, and new arrivals were permitted to make a public profession of their faith, a *reconnaissance*, and from 1685 both terms were used to indicate the procedure of acceptance into the English congregation.[65]

Claude CdeC, his wife Marie and four of their children, Pierre/Peter, Susanne, Renée and Jeanne/Jane, made their *reconnaissances* at the French Church of the Savoy on 30 June 1687.[66] Of the other four children, Thomas and Gabriel had arrived earlier, and the two eldest daughters, Marguerite/Margaret and Marie, presumably managed separately. Marguerite had married Stephen de Borde in London two years earlier, and Marie had probably married Georges Gosselin/Goslin while they were still in France.[67]

As Ball observes, there is a discrepancy in the ages given for Claude and members of his family in the church record. In 1687 Claude would have been about sixty-seven, his wife Marie fifty-nine, and their son Pierre thirty-four. The record says, however, that Claude and his wife Marie were sixty-four and fifty-five, while Pierre is described as twenty-five and the daughters' ages are similarly understated. Ball suggests that the ages recorded were not those at the time of the new arrivals were accepted, but rather those which they had reached when the pastors in France provided their certificates of membership of the congregation.[68]

If that interpretation is correct, then Claude and Marie, their daughter Jeanne/Jane and very probably the others who travelled with them, received their letters of accreditation in 1684, shortly before the Revocation, while Pierre had obtained his certificate several years earlier in 1678. Though Thomas and Gabriel arrived in England in the mid-1670s, and the family must have been to some degree prepared for difficulties, Pierre's *témoignage* was probably issued as part of his authority to represent the congregation at Trévières in the negotiations at Paris rather than in anticipation of absolute exile.

All eight children of Claude and Marie became denizens of England by an Act of 5 March 1691, and they were joined at that time by three of their Pierrepont cousins: Antoine/Anthony, Pierre/Peter, and Judith.[69] None of their parents, however – Claude and Marie CdeC, Antoine and Judith de Pierrepont – found it necessary to take that step.

---

[63] Gwynn, *Huguenot Heritage*, 80, and see note 44 above.

[64] The Introduction to Shaw, *Denization and Naturalization 1603-1700*, has a survey of the development of this procedure.

[65] Gwynn, "Arrival", 368-370.

[66] Minet, *Conversions et reconnaisances*, 13, cited by Ball, "Huguenot Family," 15-16.

[67] Chapter Four at 114.

[68] "Huguenot Family," 16.

[69] Shaw, *Denization and Naturalization 1603-1700*, 225-226, and Agnew, *Protestant Exiles*, 53-54. Not surprisingly, there are some copyist's errors:

- Peter, Thomas, Gabriel appear with the surname "Champon:" compare notes 70 and 71 immediately below; the army records for Thomas and Gabriel offer variations on Crespigny.
- Jane [Jeanne] appears as "Champion" while Susanne and Renee [*sic*] are on the same line, with no surname indicated. Margaret is listed under her husband, Stephen de Borde; all these are at 226.

CHAPTER THREE

Gabriel was then naturalised on 12 March 1699,[70] but Peter and Thomas waited until 1706.[71] It is clear that this final step was not considered urgent: by 1706 Pierre had been in England for twenty years, Thomas and Gabriel perhaps ten years longer; and both held full commissions in the army. There is no mention of any women of the family being naturalised. As discussed in Chapter Four, Marguerite, Marie and probably Suzanne were married during the 1680s and 1690s, Renée in 1716, and it is likely they acquired such rights as they needed by that means; Judith's husband Geronimo de Lamberty was never a British subject.

Whatever preparations they may have made, however, and despite their new legal standing, there is an impression in the *Lancaster Book* that the Champions de Crespigny did not do as well as the Pierreponts, presumably because the latter had established themselves in England well before the full Revocation. Though Claude had been a wealthy man in France,[72] he was obliged to abandon his estates, and – unlike the majority of the refugees who made their way to England – he and his family were neither merchants nor artisans who could transfer their money or their skills to a new country.[73] Claude and his family may have brought some items with them – possibly including the family portraits now at Kelmarsh Hall – but most of them would have been sold to provide basic living expenses. An account of relief payments for 1687 lists "Claudius Champion de Crespigny of Normandi 67 years," together with his wife 55 years, and their children Peter Champion 30 years old, Susanne [30 years], Renée 20 years and Joan [*i.e* Jeanne/Jane] 19 years, "Newly come over," receiving a total of £40 "for Pention and Cloaths."[74] And in the first years of the eighteenth century Marie and her daughter Renée were still listed as gentlefolk receiving pensions from the Queen's Bounty.[75]

- Marie Goslin is listed separately at 225/53. The *Lancaster Book* says that Mary CdeC married G[eorges?] Gosselin, so this is surely the same person, but it appears that she is by this time a widow.

    The formal date is given as 5 March 1698/99. At that time the New Year in England began on 25 March, so days before that were identified by two years: in this case 1698 was the official year at the time; and 1699 was the year by modern count. For practicality, I use the present-day system.

[70] Shaw, *Denization and Naturalization 1603-1700*, 281 [as Gabriell Champion de Grespigny]. The Pierrepont cousins Antoine and Stephen were naturalized two weeks earlier, on 22 February: Shaw, 264.

[71] Royal Assent was given on 19 March 1705/06: *Denization and Naturalization 1701-1800*, 49, 50 and 52. Pierre appears as Peter, and both he and Thomas are given the surname Champion de Crepigny.

[72] Galland, *L'Histoire du protestantisme*, 239, quotes a passage from the French National Archives which states that the property Claude lost by confiscation brought in the sum of 1089 *livres*: see 90 above. Galland adds that "The English made him a colonel, but he had eight children, and he died very poor." The possible colonelcy is discussed immediately below.

[73] Gwynn, "England's 'First Refugees'," 23: "Those who came to Britain included many skilled craftsmen, silversmiths, watchmakers and the like, and professional people – clergy, doctors, merchants, soldiers, teachers. There was a small sprinkling of lesser nobility." The Champions de Crespigny would have been in that last category: Claude had managed at least two estates, and his son Pierre/Daumont had practical experience of the law and politics, but neither held formal qualifications.

[74] Personal communication from Randolph Vigne, Hon Editor of the Huguenot Society, to Stephen CdeC in 1988, citing "Accounts for [relief payments to] French conformed Protestants, 3 August to 12 November 1687. The significance of "conformed" is explained below.

    The ages given for Claude, Renée and Jeanne are correct, but Marie was actually sixty years old, Pierre was thirty-two, and Susanne's was omitted in the copied text.

[75] When Huguenot refugees first arrived in England they relied on private charity, but in 1689 the joint monarchs William and Mary inaugurated the Royal Bounty with funds from the Civil List – money allocated by Parliament for personal expenses of the royal family. The Bounty was later maintained by Acts of Parliament; Gwynn, *Huguenot Heritage*, 58. During the reign of Queen Anne from 1702 to 1714 the program was known as the Queen's Bounty.

    The list of recipients is held in the library at Lambeth Palace, and an extract copy was provided to Stephen CdeC by Randolph Vigne in 1986 [note 74 immediately above]. In 1707 Marie and Renée – with the surname Champion de Crespigny – were living in Wardour Street, Soho, and the amount of the pension was £18. Marie's age is given more accurately as seventy-eight, and Renée's as thirty-seven. That is the last year of recorded payment; Marie died in 1708.

The *Lancaster Book* and other sources claim that Claude had held high rank in the French army and that he was later commissioned as a colonel in the British service. Galland also says that he was an officer in the army of Louis XIV, but there is no available account of his service in the French army nor any formal statement of the rank he attained. Neither is there any official documentation of his colonelcy in England. British regiments at that time were named after their colonels [76] and there is no record of any regiment named Champion or Crespigny. Furthermore, since Claude was sixty-five when he arrived in England, it is unlikely he was given a substantive appointment. He might have been granted some honorary or supernumerary rank as a means to provide him with a pension, but since it does not appear that he was ever naturalised it is hard to see how this could have been justified. The story of his British commission is probably false.[77]

Within the Huguenot community there was a distinction between the congregations which maintained their strict Calvinist faith and procedures and those which "conformed" to the doctrines of the Church of England and adopted the *Book of Common Prayer* as translated into French. The French Church of the Savoy had been established in 1661 under the authority of the Bishop of London, and members of its congregation, like those of other conformist churches, were part of the Anglican communion.

This was a matter of political significance. Restrictions on Roman Catholics were firm, and while the Act of Toleration of 1689 granted freedom of worship to non-conformist Protestant churches – notably Presbyterians but also Calvinists and Lutherans – the combined provisions of the Corporation and Test Acts of 1661 and 1673 required any holder of government office to receive regular Communion according to the rites of the Church of England.[78] Thanks to their Anglican association, however, members of the congregation at the Savoy had no difficulty in playing a full part in public life; the CdeCs would take advantage of the opportunities.[79]

Claude died on 10 April 1695, and his remains were placed in a family vault at the Church of England in Marylebone; space in the small French Chapel of the Savoy was limited. The exact site and nature of the Marylebone vault is uncertain, and we cannot be certain that it was acquired at this time and that it was the first resting place of Claude CdeC.

---

[76] See, for example, the two articles by Manchée on the military organisation of the Huguenot émigrés, also Lawson, *Uniforms of the British Army* I, 92-93, the account in Chapter Four at 120-122 of the varying names of the regiment in which Claude's son Thomas would serve, and the further discussion at 127.

[77] Dalton, *English Army Lists* III, 36, mentions Tho.[mas] Crespigny as a Cornet to the Colonel in Lord Cardross's Regiment of Dragoons: Chapter Four at 119-120. A note by Dalton on the following page identifies Thomas as the second son of Claude CdeC, "a French refugee officer," but though his compilation is detailed, it has no mention of Claude himself holding any British rank. Smiles' *History of the Huguenots* at 318 says that Claude "served as colonel under Marlborough," but offers no evidence.

[78] Gwynn, "England's 'First Refugees'," 23, suggests that the Declaration of Indulgence issued by James II in 1687 was an encouragement to Huguenot migration, as it indicated a degree of religious tolerance. James, however, was known to be a Roman Catholic, his Declaration was seen as preliminary to the restoration of Papacy, and it was fiercely opposed. The settlement which followed James' overthrow in 1688 confirmed the political supremacy of the Church of England and again removed the political rights both of Catholics and of Protestant non-Conformists.

[79] In 1250 Peter of Savoy, an uncle of Queen Eleanor the wife of Henry III, had a palace on the banks of the Thames along the present-day Strand. In the early sixteenth century Henry VIII constructed a hospital or hospice, and the foundation was maintained as a residence under various guises until it was demolished to make way for Waterloo Bridge in the early nineteenth century. The modern Savoy Hotel takes its name from its position on a part of the site.

The Savoy Hospital had two chapels, and in 1661, soon after the restoration of Charles II, the smaller one was approved for the use of Huguenots following the Anglican liturgy in French translation. The large Savoy Chapel survived the demolition and may still be seen, but the small one was destroyed.

See Cowie, "The Savoy; palace and hospital."

CHAPTER THREE

It was maintained through much of the eighteenth century, for entries in the *Consolations Book* added by Philip the son of Thomas CdeC tell of the deaths of his father in 1712, of his brother William in 1721, and of his mother Magdalen nee Granger in 1730, all being "buried in our Vault in Marylebone Church Yard." In his will of 1738 Pierre the brother of Thomas also requested burial in the family vault, and the last member of the family to be interred there was Pierre's nephew Claude of South Sea House, who died in 1782.

At the time of Claude's death, his eldest son Pierre was forty-two years old and held a respected position among the French Protestant community in London. Thomas, age thirty, and Gabriel, twenty-nine, were both on military service in the Netherlands. All three brothers had been made free denizens of England by an Act of Parliament passed on 5 March 1690; none had yet been naturalised, but that did not prevent Thomas and Gabriel from holding commissions. William of Orange had created a number of Huguenot regiments to assist his seizure of the British crown from James II and in the subsequent wars against Louis XIV; Thomas and Gabriel, however, were officers of the British army, not of these ancillary units.[80]

In the following year, 1696, Pierre, Thomas and Gabriel presented their family documents to the College of Arms, and on 4 May 1697 the College issued its Certificate. Such registration was valuable as a means to establish the identity and legitimacy for members of a family who had so lately arrived and whose records were largely inaccessible in France.[81] Confirming the tradition of the *Pedigree Book*, it also recognised the claim of gentry and heraldry in the new country, and formed a most satisfactory memorial to three hundred years of ancestors.

A Note on the Question of Compensation:

In his article on the CdeC family in Camberwell, Marks suggests in passing that

> [Philip (1704-1765)] may also have received some compensation from the French government for the family's confiscated estates, but this would probably not have amounted to very much.[82]

I have looked widely for any source or support for this possibility, but find none.

In the years following the Revocation, there was some low-level revival of Protestantism in France, and the death of Louis XIV in 1715 brought a brief relaxation of the oppression. The Reformed Religion was nonetheless still illegal, and the government of Louis XV could be just as harsh. Among major examples:

> An edict of 1724 forbade heretical religious assemblies, under penalty of sentence to perpetual [service as oarsmen in the naval] galleys for men and life imprisonment for women. For Protestant preachers the punishment was death..... In 1749 the parlement of Bordeaux ordered forty-six persons to separate for concubinage, that is, for being married by Protestant rites, and declared their children illegitimate and incapable of inheriting their property.[83]

The threat of such random oppression remained until 1787, when Louis XVI signed the Edict of Versailles granting civil rights to non-Catholics, including official recognition of their marriages; the Huguenot church itself, however, was not accepted.

In these circumstances it is most unlikely that the royal government of France, which was always in financial difficulty, would have embarked on any form of compensation scheme. Even on a limited scale, it was an unnecessary extravagance.

---

[80] See, for example, Child, *British Army of William III*, 132, Gwynn, *Huguenot Heritage*, 131 and 148, and Manchée, "Huguenot Soldiers" and "The Huguenot Regiments;" also note 41 to Chapter Four.

[81] Fifty years later, the Certificate from the College provided helpful authority for the legitimacy of their youngest sister Jeanne/Jane when she faced problems overseas: Chapter Four at 117-118.

[82] Marks, "The de Crespigny Family in Camberwell," 3.

[83] Cobban, *History of Modern France*, 59.

In private matters, moreover, several Huguenot wills of eighteenth century England refer – with varying degrees of indignation – to estates abandoned in France, many of which had been appropriated by relatives who had chosen to abjure their Protestant faith.[84]

The closest any French government got to recognition of the Hugueots – but with no reference to compensation – was the Declaration of the Rights of Man and Citizen proclaimed by the revolutionary government of 1789. This promised equal treatment to all of Protestant faith, and its provisions were confirmed by a law of 15 December 1790, whereby

> All persons born in a foreign country and descending in any degree of a French man or woman expatriated for religious reason are declared French nationals (*naturels français*) and will benefit from rights attached to that quality if they come back to France, establish their domicile there and take the civic oath.

Though there would surely have been difficulty in proving a legal descent after two hundred years, these provisions were largely confirmed by the Nationality Law of the Third Republic in 1889. In the aftermath of the Second World War, however, on 19 October 1945 the Provisional Government of the French Republic published an *Ordonnance* of nationality omitting that right of return. Descendants of Huguenot exiles must now qualify in the same way as any other foreigners.

Ultimately, we must accept that no recompense was paid for the loss of the family estates at Crespigny or Vierville, and none may be expected in the future.[85]

---

[84] *E.g.* Vigne, "Testaments of Faith," 275-277.

[85] We may note that the *Lancaster Book*, in its encomium of Philip, son of Thomas and grandson of Claude CdeC and Marie nee de Vierville, refers to the family estates having been confiscated and makes no mention of any payment: Chapter Five at 147.

Shield of Pierre Champion de Crespigny, Director of the French Hospital La Providence *1718-1739*

This is among a collection of shields which were formerly hung in the Court Room of the Hospital, but which are now displayed on the staircase of the present building at Rochester in Kent.

Though the shield is shown with a gold background to the first and fourth quarters and gold and black bars in the second and third, this surely reflects the material- brass or copper – from which it is made. The Champion/CdeC arms are a black lion on a white ground, and the Vierville family had blue and white bars; there is no reason to believe that Pierre used different colours.

Source: Murchoch and Vigne, The French Hospital in England

CHAPTER FOUR

The First Generation in England (*c*.1685-*c*.1750)

Introductory
Chronology
Pierre and his sisters
Thomas, his wife Magdalen, and their family
Gabriel, his wife Elizabeth, and their children

Introductory
The first version of this work, *Champions in Normandy*, was prepared in 1988 and offered an account of the CdeC lineage until the Revocation of the Edict of Nantes by Louis XIV in 1685 and the consequent emigration to England. The study effectively concluded at the end of Chapter Three above.

In one regard, such a stopping place is a sensible one, for the departure from France was permanent, and the history of the family for the next hundred and fifty years would be played out in England. Some members visited France and some made longer stays, voluntary or forced, but from the end of the seventeenth century this was a British family and later an Australian one.

On the other hand, the record of the first century in England is worthy of study. How did a group of minor gentry from provincial Normandy make their way so successfully in a new country? And they were successful: within a couple of generations members of the family had acquired political influence and seats in Parliament, high office in the state, education at Oxford and Cambridge, and very substantial wealth. They were not noble – the Champions never were and a baronetcy, while pleasant, does not entail membership of the House of Lords – but they were accepted and respected by the highest levels of society. It is a remarkable achievement, and while the two incidents are little more than an accidental juxtaposition one may consider the trials of Pierre/Daumont CdeC in the late 1670s and early 1680s, arguing the case of his small Protestant congregation on the eve of its extinction by the very king whose favour he sought; and observe that fifty years later his nephew Philip was among a distinguished group of courtiers and officials gathered to proclaim and celebrate the accession of George II.[1]

Thirty years ago, though I knew that there was a great deal of information available in England, little was accessible from Australia, while Eileen Ball's "History of the Huguenot Family of Champion de Crespigny" had already given a sensitive account of the period. Her essay was published in 1973, however, and there is opportunity for further consideration.

Quantities of additional material, moreover, both primary and secondary, can now be found on the internet, while email communication makes consultation with colleagues and advisers far more swift and straightforward. Sometimes the new information raises as many questions as it answers, and there are still large gaps in the records, but it is nonetheless possible to piece together a basic chronology of individual lives, and one can make some sympathetic guesses on the real experience behind the documents. So the present chapter and the next attempt an historical reconstruction of the history of the lineage in England from the end of the seventeenth to the beginning of the nineteenth century.

It may be seen from the accompanying Table III that although Claude CdeC and Marie nee de Vierville had eight children, and all except their eldest son Pierre were married, only three –

---

[1] Chapter Three at 97-100 and Chapter Five at 148-149.

CHAPTER FOUR

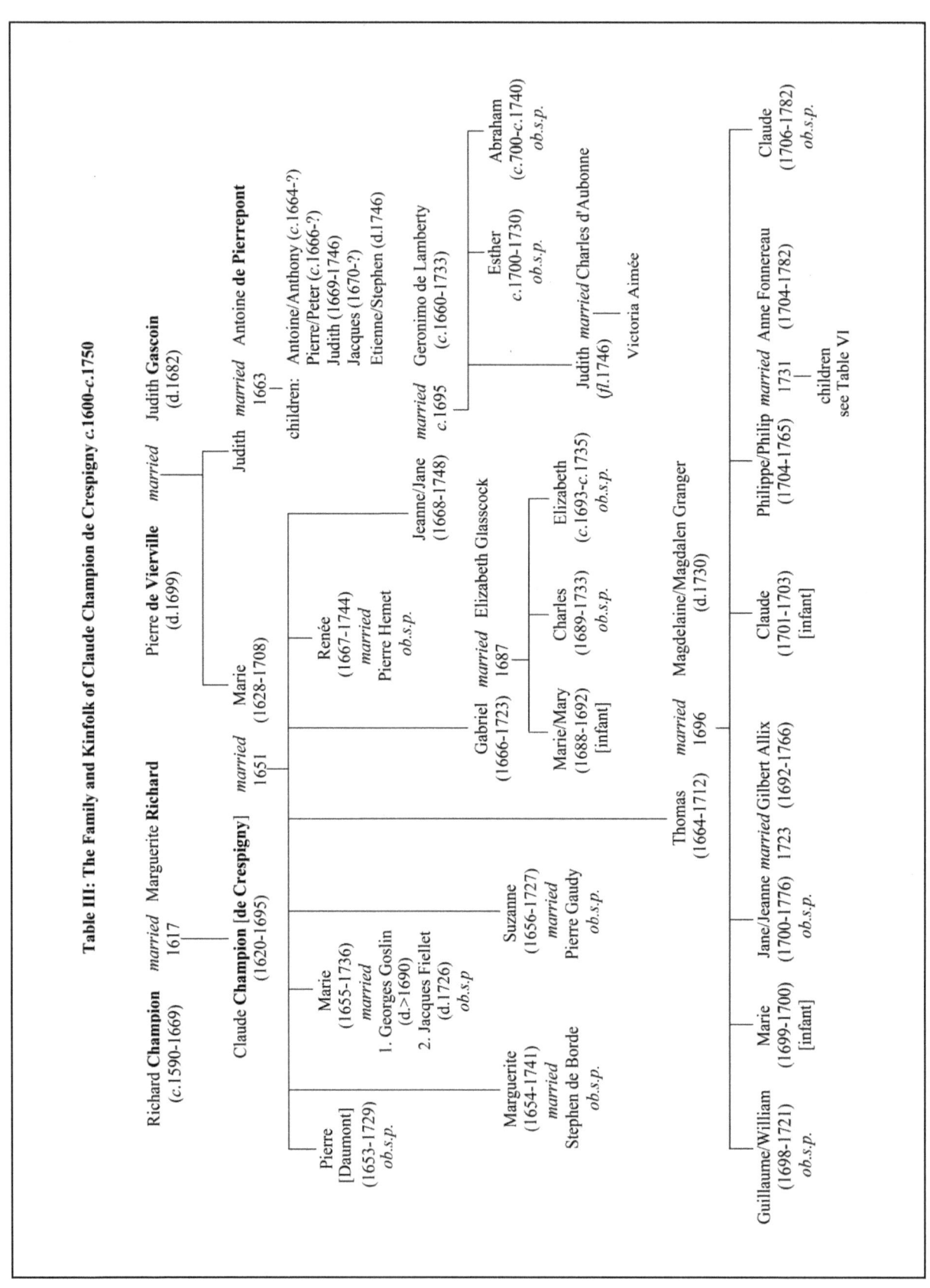

Thomas, Gabriel and Jeanne/Jane – had children themselves. Gabriel, however, had no grandchildren, and of Thomas' six children only Philip had descendants. Jeanne had three children, but only her daughter Judith had a child, Victoria Aimée. That branch of the family settled in Switzerland, and though there was contact through the first generation the distance eventually had effect, and changes of name through marriage mean that it is impracticable to trace these now very distant cousins.

In 1805 Claude CdeC, grandson of Thomas through his son Philip, was awarded a baronetcy, but the last of his descendants in the male line was Sir Vivian Other Tyrrell the eighth baronet, who died in 1952. The present English-Australian family of the Champion de Crespigny surname, therefore, trace their lineage back to Claude's younger brother Philip, son of Philip, grandson of Thomas and great-grandson of Claude CdeC and Marie nee de Vierville.

As I remark at the beginning of this work, the development and use of the surname has been erratic, and for much of the period we are dealing with in the early eighteenth century it appears as Crespigny, with Champion used rather as a given name.

Pierre, Thomas and Gabriel, for example, are certified by the College of Arms as Champion de Crespigny, but while Pierre used the full surname in his will, his brothers Thomas and Gabriel used plain Crespigny in their military careers. Their children followed suit, and for most of the eighteenth century, the effective surname was Crespigny, with occasional excursions into Champion Crespigny and Champion de Crespigny. When Thomas' son Philip acquired his great house at Camberwell in 1755, however, he named it Champion Lodge.[2]

The full version of the surname was revived by the first baronet, who styled himself Sir Claude Champion de Crespigny.[3] Other members of the family, notably Sir Claude's brother Philip and his descendants through his son Charles Fox and grandson Philip Robert, ancestor of the family in Australia, continued to use the short form Crespigny, sometimes Champion Crespigny, until late in the nineteenth century.

Faced with this confusion, while I refer to the general lineage as CdeC, I normally accept the usage of the person I am dealing with, and I sometimes quote erratic spelling in official documents just as it stands – the name is quite recognisable.

Chronology 1680-1740[*]

1686	Gabriel CdeC joins the British Army, probably as a Gentleman Volunteer
c.1687	Gabriel CdeC marries Elizabeth nee Glasscock
1688	William of Orange and his wife Mary seize the British throne from James II
1688-97	War of the League of Augsburg or War of the English Succession
1689-90	Thomas CdeC is commissioned as a Cornet in Lord Cardross's Regiment of Dragoons, later commanded by Lord Cunningham
1690	Pierre, Thomas and Gabriel CdeC, with their sisters Margaret, Marie, Susanne, Renée and Jeanne/Jane are granted denization
1691	Gabriel is commissioned as a Lieutenant acting Captain in the 1st Foot Guards
1694	Thomas on military service in Flanders against the French
1695	death of Claude CdeC
	Gabriel CdeC is wounded at Namur
1696	Thomas becomes Captain-Lieutenant in Cunningham's regiment, later commanded by Lord Jedburgh; he marries Magdalen nee Granger

---

[2] Chapter Five at 165.
[3] Grayden, *Chronicle*, 11, provides a photocopy.
[*] Items in blue are established historical facts; items in normal font relate to the family.

CHAPTER FOUR

1697	The College of Arms certifies the noble descent of the family
1698	birth of Thomas' son Guillaume/William at Bruges
1699	Gabriel is naturalised as an English citizen
1699-1704	Thomas is stationed with his regiment in Scotland
1701	Gabriel joins the Earl of Donegall's Regiment, the 35th Foot.
1702-15	War of the Spanish Succession
1704	birth of Thomas' son Philip (1704-1765) at London
1704-05	Gabriel with the garrison of Gibraltar under siege from Spanish and French forces
1705	Pierre and Thomas are naturalised as English citizens
	Thomas becomes a Gentleman Volunteer in Sir Charles Hotham's Regiment of Foot
1706	birth of Thomas' son Claude (1706-1782); Thomas goes with his regiment to Spain; his and Gabriel's regiments take part in the capture of Alicante; Thomas' regiment then remains in garrison there
1707	Gabriel's regiment is in the field army defeated at Almansa; the survivors are brought back to Ireland
	at a meeting of the Board of General Officers in London, Gabriel is assaulted by his fellow-officer Thomas Caulfeild; Caulfeild is arrested, but the matter is later dropped
1708	death of Marie CdeC nee de Vierville
1708-1709	Thomas' regiment is besieged at Alicante
1710	Thomas is promoted Captain in Sir Charles Hotham's Regiment
1712	Thomas dies at London; his widow Magdalen is granted a pension
1713	Thomas' son Guillaume/William is apprenticed to a lawyer of the Inner Temple
1718	Pierre CdeC becomes a founding Director of the French Hospital in London
	Thomas' son Philip is apprenticed to a lawyer at the Court of Arches
1721	death of Thomas' son Guillaume/William
1730	death of Magdalen nee Granger, widow of Thomas CdeC
1739	death of Pierre CdeC

Pierre and his sisters

Though Thomas and Gabriel were the third and fifth of the children born to Claude and Marie CdeC, it is more helpful to deal with them separately. Both served as officers in the British Army, so their experiences were different to those of their elder brother Pierre and their sisters. I have therefore placed them in two separate and later sections of this chapter.

Pierre [also known as Daumont] was born in 1653. In his late twenties he may have acted as his father's agent at the estate in Crespigny, and during the late 1670s and early 1680s, as the Huguenot congregation of Trévières was in dispute with the neighbouring church of Vaucelles, he acted on their behalf before the royal Council.[4]

Within a couple of years of the Revocation of the Edict of Nantes, however, the situation in France had become impossible for any true Protestant, and Pierre left for England with other members of the family. In June 1687 he and his parents and his sisters Susanne, Renée and Jeanne/Jane were formally accepted into the French Church of the Savoy.

Now in his mid-thirties, Pierre had demonstrated his abilities during the negotiations relating to Trévières and Vaucelles in France, and he became a leader of the exiled community. He was a member of the council of the General Assembly of French Churches in London, an association of both conformist and non-conformist congregations which was particularly involved in relief and charity work, and he was a founding Director of the French

---

[4] Chapter One at 28-31 and Chapter Three at 100-101.

Protestant Hospital. Formally incorporated under royal charter on 24 July 1718 as "The Hospital for Poor French Protestants and their Descendants Residing in Great Britain, it has been commonly known as *La Providence*.⁵

The Seal of the French Protestant Hospital La Providence
showing Elijah being fed by ravens, with the motto Dominus provedebit
*"The Lord will Provide"*⁶

Pierre was also involved in matters of personal administration among the Huguenot community: there are several cases where he appears as a witness, as an executor, as maker of an affidavit or as the provider of a certified translation. There is no evidence that he was formally licenced, but he was no doubt paid for his services. Surviving letters to him and documents in his own hand were written in French, but he certainly controlled the English language, and he held general respect among both migrant and native communities.

Never married, Pierre CdeC died of apoplexy – a stroke – on 22 December 1739 at the age of eighty-six.⁷ He mentions in his will of 10 August that year – translated into English for probate – that he had recently suffered heavy financial losses.⁸ Individual bequests amounted to just over £1000, and the remainder was left equally to his nephews Philip and Claude, sons of Thomas; its value cannot be quantified, but it may not have been a great amount. Besides money to his servant and his kinsfolk, he gave £20 to the French Church of the Savoy and £20 to the *Maison de Charité*/House of Charity in Soho. He asked that his body be placed in the family vault at Marylebone with that of his parents, and this was done on 27 December.

---

5   There is some confusion about Pierre's appointments. Manchée, "Marylebone and its Huguenot Associations," 76, cites Smiles' *History of the Huguenots*, but gives no pagination and I can find no such statement in that work. The *Lancaster Book*, however, describes Pierre as a member of "the Committee of French Churches in London," and this surely refers to the General Assembly of the French Churches in London, which was formed in the 1690s: Gwynn, *Huguenot Heritage*, 106-107.

   The Gentleman's Magazine 9, 661, records Pierre's death in 1739 and refers to him there as a member of the Committee of the French Churches and Poor in London.

   On Pierre's appointment as one of the thirty-seven initial directors of the French Hospital, see Murdoch and Vigne, *French Hospital*, 31 and 89. In 1965 Pierre's descendant Stephen CdeC likewise became a Director, and in 1987 he was followed by his daughter Elizabeth Louise Willis.

6   The story of Elijah is in the First Book of Kings in the *Old Testament*. Chapter XVII tells how in a time of drought he was sent by God to the brook Cherith near the River Jordan, and verse 6 describes how God sent ravens with bread and meat each morning and evening. Later in the chapter we are told that he appealed to God to restore a child to life, and this was done. He is regarded as one of the greatest of the prophets. The same motif appears in the front pages of the *Consolations Book*: Chapter One at 17-18.

7   The cause of death is given by his nephew and executor Philip in a letter of 24 December to Pierre's sister Jane de Lamberty, advising her of a bequest of £10. He mentions also the financial difficulties of his aunt [Marguerite/Margaret] de Borde/s as below.

8   The *Reveley Book* suggests this is a reference to the loss of the family estates in France, but that was fifty years in the past. It is probable that the complaint reflects some more immediate misfortune – the failure of a bank or some ill-placed investment. Finance at that time could be very erratic, and while the South Sea Bubble [Chapter Five at 141] was the most dramatic, it was not the only source of risk.

CHAPTER FOUR

Marguerite/Margaret was born in 1654. She arrived in England in 1685, and on 16 December of that year she married Stephen [Etienne] de Bordes at St Botolph's Church in Aldgate, London. He too was an émigré: when members of the family received denization in March 1691, Stephen de Borde was listed with his wife Margaret.[9]

Stephen and Marguerite had no children, and Stephen died before 1733: in that year Marguerite served as godmother to Jane, first child of her nephew Philip CdeC and Anne nee Fonnereau, and she is described as a widow at that time. Financially, she was in more difficulty than her sisters, and in his will of 1739 her brother Pierre left her £100 and all his furniture. Marguerite herself died two years later at the age of eighty-seven.

Marie/Mary, born in 1655, was married twice. The *Lancaster Book* gives the name of her first husband as a G[eorge/s] Gosselin, but the act of denization in March 1691 lists Mary Goslin alone: this is surely her, and she is already a widow.[10]

On 19 May 1698 Marie Champion married Jacques Feillet at the Chapel of Hungerford Market, now the site of Charing Cross railway station in London.[11] The will of Jacob Feillet, leaving his property to his wife Mary, was proved on 22 May 1728.

Marie died in 1736 at the age of eighty; her will had been signed on 17 April of that year and was proved on 7 June. With no surviving children by either of her marriages, she left a life interest in her estate to her brother Pierre and thereafter to her nephews Philip and Claude, sons of her late brother Thomas. Individual bequests included the amounts of £50 to her sisters Margaret Debordes and Jane Lamberti, and to her niece Jane/Jeanne married to Gilbert Allix; £25 to Frances Goslin – a kinswoman of her first husband – and £25 to be shared by her cousins de Pierrepont. In addition she gave

> my late first husband [Mr] Goslin's Picture set with Diamonds to my Nephew Philip upon Condition that it shall be preserved in his family so, without taking the Diamonds of[f]. And if he dyes without Children I desire it may go to his Brother Claude upon the same Condition.

As a final item, she left a pearl necklace to her great-niece Susanna de Crespigny, daughter of Philip – Susanna had been born just six months earlier, on 13 November 1735.

Susanne/Susanna, whose name also appears as Suzanne and as Sussanna, was born in 1656. In 1687, together with her parents, her elder brother Pierre/Peter and her younger sisters Renée and Jeanne/Jane, she is listed among recent immigrants receiving relief payments.[12] Thirty years old at that time, she was apparently still single. She later married Pierre Gaudy, but they had no children. There is no further information about her husband, but he evidently died some time before 1727, for in her will of 9 January that year Susanna describes herself as a widow, living in the parish of St James, London.

Susanna remarks at the beginning of the document that she is of sound mind but infirm body, and she died just a few days later; probate of her will – written in French but formally translated – was granted on 2 February.

Individual bequests were comparatively modest: £5 to the poor; £10 to her brother Gabriel and £5 to his daughter Elizabeth; £10 to her sister Marguerite de Bordes, and £5 to her sister-in-law Madam de Crespigny – presumably Magdelaine nee Granger the widow of

---

[9] The parish register of St Botolph's has the name of the wife as Margaretta Decampion and the husband as Stephen Debordes. Shaw, *Denization and Naturalization 1603-1700*, 226, has the surname as de Borde, and the *Lancaster Book* agrees. It occasionally appears also as de Bordes.
The French given name Etienne is regularly rendered into English as Stephen.

[10] Shaw, *Denization and Naturalization 1603-1700*, 225, and note 69 to Chapter Three at 103-104. Mary's will of 1736 gives the surname of her late husband as Goslin; it may have been anglicised.

[11] National Archives of the UK, *England & Wales, Non-Conformist and Non-Parochial Registers, 1567-1970*, piece 4550.

[12] Chapter Three at 104.

First Generation in England

Thomas[13] – together with her silver plate. Her cousins Pierrepont were left "the Room ready furnished in which I lye and all my Kitchen stuff as well Brass and Tin as Iron."

But as to my other sisters [Marie] Fiellet, [Renée] Hemet and [Jeanne/Jane] de Lamberti as they are by the Grace of God in a good State of Fortune I desire them to accept each of them a Ring of 100 Guineas as a token of my love.[14]

The balance of her estate, including funds in the South Sea Company,[15] was left to her brother Pierre, whom she also named as executor.

Renée was born in 1661. In 1707, when she was thirty-seven years old, she and her mother Marie nee de Vierville were recipients of the Queen's Bounty and living at Wardour Street in Soho[16] In 1716, now in her mid-forties, she married Pierre Hemet, with licence from the Vicar General of the Diocese of Canterbury dated 16 October. Predictably, they had no children.

Members of the Haymet family of Caen made their *reconnaissances* at the French Church of the Savoy on 26 June and 27 November 1687. The head of the family was Adrien, with his wife Jacqueline, and one of their sons was Pierre, whose age at the time of his *témoignage* was 17 years.[17] Claude and Marie CdeC and four of their children, including Renée, had been received into the congregation on 30 June. Peter Hemet of Caen is then recorded as obtaining denization by the Act of 5 March 1691 – the same day as Renée and her brothers and sisters – and naturalization on 19 March 1706, the same day as the approvals for Peter and Thomas CdeC. We may assume that Haymet and Hemet both refer to the original French surname Hémet, and that Pierre/Peter is the future husband of Renée.[18] From the comment in the will of Susanna as above, he appears to have been prosperous.

The date of Pierre Hemet's death is not known, but Renée died in 1744 at the age of eighty-three. She was buried in the family vault at Marylebone on 4 December.

Jeanne/Jane, whose name is sometimes rendered in English as Joan, was born in 1668. In 1687 she and her parents and other members of the family received relief payments as new arrivals in England. Sometime after that, probably in the 1690s, she married Giovanni Gerolamo Arconati Lamberti de Saint Leo, regularly known as Geronimo de Lamberty.[19]

Born at Grisons, now a canton in the east of Switzerland, about 1660, from a family of Italian background, de Lamberty had a varied career as a journalist, political agent and spy.[20] He first became known in Italy, where he published several scandalous libels and was accused of three murders. He spent time in prison but was either released or escaped, and by the early 1680s he was living in Geneva, at that time an independent state within the Swiss

---

[13] It is possible, but highly unlikely, that this is a reference to the wife of Susanne's brother Gabriel, Elizabeth nee Glasscock. That family was now in Ireland, where Gabriel had died four years earlier. The date of Elizabeth's death is not known, but it is very likely that she too was dead; Magdelaine CdeC nee Granger, however, lived until 1730. In any case, Ireland was a long way to send silver plate and, as below at 133, the family in England appears to have had little contact with Gabriel's family.

[14] Though the explanation makes sense, the items are strange: a guinea was twenty-one shillings – just over £1; so a single ring of 100 guineas was worth more than all the previous monetary bequests put together.

[15] On the South Sea Company, see below at 125 and, in further detail, Chapter Five at 141.

[16] See note 75 to Chapter Three at 104.

[17] Minet, *Conversions et reconnaisances*, 28. For discussion of these terms, see Chapter Three at 104.

[18] Shaw, *Denization and Naturalization 1603-1700*, 226, and *1701-1800*, 54. Hemet would be the anglicised form of Hémet, and "Haymet" a phonetic rendering.

[19] That form of the name appears on his will as held in London, but he also used the French name Guillaume, and the surname frequently appears as de Lamberti.

The wedding took place at the church of St Marylebone: 117 below.

[20] There is a biography of de Lamberty in the online *Dictionnaire des journalistes* at http://dictionnaire-journalistes.gazettes18e.fr/journaliste/447-guillaume-de-lamberty.

CHAPTER FOUR

Confederacy.[21] He offered his services to the French and possibly also to the Spanish, but neither made great use of them, and the local Calvinist church rejected him.

In 1685 de Lamberty moved to Amsterdam, where he became a local assistant to envoys from several countries. He published papers on current affairs and served for a time as editor of *Nouvelles des cours de l'Europe*, a journal which was essentially hostile to French policy. In 1692 he became secretary to the English Ambassador to the Dutch United Provinces, and he evidently spent time in England, for in 1702 he published an account of the overthrow of James II, the accession of William III, and the politics which had followed.[22]

Map Fourteen: The southwest of Lake Geneva [Lac Leman]
showing Nyon in the upper centre
Detail from Michelin France *2003 sheet 112*

It was no doubt during one of his visits to England that de Lamberty met and married Jane CdeC, and she accompanied him when he returned to Holland. He had been approved by the British government, and while he may not have been sufficiently puritanical to satisfy the church at Geneva he was certainly Protestant and opposed to the ambitions of Louis XIV. He continued to act as a diplomatic agent and to provide information to the British and also to Hanover and Sweden.[23] Presumably through the good will of the Elector of Hanover, he was

---

[21] The present-day federal state of Switzerland was established only in the mid-nineteenth century. Before that, individual cantons were self-governing, supporting one another through the Swiss Confederacy.

[22] *Mémoires de la dernière révolution d'Angleterre: contenant l'abdication de Jacques II, l'avènement de S.M. le Roi Guillaume III à la couronne, & plusieurs choses arrivées sous son règne*, 2 volumes, The Hague 1702 [Google Books].

[23] Hanover was an effectively independent state within the Holy Roman Empire. Elector George, who ruled from 1708, came to the throne of Britain in 1714 as King George I, and the two states were connected by personal rule until the accession of Queen Victoria in 1837. [Hanover then held to the Salic Law, refusing to accept a woman ruler, and the inheritance passed to Victoria's uncle the Duke of Cumberland.]

granted title as a Baron of the Holy Roman Empire, and in 1723 he was named representative of the King of Sweden to Geneva and to Bern, another canton of the Swiss Confederacy.

In the early 1730s Geronimo and Jane de Lamberty went to live at Nyon, close to Geneva. Their daughter Judith had married Charles d'Aubonne, member of a leading local family, and that was very likely the reason for the move.[24]

The "Will of the Noble Geronimo de Lamberty, Lord Baron of the Holy Roman Empire and Lord Resident or Ambassador of the ... King of Sweden at the Republics of Bern and Geneva" was composed in French and signed in 1729. Geronimo died at Nyon on 9 January 1733 and the will was proven there, while a certified translation by Philip Crespigny, Notary Public, was lodged in England.[25] There were bequests to his "well-beloved and lawful wife Dame Jane Champion de Crespigny," to his son Abraham de Lamberty and his daughter Judith the wife of Charles d'Aubonne; there was also a reference to "my late daughter Esther," but she had evidently not married or had children.

Besides essays, articles and correspondence, de Lamberty's major work, in fourteen volumes, was his *Mémoires pour servir à l'histoire du XVIIIe siècle, contenant les négociations, traitez, résolutions et autres documens authentiques concernant les affaires d'État; liez par une narration historique des principaux événemens dont ils ont été précédez ou suivis.* Published at The Hague and Amsterdam from 1727 to 1740 and covering the first years of the century, it is a vast collection of political and diplomatic material relating to every country in Europe and varying from official documents to reports by anonymous correspondents in Vienna, Berlin, Dresden, Hamburg, Copenhagen and other cities and capitals.[26] All but overwhelming in its detail, the model was followed by others, but was ultimately too exhaustive and exhausting to maintain.

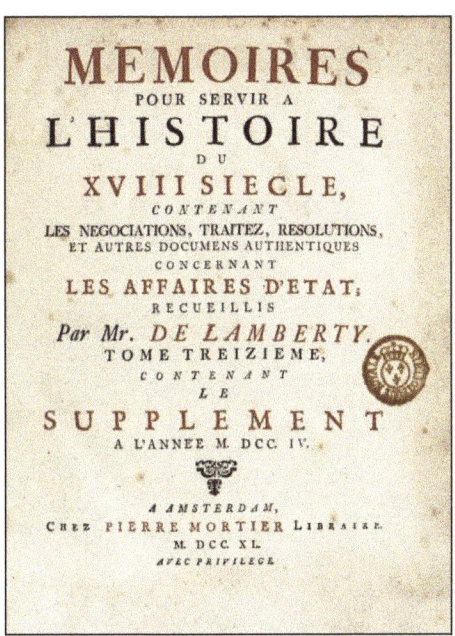

Jane de Lamberty continued to live at Nyon after her husband's death but was later involved in a dispute with Mme d'Aubonne, mother of her son-in-law Charles. In March 1736 Judith, wife of Charles, wrote to her cousin Claude Crespigny in London, evidently telling him that

---

[24] Aubonne is a town on Lake Geneva in the canton of Vaud, twenty-five kilometres from Nyon and forty-five from the city of Geneva. Jane's will, however, describes Charles as a Burgess of Nyon. The will mentions also that "the worshipful" Charles d'Aubonne had at some time been an officer in the service of the king of France.

[25] UK National Archives reference PROB 11/659/82.

[26] See, for example, http://gallica.bnf.fr/ark:/12148/bpt6k9605190k/.

Chapter Four

Mme d'Aubonne her mother-in-law was accusing Jane of not having been properly married and possibly of being illegitimate. Claude passed the matter to his brother Philip, a qualified lawyer, and Philip wrote to his uncle Pierre, brother to Jane, telling him of the situation:

> You will see that it is necessary to send authentic certificates of her marriage and also proofs of her birth. As you may have some documents referring to both, could you please examine them and also have someone visit the Marylebone Registry of Weddings. It will not be necessary to get a copy because, as we understand from Mme d'Aubonne's [Judith's] letter we shall need more authentic ones; that is to say, certified by notaries and possibly confirmed by sworn affidavits. The birth and the genealogy can be clearly confirmed by the Certificates from the College of Arms,[27] but it will all cost money – nonetheless we shall have to put up with it.
>
> The sooner these enquiries are made, the better; for I fear that any delays may have consequences.....

Philip observes that the whole affair is *factueux* [factious=petty and vicious], but that "we do not know what effect [the accusations] may have in the country where she is." He adds that Jane is particularly vulnerable on account of her age, her physical condition and her situation – as an elderly widow in a foreign country – and that he will do his utmost on her behalf. His efforts and those of the family were evidently successful, for Jane remained at Nyon until her death. When her brother Pierre died in 1739 he left her £10 in his will, the same amount as to her sister Renee and her cousin Judith de Pierrepont.

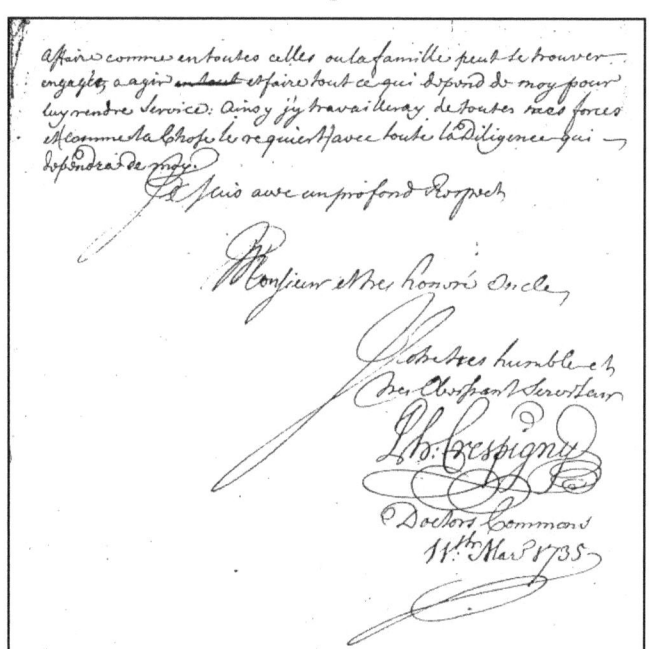

Second page of the letter written to Pierre by his nephew Philip CdeC on 11 March 1735/36 concerning the difficulties being encountered by Jane, Pierre's sister and Philip's aunt. The letter is in French, and Philip concludes: I am, with profound respect,
Monsieur and most honoured uncle,
Your very humble and most obedient servant,
Ph: Crespigny [at] Doctors Commons

The "Will of the Honorable Jane Champion de Crespigny, Baroness Dowager de Lamberty" was dictated by her to Urban Lovedil[?], a Notary and Counsellor of the city of Nyon, on 30 November 1746. Dictation was necessary because, although she was in good health and good

---

[27] On the Certificate from the College of Arms, see Chapter One at 26-17 and Chapter Three at 106.

understanding, she had been "deprived of her sight for some years past" – to such an extent that she could not sign the paper but had its content read to her repeatedly before witnesses so that they could confirm her assent. Following her death two years later, the will was proved at Nyon in August 1748; a certified translation was proved at London on 18 March 1749.[28]

Besides bequests to hospitals at Nyon and to the family where she was living and was cared for, Jane left her estate to her daughter Judith, wife of Charles d'Aubonne, with mention also of her grand-daughter Victoria Aimée. Since there is no reference to her son Abraham, he had evidently died some time after Geronimo, without being married or leaving children.

Victoria Aimée was thus the only descendant of Geronimo and Jane CdeC de Lamberty and, given that she would have changed her surname on marriage and/or may have died without children, there is no good way to trace her descendants.

Thomas, his wife Magdalen, and their family
As discussed at the beginning of the previous section, I deal with Thomas and Gabriel independently, for their military experiences distinguish them from their elder brother Pierre and their sisters. Since Pierre never married, moreover, while Gabriel had no grandchildren, Thomas and his wife Magdalen nee Granger are the ancestors of all those with the surname CdeC at the present day. This section also considers Thomas' children other than Philip (1704-1765) and Claude (1706-1782): their more significant careers are considered in Chapter Five. Gabriel and his family are discussed in a separate section below.

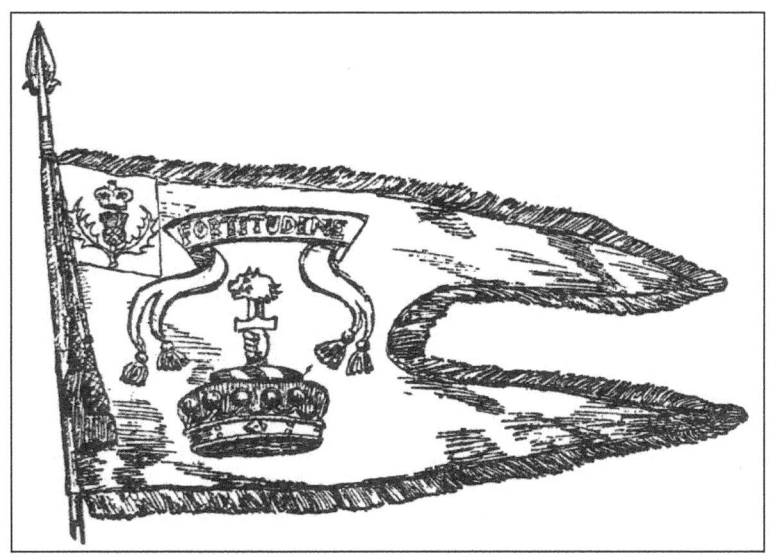

Guidon of Cardross's Dragoons 1689-1690
From Lawson, Uniforms of the British Army *I, 94, with comment at xiv:*
    This Guidon is in the National Museum of Antiquities of Scotland, and is of red silk with gold fringe and tassels. Motto in gold on red scroll edged gold. The orle [the twist of cloth above the coronet] is white, black, blue, red and gold. A gold thistle crowned on blue [appears] in the upper canton.
The Catalogue *of the Museum, published in 1892, lists the item under Banners and Flags as:*
    pennon of regiment of cavalry, raised by Lord Cardross in 1688, with hand displayed with spear, boar's head impaled, coronet, and in upper corner thistle.
    It is identified as a presentation from the Earl of Buchan in 1781.
The picture is not entirely clear, but the central design shows a coronet with a red lining, surmounted by the multi-coloured orle: above that is a hand holding a dagger, and on the tip of the dagger is a boar's head; the motto of a scroll is Fortitudine*: "By Fortitude." This was the crest and motto of Henry Eskine (1650-1693), third Lord Cardross. His son David, fourth Lord Cardross, became the Earl of Buchan, and Cardross is now a secondary title of that peerage.*
    This flag would have been carried by Cornet Thomas Crespigny.

---

[28] UK National Archives reference PROB 11/768/355..

CHAPTER FOUR

Born in 1664, **Thomas** was sent to England in 1676 when he was twelve years old. He was probably cared for by the Pierrepont family, who were already established in London, and he was followed two years later by his younger brother Gabriel.

On 7 August 1689 Thomas was commissioned as a Cornet in Lord Cardross's Regiment of Dragoons.[29] Cornet was the lowest commissioned rank in a cavalry regiment, equivalent to a present-day Second Lieutenant; his duties included carrying the troop flag, the guidon.

Thomas was twenty-five years old at that time, and he may previously have served in the ranks, possibly as a Volunteer.[30] Dalton's *English Army Lists* states that Cardross's Regiment was disbanded in December 1690, but it was in fact absorbed into a new formation under Colonel Richard Cunningham.[31] The regiment was listed on the "Scottish Establishment:" the armies of England and Scotland were formally separated until the Act of Union in 1707.

Dragoons at this time were mounted infantry, travelling on horseback but fighting on foot. It appears, however, that Cardross' troopers had been equipped as heavy cavalry and that they retained that function under Cunningham. The regiment had served against Jacobite supporters of the deposed King James II, and although that opposition had been quelled by the end of 1690 it remained in Scotland until 1694 when it was sent to face the French in Flanders.

On 10 January 1695/96 Thomas was transferred to be Captain-Lieutenant in Lord Lorne's Regiment of Foot.[32] Captaincy of the first company in a regiment was formally held by the regimental colonel, so a captain-lieutenant commanded that unit on his behalf. When he was made a full captain, he was credited with seniority for his time in rank.

The appointment was clearly a promotion, though it is probable Thomas had already risen from Cornet to regular Lieutenant under Cunningham. Less than a month later, on 7 February, he was commissioned back into his former regiment at his new rank. It is likely the transfer and promotion were matters of paperwork, and that he never physically joined Lorne's regiment. Both Lorne's and Cunningham's regiments were stationed in Flanders, but Cunningham's was in winter quarters near Ghent and did not see action until June.[33]

A few months later, on 1 October 1696 Sir Richard Cunningham was succeeded as Colonel by William Ker, Lord Jedburgh, and the regiment became known as Jedburgh's Dragoons. In 1703 William Ker became Marquess of Lothian and the name was changed again to acknowledge his new title.[34]

---

[29] *Calendar of State Papers, Domestic* for Feb 1689-Apr 1690 at 212, cited by Grayden, *Chronicle*, 8.
Thomas' appointment is also mentioned by Dalton, *English Army Lists* III, 36, and a note at 37 refers to his later position as Captain-Lieutenant to Lord Jedburgh as below. See also note 76 to Chapter Three.

[30] On Volunteer service as a route to military commission, see below at 123.

[31] Dalton, *English Army Lists* III, 36, but *cf.* Lawson, *Uniforms of the British Army* I, 92-93: the regiment was later known as the 7th (The Queens Own) Regiment of Dragoons and, from 1807, as Hussars. A detailed history, including an account of the official raising of the regiment in December 1690, is at the web-page of the 7th Dragoons: http://www.britishempire.co.uk/forces/armyunits/britishcavalry/7thdragoons.html.

[32] *Calendar of State Papers, Domestic* for 1694-1695 and *Home Office Military Entry Book* 4:108; Grayden, *Chronicle*, 8. Lord Lorne was a supplementary title held by Archibald Campbell, Earl of Argyll, a leading supporter of King William who was made Duke in 1701.
Thomas' appointment as Captain-Lieutenant is mentioned [as Thomas Crepignie] by Dalton, *English Army Lists* IV, 61. *English Army Lists* V, 207, has the Muster Roll of the Marquess of Lothian's Regiment of Dragoons for September 1703, and Thomas Crepigny is listed there as Captain-Lieutenant of the Marquess of Lothian's Troop stationed at Jedburgh.

[33] See the web-page of the 7th Dragoons as cited in note 31 above.

[34] The surname appears both as Ker and as Kerr. Dalton, *English Army Lists* III, 38 note 1, has a short account of his career. *English Army Lists* IV, 120, records his succession to Sir Richard Cunningham, noting at 3 that he became Marquess of Lothian in 1703. The web-site of the 7th Dragoons [as note 31 above] has a list of the regiment's colonels; Lawson, *Uniforms of the British Army* I, 92-93, lists the resulting changes of name.

At the time of his promotion and transfers, Thomas was granted leave to return to London, for on 11 February 1696 the Vicar-General's Office of the Archbishop of Canterbury approved the Allegation for a Marriage Licence submitted by Thomas Champion and Magdalen Granger, who certified there was no impediment to their union, and the Register of St Mary Magdalene at Old Fish Street recorded their wedding on the following day.[35] The French form of the personal name of Thomas' wife was Madelaine, and the *Lancaster Book* writes Magdelaine, but she is more commonly referred to by the English form as Magdalen.

Madelaine/Magdalen Granger was a daughter of Israel Granger and his wife Marie nee Billon, from Alençon in the south of Lower Normandy.[36] The family had been prosperous merchants with landed estates and, like the Champions, had reached the edges of *noblesse*. They were also Huguenots, however, and when Louis XIV revoked the Edict of Nantes the family was scattered. Israel and Marie migrated to England, and though their possessions in France were forfeited they were able to bring some money with them. There is no record of their joining the congregation at the Savoy, but their daughters Marthe and Madelaine made their *reconnaissances* on 14 July 1687.[37] Other members of the family remained in France as registered Protestants, some joined the Roman Catholic communion, and a few were able to temporise until they managed to emigrate.[38]

In November 1696, some months after the wedding, an official pass was issued for Magdalen Crepigny, described as a French Protestant, to go to Flanders, no doubt to join her husband Thomas. Thereafter, assuming he was close to his wife at the relevant times, one may trace Thomas' movements in the British service by the places of birth recorded for his children in the *Consolations Book*:[39]

- Guillaume/William was born at Bruges on 18 December [N.S.] 1698,[40] and was baptised 21 December by Mr Durant, Chaplain of the Regiment of M de Miremont;[41]

---

[35] Grayden, *Chronicle*, 8, cites the Allegation and also the Register at 136.

[36] There is an account of the Granger family at http://pinsonnais.free.fr/genea/index.php?id=granger, part of a website maintained by M Amaury de la Pinsonnais, with additional information gathered by Pastor Denis Vatinel. In that genealogy, Madelaine/Magdalen's father Israel is identified as Israël Granger III. He and his wife Marie had nine children, six of whom died young, and it appears that Marthe and Madelaine were the only two to accompany their parents to England.

The website says that Marthe Granger was baptised at Alençon on 21 March 1666 and that Madeleine was baptised on 17 April of the following year. 1667. The *Lancaster Book* says that Madelaine/Magdalen was sixty-six when she died in 1730, which would mean she was born in 1664. I prefer the date of 1667.

[37] Minet, *Conversions et reconnaisances*, 26. The spelling of the surname appears as Grangay, a phonetic treatment similar to that of Hémet: 113 and note 18 above.

[38] Agnew, *Protestant Exiles from France* III, 251, records how Paul Desnoës Granger, son of Israel Granger of Alençon, was one of a number of Protestants who were obliged to express their regrets and receive pardon for having attended mass according to the rites of the Roman Catholic church. Paul's ceremony was held on 7 July 1699 on Guernsey in the Channel Islands – then as now British territory – and he was naturalised in 1701. He had evidently remained in France for some years and had been obliged to conform to the demands of Catholicism. His father Israel, however, is not the same person as the father of Marthe and Madelaine: they were cousins but had no close connection.

[39] On the *Consolations Book*, see Chapter One at 17-18.

[40] New Style, abbreviated N.S., refers to the modern Gregorian calendar, which was established at Rome in 1582 by order of Pope Gregory XIII, and spread thereafter across Europe. The system was designed to amend an error in the calendar promulgated by Julius Caesar towards the end of the first century BC. The Julian calendar slightly exaggerates the relationship between the rotations of the earth on its axis and its orbit about the sun: this was adjusted by cancelling the leap-day [29 February] for most century years: thus 7 December in Old Style became 18 December in New Style. The system was not adopted in England until 1752, so dates there and on the Continent had to be identified by their relevant system.

[41] Armand de Bourbon, Marquis de Miremont (1656-1732) came to England as a Huguenot at the Revocation of the Edict of Nantes and became commander of a corps established for refugees seeking service with the British army. In 1688 he supported William of Orange against James II and took part in campaigns against the armies of Louis XIV. In 1695 he raised a regiment of dragoons on the Irish establishment.

CHAPTER FOUR

- Marie was born at Dumfries in Scotland on 26 March [Old Style] 1699 – she died exactly one year later, on her first birthday;
- Jane/Jeanne was born at Jedburgh in Scotland on 5 March 1700;
- Claude was born at Jedburgh on 3 October 1701 – he died 28 February 1703;
- Philip/Philippe was born at St James, London, on 3 December 1704;
- Claude was born at St James on 5 April 1706.

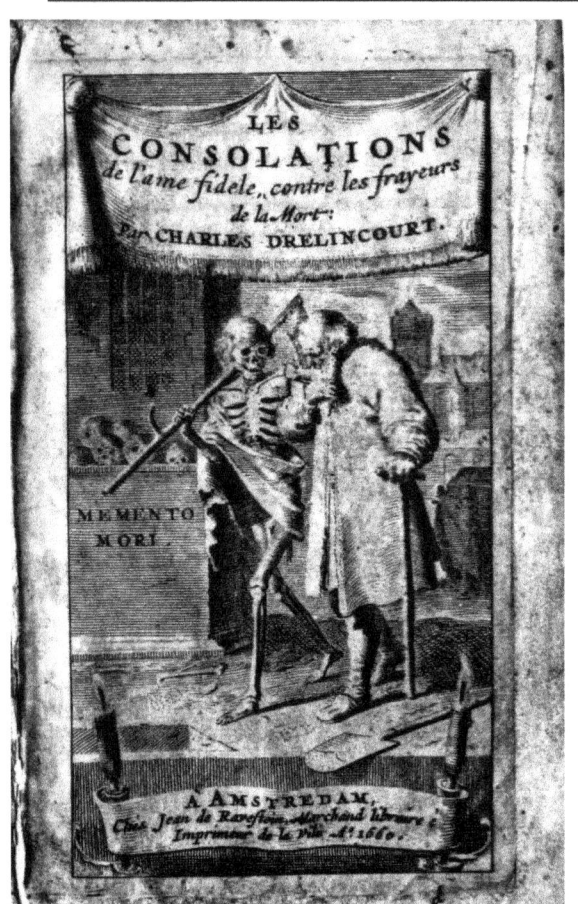 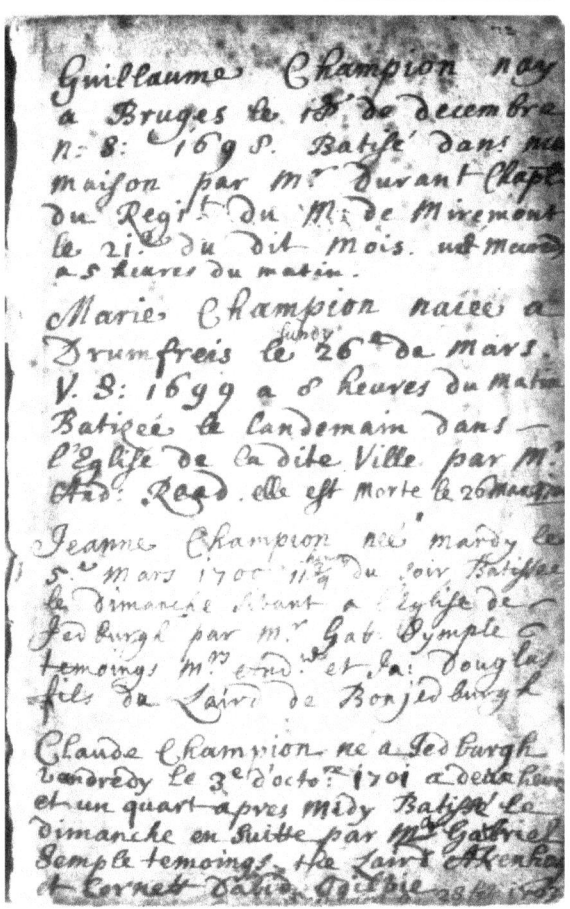

Front pages of the Consolations Book
*Left: the first title page; the second title page is shown in Chapter One at 18,
with discussion of the compilation at 17.
Right: notes by Thomas CdeC, recording births and baptism of his children:
Guillaume at Bruges in 1698,
Marie at Dumfries in 1699 – and her death there twelve months later,
Jeanne at Jedburgh in 1700,
and [the first] Claude at Jedburgh in 1701 – with a small note at the bottom of his death.*

Since 1683 it had normally been required that officers of the British army should purchase their commissions, with ranks priced at different levels. One reason for the system, following the experience of the Civil War, was that it ensured the army would be controlled by men of property who were unlikely to support political or social disruption. Formally speaking, the payment was a guarantee of good conduct: in normal circumstances, when an officer left the

---

Though Thomas was an officer of the British army, it was natural for him to call upon the services of a chaplain from a neighbouring Huguenot regiment. M Durant would have been a minister of the Reformed Church, while the chaplain in Thomas' own [Scottish] regiment was naturally Presbyterian.

service he could expect to receive the value of his commission to assist in his retirement. Bad performance, however, could lead to him being "cashiered:" deprived of his commission without reimbursement.

We cannot tell how much may have been paid for Thomas to become a cornet and then a lieutenant. The lowest price for commission as a cornet was £200, that for a lieutenant was a minimum of £250, and positions in distinguished regiments were a great deal higher: a lieutenancy with command of a company in a Guards regiment cost more than £1,500.[42] Thomas' commission as a cornet in a Scottish regiment of dragoons was probably at the lower end of the scale, and the family may have received some assistance from their Pierrepont cousins. This was a very basic grade, but we can be reasonably sure that the appointments to Captain-Lieutenant owed a good deal to the Granger family of his new wife: the juxtaposition of the wedding and the promotions and transfers appears too close to be coincidental.

In 1704, however, it appears that Thomas cashed in his position with Lothian's regiment and returned to London, where his sons Philip and the second Claude would be born. His will – leaving everything to his wife Magdalen – is dated at London on 24 June.[43]

In 1705 Thomas joined Sir Charles Hotham's Regiment of Foot as a Gentleman Volunteer.

The position of Gentleman Volunteer, later known more commonly as gentleman ranker, was a slightly anomalous development of the system of purchase. A Volunteer served as a private soldier with the understanding that he was worthy of being an officer and might later be granted a commission without the requirement to pay for it.[44] He took part in operations with the "other-ranks" but was entitled to attend the officers' mess.

With his record in Flanders, Thomas could hope that service as a Volunteer would enable him to acquire a new commission without cost. Sir Charles Hotham's command was formally established in March 1705, but was probably recruiting for some months before that date.[45] The regiment was sent to Spain in 1706, and when the port city of Alicante was captured it formed part of the garrison. Initial British success, however, was halted by a heavy defeat at the battle of Almansa in April 1707. The French and Spanish forces now held the initiative, and after a series of local successes they came to invest Alicante in November 1708.

The siege saw a remarkable act of courage. Based upon a tall rock, the fortress held out for several months, but during that time the enemy dug a mine underneath and filled it with fifty tons of gunpowder. The commanding General John Richards was invited to surrender, and two of his officers were allowed to inspect the work, but he refused to concede. On 3 March, as the fuse was lit, Richards and his staff took position on the parade ground directly above; they were lost in the explosion. The rest of the garrison, however, had been placed in secure positions, and they maintained the defence for six more weeks until a fleet arrived to bring relief. Rather than providing reinforcements, however, the British admiral negotiated surrender, and though the survivors were successfully withdrawn the position they had held so bravely was lost.[46]

---

[42] Scouller, *Armies of Queen Anne*, 138-139. Bruce, *Purchase System* provides a history.
[43] Thomas' will is cited, with a copy of the translation from the original French, by Grayden, *Chronicle*, 8.
[44] An example of the possibility is provided by Manchée, "The Huguenot Regiments (Supplemental Notes)," at 398, where he cites the petition of Peter Garric [future father of the celebrated actor David Garrick]:
> Having served as Volontier in the Earl of Donnegal's Regmt and behav'd himself very well at the Siege of Gibraltar prays a Commission in the new Regts.

Requests such as these might be granted by the commanding general.

[This Earl of Donegall's Regiment, the 35th Foot, was that in which Thomas' brother Gabriel was serving as a Captain: below at 129.]

[45] The formation of the regiment is recorded in Dalton, *English Army Lists* V, 192-193.
[46] See Chandler, "The Siege of Alicante," and the article "Signal Instance of English Fortitude," in *Chambers' Edinburgh Journal* III:146 (15 Nov 1834) at 335.

CHAPTER FOUR

Hotham's regiment had suffered such heavy casualties during the campaign that it was disbanded in 1713, but Thomas had indeed gained his commission as a Lieutenant – probably at the time of the siege, for there were surely vacancies among the ranks of the officers[47] – and in April 1710 he was promoted Captain.[48]

Map Fifteen: Spain in the early eighteenth century

Two years later, on 17 July 1712, Thomas died at the age of forty-eight. He had returned to London by that time, and he was interred in the family vault at Marylebone. His will of 1704, leaving everything to Magdalen, was proven at London on 6 October 1712.

In a document dated 20 September 1712, however, Sir Charles Hotham certifies that Thomas Champion de Crespigny had served as Captain in his regiment, and adds that:

> he left a poor widdow [*sic*] and four Children in a very distressed Condition, so that she stands in great need of Her Majesty's [Queen Anne's] most Gracious Bounty, and of the Pension commonly allowed to the Officers widdows.[49]

Of six children born to Thomas and Magdalen, four now remained: William/Guillaume (born 1698), Jane (born 1700), Philip (born 1704) and Claude (born 1706).[50]

---

[47] Stephen CdeC has provided me with a photocopy of a certificate from Lord Lothian, dated 20 January 1708/09, confirming the nine years' service of Thomas Champion de Crespigny [to 1704]; this was evidently Thomas' own copy, kept by the family, for there is a note that the original was in the War Office.

Another certificate, this from Sir Charles Hotham and likewise dated 20 January 1709, attests to Thomas' service as a Volunteer.

The testimonials probably relate to recommendations for his commission as a Lieutenant.

[48] Dalton, *English Army Lists* VI, 169-170 records the disbandment of Sir Charles Hotham's regiment in 1713; the entry refers to Thomas Crepigny as a Captain, having held that rank since 12 April 1710.

[49] Like the certificates cited in note 47 above, this is a family copy, with the original held at the War Office.

[50] Above at 121-122. Marie (1699-1700) and Claude (1701-1703) had died in infancy.

Magdalen CdeC nee Granger did receive a pension of £26 a year, being the regular rate for the widow of a captain.[51] On 15 June 1713, moreover, nine months after Thomas' death, the government granted her stock in the South Sea Company valued at £333.18.9; the amount was due for Thomas' clothing and other expenses during the period to 24 June 1712.[52]

Established in 1711, the South Sea Company had been formally constituted as an enterprise to trade with South America – hence the name – but it was actually intended to serve as an institution dealing with government finances and particularly the national debt. In competition with the Bank of England it was arranged that holders of official debt could be reimbursed with shares in the Company. The government paid annual interest and a fee, and the money was available for distribution as a dividend to shareholders. It was an ingenious arrangement but open to corruption, and the celebrated "South Sea Bubble" of 1720 caused widespread financial ruin and brought down the government.[53]

We may assume that Thomas' widow Magdalen realised on the shares soon after she had received them. It is impossible to make a good judgement of the value of £333 in present-day currency,[54] but the money was surely useful – albeit a late payment for expenses already incurred. In that same year 1713 the family paid £150 for Thomas' eldest son William, now fifteen years old, to be an apprentice of Edward Mills, a lawyer of the Inner Temple. Five years later in 1718 Philip de Crespigny was apprenticed to Charles Garrett, Procurator of the Arches Court of Canterbury; the fee was £126.[55] Given that Philip was apprenticed when he was thirteen, it is possible William's indenture had had to wait until money had come from the government by way of the South Sea Company.

In March of 1714, however, the financial situation changed. Magdalen's father Israel Granger had died in 1700, but her mother Marie continued in control of the family property until her death. Composed on 18 February 1711/12, her will was proved on 7 March 1713/14.

Marie Granger divided her property into two equal parts, both in the form of annuities. One half went to Magdalen direct; the other was to support the children of her elder daughter Marthe/Martha by her husband Fleurand Dauteuil: their sons Fleurand and André/Andrew, and their daughter Martha Susanna. Marthe had died in 1711,[56] but her mother was insistent the children's father had no authority for "inter-meddling or intervening" in any of the arrangements. Magdalen had full control on behalf of her nephews and niece; and Fleurand died in any case a few years later.[57]

In similar fashion, Magdalen's annuities were left to her absolute discretion, and upon her death to her children in trust, with her husband Thomas likewise forbidden to interfere. The

---

[51] See, for example, *Calendar of Treasury Books*, Volume 29, 1714-1715, pages cxiii-cxlii: Declared Accounts: Army: Pensions to Officers' Widows [Audit Office: Bundle 233, Roll 810 A.O. 1/233/810] 25 October 1714 to 24 December 1715, citing Crespigny and six others of Sir Charles Hotham's Regiment.

A later accounting, in Bundle 233, Roll 811, relating to 22 April 1723, identifies £26 *per annum* paid to Mary Crespigny, widow of a captain in Sir Charles Hotham's Regiment; Mary is miswritten for Magdalen.

[52] *Calendar of Treasury Books*, Volume XXVII Part 2, page 249; cited by Grayden, *Chronicle*, 8. The authority for payment is issued by Robert Harley, Earl of Oxford and Lord Treasurer, to John Howe the Paymaster General of Guards and Garrisons.

[53] On the South Sea Company and the Bubble, see further in Chapter Five at 141.

[54] The web-site measuringworth.com has figures varying from £45,000 [AUD $75,000], through £670,000 to £1,170,000,000 depending whether comparison is by purchasing power, labour value or income value.

[55] Philip's career in law is discussed in Chapter Five at 147-156.

[56] There are indications that her second son Andrew was born in that year, so she may have died in childbirth.

[57] Fleurand's will was proved in February 1718. His considerable estate was divided among his children.

The English translation of the will indexes Fleurand's surname as de Meausse Dauteville – evidently adapted from French d'Auteville. It had already suffered a form of abbreviation, for Dalton, *English Army Lists* VI, 273, has Florand D'Auteuil as a Captain in the Marquis de Montandre's Regiment of Foot in Spain in 1708. So the original full surname of de Meausse d'Auteville was first abbreviated to d'Auteuil and then Anglicised to Dauteuil.

Chapter Four

capital could be redeemed only when the children reached the age of twenty-one. Thomas' death meant the restrictions were unnecessary, but they represent a very firm feminism. We may in any case assume that the situation of his widow and children was now much easier.

William, however, died on 12 September 1721. Twenty-three years old, he had not married and he left no children. He was buried in the family vault at Marylebone.[58]

Magdalen died on 8 May 1730 and was also buried in the family vault.[59] Her will, dated 19 February 1729, left £700 each to her two sons Philip and Claude; £200 to her brother-in-law Pierre/Peter CdeC; £10 to her sister-in-law Marguerite de Borde; £10 each to her daughter Jane Allix and her husband Gilbert as immediately below; £10 to the poor; and the residue of her estate to Philip and Claude.

Jane/Jeanne, born on 5 March 1700 to Thomas and Magdalen, married Gilbert Allix in St Martin Orgar Church, London, on 10 September 1723.[60]

Born in 1692 and baptised on 1 January 1693, Gilbert was a son of the Reverend Pierre Allix (1641-1717), who had been pastor at Alençon but moved to England after the Revocation and became minister of a French church at Aldgate in London. In 1690 he graduated as a Doctor of Divinity of Cambridge and became Treasurer of Salisbury Cathedral under Bishop Gilbert Burnet, serving there until his death. He was widely recognised as a scholar of early biblical texts.

Gilbert was presumably named after his father's episcopal patron, but he did not maintain a strong religious connection. He became a merchant in London, dealing in textiles through a company called Gilbert Allix and [Daniel] Crespin.[61] In 1735 Gilbert Allix – and presumably his wife Jane – were recorded living in the parish of St Benet Fink in Broadstreet Ward, near Threadneedle Street in the City of London,[62]

Gilbert died in 1767, his will was proved on 3 July, and it appears that his widow Jane then moved to stay with one or other of the members of her family. In 1773 she composed an informal will at Camberwell; no doubt at Champion Lodge, which had been purchased by her late brother Philip in 1755 and was now occupied by his son Claude, future baronet.[63] The first provisions were that she should be buried in the parish where she died, and that the

---

[58] William's death is recorded by his brother Philip in the *Consolations Book*. The Register of St Marylebone Church for 17 September 1721, cited by Grayden, *Chronicle*, 8, lists a burial of the de Crespigny family. No given name is apparent, and Grayden reads the prefix as "Mrs." He suggests that it may have been Elizabeth nee Glasscock, wife of Gabriel as below, but *Boyd's London Burial Index* confirms that it was William CdeC, who had died just five days earlier.

[59] An entry in the *Consolations Book* made by her son Philip gives the date of her death and the fact of her interment. The Register of St Marylebone Church, cited by Grayden, *Chronicle*, 8, says that she was buried on 12 May, four days after her death. The *Lancaster Book* says that Magdalen was sixty-six when she died, so she was born about 1664, very close to Thomas.

[60] St Martin Orgar, near Canon Street in the City of London, is one of the churches mentioned in the nursery rhyme "Oranges and Lemons." It had been largely destroyed in the Great Fire of 1666, but the tower and part of the nave remained, and they were home to a Huguenot congregation through the eighteenth century.

Not surprisingly, there was already a connection between the two families: Elizabeth nee Granger, a cousin of Magdalen's father Israel, had married Daniel Allix, who was probably a brother of Gilbert's father Pierre: http://pinsonnais.free.fr/genea/index.php?id=granger&page=3.

[61] E.g. *Textile history and economic history: essays in honour of Miss Julia de Lacy Mann*, edited by N B Harte and K G Ponting, Manchester UP, 1973, 95-96 [Harte, "The Rise of Protection and the English Linen Trade 1690-1790]; also David Ormrod, *The Rise of Commercial Empires: England and the Netherlands in the age of mercantilism, 1650–1770*, Cambridge UP 2003, 176. [The latter work also mentions Claude Fonnereau, future father-in-law of Thomas's son Philip, as a merchant in this field.]

Gilbert Allix and Daniel Crespin were subscribers to *A Calculation of Foreign Exchanges, as transacted on the Royal Exchange of London*, a set of tables compiled by Edward Oldenburgh and published in 1741.

[62] *City of London Land Tax Records, 1692-1932*, Broad Street 1735 at 21.

[63] On the purchase of Champion Lodge, see Chapter Five at 153-154. Philip had died in 1765.

funeral should be simple, with just one horse and coach and no funerary rings.[64] On 30 May 1776 she was buried at St Swithin's Anglican Church, Walcot, near Bath in Somerset, where her brother Claude had a property.[65] The unofficial will was proven on 6 June 1776.[66]

The document makes no mention of any children. Family bequests included £100 to her sister Crespigny – that is Anne nee Fonnereau the widow of her brother Philip – £200 and a snuffbox to her brother Claude of South Sea House and £100 each to her niece Jane, married to Henry Reveley and to their son Hugh; there were smaller legacies to members of the Allix family and others. The balance of the estate, which may have been substantial, was left to her nephew Claude,[67] who was named as sole executor, with another £100 and some shares to his son William, future second baronet, at that time ten years old.

A soldier of the 35th Foot, showing the buff facings and lining of the coat
This is an illustration from 1742, but the style of uniform was little changed from the beginning of the century. Known first as Donegall's and later as Gorges', this was the regiment of Gabriel CdeC from 1701 to 1711.

Gabriel, his wife Elizabeth, and their children

Gabriel, younger brother of Pierre and Thomas, was born in 1666.[68] The *Reveley and South Sea* books state that he married Elizabeth Glasscock, and they are followed by the *Lancaster Book*, which identifies Elizabeth as the daughter of W[illiam] Glasscock, and states that the couple had two children, Charles and Elizabeth.[69] Records, however, are erratic.

The Register of Westminster St Margaret, Middlesex, records the christening of Mary, daughter of Gabriel, on 30 March 1688, but the name of the mother is given as Isabella.[70] One year later, however, on 6 April 1689, the same office recorded the baptism of Charles

---

[64] From the sixteenth to the early twentieth century it was customary to give funerary rings as mementos to members of a dead person's family and sometimes to those attending the funeral. Jane Allix made one exception to her prohibition: one ring should be given to John Torriano.

John Samuel Torriano (1751-1825) was twenty-five at the time. He had been commissioned as a lieutenant of artillery for the East India Company in 1768, and in 1776 he was engaged in the Mahratta War, where he was recognised for excellent conduct. Jane Allix had evidently known him as a boy and left him a memento.

[65] See Chapter Five at 145.

[66] The document begins "In case I should not make a will in proper form I desire this should take place….."

In an impressive display of flexibility, the judge responsible for granting probate called two women – possibly servants – from London and from Bath to attest that they knew the late Jane Allix and could certify that the writing in the document was hers. He then confirmed the will.

[67] Claude is identified as Dr Claude Crespigny; he had a doctorate of Laws from Cambridge: Chapter Five at 162.

[68] The *Lancaster Book* does not give Gabriel's date of birth nor his age at death, but Stephen CdeC notes that records held at the College of Arms indicate Gabriel was born at Vierville[-sur-Mer] on 6 August 1666.

[69] The surname appears both as Glasscock and as Glascock; I follow the family books.

[70] The christening is recorded at page 24 of the Register published by the Harleian Society, cited by Grayden, *Chronicle*, 9a; an image of the original page may now be found online.

CHAPTER FOUR

Crepigny, and this time the parents are identified as Gabriel and Elizabeth. It is certain that the 1688 entry has miswritten "Isabella" for "Elizabeth," and that Elizabeth nee Glasscock was Gabriel's first and only wife.

The Westminster Burial Register then records the burial of Mary Crispigny at St Martin-in-the-Fields on 22 March 1692; she would have been just three years old.[71]

The Glasscocks of Essex had risen to prosperity in Tudor times and were granted arms in 1571. During the seventeenth century some had been knighted and others had held seats in Parliament, and it was now a widespread and well-established family. The Farnham branch was recognised in a heraldic Visitation of 1664, and at that time William Glasscock, a Justice of the Peace, was recorded with a son named William and two daughters Mary and Elizabeth. It is likely that this Elizabeth, born in the early 1660s, became the wife of Gabriel CdeC; she would have been a little older than her husband.[72]

Gabriel had joined the army in 1686, perhaps a year before his marriage.[73] He was first enrolled as a Gentleman Volunteer, effectively an officer cadet,[74] but the *Calendar of State Papers, Domestic* for 23 October 1691 records the commission of Gabriel Crespigny, gentleman, as Lieutenant under Lieutenant-Colonel James Harrison in the 1st Foot Guards, with authority to command a company as a Captain of Foot.[75] This was a similar appointment to that held by Gabriel's brother Thomas as Captain-Lieutenant in Lord Lorne's and then Lord Cardross's regiments; the 1st Foot Guards, however, was the senior infantry regiment of the army – in 1815 it would be renamed the Grenadier Guards – and the cost of the commission would have been more than £1,500.[76] It seems certain he had support from his wife's family.

An entry for 6 February 1694/95 in the *Calendar of State Papers, Domestic*, mentions passes for Gabriel Crespigny and other officers to travel to Holland or Flanders; and another for 10 January 1695/96 refers to passes issued to Mrs Elizabeth Crespigny, accompanied by two children and a maid, to travel to Flanders.[77] This was surely so that Elizabeth could join her husband Gabriel on service, and – Mary being dead – the two children were Charles and Elizabeth, this second daughter being named after her mother. There appears to be no record of Elizabeth's birth or baptism, but it was presumably about 1693.

A note by Dalton says that Gabriel was wounded at the assault of Terra Nova, Namur, on 20 August 1695. Now in Belgium, Namur was at that time on the contested border between France and the Netherlands and had been captured by the French in 1692. The main fortress of Terra Nova had been rebuilt by Louis XIV's celebrated engineer Vauban, but it was stormed and captured, and the city itself surrendered a few days later. Namur is a battle honour of several regiments, including the Grenadier Guards.

---

[71] Members of a family named Silverthorne or Thorne have claimed that Mary in fact grew to adulthood, but that about 1710 she married a groom named Oliver [Silver?]Thorne, was disowned by her family and emigrated with her husband and children to America. A statement of this legend from Steve Thorne, "Secret Silverthornes" – with a bonus connection to an Indian princess – is at http://www.genealogy.com/ forum/ surnames/topics/silverthorn/321/. No documentary evidence, however, has been found to support that story, and there is no other person to whom the burial record above can reasonably refer.

[72] The Glasscock family is discussed in historyofparliamentonline.org/volume/1660-1690/member/Glasscock -william-1617-88 [Paula Watson]. A short tree of the Glasscocks of Farnham is given by Bysshe, the Clarenceux King of Arms, in his *Visitation of the County of Essex*, 39, preceded by that of a senior branch at 38. On visitations, see the Introduction at 1.

[73] The Treasury Warrant of December 1714, cited immediately refers to Gabriel's service "upwards of 28 years." That indicates he had joined the army in 1686, when he was twenty years old.

[74] See the discussion of Thomas' career at 123 above.

[75] *Calendar of State Papers, Domestic* at 68 and 72: Grayden, *Chronicle*, 9, also Dalton, *English Army Lists* III, 188, with the surname as Crepigney.

[76] Above at 123.

[77] The *Calendar* is cited by Grayden, *Chronicle*, 9.

The Siege of Namur in 1695 by Jan van Huchtenburg
The foreground shows King William of Britain, in the centre dressed in grey,
consulting with the Elector Maximilian of Bavaria

A Treasury Warrant dated 23 December 1714 provides a summary of Gabriel's further career:
> Royal warrant dated St. James's to the Lord Lieutenant of Ireland to insert on the Establishment of French pensioners an allowance of 5s. a day to Capt. Gabriel Crepigny, he having been upwards of 28 years in the Army, 22 thereof as Captain, during which time he has been a very great sufferer by divers wounds received in Flanders, Spain and Portugal, and afterwards as he was raising recruits in Lancashire for Lieut. Gen. Gorge's Regiment of Foot and as he was bringing away the recruits which were delivered over to him by the Mayor of Wigan he was assaulted by the inhabitants of that place, who not only broke one of his ribs but likewise gave him several other wounds to the very great hazard of his life insomuch that he lay a considerable time in the physician's and surgeon's hands for the recovery of his health: upon which he petitioned the late Queen [Anne] for redress and was referred to the Board of General Officers, who reported that he was a fit object for compassion and might deserve her Majesty's leave to dispose of his commission for discharging of his debts and to merit a pension for the support of himself and his family, but the death of the said Queen soon after prevented the intended benefit.[78]

The events at Wigan and other matters are considered below.

We do not know why Gabriel left the 1st Foot Guards. The wounds he received at Namur could have kept him from active service for a time, and he may have found it necessary for financial reasons to transfer to the regular infantry, taking profit from the sale of his commission in the Guards. Given that his new regiment was overseas from 1702 to 1703, with only a brief period in England in 1703-1704, he probably joined at the time of its first formation in 1701.

The regiment was raised at Belfast by Arthur Chichester, Earl of Donegall, and was first known as Donegall's Regiment.[79] Numbered as the 35th Foot, the unit was strongly Protestant and received special permission from King William III to bear orange facings on its uniform.. Not all regiments had numbers, and they were commonly known by the name of their current

---

[78] *Out Letters* (*Ireland*) IX, p. 602; *Calendar of Treasury Books* XXIX, 222; Grayden, *Chronicle*, 9. On the Board of General Officers, see below at 131.
Queen Anne died on 1 August 1714, succeeded by her distant cousin George I, first of the Hanoverian monarchs. It is not surprising that matters such as this were delayed during the period of change

[79] Though the county in Ireland is Donegal, the title of the fief is Donegall.

colonel. The system was confusing, but it was maintained until 1751 when all regiments were numbered.[80]

As the War of the Spanish Succession broke out in 1702 Donegall's Regiment and five others were specified for "sea service:" amphibious attacks on enemy ports and shore positions. They made an unsuccessful assault on Cadiz in August 1702, then transferred to the West Indies, returning to England in the autumn of 1703. The regiment went back to Spain in 1704, and was sent in November to join in the defence of Gibraltar: the rock had been captured in August but was soon under strong attack from combined Spanish and French forces, and the siege was not lifted until the following April.

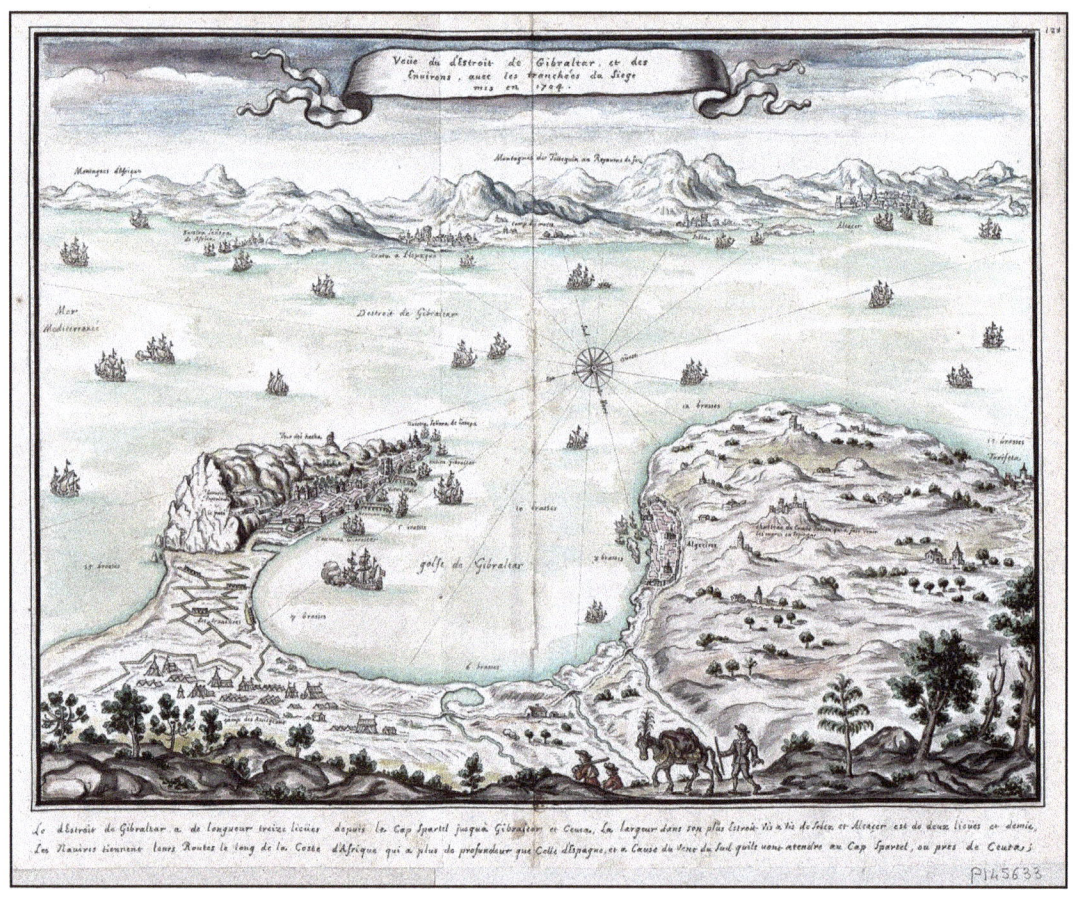

The Siege of Gibraltar 1704
panorama by Louis Boudan from the Bibliothèque nationale *of France*
The rock, fortress and town of Gibraltar is on the left, facing the Spanish town of Algeciras across the bay. The Franco-Spanish camp is shown at the lower left, with siege-lines approaching the British defences. The strait of Gibraltar is in the middle distance, and then the mountains of Tangier on the African shore.

Later in 1705 the regiment took part in the capture of Barcelona, but in April 1706 Lord Donegall was killed in action during its defence. He was succeeded by Brigadier-General Sir Richard Lord Gorges (*c.* 1619-1712) an English baronet who was also a baron in the peerage of Ireland, and it was then identified as Gorges' Regiment.

From June to September 1706, General Gorges held command in the attack and capture of Alicante, so Gabriel and his brother Thomas were engaged in the same operation, though

---

[80]. The 35th Foot later became part of the Royal Sussex Regiment. Trimen, *Historical Memoir*, provides a detailed history.

As to the potential for confusion in the system, we have seen above at 120-121 how Thomas was commissioned into Lord Cardross's Regiment in 1689, which became Sir Richard Cunningham's in the following year, changed its name in 1696 to that of its new colonel William Ker, Lord Jedburgh; and was renamed once more when William Ker became Marquess of Lothian in 1703.

in different units. They were separated again at the end of the year, for Thomas was in Sir Charles Hotham's Regiment which remained in garrison at Alicante, while Gorges' Regiment went to join the main force in field operations.

In April 1707, however, the Anglo-Portuguese army was heavily defeated at the battle of Almansa and the advantage of the campaign transferred to the favour of the Bourbon Spanish. Gorges' regiment lost its colours and most of the officers and men were killed or captured.[81] The unit was brought back to Ireland to be re-formed, and it remained there for the rest of the war.[82]

The Battle of Almansa, 25 April 1707
Landscape by Filippo Pallotta, figures by Buonaventura Ligli

Soon after the return from Spain, however, the Board of General Officers at London – forerunner of the modern Army Council and designed to serve as the chief authority for discipline, disputes, recruitment and the provision of supplies – held an enquiry. Its concern was not with the defeat at Alamansa, but with the conduct and circumstances of William Caulfeild, Viscount Charlemont in the peerage of Ireland, who had been Colonel of the 36th Foot at the time of the attack on Barcelona in September 1705.

Like the 35th Foot, where Gabriel was Captain, the 36th had been raised in Ireland. Both regiments took part in the attack on Cadiz in 1702, and they had served together in the West Indies and in Spain, including the capture of Barcelona and the defeat at Almansa. There were suggestions, however, that during an assault on Fort Monjuïc at Barcelona Charlemont had failed to press the attack as hard as he should, and he soon afterwards resigned his commission, apparently under pressure from Charles Mordaunt Lord Peterborough, general commander of land forces.

The first meeting of the Board to consider the matter was held on 15 December 1707, and there followed a number of meetings, with letters of justification, arguments and witnesses on both sides.[83] Eventually, at its meeting of 24 March the Board found that Peterborough had behaved properly, but that he had been deceived by the false report of a message from Queen Anne ordering Charlemont to relinquish his colonelcy. Charlemont for his part had decided to quit the appointment rather than sell it, as he expected a greater

---

[81] Dalton, *English Army Lists* VI, 361-373, presents a list of the casualties at the battle; those of Brigadier-General Gorges' regiment are at 368; they do not include Gabriel CdeC. Ball, "Huguenot Family," 33, cites a report to the House of Lords indicating Gabriel was not at the battle; no explanation is given.

As below, Gabriel had been wounded in the assault on Barcelona, and may not yet have been fit for action; it is also possible that he had already been sent back to England or Ireland to engage in recruiting.

On the subsequent siege of Alicante, where Thomas was part of the garrison, see 123 above.

[82] Dalton, *English Army Lists* VI, 138, mentions two new lieutenants appointed in 1708 to serve under Captain Crepigny in the reconstructed regiment.

[83] The progress of the enquiry is recorded in *Proceedings of the Board of General Officers* [PGO] WO 70/1 1706 Feb-1711 Mar, 77-144.

promotion in England. Despite some confusing evidence, the Board also found that Charlemont had behaved with good sense, energy and courage at the attack on Barcelona.

At its meeting of 9 February 1708, however, a letter written by Captain Crespigny had been presented in which he complained to Colonel Phineas Bowles, commander of another regiment, that after Colonel Lord Donegall was killed on 10 April 1706 Viscount Charlemont had appropriated a quantity of his goods and papers. It appears that this matter had come to the notice of Lord Peterborough, and was the initial reason for his summoning Charlemont to discuss his position.

The minutes of the meeting then record that[84]
> After which all Persons being ordered to withdraw, as they were passing out, Mr Caulfeild, Son to the Lord Charlemont, gave Capt Crepigny several blows over the Face and Head with a Cane. Whereupon Mr Caulfeild was sent Prisoner to the Guard, to be kept there until Her Ma^{tys} or the Princes Pleasure should be known.[85]
> The Disorder being then over.....[86]

Born in 1685, Thomas Caulfeild was the second son of Viscount Charlemont, and became an Ensign in his father's command at the age of sixteen. Like a Cornet in the cavalry – the rank at one time held by Gabriel's brother Thomas – Ensign was the lowest commissioned rank in the infantry, equivalent to a Second Lieutenant at the present day. There is no record of any promotion, but he had probably become a full Lieutenant when the regiment was in Spain.

At the time of the incident Gabriel Crespigny was forty years old with twenty years active service. Thomas Caulfeild was twenty-one; he had seen combat at Cadiz in 1702, followed by two years in Spain.

Two weeks later, on 27 February, Captain Crepigny was called as a witness. Nothing was said about his original complaint to Colonel Bowles, and the only questions concerned the day of the attack on Fort Monjuïc. In this regard, his evidence was not notable, but he did say that as he was returning for treatment of wounds suffered in the attack he had seen Lord Charlemont appropriately at the head of his men. There is no indication of resentment or revenge for the recent assault.

On the other hand, though Caulfeild was presumably released from his detention after a short time, the affair was not forgotten, and at its meeting on 5 May the Board agreed to a very strong form of words:[87]

> May It Please your Royal Highness:
> The General Officers of the Army, having, in pursuance of your Royal Highness's Command, taken into Consideration the Difference between Mr Caulfeild and Capt Crepigny, They humbly Report as their Opinion, that the said Mr Caulfeild, having struck Capt Crepigny in the Guard-Chamber with a Cane, during the Time the General Officers were sitting, the least thing the said Mr Caulfeild can do, to Repair so great an Injury and Affront to a Gentleman's Honour, is, in the said Guard-Chamber, during the Sitting of the Board, on his Knees, to ask pardon of Capt Crepigny, who is at the same time to have a Cane in his Hand, with Liberty to use it, as he pleases.

Though Gabriel may have been gratified by the show of support, the matter went no further. Prince George was in poor health and under pressure on other fronts; he died on 28 October without having found time or occasion to confirm or amend the Board's recommendation.

The final reference to the incident appears in the minutes of a meeting on 26 October, six months after the Board had made its recommendation and just two days before the prince's death:[88]

---

[84] *Proceedings* at 98.
[85] Prince George of Denmark, husband of Queen Anne, held formal authority over all English military forces.
[86] One is reminded of the film *Dr Strangelove*: "Gentlemen! You can't fight in here. This is the War Room."
[87] *Proceedings* at 167.

> Capt Crepigny [was] called in on his Petition for Satisfaction from Mr Caulfeild, and [was] told that Lt-Gen Seymour not being at the Board, who presided when the matter was first under Consideration, and had attended the Prince. Therefore the Pet[itioner] could not be then informed what Directions His Royal Highness had given therein.

Lieutenant-General William Seymour was Colonel of The Queen's Regiment of Foot, now part of the Royal Marines. He had presided at the Board Meeting of 5 May, but later joined his regiment in Spain; in September he and his men had taken part in the capture of the Mediterranean island of Minorca. Since there had been no written reply from the prince, nor any report of what he might have said, the matter was left to lie.

Thomas Caulfeild later transferred to the marines: since his original regiment had been on sea service the change was appropriate. In 1710 he was sent with his unit to America to support colonial militia troops of New England in an attack on French-held Nova Scotia. Distinguishing himself in the campaign, he was named Lieutenant-Governor of the newly-acquired province and held charge there until his death in 1717 at the age of thirty-two.

Just a few years after this imperfect vindication, Gabriel suffered the injuries which obliged him to leave the army. The Treasury Warrant is dated to December 1714, but the incident probably took place in 1711, for his petition for assistance was first heard by the Board of General Officers on 10 February 1712.[89]

The Warrant says that he was recruiting at Wigan when he was attacked by local rioters and so severely wounded that he was in danger of death, was a long time recovering and required expensive treatment at Bath.[90]

Wigan is in Lancashire, just north of Manchester and Liverpool, and was presumably considered a suitable region for recruitment into a unit based on Belfast just across the Irish Sea. The men had very likely been gathered by varying levels of force and deception – the press-gang system did not apply only to the Navy, and the "King's Shilling" was sometimes taken through trickery. Still more to the point, authorities such as mayors and magistrates frequently took advantage of the process to forcibly enlist local trouble-makers and men who were unemployed – but friends of the unwilling recruits often came to their rescue.[91]

Scouller observes that "Regiments were kept in anything approaching fighting trim only by the diligent work of their own recruiting officers..." and the work of officers such as Gabriel Crespigny was essential to the maintenance of an effective army. The War of the Spanish Succession was now in its tenth year, however, and though the Duke of Marlborough had gained a magnificent victory at Blenheim in 1704 his most recent success at Malplaquet in 1709 was accompanied by very high casualties. As people tired of the constant conflict, the army lost much of its popularity.[92]

Eventually, some three years after the incident at Wigan and almost two years since he had submitted his request for assistance, Gabriel was authorised to dispose of his commission as a means to discharge the debts he had incurred, and was approved for a pension of five shillings a day. This represented an annual income of just over £90 and was effectively half-

---

[88] *Proceedings* at 206-207.
[89] The Warrant is quoted at 129 above. Scouller, *Armies of Queen Anne*, refers to the case at 124, and his footnote gives the date of the meeting; PGO WO 71/2 [March 1711 to April 1714].
[90] Warrant Books in *Calendar of Treasury Books*, Volume 29, 1714-1715, 222.
[91] Scouller, *Armies of Queen Anne*, 108-109 and 122-125, discusses the procedures and problems of recruiting. The passage quoted is at 124.
[92] Manchée, "Huguenot Soldiers and Service," 258-259, discusses Gabriel's difficulties, but appears to relate them to Jacobite sentiment in the north of England. There is no reason to believe, however, that Wigan was particularly attracted to the cause of the Old Pretender, son of the deposed James II (who had died in 1701), and Jacobite rebellion did not break out until 1715. It is more likely that the rioters simply opposed the foreign war.

pay.[93] Despite his visit to Bath for treatment, Gabriel had by this time settled in Ireland – presumably on account of the connection with Lord Gorges' Regiment – and a Warrant for his pay was sent to the Lord Lieutenant of that kingdom in December 1714. On 22 December 1715, one year later, another was sent to confirm the first, requiring that Gabriel and two others be placed on the Establishment of French Pensioners in Ireland. The original authorisation had been "by some mistake left out..." and they were now entitled to three delayed instalments.[94] It cannot have been easy for the family to have waited so long.[95]

Gabriel died in Ireland in 1722; it is not known when his wife Elizabeth nee Glasscock died, but it was probably also in Ireland and before 1730. The couple had three children: Mary who had died an infant in 1692; Charles who died unmarried at Dublin in Ireland in 1733; and Elizabeth, who survived her brother but also died unmarried in Ireland.

Charles Crespigny was appointed an Ensign in the Earl of Barrymore's Regiment of Foot on 6 April 1706.[96] He was probably born about 1689, so would have been some eighteen years old at that time. Like his uncle Thomas and possibly his father Gabriel, he may have received his commission after service as a Volunteer.

Barrymore's was a new raising, as a previous unit under his command had been changed from infantry to dragoons. The regiment was sent to Portugal in 1708, and in May 1709 took part in the Battle on the Caya, also known as the Battle of La Gudiña. When the allied Portuguese cavalry was driven from the field three British regiments made a counter-attack, but were surrounded and compelled to surrender. In the following year the officers and men were exchanged for French troops captured during the Duke of Marlborough's victories in northern Europe, and the regiment was then transferred to join the garrison of Gibraltar.[97] In 1714, still with the rank of Lieutenant, Charles Crespigny transferred to the regiment commanded by General Thomas Meredith, but both his new unit and his old remained at Gibraltar until 1728. The fortress was twice attacked by Spanish forces, briefly in 1720 but for six months from January to June in 1727.[98]

Unfortunately, with one strange exception, there appears to be no further information about Charles Crespigny' military career, nor when he may have left the army.

The exception is a mention in the will of Captain John Bennett (1670-1717), a naval officer whose family was based at Poole in Dorset, but who died at Barking in Essex.[99] Captain Bennett made his will the year before he died: one of the beneficiaries was "Captain Cripiny of Barking," who received £10; while "Chas Crepigny'" served as a witness. Leaving aside the legal uncertainty of the beneficiary of a will being also a witness, it is hard to imagine what Charles Crespigny could have been be doing in Essex at that time; and the

---

[93] Trimen, *Historical Memoir*, 21, notes that in 1736 a captain in active service received nine shillings and six pence a day, and the amount had varied little over time.

[94] *Calendar of Treasury Books*, Volume 29 at 861; Grayden, *Chronicle*, 9.

[95] Scouller, as above, says there is no evidence to show that Gabriel received the relief that he sought. In fact he did, but it was a long time coming.

[96] Dalton, *English Army Lists* V, 70, with the name of the regiment miswritten as Barimore's.

In 1751, when regiments ceased to be identified by the names of their colonels, this unit became the 13th Regiment of Foot. It was later known as the Somerset Light Infantry (Prince Albert's): Chant, *Handbook of British Regiments*, 142.

[97] There is an account of the action at the Caya and the subsequent exchange of prisoners in Carter, *Historical Record of the Thirteenth*, 31-32.

[98] Dalton, *George the First's Army* I, 160. As Colonel of a different regiment, Thomas Meredith [or Meredyth] had also been captured at the Caya. He was later promoted to Lieutenant-General and took command of the 20th Foot in 1714. He died in 1719 and was succeeded by William Egerton.

The 20th Foot later became the Lancashire Fusiliers. The history has been compiled by Major Smyth.

[99] See Michael Wand, "*Captain Bennett Investigated: an account of a historical enquiry into Capt John Bennett (1670-1717)*" at *www.foxearth.org.uk/CaptainBennett.html*.

puzzle is made the more complex by the fact that in 1716 "C Crepigny" – apparently acting as a Churchwarden – signed the Vestry Minutes of St Margaret's Church in Barking. Though no other Charles Crespigny is known at the time, it is hard to make a connection.

Charles Crespigny died at Dublin in Ireland on 1 October 1733. His will, proven on 11 February 1734, describes him as a bachelor and gives his rank as Lieutenant. His sister Elizabeth, described as a spinster and his only next of kin, was his executor. The will refers, however, to "goods in divers jurisdictions" – presumably including England, and possibly Essex or Gibraltar; an inventory was due to be delivered in the following August.[100]

Little is known of Charles' sister **Elizabeth** save that was born about 1693, that forty years later she was unmarried and living in Dublin, and that she outlived her brother. Ball, however, cites a letter from Elizabeth preserved in the Fairfax family papers in the British Museum manuscript collection.[101] Dated about 1734, it is addressed to Betty [Elizabeth] Fairfax, referring to her as "Cosen [*sic*=cousin]" and thanking her for her care. She is in poor circumstances, having been obliged to sell most of her possessions, and though she is the "chife Creditter" of her brother Charles' will, he left many debts. Her cousin Harry Glasscock had sent her a pocket-book of "notes" – IOU's – before his recent death, and she was hoping for assistance in redeeming them. She suggests that her cousin Claude [presumably Claude of South Sea House] might be able to help through his contacts in London. Other than that, Elizabeth makes no mention of her CdeC relations, but refers to another Glasscock cousin, William. It is probable that Betty Fairfax the recipient of the letter was born Glasscock.

I have no access to the Fairfax papers, and cannot check the document itself, but Ball's description is convincing. She observes that the handwriting is unskilled and that "the letter reveals Elizabeth to be a rather poorly educated and not very accomplished spinster."

It is possible that Elizabeth died soon after this, without further contact to her Crespigny relatives. When her uncle Pierre/Peter made his will in August 1736 he left small bequests to his sisters, and to his nephews and niece the children of his brother Thomas, but he made no mention of Gabriel's daughter, his niece Elizabeth.

An indenture of 1716 records the apprenticeship of Harry Glasscock of Hassobury in Essex, son of William Glasscock, to Thomas Horsnell of the Inner Temple. The contract was presumably the same as that for Thomas' son Guillaume/William in 1713, though the fee for William was £150 and Harry Glasscock paid only £10; this may reflect the reputation and influence of the master.[102] Such engagements were commonly taken up by young men in their mid-teens – William CdeC and his brother Philip were indentured at the ages of fifteen and thirteen – so Harry Glasscock would have been born about 1703.

Based on the record of the heralds' Visitation of 1664, I have suggested that Elizabeth CdeC nee Glasscock was the daughter of William Glasscock of Farnham, who had also a son named William.[103] It seems possible this younger William had two sons: one named William after his father and grandfather, the other the apprentice Harry; and both were first cousins to Elizabeth and Charles CdeC the children of Elizabeth nee Glasscock.

This indeed can be no more than a tentative proposal, for several men of the Glasscock family had the personal name William, and there were other women called Elizabeth. What does seem clear, however, is that Gabriel's wife came from a substantial family of English background.

---

[100] Grayden, *Chronicle*, 9.
[101] "Huguenot Family," 37-39, citing Manuscript Room, British Museum – Addition Catalogues Vol. 12 (1854-1875) Ref. 21554 f. 15.
[102] *Britain, Country Apprentices 1700-1808*: National Archives reference (IR1 series) 5f94; Society of Genealogists volume 12, page 2214, number 81366. On William CdeC's indenture, see 125 above.
[103] Above at 128.

CHAPTER FOUR

Table IV: Putative kinship of Elizabeth Champion de Crespigny and the Glasscock family of Essex[104]

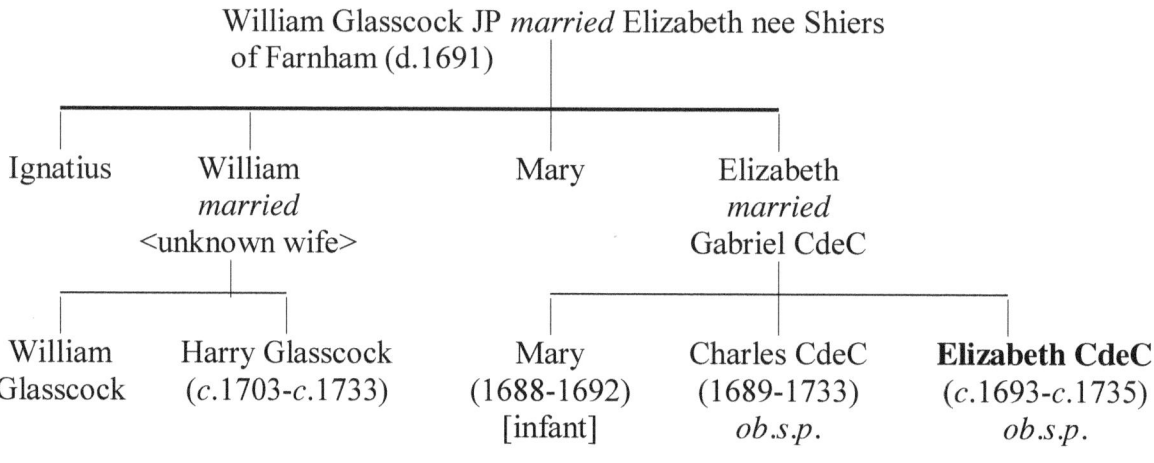

In the end, this is a sad story. Gabriel's marriage to a native English family was unusual: his brother Thomas and his sisters Marguerite, Marie, Susanne and Renée all married within the Huguenot community in England,[105] and the tradition was followed by Thomas's daughter Jane/Jeanne and his son Philip. The English connection, and some money from his wife's kinfolk, may have been useful to Gabriel's early career in the army, but the transfer of his commission from a Guards regiment to a newly-raised unit in Ireland indicates there were financial problems, and it does not appear that support from the Glasscock family was continued. By the time that he was injured at Wigan and compelled to retire from the army his situation and that of his family had become quite precarious. We may observe, moreover, that while Thomas's sons William, Philip and Claude found opportunity in civil professional life, Gabriel's son Charles followed his father into the army and gained only a low-ranking commission as lieutenant. Regardless of any connection to Captain Bennett in Essex, or any property he may have laid claim to, it is clear from his sister Elizabeth's letter that his debts were more important.

At the same time, moreover, the move to Ireland created a separation from both the Glasscocks and the Crespignys in England. One has only negative evidence, for many letters and documents are no longer available and we do not know how Betty Fairfax replied or whether Elizabeth was able to realise on her cousin Harry's notes – with or without the assistance of Claude of South Sea House – but the omission from Pierre's will may be significant. From the fragments we have, however, there is considerable contrast between the Fairfax correspondence of 1734 and the concern showed by Elizabeth's cousin Philip when his aunt Jeanne de Lamberty faced problems in Switzerland just one year later.[106] In comparison with that most active intervention, Elizabeth in Ireland seems lonely and unsupported.

---

[104] The first two generations are based upon Bysshe, *Visitation of Essex*, 39 [as in note 72 above]; the third is speculative.

We must note, however, that when William Glasscock of Farnham died in 1691, his will probated on 19 June made bequests to his wife Elizabeth and his daughter Mary, but contained no mention of his daughter Elizabeth. It is possible that this Elizabeth was already dead; or her father believed she and her husband Gabriel had already received their proper share of her entitlement at the time of their marriage; or there was disagreement within the family.

[105] Gabriel's other sister Jeanne/Jane, of course, married Geronimo de Lamberty; again, definitely not English. In her case, however, the family connection was maintained, even at a distance.

[106] Above at 117-118.

Chapter Five

English Establishment 1730-1805

Introductory
Chronology c.1700-1800
Philip and Claude, sons of Thomas
    Claude Crespigny (1706-1782) of South Sea House
    Philip Crespigny (1704-1765) of Doctors Commons and Champion Lodge
The children of Philip Crespigny and Anne nee Fonnereau
    Susanna (1735-1766)
    Anne (1739-1782)
    Jane (1742-1829)
    Claude (1734-1818) the first baronet
    Philip (1738-1803) the Member of Parliament
        The children of Philip the younger
Epilogue

Introductory
Chapter Four has discussed the first generation of settlers in England, notably the brothers Pierre, Thomas and Gabriel, sons of Claude Champion de Crespigny and his wife Marie nee de Vierville. Pierre, however, never married, and Gabriel had no grandchildren, so the story of the next generation is primarily concerned with the two surviving sons of Thomas, Philip and Claude. Again, only Philip would marry and have children: his wife Anne was the daughter of the wealthy merchant Claude Fonnereau, but he had a successful career in his own right as a lawyer. Philip and Anne's eldest son Claude became Receiver of the Droits of Admiralty and was made a baronet in 1805; their second son, Philip the younger, became a King's Proctor and a Member of Parliament.

    My concern in this chapter is with the history of the family through the eighteenth century, and I do not offer great detail on the children and further descendants of Claude and Philip; many of them are discussed by Anne's Family History. We may note, however, that the male lineage of Sir Claude ended with the death of the eighth baronet in 1952. When Claude's brother Philip died in 1803 he left thirteen children by four marriages, but only his son Charles Fox CdeC maintained a male lineage: he is the ancestor of all who bear the CdeC surname at the present day.

*Chronology c.1700-1800**

1698	birth of Guillaume/William, son of Thomas CdeC and Magdalen nee Granger, at Bruges
1704	birth of Thomas and Magdalen's son Philip at London
1706	birth of Thomas and Magdalen's son Claude at London
1712	death of Thomas CdeC
1713	Guillaume/William is apprenticed to a lawyer of the Inner Temple
1718	Philip is apprenticed to a lawyer at the Court of Arches, dealing with probate, divorce and admiralty cases
1720	the South Sea Bubble
1721	death of Guillaume/William; Thomas' son Claude becomes a junior clerk at South Sea House

---

*   Items in blue are general historical facts; items in normal font relate to the CdeC family.

CHAPTER FIVE

Table V: Descendants of Thomas Champion [de] Crespigny *c.*1700-1800

Thomas Crespigny *married* Magdalen nee Granger
(1664-1712)   1696   (1667-1730)

- four other children
  none with issue
  see Table III
- Philip *married* Anne nee Fonnereau
  (1704-1765) 1731   (1704-1782)
- Claude
  (1706-1782)
  ob.s.p.

Children of Philip and Anne:

- Jane (1733-1734) *infant*
- Anne (1736-1737) *infant*
- Anne (1739-1797) *ob.s.p.*
  married
  (1) Bonouvrier Glover (1735-1780)
  (2) James Gladell Vernon (*c.*1746-1819)
- Susanna (1735-1766) *married* 1765 Richard Sutton [later a baronet] [*one child died in infancy*]
- Claude (1734-1818) [created baronet 1805] *married* Mary nee Clark (1747-1812)
  - William (1765-1829) [second baronet] *had issue*
    - **the Baronet lineage**
- Jane (1742-1829) *married* Henry Reveley (1737-1798)
  - Hugh Reveley (1772-1851)
  - 1 other son, 2 daughters
- Philip (1738-1803) *married*
  (1) Sarah nee Cocksedge (d.1768): 2 sons, 2 daughters
  (2) Betsy Hodges nee Handley (d.1772): 1 son [*infant*]
  (3) Clarissa Sarah nee Brooke (d.1782): 3 daughters
  (4) Dorothy nee Scott (d.1837): 2 sons, 1 daughter

Notes:
1. The male line of the baronet lineage – and the title – ended with the death of Sir Vivian Tyrrell CdeC, eighth baronet, in 1952.
2. Though Philip had children by all four of his wives, only one – Charles Fox CdeC (1785-1875) born to Dorothy nee Scott – has present-day descendants in a male lineage.
3. Charles Fox CdeC's third son, Philip [Robert] Champion [de] Crespigny (1817-1889) arrived in Australia in 1852 with his wife Charlotte Frances nee Dana and their two children Ada Isadora Charlotte and Philip. Through this son Philip (1850-1927), Philip Robert is the ancestor of the main line of the Champion de Crespigny family in Australia.

ENGLISH ESTABLISHMENT

*c.*1727	Philip qualifies as a Proctor at the Court of Arches
1730	death of Magdalen nee Granger, widow of Thomas CdeC
1731	Philip marries Anne nee Fonnereau
	Claude is appointed First Clerk in the Secretary's office of the South Sea Company
1733	Philip becomes Marshal of the Court of Admiralty
1734-65	Philip serves as Secretary to the French Hospital *La Providence*
1734	birth of Philip's eldest son Claude, future baronet
1738	birth of Philip's second son, also named Philip [Philip the younger]
1739	Philip is appointed Supernumerary Proctor of the Arches Court and of the High Court of the Admiralty
1741	Philip leases a house at Denmark Hill in Camberwell
1745	Claude pursues the absconding clerk Thomas Shuttleworth
	Philip is appointed Admiralty Proctor
1753	Claude is appointed Secretary to the South Sea Company
	Philip buys properties in Suffolk
1755	Philip purchases his leased house at Camberwell and names it Champion Lodge
1756-63	Britain is engaged in the Seven Years War against France and Spain
1757-63	Philip's son Claude is a Fellow of Trinity Hall, Cambridge
1759	Philip the younger becomes a Proctor at the Court of Arches
1762	Philip the younger marries his first wife Sarah nee Cocksedge
1763	Philip's son Claude becomes an Advocate at the Court of Arches
1762	birth of Philip the younger's first son Thomas
1764	Philip's son Claude marries Mary nee Clark, widow of Isaac Heaton
1765	birth of William, son of Claude and Mary nee Clark, and future second baronet
	death of Philip the Admiralty Proctor
	birth of Philip the younger's second son, also named Philip
1759	Philip the younger is made a King's Proctor at the Court of Admiralty
1768	death of Sarah nee Cocksedge, first wife of Philip the younger
1771	Philip the younger marries his second wife Betsy Hodges nee Handley
1772	death of Betsy nee Handley, second wife of Philip the younger
1774	Philip the younger marries his third wife Clarissa nee Brooke
	Philip the younger and his uncle Thomas Fonnereau are elected as Members of Parliament for the borough of Sudbury, but are unseated following a petition
1775	revolt of the American colonies against Britain
1780	Philip the younger is elected a Member of Parliament for the borough of Aldeburgh, and controls that constituency thereafter
1781	General Cornwallis compelled to surrender to American and French forces at Yorktown
1782	death of Claude of South Sea House; death of Anne Crespigny nee Fonnereau
	Philip's son Claude is appointed Receiver of the Droits of the Admiralty
	death of Clarissa nee Brooke, third wife of Philip the younger
1783	Philip the younger marries his fourth wife Dorothy nee Scott; birth of Philip and Dorothy's first son George
	the Treaty of Paris confirms the independence of the American colonies
1784	birth of Elizabeth/Eliza, daughter of Philip the younger and Dorothy nee Scott
1785	birth of Charles Fox CdeC, second son of Philip the younger and Dorothy nee Scott
1789	the fall of the Bastille in Paris on 14 July marks the beginning of the French Revolution

CHAPTER FIVE

1790   Philip leaves Parliament, but continues to arrange the election of supporters of Charles James Fox at Aldeburgh
1793-1802   Britain at war against Revolutionary and then Napoleonic France; concluded by the Treaty of Amiens in 1802
1803   death of Philip the younger
    Britain declares war against Napoleonic France, ending the Peace of Amiens
    Philip, son of Philip the younger, is interned at Verdun; while in France he marries Emilia nee Wade; they escape in 1811
1804   Claude and Mary nee Clark receive the Prince of Wales, future George IV, at a fete held at Champion Lodge
    Eliza, daughter of Philip the younger, elopes with Richard Hussey Vivian, future Baron Vivian
1805   Sir Claude Champion de Crespigny is made a baronet
1812   death of Mary, Lady Champion de Crespigny
1813   George, eldest son of Philip and Dorothy nee Scott, is killed in action in Spain
1815   the victory of the Duke of Wellington at Waterloo ends the Napoleonic Wars
1818   death of Sir Claude CdeC, first baronet, succeeded by his son Sir William

Philip and Claude, sons of Thomas

We have noted that after the death of Thomas CdeC in 1712, his widow Magdalen nee Granger received £333 worth of stock in the South Sea Company as reimbursement for some of her late husband's expenses during his last years of military service. Soon afterwards the couple's son William was apprenticed to a lawyer of the Inner Temple at the cost of £150, and five years later his brother Philip was indentured to a procurator at the Court of Arches; this required £126.

These arrangements were very likely made with the guidance of Thomas' elder brother Pierre, and perhaps also with the assistance of Magdalen's family the Grangers. In any case they show remarkable imagination and forethought; though William died sadly young, Philip would make the most of his opportunity.

The third surviving son, Claude, born in 1706, joined the South Sea Company and rose to become its Secretary. He was younger than Philip, but it is convenient to consider him first.

Claude Crespigny (1706-1782) of South Sea House

The South Sea Company, formally known as "The Governor and Company of the Merchants of Great Britain, trading to the South Seas and other Parts of America, and for the Encouragement of Fishing," had been established in 1711. Despite its title, however, and some commercial activity in South America and elsewhere, the core activity of the company was the management of British government debt.

The Glorious Revolution of 1688, which saw the expulsion of James II and confirmation of parliamentary power, also brought a new arrangement for state finances. Through the Bank of England, established in 1694 as a private enterprise under royal charter, the government borrowed money from private investors, while the state itself provided excellent security.

> The subscribers would earn interest on their deposits; the corporation would make a profit by charging a higher rate on its loans to the government; and the government would be assured in perpetuity of a steady source of finance.[1]

The success of the system meant that during all the eighteenth century the British government had access to resources unmatched by any other European power. Some rival states were forced into bankruptcy, others borrowed at need or demanded loans without good security, and many sold rights, privileges, offices and annuities which extended liabilities into the

---

[1] Davies, *The Isles*, 558.

future without serious prospect of payment. The most dramatic example came at the end of the century, after French military and naval forces had supported the American colonists against Britain. The cost of that intervention brought a financial crisis in France which led to the calling of the Estates-General in 1789 and the subsequent Revolution. In contrast, despite the defeat and the loss of its colonies the British government remained financially stable, and during the years of conflict which followed, first against Revolutionary France and then against the empire of Napoleon, Britain not only maintained a powerful navy and an effective army, but provided subsidies to its allies.

The South Sea Company was established primarily as a rival to the Bank of England, which had begun as an essentially private company. When a Tory government came to power in 1710 the Bank was considered too close to the former Whig regime and the new Treasurer Robert Harley, Earl of Oxford, arranged a second establishment to deal with government debt. It was in these circumstances that Thomas Crespigny's estate was paid with South Sea Company shares in 1713.[2]

A few years later, as the Company took an increasing share of official finance, there was great enthusiasm accompanied by a high level of corruption and insider trading, while reports of enormous profits led to a vast inflation of value in the South Sea Company and many others. There was no substance to such expectations, however, the Bubble burst in 1720, and as South Sea shares fell from more than £1000 to their former level of £100 many people were ruined. There followed a great political scandal and a long Whig supremacy under Prime Minister Walpole.

Though most histories place emphasis on the Bubble and the Company's position at the centre of the disaster, the South Sea Company continued to function for another 130 years as it was originally designed: issuing shares to raise money; lending that money to the government; and using the interest received on the loan to pay dividends on the shares. No longer a source of excitement, it was a substantial organisation whose stock provided steady dividends and was traded at a rate comparable to the East India Company and the Bank of England itself.[3]

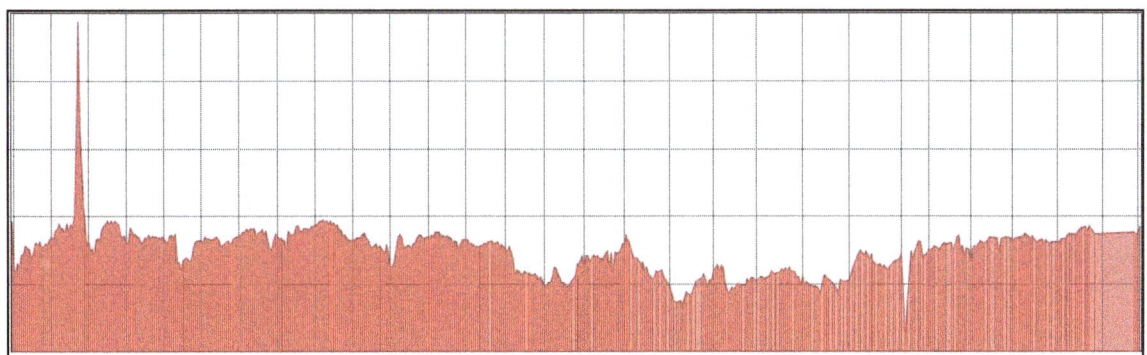

Price of stock in the South Sea Company from 1711 to 1855
adapted from Taylor, "The South Seas Company"
The y-axis of the graph is in log-scale. The Bubble of 1720 may be noted on the left. Thereafter the value remains reasonably steady, with dips indicating periods when government bonds appeared less risky than usual and so the value of dividends – and stock prices in consequence – were reduced.

The Company did make some early attempts to engage in the trade for which it had formally been established. By the Treaty of Utrecht which ended the War of the Spanish Succession in 1713, the Spanish government granted a contract – *Asiento* – to bring slaves from Africa to

---
[2] Chapter Four at 125.
[3] Bryan Taylor, "Complete Histories – The South Seas Company – The Forgotten ETF," posted in *Stock Histories, Stock Scams* at https://www.globalfinancialdata.com/gfdblog/?p=986.

work in the silver mines of America. There was also approval for one ship each year to bring in other commodities, while the possibility of contraband offered further profits. In practice, however, though the Company arranged almost a hundred passages, carrying more than thirty thousand slaves with a mortality of "only" eleven per cent, the enterprise was bedevilled by argument with the Spanish government and occasionally interrupted by war and piracy. Overall profit was small, and the program was wound down after 1731.[4]

Besides this, from 1724 the Company was engaged in hunting whales in the far north Atlantic. Though somewhat contradictory for an enterprise supposed to trade in the south, the project was supported and subsidised by the government. Eight years of operations, however, saw the accumulation of a substantial loss, and this program too ended in the early 1730s.

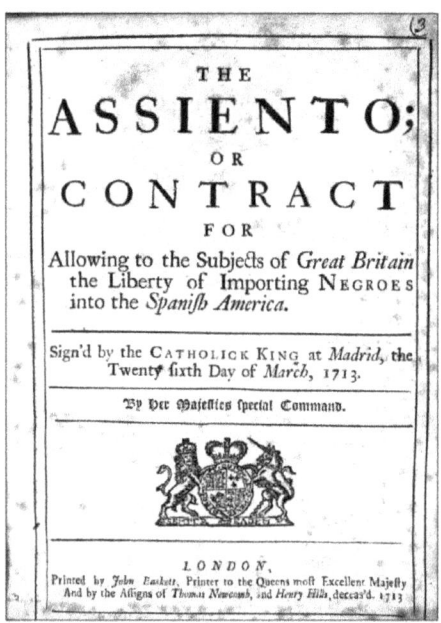 

Left: Cover of the English translation of the Asiento *contract agreed with Spain, allowing the importation of negro slaves to the Spanish colonies of America.*
Right: Trade label of the South Sea Company, identifying the finest quality English serge cloth. The coat of arms is a variant of the Company's, showing the royal arms of England impaled with those of Scotland in the upper left, two fish [herring] in the upper right, and a formalised map of the Americas; the Latin motto means "My hope, Lord, is in Thee." SS&FC at the base are initials for "South Sea and Fishery Company."

Claude Crespigny joined the staff of the South Sea Company in 1721, a few months after the collapse of the Bubble.[5] He was fifteen years old, the same age as his brother Philip had been when he was indentured at the Court of Arches, though Claude was probably not a formal apprentice but simply a junior clerk at a very low salary.[6]

The following ten years were turbulent, initially from the aftermath of the Bubble entailing massive financial and administrative restructuring, and then from continual difficulties regarding the trade – both legal and doubtful – with the Spanish colonies. Claude, however, was evidently competent and recognised for his ability and in April 1731 *The Gentleman's Magazine* recorded his promotion to be First [*i.e.* chief] Clerk in the Secretary's office; he was then twenty-five years old.[7] There were considerable questions of policy in play at that time, with fierce debates among the directors and a series of disputed elections,

---

[4] Helen Paul, "The South Sea Company's Slaving Activities" at https://archive.is/8b62.
[5] Recording Claude's death, *The Gentleman's Magazine* for October 1782 noted that he had been in the secretary's office of the company for almost sixty-two years: volume 52 at 503.
[6] The pay and expenses of clerks are discussed by White, *Great and Monstrous Thing*, 408-410.
[7] *The Gentleman's Magazine* volume 1 at 503.

while the South Sea Company ceased its overseas operations soon afterwards. Members of the modern family may be pleased to note that their kinsman saw the end of involvement in the slave trade, though the decisions were taken above his level. In any event, from the mid-1730s the Company reverted to its original real purpose, to serve as a clearing house receiving interest payments for its holdings of government debt and distributing the proceeds to its shareholders.[8]

In May 1745 Thomas Shuttleworth, an employee of the Company, embezzled the very considerable sum of twenty thousand pounds and fled to Amsterdam. He was thought to be headed for Italy, and the directors offered two hundred pounds to anyone who captured him. They also sent Claude Crespigny, and it was reported in July that he had recovered a banker's draft for ten thousand pounds originally intended for Mr Shuttleworth.[9]

In October 1753 *The Gentleman's Magazine* reported that Claude Crespigny Esquire had been chosen Secretary to the South Sea Company, replacing Mr Smith, who had died in that office.[10] Claude too would die in office, but he was Secretary – Chief Executive Officer – of this major financial institution for almost thirty years.

South Sea House in Threadneedle Street, London, in the early nineteenth century
Drawn by Thomas H Shepherd, engraved by A Cruse
The South Sea House, headquarters of the Company from the early eighteenth century, burned down in 1826. This picture from the early 1820s, however, shows the original building where Claude Crespigny served as Secretary and – later – the writer Charles Lamb as a clerk.

The South Sea Company maintained its financial function until the middle of the nineteenth century, though its holdings by then were only a small fraction of the whole national debt and its significance had diminished accordingly. In 1853 the Chancellor of the Exchequer and

---

[8] Sperling, *The South Sea Company*, has a detailed essay on the financial affairs of the Company, with particular attention to the circumstances of the Bubble, to the complex dealings with Spain and to the debates andconflicts of the 1730s.

[9] The affair was reported in several papers of the time, including *The London Evening Post, St James's Evening Post, The General Evening Post* and *The Penny London Post or Morning Advertiser*: 17th and 18th Century Burney Collection, tinyurl.galegroup.com/tinyurl/4Vhqe5.

[10] Volume 23, page 492: the item concludes "(Smith, dec.)."

CHAPTER FIVE

future Prime Minister William Gladstone arranged the conversion of South Sea stock into government bonds or bills. The directors accepted the terms and the Company was liquidated in July 1855: the final settlement paid just under £120 for every £100 share.[11]

The Dividend Hall of South Sea House 1810
Architectural details by Augustus Charles Pugin, figures by Thomas Rowlandson
from Rudolph Ackermann's Microcosm of London *volume III*

The writer Charles Lamb (1775-1851) was a clerk in the Examiner's Office at South Sea House for a few months in 1791 and 1792, ten years after the end of Claude's tenure as Secretary. In 1823, when he published his *Essays of Elia*, he wrote of "The South Sea House" as deserted and derelict:

> This was once a house of trade, – a centre of busy interests. The throng of merchants was here – the quick pulse of gain – and here some forms of business are still kept up, though the soul be long since fled. Here are still to be seen stately porticos; imposing staircases; offices roomy as the state apartments in palaces deserted, or thinly peopled with a few straggling clerks; the still more sacred interiors of court and committee rooms, with venerable faces of beadles, doorkeepers – directors seated in form on solemn days (to proclaim a dead dividend,) at long worm-eaten tables, that have been mahogany, with tarnished gilt-leather coverings, supporting massy silver inkstands long since dry .....
>
> Such is the South-Sea House. At least, such it was forty years ago, when I knew it, – a magnificent relic!

It is an agreeable piece of writing, slightly confused by reference to the Bubble of seventy years earlier, and one cannot be sure that all Lamb's recollections are correct or whether the essay was composed for effect.[12]

---

[11] Sperling, *The South Sea Company*, 48-49.
[12] Several items in the essay are confusing, particularly as to time. Though he was a sixteen-year-old clerk in 1791-92 and published the piece in 1823, Lamb claims to be thinking of the House from "forty years back;" while his reference to the time of the Bubble is sufficiently confusing that the Wikipedia entry for

Claude Crespigny (1706-1782), Secretary of the South Sea Company 1753-1782
Portrait at Kelmarsh Hall, Northamptonshire, attributed to Jean-Baptiste van Loo

In contrast to the sad picture presented by Lamb's essay, Claude Crespigny appears to have been a man of energy and style, well-read, with a wide circle of acquaintances and a reputation for wit. He was obviously proud of his association, for he identified himself as Claude Crespigny of South Sea House even before he became Secretary.[13]

In 1760, following his late uncle Pierre, Claude became a Director of the French Hospital *La Providence*, and he continued in that office until his death. He never married, but was close to his brother Philip and his family: he formally joined the conveyance when Philip purchased Champion Lodge in Camberwell in 1755.[14] He had an official residence in South Sea House, but he also owned a house and property in the area of the Vineyard at Bath.[15]

---

his *Essays* is quite anachronistic: "Its subsequent downfall in a pyramid scheme after Lamb left (the South Sea Bubble) would be contrasted to the company's prosperity in the first Elia essay."

[13] The bookplate of the copy of *Hermippus redivivus* – as illustrated on the next page – may be dated by the inscription recording the book as a gift made in 1745, when Claude was still First Clerk and eight years before his appointment as Secretary.

[14] Champion Lodge is discussed below at 153-154.

[15] Claude identifies the holding in his will.

Chapter Five

Above: *The bookplate of Hugh Reveley (1772-1851)*

Below: *The back spine and front endpaper of Johann Heinrich Cohausen (1665-1750), Hermippus redivivus: or, the sage's triumph over old age and the grave. Wherein, a method is laid down for prolonging the life and vigour of man. Including a commentary upon an antient inscription, in which this great secret is revealed; supported by numerous authorities. The whole interspersed with a great variety of remarkable, and well attested relations; printed for J. Nourse, London 1744.*

The spine shows the CdeC crest at the top and then a series of intertwined Cs, used by Claude Crespigny as a badge.

The left of the endpaper has the bookplate of Claude Crespigny of South Sea House, *with a note "This book was given me by the Hon.ble John Spencer Esq.r A.o 1745." John Spencer (1708-1746) was the youngest son of the Earl of Sunderland and his wife Lady Anne Churchill, daughter of the first Duke of Marlborough. Member of Parliament for Woodstock from 1732 until his death, John Spencer is an ancestor of the present Earls Spencer and of the late Diana, Princess of Wales.*

The right of the endpaper has Claude Crespigny's signature in ink on the upper right, and the pencilled signature Hugh Reveley *with a largely illegible subscript, possibly "Temple" as in the Inner or the Middle Temple of the Inns of Court in London.*

The book is now held in the Princeton University Library: https://blogs.princeton.edu/notabilia/2011/12/22/claude-crespigny-of-the-south-sea-house/ compiled by Stephen Ferguson.

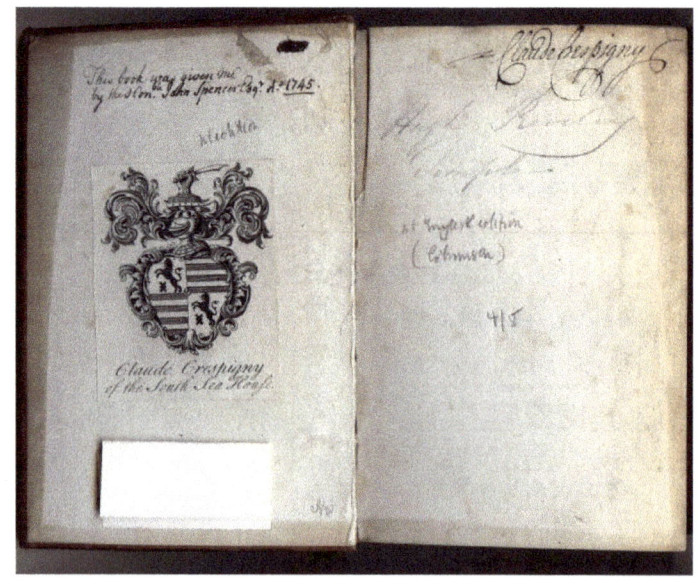

Claude Crespigny died at the age of seventy-six on 6 October 1782 at Champion Lodge in Camberwell, now the residence of his nephew Claude the future first baronet. He was buried in the family vault at Marylebone on 11 October.[16]

His will and two codicils were proved on 15 October. Apart from bequests to the charity schools of Camberwell and some personal gifts "for mourning" or remembrance, he left the house at Bath to his nephew Claude, while the remainder of his property, "whether in the ffunds or in ffurniture," was to be divided equally between his nephews Claude and Philip and his nieces Anne – widow of Bonouvrier Glover – and Jane, now married to Henry Reveley. A major exception was the grant of "my library of books wherever they are" to his great-nephew and godson Hugh Reveley, together with ten pounds "to help fit up his chambers when he goes to college." In 1782 Hugh was just ten years old, but the ambition is obvious and was duly fulfilled. Hugh Reveley graduated as a Bachelor of Civil Law from Christ Church, Oxford, in 1799, and was later a magistrate, Deputy Lieutenant and High Sheriff of his home county Merioneth in Wales. He died in 1851.[17]

Philip Crespigny (1704-1765) of Doctors Commons and Champion Lodge
The *Lancaster Book* remarks of Philip:
> By his talents he accumulated a considerable fortune, for tho' [he was] the representative of his family, his patrimony was very small the French estates of his grandfather having been confiscated.

In 1718, when Philip's mother Magdalen nee Granger paid to indenture him with Charles Garrett, Procurator of the Arches Court of Canterbury, she was arranging his entry into a different area of law to that of his elder brother William. Williams's apprenticeship at the Inner Temple would have qualified him as a solicitor in the regular courts of England, governed by the Common Law; his death in 1721, however, ended that possibility. Philip's practice was based upon the Roman tradition.

Besides its jurisdiction over members of the clergy in the archdiocese of Canterbury, governing all the southern part of England, the Court of Arches had authority over death and marriage, notably the probate of wills and questions of divorce. By a slightly surprising quirk, moreover, practitioners were authorised to deal with cases of admiralty law: given that these commonly involved international affairs, they were based on Roman law rather than English Common Law. The separate jurisdiction developed in medieval times and continued into the nineteenth century.[18]

Practitioners in these courts were divided in similar fashion to those working in the Common Law. Advocates were trained in Roman law at Oxford or Cambridge, and their role was similar to that of barristers. Proctors, on the other hand, were analogous to solicitors and entry to their ranks was based upon a seven-year term of service as an articled clerk. Since there were only thirty-four Proctors, and each was allowed just one such apprentice at a time,

---

[16] As below at 153-154, Champion Lodge had been bought by Claude's brother Philip in 1755. Following Philip's death in 1765, it became the home of his son Claude the future baronet.
The burial is recorded in the Register of St Marylebone Church, cited by Grayden, *Chronicle*, 8. Claude was the last member of the family to be interred there.

[17] See, for example, Burke, *Genealogical and Heraldic History of Commoners* III, 132-133. On his library inherited from Claude Crespigny, see also Chapter One at 21.

[18] In 1857 the separate ecclesiastical jurisdiction over wills and testaments was abolished by the Court of Probate Act, while the Matrimonial Causes Act created a new court to deal with divorce. Both these fields were now opened to practitioners of the Common Law, and members of the College lost their special authority. In 1859 the High Court of Admiralty Act opened that court too, and the remnant ecclesiastical matters handled by the Court of Arches followed a few years later. The purpose of the College thus came to an end, and the buildings of Doctors Commons were demolished in 1865.

CHAPTER FIVE

Philip was fortunate to have obtained a vacancy; there may have been family assistance. At the same time, however, he was also required to have a good classical education, best provided by a grammar school, so someone in the family – and again one may suspect the influence of his uncle Pierre – had worked to prepare the young man.[19]

In similar fashion to the Inns of Court which have survived to the present day, advocates and proctors were based at Doctors Commons, headquarters of the College of Doctors of Law *exercent* in the Ecclesiastical and Admiralty Courts, also known as the College of Civilians. There were offices and apartments in the compound, and a court to hear civil cases.

A Court Sitting in the Common Hall of Doctors Commons 1808
Architectural details by Augustus Charles Pugin, figures by Thomas Rowlandson
from Rudolph Ackermann's Microcosm of London *volume I*

As with modern legal practice, there was a quantity of work available which did not require attendance at court, and the work of a Proctor, particularly dealing with wills and other financial documents, could be extremely profitable. Since Philip and his family had good connection with the Huguenot community, he surely obtained a deal of business through those contacts.[20]

An early example may be seen in the account by the *London Gazette* of the ceremonies held on 15 June 1727 to announce the accession of King George II following the death of his father George I. "The principal Officers of State, a great Number of the Nobility, and other Persons of Distinction" attended a series of proclamations, first at Leicester House, then at Charing Cross, with a final gathering at the Royal Exchange within the City of London. The

---

[19] The procedures for entry to the position of Proctor are discussed in some detail by O'Day, *Professions in Early Modern England*, 156-157, and also by *The Penny Cyclopædia* XIX, 34.

[20] In "Some Huguenot Wills" at 130, Lefroy remarks on a large number of these and other documents of the 1770s which were coming on the market from "the same firm of Proctors, Messrs Crespigny and Greene, afterwards Wittenoom and Crespigny" of Doctors Commons, presumably as the result of a clearance of old files. The documents were acquired by the Huguenot Society and held at the French Hospital.

The Crespigny concerned was Philip's son Philip the younger (1738-1803) as below, and the wills had been proven in Holland. It is clear that the firm had maintained a substantial business – and overseas connections – with Huguenot clients.

ENGLISH ESTABLISHMENT

Gazette goes on to list the names of those present, and within this gathering of the great and the good appears the name of Ph[ilip] Crespigny; he was at that time just twenty-three years old and quite newly qualified as a Proctor at Doctors Commons.

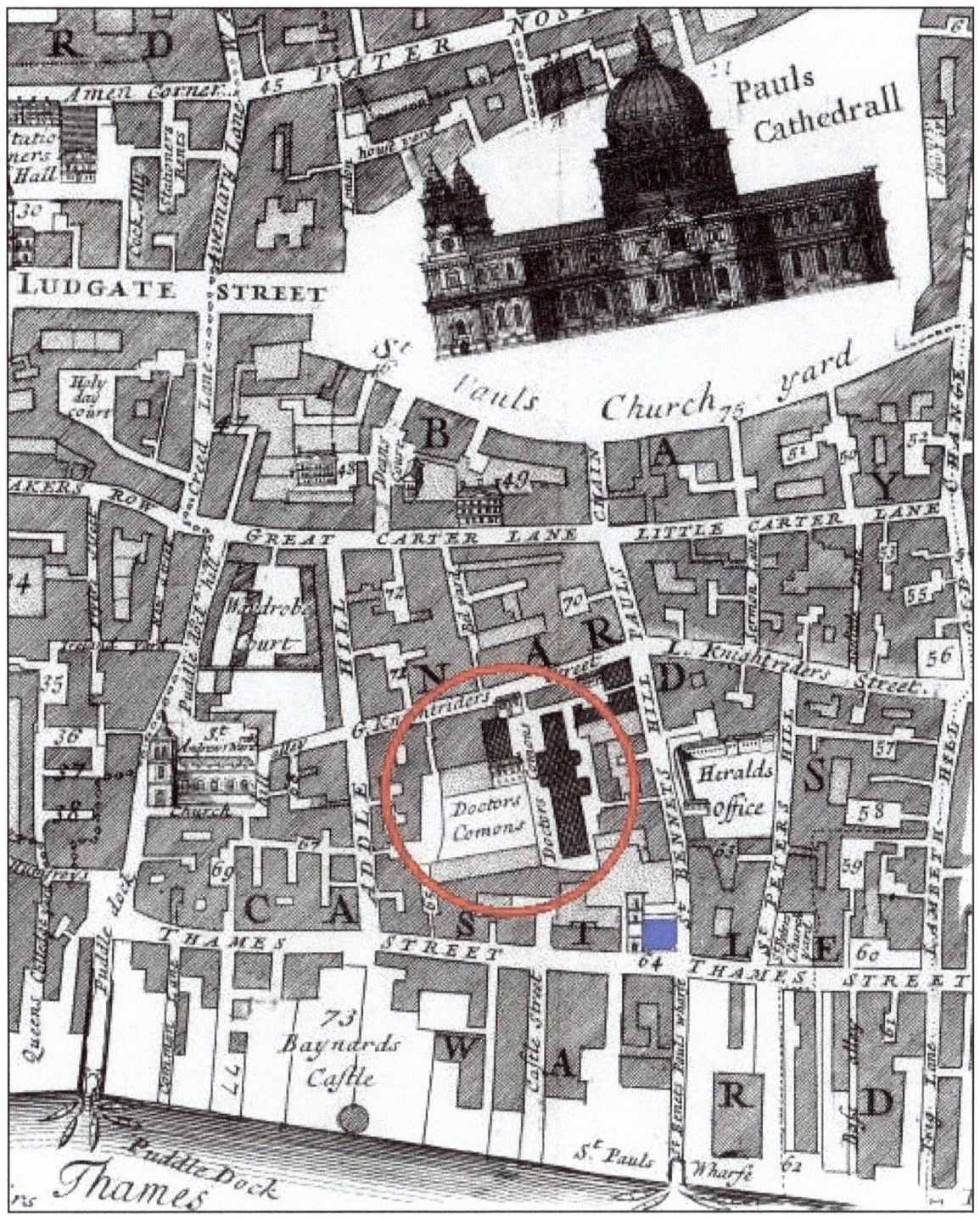

Map Sixteen: Doctors Commons [circled] between St Paul's Cathedral and the Thames, with the Heralds' Office or College of Arms close by to the east.
The church of St Benet's Paul's Wharf[e] is marked in blue: see further below.
Detail from John Strype, A Survey of the Cities of London and Westminster, *1720*

Immediately before his name in the list is that of Claud[e/ius] Amyand, and it is very likely through his agency that Philip gained his entrée. A Huguenot born about 1680, Claudius Amyand was naturalised in England in 1698, served as a military doctor during the War of the Spanish Succession and then held a series of senior civilian posts. In 1715 he was

Chapter Five

appointed Sergeant Surgeon, chief medical officer in the royal household. Elected a Fellow of the Royal Society, he served both George I and George II until his death in 1740.[21]

Given Pierre CdeC's position with the French Hospital, we may assume the two men knew one another well and that Dr Amyand invited Pierre's nephew to the royal occasion. It was a minor matter, but it indicates the connections available to a young man with helpful patrons. Four years later Philip married Anne, daughter of Claude Fonnereau.

Claude Fonnereau (1677-1740) c.1725
Portrait by an unknown artist, held by the Colchester and Ipswich Museums Service

The Fonnereau family was also Huguenot in origin. Zacharie Fonnereau, father of Claude and grandfather of Anne, had been a linen merchant of La Rochelle with interests in England and northern Europe, notably at Hamburg. The family moved to England at the Revocation, maintaining their trading interests and their considerable wealth. Born in 1677, Zacharie's son Claude is said to have been sent to England at the age of twelve – the same pattern as may be observed with Thomas and Gabriel CdeC. He received his certificate of denization in 1693 and was naturalised in 1698. In the latter year he married Elizabeth Bureau, also from a Rochellais family, and they had eight children.

There is one major uncertainty about the emigration. Most sources state simply that the arrangements were made by Zacharie, and that it was he who brought the family to England and arranged the transfer of business. The Cobbold website, however, states that Zacharie

---

[21] An early practitioner of vaccination against smallpox, in 1735 Claude Amyand carried out the first successful appendectomy that has been recorded.

died in 1678, the year after Claude's birth, so he could not have been involved in the move. I have not been able to confirm the source for this date of death, but I note negative evidence: the death of Claude's mother Marguerite nee Chateigner is recorded in London on 1 October 1720, but there is no account of the death of Zacharie/Zachary in any English sources.[22]

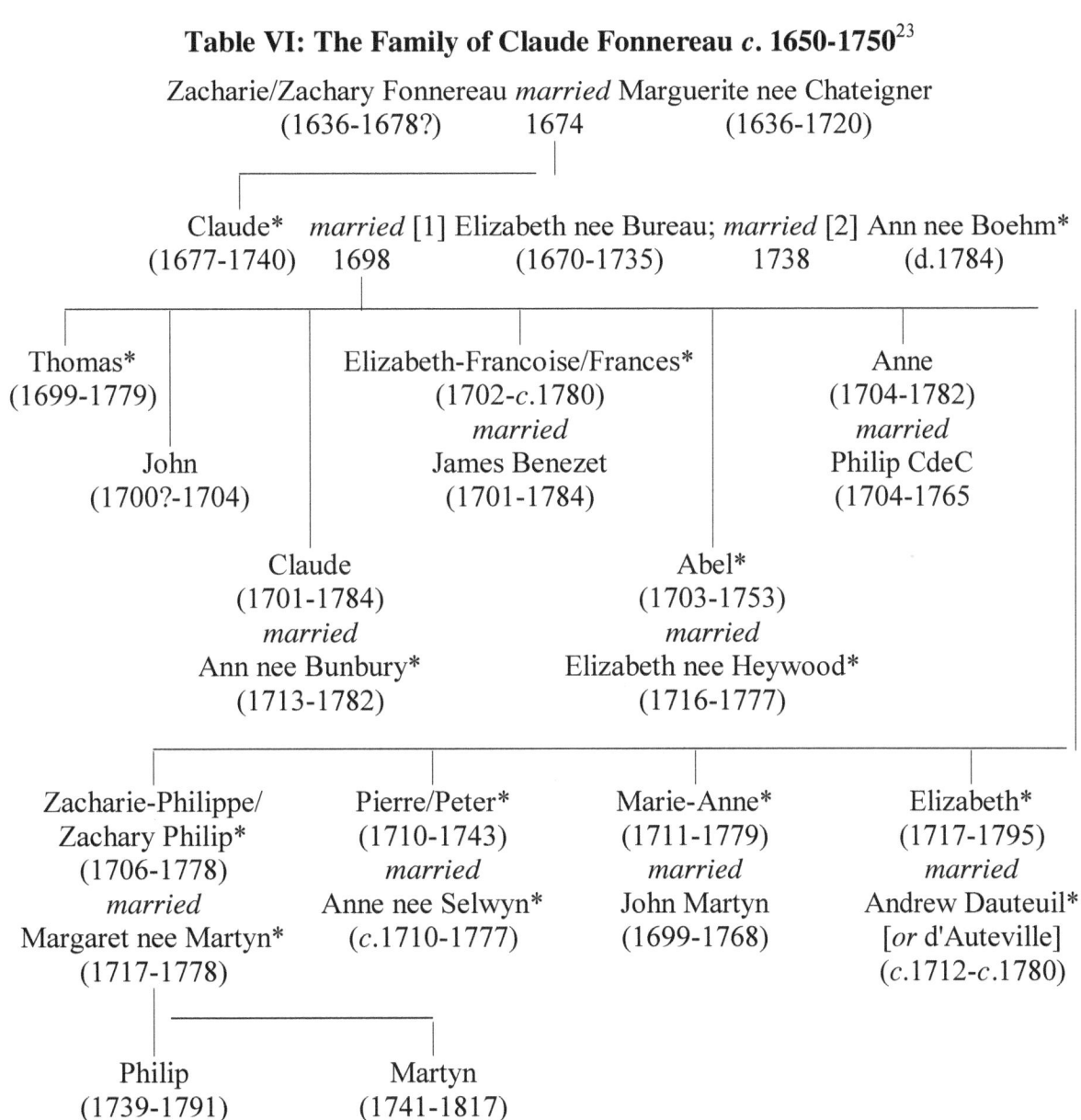

Table VI: The Family of Claude Fonnereau c. 1650-1750[23]

Individuals whose names are marked with an asterisk* served as sureties or godparents for one or other of the children of Philip CdeC and Anne nee Fonnereau. See Table VII below.

I have identified Philip and Martyn, sons of Zachary Philip Fonnereau, because they were associated with the political career of Philip Crespigny the younger. I do not extend the table to include other members of the family in that generation.

---

[22] *Visitations*, 44, states clearly that Marguerite died on 1 October 1720 and was buried at St Stephen's Walbrook. There is no such information for her husband.

[23] Genealogies of the Fonnereau family are given by Agnew, *Protestant Exiles* II, 399-400, by Howard and Crisp, *Visitation*, 44-47, and by Lart, *Huguenot Pedigrees* I, 37-39. There is a summary in Burke, *Genealogical and Heraldic History of Commoners* II, 108. Additional information is available on the internet, including particularly the Fonnereau and other family trees on the web-site ancestry.co.uk, and the Cobbold Family History Trust. I have attempted to resolve a number of contradictions.

CHAPTER FIVE

It is difficult to speculate without further details, but on present evidence it appears that Claude's mother Marguerite would have been responsible for the resettlement, with all its commercial and financial implications. There have been other successful business-women in such times, but this was a notable achievement.

Anne Fonnereau, sixth child and second daughter of Claude and Elizabeth nee Bureau, was born on 12 October 1704. On 5 February 1731 she married Philip Crespigny in a ceremony at St Pauls' Cathedral; both husband and wife were twenty-seven years old, with Anne two months the elder. By the contract of marriage, witnessed by Philip's brother-in-law Gilbert Allix and by Anne's brother Abel Fonnereau, Claude Fonnereau granted Philip £2000 and a "yearly rent" of £200; the same amount was provided for Anne and her children, with a further £300 annually for Anne herself, free from any "intermeddling of her husband."[24]

As the settlement indicates, Claude Fonnereau was very well off. When he died in 1740 *The Gentleman's Magazine* listed bequests to his nine children totalling £165,000, with a legacy and an additional income of £400 a year to his wife; at interest of 2½% this required a capital sum of another £13,500.[25] Anyone worth £100,000 was regarded as "plum" –rich – and with his landed properties Claude Fonnereau had more than double that. Philip had gained an impressive marital connection.

Bookplate of Philip Champion [de] Crespigny (1708-1765)
married to Anne, daughter of Claude Fonnereau
The Lancaster Book *marks the marriage with the standard shield showing the arms of Champion [de] Crespigny impaling those of Fonnereau. Philip's bookplate, however, with impressive ornamentation, is more worthy of the union.*
Sources: *Stephen CdeC, "Bookplates and Family Trees," and Murdoch and Vigne,* French Hospital.

---

[24] *Visitations* has the details of Anne's marriage to Philip Champion Crespigny at 46, giving the date as 1730/1 in the Old Style, 1731 by the modern calendar. *Huguenot Pedigrees* has the year as 1734/5, but this is certainly wrong: Philip and Anne's daughter Jane was born in 1733 and Claude the future first baronet in 1734. [Lart also fails to mention Anne's elder brother Abel, fifth child of Claude and Elizabeth.]

The marriage contract is cited by Ball, "Huguenot Family," 41, from a photocopy of the original document provided by Stephen CdeC. It is also mentioned in Philip's will of 1762: Grayden, *Chronicle*, 10.

[25] *The Gentleman's Magazine* 10 at 204.

As with the royal ceremony of 1727, Philip may well have owed his contact with the Fonnereau family to his uncle Pierre, for in 1718 Claude Fonnereau had donated £10 towards the foundation of the French Hospital, where Pierre was one of the Directors. On the other hand, though he was now qualified as a Proctor, Philip had no inherited wealth: his father Thomas was long dead and his late mother Magdalen nee Granger had relied upon a soldier widow's half-pay. We may assume that he and Anne were fond of one another, but that was not enough for a father to approve a potential son-in-law and there must have been questions in Claude Fonnereau's mind. He approved Philip's suit nonetheless, and it does not appear that either he or his daughter found reason to regret that quite courageous decision.

Besides this excellent marriage, Philip achieved a successful and properous career in law. While his private practice dealt with wills and other civil matters, he also held government office. In 1733 he was named Marshal of the High Court of Admiralty, receiving fees for cases taken on behalf of the government.[26] This is a considerable appointment for a young man recently out of articles and not yet thirty years old, and argues a degree of ability and again perhaps personal influence. In 1739 he was appointed a Supernumerary Proctor of the Arches Court and of the Court of Admiralty, and in 1745 he became Admiralty Proctor at a higher rate of income. He also held appointment as Proctor to the Courts of Chivalry at the College of Arms; this, however, was a sinecure, for the court had not sat since the early years of the century, and indeed would not be called again until 1954.[27]

In his will of 1762 Philip refers to a house at Knight Rider Street held under lease from the Dean and Chapter of St Paul's Cathedral. Knightriders Street was immediately adjacent to Doctors Commons, and it is very likely that the property had been leased since the time of his marriage and served as his residence in London.

Champion Lodge at Denmark Hill, Camberwell, about 1800

In 1741, however, the family moved to Denmark Hill in Camberwell. At that time a small village on the road to Brighton, Camberwell was one of the first places south of the river with attractive and healthy rising ground. There were some impressive mansions and good quality

---

[26] Philip's appointment as Marshal by the Board of Admiralty was noted in the *Daily Journal* of London for Monday 6 August. It was remarked there that the place was worth some £600 a year; another entry, on 11 August, mentioned £700. His further appointments, as below, are noted also by 'Admiralty court', in Sainty, J C [editor], *Office-Holders in Modern Britain: Volume 4, Admiralty Officials 1660-1870*, London 1975, 95-99; from *British History Online* http://www.british-history.ac.uk/office-holders/vol4/pp95-99.

[27] Squibb, *High Court of Chivalry*, xxv-xxvi and Chapter VII.

CHAPTER FIVE

neighbours nearby, and a view of St Paul's Cathedral in the distance. The house Philip chose had been built in 1717 – there were rainwater downpipes marked with that date. He initially took a twenty-one year lease, but then purchased the full freehold with sixteen acres in 1755. The cost was £2075, and he renamed it Champion Lodge.[28] Allport's account of Camberwell describes the house and its garden, including its fine cedar trees, and records that there was ornamental ironwork at the west front of the building, elegantly designed with joined CCs and the family coat of arms: CdeC impaling Fonnereau.[29]

In 1732 Claude Fonnereau had acquired Christchurch, a grand Tudor mansion at Ipswich, with two other properties in Suffolk. Following that interest, in 1753 – even before he bought Champion Lodge – Philip purchased Broughton Hall and supplementary estates near Stowmarket, a few miles to the northwest.[30] Claude Fonnereau also gained influence in the two boroughs of Sudbury and Aldeburgh, each entitled to send two members to Parliament; his family and associates took later advantage of these political possibilities.[31]

Like his brother Claude of South Sea House, Philip appears to have been an agreeable and convivial man. He became Secretary of the French Hospital in London in 1734, formally responsible for supervision of all its activities, and he held that office for thirty years until his death.[32] At Camberwell he was active in the Anglican community and became a member of the board of the Greencoat School, a charity institution for elementary education.[33] He also belonged to the Camberwell Club which met at the Grove House Tavern – described as large and commodious, with fine gardens and a fashionable assembly room. Philip's brother Claude and their brother-in-law Gilbert Allix were also members, and among other entertainments the company placed eccentric bets:[34]

30 April 1750: Mr Allix lays a bottle of wine with Dr Ducarel that the Jesuits' account of the Longitude is in the *Daily Advertiser*. Dr Ducarel lays it is in the *General Advertiser*, and not in the *Daily*; Allix lost.[35]

26 July 1750: Mr [Philip] Crespigny lays a bottle that two new Bishops will not be made before Dr Lynch is made a Bishop; on 15 April 1752 Mr Crespigny acknowledged that he had lost the wager.

---

[28] Marks, "Family in Camberwell," 2-3. The last entry in the *Consolations Book* records the birth of Philip's youngest child Jane at Camberwell on 12 October 1742: Chapter One at 17-18.

Walford, *Old and New London* 6, discusses Camberwell at 269-286. At 278 he states that the house was built in 1717 by "Claude de Crespigny," and the *Camberwell History Guide* agrees about the date and the family: http://www.southlondonguide.co.uk/camberwell/history.htm. Both, however, are mistaken. The house was indeed constructed at that time, but it was first leased and then purchased by Philip from Henry Cornelison. Marks has the history correctly.

We may observe that Philip consistently used the short surname Crespigny, but reflected the original in the name of his new residence.

[29] *Collections* 81-83. Allport notes that at the time of his writing in 1841 the house had been demolished and the site was being prepared for housing: below at 165.

[30] Kirby, *Suffolk Traveller*, 204 and 209. Philip subscribed for three copies of this second edition, and his brother Claude for one.

[31] Below at 171-173.

[32] Murdoch and Vigne, *French Hospital*, 30-31, notes Philip's service and the duties it entailed.

[33] Walford, *Old and New London* 6, 278. The school had been founded in 1721 by the same Henry Cornelison from whom Philip had acquired Champion Lodge.

[34] Marks, "Family in Camberwell," 2-3, mentions the club. Some wagers are listed in *Notes and Queries* 3:11, 149-150, others in Blanch, *Parish of Camerwell*, 306-307, which also has an account of the tavern.

[35] Dr Andrew Coltée Ducarel (1713-1785) was of Huguenot descent. In 1765, acting as a surrogate judge at the Court of Arches, he granted probate for Philip Crespigny's will.

The Jesuit mission to Qing dynasty China was at this time engaged in mapping the empire and calculating the longitude and latitude of cities, a work facilitated by the vast expanse of the North China plain. The problem of gauging longitude at sea, however, was not solved until John Harrison developed his chronometer in the 1760s and 1770s.

25 June 1751: Mr Woodbridge lays a bottle that a Prince will be born. Mr C. Crespigny lays a Princess; lost by Mr Woodbridge. [Princess Caroline Matilda was born on 22 July 1751; she was the posthumous daughter of Frederick Prince of Wales, son of George II and father of George III, who had died on 30 March.]

Philip Crespigny (1704-1765), Procurator-General of the Arches Court of Canterbury
Portrait at Kelmarsh Hall, Northamptonshire, attributed to Jean-Baptiste van Loo

There is also a letter preserved to his friend Dr Andrew Ducarel, who was an Advocate at the Court of Arches, a noted antiquary and archivist, and later Librarian of Lambeth Palace for the Archbishop of Canterbury. Writing from Southampton in August 1753, Philip discusses the tale of William Rufus, son of the Conqueror, killed by an arrow in the New Forest in 1100. It was believed that the arrow glanced off an oak, fatally changing its flight, and Philip promises to try to collect a piece of the roots of the ancient tree "having seen two or three pieces of it made into tobacco-stoppers."[36] He concludes with a postscript:

We all bathe in the sea daily, and drink the salt water, which agrees exceedingly with us.

Philip Crespigny died on 11 February 1765 at the age of sixty and was interred in the family vault at Marylebone.

---

[36] Nicholls, Illustrations of Literary History IV, 599-600.

CHAPTER FIVE

Philip's will named his elder son Claude, future baronet, as residual legatee, so it is not possible to assess its total value. He did, however, leave bequests amounting to thousands of pounds, and besides Champion Lodge and other leaseholds in Camberwell he mentions "several Manors and Lordships" in different parishes of Suffolk, two estates in Kent, another in Surrey, two houses at Limehouse in London, and the right to nominate a rector to the living of Stockport in Cheshire. This is a great deal of property acquired in one generation – and it does not include the holdings of his wife Anne, who survived him by seventeen years and left a lengthy will of her own. The *Lancaster Book* was justified in its praise.

Table VII: The Godparents of Philip CdeC's children with Anne nee Fonnereau
based upon Philip's entries in the Consolations Book

1733	Jane I	Claude Fonnereau, Anne's father
	(d.1734)	Jane Allix nee CdeC, Philip's sister
		Margaret Debordes/de Borde nee CdeC, Philip's aunt
1734	Claude	Pierre/Peter CdeC, Philip's uncle
		Claude CdeC, Philip's brother
		Elizabeth-Frances Benezet nee Fonnereau, Anne's sister
1735	Susanna	Thomas Fonnereau, Anne's brother
		[Philip Fonnereau, Anne's brother, acted as proxy]
		Martha Susanna Hebert, Philip's cousin[37]
		Anne Fonnereau [nee Bunbury], wife of Anne's brother Claude
		[her mother Anne CdeC/Fonnereau acted as proxy]
1736	Anne I	Gilbert Allix, husband of Philip's sister Jane
	(d.1737)	Mary Anne/Marie-Anne Fonnereau, Anne's sister
		Mrs Elizabeth Fonnereau, wife of Anne's brother Abel Fonnereau
1738	Philip	Zachary Philip Fonnereau, Anne's brother
		Andrew Dauteuil, Philip's cousin
		Elizabeth Fonnereau, Anne's sister[38]
1739	Anne II	Abel Fonnereau, Anne's brother
		Mrs Anne Fonnereau nee Boehm, Anne's step-mother]
		Mrs Anne Fonnereau nee Selwyn, wife of Anne's brother Peter Fonnereau
1742	Jane II	Peter Fonnereau, Anne's brother
		Jane Allix, Philip's sister[39]
		Margaret Fonnereau nee Martyn, wife of Anne's brother Zachary Philip

All the children except the second Jane were baptised at St Benet's Paul's Wharf; Jane II was baptised at St Giles Church in Camberwell, close to the new residence of Philip and his family at Champion Lodge.

---

[37] Martha Susanna nee Dauteuil (1708-1770) was the daughter of Marthe/Martha nee Granger, sister of Philip's mother Magdalen: Chapter Four at 125. Born in 1707, she married Thomas Hebert, probably of Huguenot origin [Hébert?: *cf.* Chapter Four at 115], at St Benet's Paul's Wharf on 9 June 1731.

The will of Susanna Hebert of Stoke Newington in north London was written on 13 December 1770 and proved on 31 December. She made small bequests to her brother Andrew and to her cousins Jane Allix, Claude Crespigny [of South Sea House] and Anne Crespigny nee Fonnereau. The remainder went to her daughter Elizabeth Hebert; she appears to have been the only child, and was evidently unmarried, for there is no mention of her husband, nor of any other children or any grandchildren.

[38] Andrew/Andre Dauteuil was a brother of Martha Susanna: note 37 immediately above.

Andrew Dauteuil later married Elizabeth Fonnereau the younger sister of Anne. The bond was sworn at St Martin-in-the-Fields on 28 July 1742.

[39] As above, Jane Allix nee CdeC had earlier been godmother to Philip and Anne's first child Jane I, who died when just a few months old.

The children of Philip Crespigny and Anne nee Fonnereau
Philip Crespigny continued the family record commenced by his father Thomas in the front leaves of the *Consolations Book*. From that information, Table VII provides a summary of the birth order of his children by Anne nee Fonnereau and the names of their "sureties" or godparents. It may be observed that all the godparents were members of the Crespigny or Fonnereau families: the most distant are cousins or relatives by marriage.

It is most convenient to deal first with the daughters and then with the two sons, Claude the first baronet and his younger brother Philip, ancestor of the Australian lineage.

Susanna was born on 13 November 1735. On 28 June 1765 she married Richard Sutton, a barrister of the Inner Temple, at the church of St Giles in Camberwell. She died, however, just under one year later, on 12 June 1766. It seems certain that her death came from complications of child-birth, for the will of her mother Anne observes that she had died "leaving only one child who is since also dead intestate and without issue." Since there is no mention of the name of the child, nor even of its sex, it is likely the infant died soon after birth.

Born in 1733, Richard Sutton later became a Member of Parliament and was made a baronet in 1772. He was married twice more, with children, and died in 1802.

St Giles Church, Camberwell in 1750 [destroyed by fire in 1841]
from Walford, Old and New London

Anne was born on 10 October 1739. On 24 April 1765 she married Bonouvrier Glover, an officer of the Royal Navy. This wedding too was held at St Giles Church in Camberwell and, like that of Susanna, it took place just a few months after the death of her father Philip in February of that year.

Bonouvrier was the son of Richard Glover, who was a Member of Parliament and a poet of some note – though opinions varied about the quality of his work. The family company was engaged in trade with Hamburg, but despite his personal name – French for "good worker" – there does not appear to have been a direct Huguenot connection.[40]

---

[40] His personal name appears in variants, such as "Bonovier," and the surname is sometimes miswritten Grover.

CHAPTER FIVE

Left: Susanna nee Crespigny (1735-1766), first wife of Richard Sutton, portrait possibly by Thomas Beach.

> *This painting and that of Betsy Hodges nee Handley, second wife of Philip the younger [below at 167], both of which are at Kelmarsh Hall, have been loosely attributed to the celebrated painter George Romney or his school. In a personal communication to Anne Young, however, Alex Kidson, Research Fellow of the Romney Society and compiler of a complete catalogue of Romney's work, rejects the suggestion:*
>> I'm afraid that beyond saying those two portraits are definitely not by Romney, nor even very close to his painting style, I cannot really be of much help. I would agree that the date of both is around 1770. I'd guess that both pictures - plus a third one in the Kelmarsh collection, of Claude de Crespigny [*i.e.* the first baronet, below at 165] - are all by the same artist and were done at the same time as part of a single commission. (They are all the same size.) I cannot put a name to the artist, rather to my irritation. The portrait of Susanna is an essay in the manner of Gainsborough whereas the one of Betsy is in the mode of Reynolds, so we are talking an eclectic, probably youthful portraitist still searching for his own idiom. Thomas Beach, a pupil of Reynolds, who was making his name at Bath around 1770, comes to mind. I have seen essays by him in the manner of Romney too around this date and Bath was a centre of fashion that the Crespignys might have visited.

Right Anne nee Crespigny (1739-1797): portrait in pastel by Catherine/Katherine Read.
> *Catherine Read (1723-1778) was active in London from 1753, and this portrait probably dates from the early 1760s, when Anne was in her twenties, shortly before her marriage to Bonouvrier Glover.*
> *Source: Jeffares,* Dictionary of Pastellists before 1800 *at* www.pastellists.com/articles/read.pdf, *4-5 [a confused entry].*
> *This was item 124 in a sale catalogue of The Anderson Galleries of New York in 1927; it was described as "Lady Ann de Crespigny, a pastel portrait on paper, stretched on canvas," offered by Xavier Haas of Nice in France:* https://archive.org/stream/paintingssculptu00ande/paintingssculptu00andedjvu.txt.
>> *Four years later the same work was presented for auction by Plaza Art Galleries of New York as item 24 of* Important Paintings by European and American Artists *from the estate of the late Rita de Acosta Lydig:* https://archive.org/stream/importantpaintin00orei/importantpaintin00orei_djvu.txt.
>> *Though attributions appear firm, one should note the similarity – including hairstyling and an earring – to the portrait of Betsy Hodges nee Handley, second wife of Philip CdeC (1738-1803) at 167 below.*

Also born in 1739, Bonouvrier Glover served as a midshipman in the 1750s and was promoted Lieutenant of the *Hind* in 1760 during the Seven Years War (1756-1763). In 1762 he became Commander of the *Favourite*, but the ship was paid off at the end of the war. Soon after his marriage, in June 1765 Bonouvrier was named Captain of the *Unicorn*; though he was not in command, the appointment meant that he was now a full Captain with seniority from that time. In 1770-1771 he was in charge of the recommissioning of *HMS Tartar*, an elderly vessel of 28 guns, then at Spithead, the naval base by Portsmouth, but it was not until 1778 that he held command of his own ship, the frigate *Janus* of 44 guns, and sailed her to join the West Indies squadron.

On 20 March 1780, as part of a flotilla commanded by William Cornwallis, future admiral and a personal friend of Glover, the *Janus* took part in an attack on a French convoy passing north of Hispaniola near the border of present-day Haiti and the Dominican Republic. While Cornwallis had three ships under his command, however, the convoy was defended by five French warships, three of them larger than any of the British, and the raiders were forced onto the defensive. Captain Glover was seriously ill at the time, and he died of natural causes during the engagement. The *Janus* was fought successfully by Lieutenant George Stephens, but Cornwallis is said to have resented the fact that Stephens had left his captain below and thus denied him the honour of dying on his own quarterdeck.[41]

Left: HMS Argo, *a frigate of the same* Roebuck *class as the* Janus, *sometime commanded by Bonouvrier Glover.*

Three years later, on 3 March 1783, Anne married James Gladell at the fashionable church of St George's Hanover Square in London. Born about 1746, he was a few years her junior.

James' mother was a member of the Vernon family, which traced its descent from William de Vernon of Normandy, who had come to England with William the Conqueror in the eleventh century; his son Richard was enfeoffed as a baron and held land at Shipbroke in Cheshire. That lineage ended in 1403, when Sir Richard Vernon rebelled and was executed by King Henry IV.[42] It was a widespread family, however, and Anne's husband James was based in East Anglia.

---

[41] See Allen, *Battles of the British Navy* I, 299-300, and *http://morethannelson.com/officer/bonovier-glover/*.
William Cornwallis' brother Charles was the general who was obliged to surrender Yorktown to the American revolutionary army in 1781.
Following the death of Captain Glover, the next commander of the Janus was Horatio Nelson, future hero of Trafalgar.

[42] The forces of the Percy family and other discontented nobility were led by Harry "Hotspur" Percy, son of the Earl of Northumberland, and received strong support in Cheshire. King Henry, however, defeated the rebels at the battle of Shrewsbury. The campaign is a central theme of Shakespeare's play *King Henry IV*; Part 1, whose central characters are Sir John Falstaff and the young Prince Hal, future Henry V.

CHAPTER FIVE

James' uncle – his mother's brother – was Francis Vernon of Orwell Park in Suffolk, who had been Member of Parliament for the seat of Ipswich from 1761 to 1768 and was made Earl of Shipbrook in 1777; Francis' father and grandfather, both named James, had been members of parliament in the late seventeenth and early eighteenth centuries, and his uncle Edward was a celebrated admiral.[43]

Francis Vernon died in 1783, a few months after James had married Anne Glover nee Crespigny. As Francis had no male heir the earldom was extinguished, but James Gladell inherited his uncle's broad estates in Lincolnshire, Norfolk and Suffolk. Following provisions of Francis' will, in May of 1784 James Gladell received royal licence to adopt the surname Vernon and the arms which had been .granted to his late uncle.[44]

The arms of Vernon and a bookplate inscribed J G Vernon

The left hand illustration shows the arms attributed to the Vernons of Shipbrook. They were adopted by Francis Vernon and then by James Gladell Vernon when he inherited his uncle's estates: Guillim and Mackenzie, Display of Heraldry, 124-125. The shield is blazoned or, on a fess azure three garbs of the first: *that is, a gold/yellow shield with three wheat-sheafs – also gold/yellow – on a blue band across the centre.*

The bookplate [from Stephen CdeC, "Bookplates and Family Trees," 94] has a black-and-white "hatched" shield – with dots for gold and sideways stripes for blue – showing Vernon impaling Champion de Crespigny with Vierville. The "lover's knot" in place of the crest is normally used by a woman, so it appears that Anne adapted her husband's plate.

Anne Vernon nee Crespigny died at the family residence in Hanover Square, London, on 2 June 1797; her will dated 7 January of that year was proved on 5 July. No children are mentioned, and her estate was complicated by a marriage indenture which granted a life interest to her husband James,[45] but she left considerable amounts of money or annuities to her relatives by blood or marriage: beneficiaries included her brother Claude the future

---

[43] Known for wearing coats made of heavy grogram cloth, Admiral Vernon was nicknamed "Old Grog." As commander in the West Indies in the 1740s he encouraged the drinking of rum diluted with water: the mixture, 4:1, limited the spoilage of the water but was not strong enough to make men drunk. The name "grog" became a generic term for a mixture of alcohol with soft or fruit drinks.

Lawrence Washington, elder brother of George the future first President of the United States, served under Vernon and named the family home Mount Vernon in his honour.

[44] *Lincs to the Past.com*: Vernon family: records *re* their estates in Lincolnshire & Norfolk; Reference Name MISC DEP 128. The *London Gazette*, issue 12540, May 4 to May 8, 1784, records the change of surname and the adoption of the arms.

[45] Details of the contract and the amounts involved, both land and government bonds, are given in the first part of Anne's will. It was a tripartite agreement between James – then known by his original surname of Gladell, Anne herself, and two guarantors: Anne's brother-in-law Sir Richard Sutton, widower of her late sister Susanna; and George Stainforth, who presumably represented the Vernon/Gladell interests.

baronet, his wife Mary nee Clark, their son William, and his son William Other who was also her godson; her nephews Thomas and Philip and her nieces Clarissa/Clara, Maria, Fanny and Elizabeth – being the sons and daughters of her brother Philip;[46] her sister Jane and her husband Henry Reveley. She also left money to her former brother-in-law Richard Glover and to her widowed aunt by marriage, Alice the Dowager Countess of Shipbrook. Thomas and Philip, sons of her brother Philip by his first wife Sarah nee Cocksedge, were executors.

Jane Crespigny was born at Champion Lodge in Camberwell on 12 October 1742 and was baptised at St Giles' Church. In September 1771 she married Henry Reveley, and their first child, Hugh, was born on 15 July in the following year. He was baptised on 6 August, and Claude Crespigny of South Sea House was one of his godparents.

Henry Reveley came from a landed family of Yorkshire, but the family spent time in Spain and he was born at Alicante in 1737. He was connected to the royal household, serving as a Gentleman Usher to Queen Charlotte the consort of George III, and he held a contract to provide grain to the royal stables under the Master of the Horse. In 1775 he became a Director of the South Sea Company and in 1784 he was appointed a Commissioner of Excise, with an annual net salary of £1000. He was known as a fine musician and a connoisseur of art, with an impressive collection of drawings and etchings.

Henry Reveley died in 1798, leaving all his property to his widow Jane, ,who lived until 1829. Their son Hugh, having graduated in law from Oxford and been called to the bar, became assistant to Lord Redesdale the Chancellor of Ireland. In 1803 Hugh married Jane Hartley-Owen, and through her inherited the estate of Bryn-y-Gwyn near Dolgelley in Wales. He built a house and took up residence there, and he was High Sheriff of Merionethshire in 1811. The connection with the CdeC cousins continued, and the records of the *Reveley Book* were maintained, probably by Hugh's son Henry John Reveley, grandson of Jane nee Crespigny: this is discussed further in Chapter One.

The "Back Court" at Trinity Hall in the eighteenth century
showing the Master's Lodge on the right and the Old Library on the left

---

[46] Strangely, three of Philip's children are not mentioned in the will. They are Anne, daughter of Sarah nee Cocksedge, born in 1768 – though she may have received a separate gift – and George and Charles Fox the sons of Dorothea nee Scott, born in 1783 and 1785 respectively; their sister Elizabeth/Eliza, however, is listed with her three half-sisters the children of Clarissa Sarah nee Brooke.

CHAPTER FIVE

Claude (1734-1818) the first baronet, and his family

Born on 19 December 1734, **Claude** was educated at Eton and was admitted to Lincoln's Inn as a student in 1750. He became a Scholar at Trinity Hall, Cambridge – known for its legal associations – receiving a Bachelor of Laws in 1755 and a doctorate in 1763. Recognised as a classical scholar, he was elected a Fellow of the college in 1757; this, however, was largely due to the patronage of the Chancellor, Thomas Pelham-Holles, Duke of Newcastle and former Prime Minister, who was engaged in a political struggle with Dr Edward Simpson the Master of Trinity Hall.[47] In 1763 Claude was admitted as an Advocate to the Court of Arches, and he resigned the fellowship soon afterwards.

On 16 February 1764 Claude married Mary Clark, daughter of Joseph Clark and Mary nee Wilks; Claude was turning thirty and Mary was just sixteen years old. The couple lived for a time in Bath, but their son William, future second baronet, was baptised in Camberwell on 31 January of the following year.

Claude's father Philip died on 11 February 1765, a few days after the birth of his grandson. He left the greater part of his estate to Claude, with money, houses, lands and leases, but made provision for his widow Anne, Claude's mother, to remain at Champion Lodge or take other accommodation rent-free. Details are unknown, but the will of Anne nee Fonnereau, dated 1766, refers to her as "of Camberwell in the County of Surry," so she had maintained her residence there. All her bequests were monetary, with no mention of landed property.

Claude's younger brother Philip did not receive any great share of his father's estate, for he had married the wealthy heiress Sarah Cocksedge.[48] The wedding took place in November 1762, and the elder Philip signed his will a few weeks later, remarking with an obvious sense of satisfaction that he and Anne had already made gifts to the new couple, and that his son "has settled himself in Life in a very happy and advantageous Manner."

Besides the inheritance from his father, valued at some £5000 *per annum*, Claude also acquired property in East Anglia through the Fonnereau connection. His main residence was Champion Lodge in Camberwell, but in 1775 he built Crespigny House at Aldeburgh on the Suffolk coast: Aldeburgh became a pocket borough for the family, and Claude's brother Philip controlled its seats in Parliament.

Crespigny House in Aldeburgh was built for Sir Claude de Crespigny (first Baronet) in 1775. Two views from an estate agent's brochure; the house was later a school and is now divided into apartments.

Mary's father Joseph Clark had died in 1757, and Mary inherited the bulk of his estate. Her mother later married the merchant Isaac Heaton, who had a son by a previous marriage, also named Isaac.[49] The elder Isaac died in 1774 at the age of sixty-nine and his son, Mary's step-

---

[47] Venn, *Alumni Cantabrigienses* 2.2, 175. A detailed account of the intrigues is provided by Winstanley, *Cambridge in the XVIIIth Century*, 266-281, especially 278-279.

[48] See below at 167-168.

[49] On 19 February 1731 an Isaac Heaton married Sarah Watts at Little Ilford in Essex, now part of the London metropolitan area, and their son Isaac was baptised on 9 May 1734 at the Independent Meeting

brother, received the bulk of his estate, including property at Peckham, just east of Camberwell. There were no other close kin and the younger Isaac never married; when he died in 1810 his lengthy will left several bequests to Mary and her son William, while her husband, now Sir Claude, was his residual legatee and sole Executor.[50]

The Heaton family was locally significant: there was a public house called the Heaton Arms and also Heaton's Folly. A building with a tower, set in a pleasant park with a lake, it was said to have been constructed to provide work for local labourers at a time of distress. Though widely known and admired, it was demolished in the early nineteenth century.[51]

Heaton's Folly, Peckham, in 1804
from Walford, Old and New London

Besides this inherited wealth, Claude was a successful Advocate at the Court of Arches, and in 1782 he was named Receiver of the Rights and Perquisites of the Admiralty, otherwise known as Receiver of Droits. In this same year the death of his mother Anne nee Fonnereau and of his uncle Claude of South Sea House brought further property by inheritance.

The Droits of Admiralty refer to the claim of the Royal Navy to a broad variety of goods and property abandoned or lost and found at sea, together with whales, sturgeon and other large fish, and it notably included salvage and treasure, including ships and cargoes taken at sea during time of war. Given the frequent conflicts of the eighteenth century, and the general

---

House of St George in the East at Old Gravel Lane in Stepney. It is appears likely that this Isaac Heaton is the father, born about 1705, that Sarah nee Watts born about 1711 was his first wife, and that their child Isaac Heaton was Mary's future half-brother.

In that scenario Isaac Heaton was a London merchant, and the change from non-conformism to the Anglican church reflected his increasing prosperity and perhaps also the influence of his second wife.

[50] Isaac Heaton's will of 23 September 1808 was proven on 13 July 1810.

Heaton was later used as a given name by the family. Heaton CdeC (1796-1858) led an erratic life: having served in the Royal Navy during the Napoleonic wars, he was ordained as a clergyman and married to a bishop's daughter, but he also fought a duel and was later divorced and defrocked; he went to Australia and died in the goldfields of Ballarat.

[51] Walford, *Old and New London* 6 has an illustration of the Folly at 289 and discussion at 291, with an extensive quotation from the antiquarians Daniel and Samuel Lysons who described the site in 1796; see also http://www.exploringsouthwark.co.uk/heatons-folly/4593584044 with mention of the Heaton Arms, demolished in the 1990s.

The *Reveley Book*, 15a, attributes the work to the younger Isaac, whom it describes as an energetic and extravagant gardener.

CHAPTER FIVE

success of the British fleet, the Receiver's office must have been busy and profitable. The official salary was £300 a year, but many cases must have provided opportunity for additional fees.[52]

Claude's wife Mary was admired as a woman of letters, composing both prose and poetry. She kept a voluminous journal, her *Letters of Advice from a Mother to her Son* "obtained universal approbation," her verse was widely circulated, and she is believed to have been the anonymous author of a novel, *The Pavillion*. In 1801 a concert at the Theatre Royal in Haymarket, attended by many ladies of distinction, featured "NAVAL GLORY, a Grand Thanksgiving Ode, written by Mrs Crespigny, in honour of our splendid Victories."[53]

Mary was also an enthusiast of archery, and in the same year 1801 she became Patroness of the Royal Toxophilite Society; Patron was the Prince of Wales, later Prince Regent and then King George IV.

*Meeting of the Society of Royal British Archers or Royal Toxophilite Society
in Gwersyllt Park, Denbighshire.*
*1794 aquatint by Cornelis Apostool after a painting by John Emes.
The three-feather badge of the Prince of Wales appears at the base as part of the dedication.*

Having developed this royal connection, on 23 June 1804 Claude and Mary Crespigny received the Prince of Wales at a grand reception in Champion Lodge. There are several accounts of the occasion, but an early report in *The Gentleman's Magazine* describes a *fête champêtre* [country fair/garden party] attended by five hundred noble and distinguished guests. When the prince arrived with his suite at 3 pm he was welcomed with a guard of

---

[52] *The Gentleman's Magazine* 1818, 187-188, recording his death, says that Claude had held the appointment for nearly half a century; in fact, it was just over thirty-five years.

[53] An advertisement for the concert appeared in the *Morning Post* on 14 May 1801, and *Letters of Advice* may be found in Google Books. There is further detail on Lady Mary, including an account of her archery, at https://ayfamilyhistory.com/2013/05/06/a-toxophilite-mary-de-crespigny-nee-clarke-1749-1812/.

honour from the Camberwell Volunteers – Claude was the Major-Commandant – and was entertained with music and a song composed for the occasion. He was then escorted by Mrs Crespigny through winding paths, past some romantic masked gypsies, to a fairground with booths kept by pretty young ladies, while others danced in farming and gardening costumes with rakes and floral garlands. Twenty years after Marie Antoinette of France had found leisure at the *Hameau* of Versailles, and twelve years since her death under the guillotine, the royalty, nobility and gentry of Britain still enjoyed the simple country life.[54]

Fifteen months later, on 5 October 1805 the *London Gazette* reported that Claude Champion de Crespigny had been granted the dignity of a Baronet of the United Kingdom of Great Britain and Ireland. Sir Claude and Lady de Crespigny attended court, where Lady de Crespigny was noted for the elegance and richness of her dresses and the quality of her jewellery. Fitting their new status, the baronets took the full surname Champion de Crespigny, abbreviated on occasion to the more convenient de Crespigny.

Sir Claude Champion de Crespigny, first baronet, and his wife Mary nee Clark
Portraits by an unknown English artist, possibly Thomas Beach; both at Kelmarsh Hall, Northamptonshire[55]

In 1809, five years after the fete for the Prince of Wales, Sir Claude and Lady Mary held a final reception for five hundred guests at Champion Lodge and then took up residence in Lincoln's Inn Fields, a fashionable area in the City of London close to Doctors Commons and the Inns of Court. The Lodge was left empty and the contents were sold off in 1830.[56]

Mary de Crespigny died on 20 July 1812 at Richmond House in Twickenham, which had lately been purchased by her husband. Sir Claude died in London on 26 January 1818. They were both buried at the church of St Giles in Camberwell.

Marks is no doubt right to suggest that eighty years after the original purchase the country setting of Denmark Hill had become more crowded and less attractive. The Lodge remained with the family but was no longer lived in, and eventually in the 1840s Sir Claude William the third baronet had the buildings demolished and divided the land for housing.[57]

---

[54] *The Gentleman's Magazine*, 74.2, 621-622. Parallel accounts appear in most local histories of Camberwell.
[55] On Thomas Beach (1738-1806), see the comments by Alex Kidson at 158 above.
[56] The *Morning Post* of 18 March 1830 advertised a comprehensive sale of furniture and other effects, and an auction of the balance of the library, with many rare and valuable books, was announced in the issue of 10 December 1831. This last was the dispersal so bitterly regretted by Sir Claude William: Chapter One at 14.
[57] Allport, *Collections*, 81, and Marks, "Family in Camberwell," 5.

CHAPTER FIVE

*Map Seventeen: detail from the Ordnance Survey First Series Sheet 7
showing Camberwell and Peckham in the early nineteenth century*
The red hexagonal and oval show the approximate site of Champion Lodge, now demolished, and the general area of the surrounding park between two large roads; the orange diamond shows the site of St Giles Church.
The purple rectangle marks Peckham Lodge, residence of Isaac Heaton, father and son; Heaton's Folly and its park are identified to the east.

Born in 1765, **William** was fifty years old when he succeeded his father as the second baronet. He had had a successful career in his own right: educated at Eton and Trinity Hall, he gained his law degree from Cambridge in 1786 and was married in that year to Lady Sarah Windsor, a daughter of the Earl of Plymouth. With five sons and five daughters, the family lived close to Southampton and the New Forest, but there was property in Carmarthenshire, Wales, and William was a member of the North Gloucestershire militia, reaching the rank of Lieutenant-Colonel commanding. Nearer to home, he was Provincial Grand Master of the Freemasons of Hampshire.

In 1796, as Britain was allied with Prussia against revolutionary France, William was offered a diplomatic post at Berlin and a baronet's title to go with it – which would have given him precedence over his father. The arrangement fell through,, however, when King Frederick William of Prussia made peace with the French.[58]

In 1818 William stood for Parliament in the large borough of Southampton, which had a population of eight thousand with seven hundred electors.[59] It was an expensive constituency, long controlled by the Rose family, but William was successful – partly because people were unsure whether he would support the government or the opposition. It appears that William was too, for his maiden speech was generally regarded as incoherent and incompetent. Later, however, he developed a successful style as a critic of the government, and took a strong stand against those responsible for the massacre of Peterloo at Manchester in 1819, when cavalry charged a gathering of sixty thousand people calling for parliamentary reform: fifteen

---

[58] Marks, "Family at Camberwell," 4.
[59] On the electoral system of this time, see the discussion below relating to William's uncle Philip at 171.

were killed and several hundred injured. William was also a supporter of proposals to assist the poor and lower classes. He held his seat until 1826, and died on 28 December 1829.[60]

Four of William' five sons were in the Royal Navy during the Napoleonic Wars, two of them reaching the rank of Captain. Augustus James in particular, who was born in 1791, served under Admirals Nelson and Collingwood. He was a midshipman on *HMS Spartiate* at Trafalgar in 1805 and was later celebrated for saving men from drowning on three separate occasions. He died of yellow fever at Port Royal, Jamaica, in 1825; his son Claude William (1818-1868) succeeded to the baronetcy.[61] Sir Claude William's son was the energetic fourth baronet Sir Claude (1847-1935),[62] and the title ended with the death of the eighth baronet Sir Vivian Tyrrell in 1952. Those matters, however, require another history.

Philip (1738-1803) the younger, Member of Parliament
Second son of his father Philip and Anne nee Fonnereau, and younger brother of Claude, **Philip** was born on 1 April 1738. Though he too was probably educated at Eton, he did not attend a university but was apprenticed as an articled clerk at the Court of Arches under his father. Admitted as a Proctor in 1759 at the age of twenty-one, in 1768 he was appointed a King's Proctor, acting for the government in cases before the High Court of Admiralty.[63]

Philip Champion Crespigny (1738-1803)
portrait from the school of John Russell (1745-1806)
[*Both pictures at Kelmarsh Hall, Northamptonshire*]

Betsy Hodges nee Handley (1743-1772)
second wife of Philip Champion Crespigny
portrait possibly by Thomas Beach[64]

Philip had four wives. His first marriage, on 24 November 1762, was to Sarah the daughter of Thomas Henry and Lydia Cocksedge. Cocksedge is quite a common surname in East Anglia,

---

[60] On Sir William CdeC, see Marks, "Family at Camberwell," 4, and historyofparliamentonline.org/atvolume/1790-1820/member/de-crespigny-sir-william-champion-1765-1829 [Brian Murphy] volume/1790-1820/constituencies/southampton [R G Thorne and Brian Murphy] and volume/1820-1832/constituencies/Southampton [Howard Spencer and Philip Salmon].

[61] See Anne's Family History *sub voce*. Augustus James' memorial inscription in the parish church of Port Royal notes that he was in the British fleet under Nelson at the battle of Trafalgar in 1805. He would have been sixteen years old at that time.

[62] See Chapter Two at 68-69.

[63] Philip is discussed by Bell, "Huguenot Family," 52ff and at http://www.historyofparliamentonline.org/volume/1754-1790/member/crespigny-philip-champion-1803 [Mary M Drummond]. See also Anne's Family History: ayfamilyhistory.blogspot.com.au/2014/03/philip-champion-de-crespigny-1738-1803.

[64] See the comments by Alex Kidson at 158 above. But note also the similarity to the pastel portrait on that page, identified as Ann Crespigny.

CHAPTER FIVE

but Thomas Henry had been the Recorder of the borough of Thetford in Norfolk, a judicial position held by a senior lawyer. He had died earlier that year, and his will, proven on 13 March, left wide-spread holdings of property in Norfolk, Suffolk, Essex and Cambridgeshire to his daughter Sarah and thus to Philip.[65]

Philip and Sarah had four children: Thomas (1763-1799), Philip (1765-1851); Jane (1766-1785) and Anne (1768-1844). Sarah died, however, in April 1768, very likely from problems associated with the birth of her second daughter Anne; she was buried in the family vault at Marylebone.

Philip's second wife was Betsy Hodges nee Handley.[66] Her father Joseph was a medical practitioner at St Albans in Hertfordshire, where she was born in August 1743. At the age of seventeen in April 1765 she married the Reverend George Borradale, and in July 1767 she bore him a son. Early in the following year, however, she met Francis William Bellis of St Martin-in-the-Fields, engaged him in "criminal conversation," committed "the foul crime of adultery with him at several places," notably London Hotel at Leicester Fields, now Leicester Square – described as a *bagnio*[67] – and stayed with him for several days at Wine-Office Court on Fleet Street. In February 1769 George Borradale sued for divorce at the Court of Arches.[68]

There is one strange circumstance in an otherwise straightforward case: while the various proprietors and servants testified to the adulterous couple sharing a room with a single bed, the witness John Drysdale of the London Hotel also described how

> …in a day or two afterwards a gentleman, whom the deponent believes to be the Reverend George Borradale, party in this cause, and the lady by him before-mentioned, came together to the deponent's master's said house, and such lady said to the deponent, that the gentleman who was with her was her husband, that she had run away from him, and that the deponent need not be afraid to speak what he knew…

And Rebecca Wolley, a servant at Wine-Office Court, told how

> …the said lady told the deponent, that the truth was, that the said gentlemen, meaning Mr Borradale, was her husband, and that she had run away with the other gentleman [Mr Bellis], and the said lady hath confessed to the deponent, that she was a week with the said gentleman at a *bagnio*…

John Drysdale and very likely other servants were evidently given explicit permission to speak in order that they might feel free to do so without injuring the reputation of their lodging houses for discretion regarding other couples. Given such ostentatious behaviour by husband and wife, and given that divorce could be granted only on account of the husband's cruelty or the wife's adultery, we must assume a degree of collusion.[69] There would have

---

[65] Philip refers to these properties in his will of 18 March 1797, though he had made adjustments to the original holdings: Norfolk Record Officehttp://www.nationalarchives .gov.uk/a2a/records.aspx?cat= 153-wls& cid=23-19#23-19 and http://www.legislation.gov.uk/cy/changes/chron-tables/private/17 at *c123*.

[66] From the Marriage Allegation made on 29 March 1765, whereby her father formally consented to her marriage as a minor, it appears that her given names were Betsy Hodges: http://search.ancestry.com/cgi-bin/sse.dll?indiv=1&db=SurreyMarriage&h=580561&tid=&pid=&usePUB=true&usePUBJs=true&rhSource=9852. Betsy sometimes appears as Betsey, while Hodges was presumably a family surname, possibly on her mother's side: *cf.* Heaton Champion de Crespigny in note 50 above.

[67] The term *bagnio*, from the Italian *bagno*, originally described a bath-house, then indicated a coffee-house which provided Turkish baths. By the middle of the eighteenth century, however, it was a place offering rooms for long- or short-term let with no questions asked.

[68] Anonymous, *Trials for Adultery* VII, 57-77. On the types of publications dealing with divorce at this time, including *Trials for Adultery*, see Stone, *Road to Divorce*, 248-255.

[69] Stone, *Road to Divorce*, 141. Cruelty was not mentioned in this case, but at 183 Stone remarks further that "Uncontested or nominally contested suits brought by the husband were usually part of a collusive arrangement by which both parties conspired together to prepare the ground for a parliamentary divorce."

been great trouble with such a case in the 1920s and 1930s, but the court at this time had no problem approving the divorce, and the affair was immortalised in a book of salacious gossip.

While divorce in the Court of Arches allowed the couple to separate, however, it did not give either party the right to remarry. That required a private act of Parliament: it was an extremely expensive process, but the successful suit in the ecclesiastical court could prepare the ground for such an application.

Whatever may have been intended or expected, however, the situation changed when George Borradale died a few months after the conclusion of the case: his will dated 7 September 1769 was proved on 17 January 1770.[70] Being now his widow, albeit divorced, Betsy was free, and she married Philip Crespigny later in 1770 or in 1771.[71]

Betsy, however, died in May of 1772. As with Philip's first wife Sarah, her death came in consequence of childbirth. She too was buried at Marylebone. Her son Charles was baptised at St Giles Camberwell on 1 June 1772, but died when he was two years old; he was buried at St Albans, home of Betsy's parents, on 21 October 1774.

On 1 July 1774 Philip married Clarissa Sarah, youngest daughter of James and Hester Brooke; born in 1755, she was nineteen years old. The wedding was held at St Marylebone, the church where the family maintained its burial vault.

Clarissa and Philip had four children: Clarissa (1775-1836); Maria (1776-1858); Harry (1777; died in infancy) and Fanny (1779-1865). In 1780 Clarissa and her two elder daughters were painted by George Romney: the commission is recorded in his diary; it cost £50.

Portrait of Clarissa nee Brooke (1755-1782), third wife of Philip Champion Crespigny, with her daughters Clarissa and Maria 1780; painted by George Romney (1734-1802)[72]
Source: Kidson, George Romney, complete catalogue

Clarissa's father was evidently a man of private means. His obituary in 1807 makes no mention of a formal profession, but notes his literary abilities, his reputation as a fine wit, and his wide acquaintance with the leading intellectuals of his age, including Dr Samuel Johnson, the actor and theatre manager David Garrick, and the political agitator John Wilkes. This last,

---

[70] George Borradale left his estate to his son George Aris Tilden Borradale, but predictably made no mention of his former wife. George Aris Tilden matriculated at Merton College, Oxford, in 1784; he died in 1800.

[71] It is very likely that Philip met Betsy in the course of her divorce case, and it is possible that he was involved in some fashion with the legalities of the affair, but there is no further information.

[72] The painting is no longer in the possession of the family; it was last transferred from a private seller to a private buyer through Leger Galleries of London in 1986.

CHAPTER FIVE

celebrated for his opposition to the political influence of George III and particularly to the king's favourite, Prime Minister Lord Bute, founded the journal *The North Briton* to wage his campaign; for his issue number 45, criticising a royal speech, he was charged with seditious libel but the case became a symbol of free speech. When Wilkes relinquished his position as editor, James Brooke took over and maintained the magazine – with less controversy – for several years, while publishing on his own account a number of political and literary pieces and pamphlets.[73]

Clarissa died in May 1782 at the age of twenty-seven. The obituary of her father James recalls her as an amiable and accomplished lady who had died in the prime of life.[74] She was buried in the family vault at the church of St Marylebone, where she had been married just six years before.

Philip's fourth wife was Dorothy Scott, who was born on 15 November 1765 to Richard and Elizabeth Scott of Betton Strange, a village just south of Shrewsbury in Shropshire. Dorothy's father died in 1770, her brother George succeeded as a minor, and Dorothy was also a minor, aged seventeen, when she married Philip on 20 February 1783.

Dorothy's portrait was painted by George Romney in 1790: a sitting for "Mrs Chrspaney" is recorded in his diary for 2.30 in the afternoon of Wednesday 17 March; the commission was worth £42. The painting was sold through Christie's by Dorothy's great-grandson George Harrison CdeC on 27 April 1901 and realised £5,880. It is now in the Philadelphia Museum of Art in the United States.

Philip Champion Crespigny MP (1738-1803)
portrait by John Opie (1761-1807)
at Kelmarsh Hall, Northamptonshire

Dorothy nee Scott (1765-1837)
fourth wife of Philip Champion Crespigny
portrait by George Romney 1790

Philip and Dorothy had four children: George (1783-1813), Elizabeth/Eliza (1784-1831), Charles Fox or Charles James Fox (1785-1875) named for the leading politician of the day, and Dorothea, who was born in 1800 but died in that same year.

Philip was married to Dorothy for twenty years until his death in January 1803. In March of the following year she married the baronet Sir John Keane, and in November 1805, when

---

[73] Taylor, *Literary Panorama* III (March 1808), 1354-1355.
[74] *The Gentleman's Magazine*, November 1807, 1080.

she was thirty-nine years old, she bore him a son, George Michael Keane. Dorothy died in 1837 at the age of seventy-one.

In 1774 Philip Crespigny entered parliamentary politics, and in the years that followed he developed a substantial interest.

In the system of the time, each of forty counties returned two members to the House of Commons, and there were also two hundred enfranchised boroughs, most of which likewise returned two members.[75] The qualifications of electors varied. Women could not vote, but in some places all male residents could, while in others the right was restricted to freemen – not always clearly defined – and numbers ranged from a thousand to less than fifty.

There were formal procedures for elections, but practice was erratic. Voting was public, polling was held over the course of several days, and the occasion was regularly accompanied by drinking and other entertainment, with a fair possibility of violence. The level and degree of competition depended upon circumstance: local interests were often more important than questions of national importance, and many seats were uncontested, with only two candidates willing to stand. Above all, elections were expensive: though direct bribery was formally forbidden, candidates were expected to be generous, and either the voters themselves or those who controlled them expected some form of recognition. Figures varied by circumstances, but any seat cost thousands of pounds, and expenditure for some large constituencies, fiercely contested, was in the tens of thousands.

Even when the counting was over, a defeated candidate could appeal by petition to the House of Commons, disputing the legitimacy of his opponent's voters, charging him with bribery, or protesting the conduct of the contest as a whole. Either the House itself or a committee would determine the case – and at that level too there was room for negotiation and perhaps undue influence.

When Claude Fonnereau purchased his great house Christchurch near Ipswich in Suffolk he also acquired influence in the boroughs of Sudbury and Aldeburgh.[76] In 1741, the year after Claude's death, his son Thomas Fonnereau became the first of the family to benefit from this patronage. He was returned unopposed in Sudbury, accompanied by another wealthy landowner Carteret Leathes; both were supporters of Prime Minister Robert Walpole. By the time of the next General Election in 1747 Thomas had largely gained control of Aldeburgh as well: there was government interest against him, but his brother Zachary Philip took one of the two seats.

The two boroughs were very different: both returned two members to the House of Commons, but while Aldeburgh had only 50 men entitled to vote, Sudbury was a sizable town with some 800 voters and extremely difficult to control: every election was contested and the borough was known for its independence and its corruption.

At the General Election of 1774 Philip Crespigny joined his uncle Thomas Fonnereau as candidates for Sudbury. By local tradition the Mayor of the time acted as Returning Officer, with power to determine who was entitled to vote, and Fonnereau influence and money were sufficient to determine the ballot: Thomas received 181 votes and Philip 179, while their opponents had 74 and 73. Since each constituent had two votes, however, and the potential number was sixteen hundred, it was clear that many had been disfranchised; fourteen hundred votes had been counted in the election of 1768. When the unsuccessful candidates petitioned the House of Commons, Thomas Fonnereau and Philip Crespigny were unseated.

---

[75] There are many books on different aspects of the electoral system of the eighteenth century, including those by Grego, O'Gorman, Phillips and Cook. http://www.historyofparliamentonline.org has an excellent survey; the same site provides essays by various scholars on each constituency and on every member.

[76] On Christchurch, see above at 154. During the eighteenth century the name of the place now known as Aldeburgh was regularly written Aldeborough. For consistency, I use the present-day spelling.

CHAPTER FIVE

Thomas Fonnereau died in 1779, but Philip was a candidate in the election of 1780. This time he obtained 344 votes, ten more than the third-placed contender; again, however, he lost the seat on appeal.

Ten years later, in 1790, Philip managed to have his eldest son Thomas, born of Sarah nee Cocksedge, elected in Sudbury. This, however, was something of a last hurrah: Thomas Crespigny served only one term in Parliament, he did not contest the seat at the election of 1796, and he died three years later. His successor in 1796 was William Smith, a former opponent now endorsed by the Crespignys, but family influence was in decline and by 1800 another contender was able to assure his allies that "The interest of Crespigny is *extinct*."[77] In practice, the electorate was so large, and so vulnerable to outside money, that "Without government assistance it was very difficult for a private interest to survive in such an expensive borough."[78]

Map Eighteen: The County of Suffolk,
from John Cary's New and Correct English Atlas *published in 1787*
Sudbury on the west, Ipswich in the centre and Aldeburgh [Aldeborough] on the east are indicated with red; Stowmarket, the area of the elder Philip Crespigny's purchases in the 1750s, and Thetford in Norfolk, home of the younger Philip Crespigny's first wife Sarah Cocksedge, are marked with blue.

Aldeburgh, however, was small, and provided better opportunity. When Zachary Philip Fonnereau won his seat in 1747 he was obliged to share the place with a government candidate, but at the election of 1761 he was joined by his eldest son Philip and the borough remained thereafter in family control. Philip retired in 1768, but Zachary Philip's brother Thomas joined him in 1773: though he lost Sudbury on petition in the following year he

---

[77] historyofparliamentonline.org: Sudbury 1790-1820 [Winifred Stokes/R G Thorne].
[78] historyofparliamentonline.org: Sudbury 1754-1790 [J A Cannon].

remained secure in Aldeburgh. Thomas was succeeded there by his son Martyn, but Philip Crespigny followed the same insurance policy in 1780: displaced in Sudbury, he joined Martyn as a successful candidate in Aldeburgh.

Martyn did not stand at the General Election of 1784, but Philip Crespigny did, entrenching his position by introducing "honorary freeman" to vote as he wished. He did not himself stand at the election of 1790, but he had firm control of the borough and nominated candidates of his own persuasion. At his death in 1803 his will passed his interest to his brother Claude, future baronet, to act on behalf of Philip's son Charles Fox Crespigny, then aged eighteen. When Charles Fox Crespigny came of age three years later he took over management of the borough, but after the death of Sir Claude in 1818 he sold his control for £39,000.

Overall, in the seventy years which followed the election of Zachary Philip Fonnereau in 1747, Aldeburgh saw only one contested election: in 1812 the Marquess of Salisbury sponsored candidates but the Crespigny "guests" won handsomely – and each had paid £6000 for the endorsement. This was indeed a pocket borough, and lucrative too.[79]

When he first entered Parliament in 1780, Philip Crespigny supported the Tory Prime Minister Lord North, who arranged a pension for Philip's wife Clarissa nee Brooke to compensate for the expenses of his election campaign. When Clarissa died a few months later, however, the payments ceased.

In 1781 the surrender of Yorktown confirmed the loss of the American colonies, and North was forced from office in the following year. He returned to power soon afterwards in loose alliance with the radical Whig Charles James Fox (1749-1806), and Philip transferred his allegiance. His second son by his fourth wife Dorothy nee Scott, born in 1785, was baptised Charles [James] Fox. Fox may have been a godfather – one assumes he and Philip were well acquainted – but no detailed record is available. The baptism was carried out by the noted clergyman Dr John Warner, a friend of the family: one account claims that he was first baptised just as Charles and a second ceremony had to be held to add Fox; another suggests there was such confusion that Warner decided to give him all three names.[80]

In practice, Philip voted with Fox's group against governments headed first by the Earl of Shelburne and later by the long-serving Prime Minister William Pitt. Records of speeches in Parliament are incomplete, but Philip's only recorded contribution was in 1781, when he argued strongly against a bill to exclude government contractors from membership of the house – since the Fonnereaus were heavily engaged in such affairs, including the supply of foodstuffs to the garrison at Gibraltar, Philip's advocacy in their cause is not surprising. The measure passed in 1782, but Philip was not affected: the core of his career was in the Court of Arches, and his private wealth was not dependent upon official trade.

In 1781, soon after Philip had entered Parliament, the journal *English Chronicle* remarked that:

> His hauteur is so distinguished, that he is generally characterised...by the profane, though very applicable appellation, of *God Almighty*.[81]

On the other hand Dr Warner has described an evening at Champion Lodge: "... dining at Camberwell with Claude Crespigny, Phil's elder brother, Phil and many others. An immense

---

[79] historyofparliamentonline.org: Aldeburgh 1754-1790 [John Brooke] and 1790-1820 [Winifred Stokes].

[80] See the *Reveley Book* 20b-21a and Stephen CdeC, "Bookplates and Family Trees," 95.

He is commonly referred to as Charles Fox, and his will of 1867 and a codicil of 1869 have his name as Charles Fox Champion Crespigny. Venn, *Alumni Cantabrigienses* 2.2, 175, however, identifies him as "Crespigny or de Crespigny, Charles [James] Fox Champion," and a letter of 9 January 1858 to his son Philip Robert in Australia was signed with the initials CJC.

[81] Quoted by historyofparliamentonline.org: 1754-1790 Philip Champion Crespigny [Mary M Drummond]; I have not been able to find the original citation.

dinner and an ocean of claret."[82] On another occasion the two men and another friend dealt with a bottle of white wine, a bottle of port, a magnum of claret, and two bottles of burgundy.

The Gentleman's Magazine of 1803 gave Philip a generous obituary:

> He was a man of extensive knowledge, possessed a taste for literature, and wrote two numbers in the periodical paper "The World," ... though at that time Mr C. must have been very young; a proof that his taste and talents were, however, mature, as "The World" was enriched by contributions from the most distinguished wits of the period. ..... very much the man of fashion in his person and demeanour; full of anecdote, and with a turn for satirical humour that rendered him a very amusing companion.[83]

Indeed, Philip appears to have inherited his father's gregarious nature and had a wide circle of friends. He became a Freemason in 1780, the same year as he entered Parliament, and in the following year he was Grand Steward of the Royal Somerset House and Inverness Lodge. His address at that time was number 4, Old Palace Yard, an elegant residential terrace next to the houses of parliament in the Palace of Westminster.

Left: The Old Palace of Westminster, containing the houses of parliament, before it was largely destroyed by fire in 1834; the gated entrance to Old Palace Yard is on the right. Right: Numbers 6 and 7, Old Palace Yard, the last remaining building of the former terrace.

Philip was interested in houses and land: he owned a great deal and took others on leasehold. He acquired several estates in East Anglia through his first wife Sarah nee Cocksedge; at the time of his marriage to Clarissa nee Brooke he was living at Burwood House near Walton on Thames in Surrey, south of present-day Heathrow airport, and he had another place in Hertfordshire. Crespigny House at Aldeburgh in Suffolk was built by Philip's brother Claude the future baronet in 1775, but Philip naturally owned considerable property at the heart of his political position, and he held a lease on Hintlesham Hall, east of Ipswich in Suffolk and mid-way between the constituencies of Sudbury and Aldeburgh. This was the time of his marriage to Dorothy Scott in 1783: three of their four children were born at Hintlesham Hall and the family continued to use it after Philip's death.

Philip later extended his interest westwards to Bath. In the mid-1780s the local architect John Eveleigh designed a handsome terrace at Portland Place, now listed as Grade 1 by Historic England; the central house was constructed specifically for Philip Crespigny.

Still further afield, in 1794 Philip purchased the manor of Llangasty Talyllyn, with an estate of two thousand acres a few miles east of Brecon in Wales. He was High Sheriff of the County of Brecknock or Breconshire in 1796, and in his will of 1797 he described himself as living at Talyllynn House.[84] He died, however, in his house at Bath on 1 January 1803.

---

[82] Marks, "Family in Camberwell," 4. There is a biography of the talented but eccentric Dr Warner in Fyvie, *Wits, Beaux and Beauties*, 287-317, with accounts of copious eating and drinking at 313-314.
[83] *The Gentleman's Magazine* 73.1, 89.
[84] https://www.lime.org.uk/history-of-the-farm/.

Thirty-four pages long, including ten codicils, Philip's will was proved at London on 7 March 1803. In making provision for the surviving sons and daughters of his four wives, and the disposition of the settlements related to their marriages, he identified "messuages, farms, lands, tenements, hereditaments and real estate" in Suffolk – including Aldeburgh – Norfolk, Cambridgeshire, Westminster, Bath and Breconshire. George and Charles Fox, his two sons by Dorothy nee Scott, were residual legatees, while Dorothy, her brother Richard Scott, Philip's brother Claude the future baronet, and a close friend Stafford Squire Baxter were named as Executors. He was clearly a man of very real wealth.[85]

Hintlesham Hall near Ipswich in Suffolk – now a hotel – in 2004

Portland Place, Bath, in 2014: the house with the gable was built for Philip Crespigny.

---

[85] A photocopy of the will, and a typescript transcription, is provided by Grayden, *Chronicle*, 22. The manuscript is messy, with many corrections and erasures. It would present serious problems for a modern probate, but was approved with statements on oath from the executors and attorneys.

CHAPTER FIVE

Philip Crespigny's holdings in Breconshire, Wales.
An aerial view, looking towards the north, presented by Clwyd Powys Archaeological Trust
The estate extended from Cathedine, shown at the middle right, to Llangasty Talyllyn on the further left across an arm of Lake Llangors.

The children of Philip the younger:
Philip had thirteen children by his four wives, and ten of them were living when he died in 1803. Though a detailed account of the family in the nineteenth century lies beyond the scope of this work, it seems appropriate to summarise the situation in the following generation.[86]
Philip and Sarah nee Cocksedge had four children:

Thomas, born in 1763, was Philip's eldest son. He became a Scholar of Trinity Hall at Cambridge, obtained a bachelor's and then a doctoral degree in law, was admitted as an Advocate at the Court of Arches and was elected Member of Parliament for the borough of Sudbury in 1790. On 26 March 1798 he married Augusta Charlotte Thellusson; her father Peter/Pierre, a wealthy Swiss merchant of Huguenot descent, had settled in London and was a Director of the Bank of England Their wedding was held at St George's Hanover Square.

The Thellusson family had property at Bromley in Kent, now part of greater London, and Thomas and Augusta Charlotte's daughter Augusta Anne was baptised there at the church of St Peter and St Paul on 1 July 1799. One month later, however, Thomas died on 2 August 1799; he was buried at the church of St Peter and St Paul in Aldeburgh.

In 1827 Augusta Charlotte CdeC nee Thellusson married Joseph Whatley; they had no children. He died in 1844, and she in 1853.

Augusta Anne CdeC married Thomas Henry Hastings Davies in 1824. He had fought at Waterloo as an officer in the 1st Foot Guards and was later a Member of Parliament; he died in 1846. In 1851 Augusta Anne married John Somerset Russell, also a Member of Parliament; he died in 1880 and she in 1892. She had no children.

---

[86] Much of the information which follows is based upon the eighteenth edition of *Burke's Landed Gentry*, though there is additional detail on some individuals in Anne's Family History.

Philip, born in 1765, served as a Midshipman during the American Revolutionary War, but later became a Proctor at the Court of Arches and purchased Harefield House, near Uxbridge, west of London, in 1796. As the Treaty of Amiens in 1802 brought a halt to the war against Napoleon he travelled to France, but was interned there when conflict resumed in May 1803. He was held for a time at the fortress town of Verdun, but later moved to Saint-Germain-en-Laye near Paris, and managed to escape in 1811. While he was in France he met Emelia Wade, a woman of wealthy family, and they married in 1809. She died in 1832 and he in 1851; there were no children.

Jane, born in 1766, died unmarried in 1785 at the age of nineteen.

Anne, born in 1768, married Hugh Owen Barlow in 1791. Born in 1729, he was Member of Parliament for Pembroke Boroughs from 1774 until his death in 1809. They had no children and she died in 1844.

Philip and Betsy nee Handley had one child:

Charles was born in 1772 but died in 1774.

Philip and Clarissa nee Brooke had four children:

Clarissa, born in 1775, married Edward Toker of Kent in 1801, and had children. She died in 1836.

Maria, born in 1776, married Captain John Horsley of the Royal Horse Guards in 1804.

In the following year a fellow-officer published a libel against Captain Horsley. Advised by his comrades, Horsley decided to prosecute rather than fight a duel, which was illegal. King George III, however, considered that this was cowardice, and Horsley and his allies were compelled to resign their commissions.

It appears that the marriage broke down, for when Horsley went to Australia ten years later Maria did not accompany him. They had no children.

Horsley achieved considerable success in New South Wales, acquiring property near Liverpool and becoming a magistrate and Coroner. He died in 1834, but his property went to his common-law wife Jane Cross and to the several children he had by her. Maria made enquiries but gained nothing. She died at Canterbury in 1858.[87]

Harry was born in 1777 but died soon afterwards.

Fanny was born in 1778 and died unmarried in 1865; she was Executrix to the will of her sister Maria in 1858.

Philip and Dorothy nee Scott had four children:

George was born in 1783. In 1804, the year after his father's death and soon after his mother Dorothy had married again to Sir John Keane, he was commissioned by purchase as an Ensign in the 13th Regiment of Foot, the Somerset Light Infantry, which was then at garrison in Gibraltar; he was at that time aged twenty-one.[88] He later became a Captain in the 68th Foot, the Durham Light Infantry, and he was wounded in operations at Walcheren in the Netherlands in 1809.

The regiment later joined the army commanded by Arthur Wellesley, future Duke of Wellington, in the Peninsula War against Napoleon's forces in Spain, and in October 1812 George purchased a commission as Major in that regiment; he was apparently resented by the troops as a martinet. On 30 July 1813 he was killed in action near Pamplona, during the Battle of the Pyrenees. He was not married and left no children.[89]

---

[87] Anne's Family History: http://ayfamilyhistory.blogspot.com.au/search?q=Horsley.

[88] This was the same regiment in which George's cousin Charles, son of Gabriel, had served a hundred years earlier: Chapter Four at 134; it was at that time known as the Earl of Barrymore's Regiment.

[89] Anne's Family History: http://ayfamilyhistory.blogspot.com.au/search?q=George+Crespigny, also Vane, *Durham Light Infantry*, and Ward, *Faithful*.

CHAPTER FIVE

> **Eliza** [Elizabeth] was born in 1784. In 1804, at the age of twenty, she eloped from Hintlesham Hall with Richard Hussey Vivian (1775-1842) and married him at Gretna Green in Scotland. Though the family had presumably disapproved of the union, Richard Vivian became a close comrade of the Duke of Wellington, rose to be a Lieutenant-General, and commanded a brigade of cavalry at the battle of Waterloo in 1815. A knight of the order of the Bath and for some time a member of the House of Commons, he was created Baron Vivian in 1841. Eliza died in 1831, but Crespigny became a personal name of the Vivians, and several of the CdeC family have been christened Vivian.[90]
>
> **Charles** [James] **Fox** was born in 1785.[91] In 1813 he married Eliza Julia nee Trent (1797-1855).[92] They had five children, Charles John (1814-1880), George Blick/e (1815-1893), Philip Robert (1817-1889), Julia Eliza (1819-1848) and Eliza Constantia Frances (1825-1898) He inherited the greater part of his father's estate, but died in comparative poverty in 1875.
>
> Neither of Charles Fox CdeC's daughters married, but all three of his sons married and had children. Through his third son Philip Robert he is the ancestor of the major branch of the family in Australia.
>
> **Dorothea** was born in 1800 and died in infancy.

Epilogue:

By the beginning of the nineteenth century, little more than a hundred years after Claude and Marie nee de Vierville had come to Britain as impoverished refugees, their descendants had established themselves in the highest ranks of their new community. Holders of government office, members of parliament, owners of landed properties from the east of England to the north of Wales, there was no question of their position in society. The baronetcy awarded in 1805 reflected the personal favour of the Prince Regent, there were marriages with both greater and lesser nobility, and substantial estates had been acquired by one generation after another.

This, as we have observed, is a very great change from the situation which Claude and Marie and their family had left behind in France. Regardless of titles and claims to nobility, the family in Normandy had been little more than prosperous squirearchy, with limited – and often negative – contact with the government, and no role in the broader affairs of the kingdom. Claude may have served in the army, but nothing is known of his career, and though his son Pierre/Daumont was involved in a long-drawn court case at Paris, it was a minor and literally parochial affair. At the same time, members of the family had constant difficulty in justifying their status among the *noblesse*, and an eventual success in that matter was soon followed by religious persecution and exile abroad.

In the first years of that exile, the newcomers were well accepted by their co-religionists in London, and Pierre became a leader of the community. His brothers Thomas and Gabriel held commissions in the army, but their ranks were not high, their achievements were not great and both died poor. While Gabriel's family disappeared into obscurity in Ireland, however, Thomas's children achieved impressive and prosperous careers in London. Philip qualified as a lawyer in the Court of Arches and made an excellent marriage into the wealthy

---

[90] Anne's Family History: http://ayfamilyhistory.blogspot.com.au/search?q=Vivian, and see *inter alia* the entry for Vivian, Richard Hussey by Robert Hamilton Vetch in *Dictionary of National Biography, 1885-1900* and historyofparliamentonline.org/volume/1820-1832/member/vivian-sir-richard-1775-1842.

[91] On the given names of Charles [James] Fox CdeC, see note 79 above.

[92] The wedding was held at the society church of St George in Hanover Square, London. Eliza Julia was just sixteen at the time. Her father John Trent (1770-1796) had died before she was born and her mother Elizabeth nee Phipps, now the wife of Arthur Branthwayt, gave permission for the marriage.

Fonnereau family; his brother Claude, from humble beginning as a junior clerk, became the long-serving manager of a major financial institution, the South Sea Company. They had surely received support and guidance from their uncle Pierre and from their mother's family the Grangers, but both made full use of their opportunities to acquire an education and both showed a high level of administrative ability. Patronage and good connections were valuable, but other young men had the same or better advantages, and Philip and Claude's long-term success is evidence of their personal qualities. In the following generation Philip's sons Claude and Philip the younger, now with university education, maintained and developed the same tradition of professional achievement and political success.

Crespigny in Australia

The story of the family in the nineteenth century is a good deal more complex, and it seems sensible to close the present history at this point, with two branches of the Champion de Crespigny lineage established in England. We have discussed the baronetcy, and also the children of Philip the younger, whose male lineage in the present day is traced to Charles [James] Fox CdeC, born to his fourth wife Dorothy nee Scott in 1785. In conclusion, I offer a brief summary of the family which came to Australia.

Following the end of the Napoleonic Wars in 1815, Charles Fox CdeC and his wife Eliza Julia nee Trent spent several years on the continent and their third son, Philip Robert, was born at Boulogne in 1817. In 1849 Philip Robert married Charlotte Frances nee Dana. She was formerly married to John James, a solicitor of Gloucestershire, but had been divorced by Act of Parliament earlier that year. The couple's first child Ada Isadora Charlotte (1848-1927) was born before the wedding, their son Philip (1850-1927) six months after it.

Philip Robert and Charlotte Frances lived with their children near Saint Malô in Brittany until 1851, but in December of that year they sailed to Australia, arriving at Geelong in March 1852. They took Ada and Philip with them, while their new-born second son Constantine Pulteney Trent (1851-1883) remained in England under the care of his grandparents Charles Fox and Eliza Julia. He became a Lieutenant in the army, but was obliged to retire on account of ill health in 1875. He then spent a few years in Australia – meeting his parents and siblings effectively for the first time – but returned to England in 1881 and died two years later without marriage or children.

Philip Robert became a Police/Stipendiary Magistrate in Victoria, and he and Charlotte had two daughters born in Australia: Viola Julia Constantia (1855-1929) who, like her sister Ada, never married; and Helen Rosalie [Rose] (1858-1937), who married Francis Beggs (1850-1921) but had no children. Philip Robert died in 1889, after thirteen years of paralysis; his widow Charlotte nee Dana lived at the Beggs property "Eurambeen" near Ararat until her death in 1904.

Philip Robert and Charlotte's son Philip joined the Bank of Victoria, and became General Manager in 1916. His first wife was Annie Frances nee Chauncy (1857-1883), daughter of Philip LaMothe Snell Chauncy, a government surveyor; they were married in 1877 and had two sons: Philip (1879-1918), a journalist who became Chief of Staff at the Brisbane *Daily Mail*; and Constantine Trent (1882-1952), physician and pathologist in Adelaide.

In 1891, eight years after Annie Frances' death, Philip married Sophia Montgomery Grattan Beggs (1870–1936) and they had four sons: Francis George Travers [Frank] (1892-1968), a doctor in Ararat; Hugh Vivian (1897-1969), who became an Air Vice-Marshal in the Royal Air Force; Royalieu Dana [Roy] (1905-1985), farmer and grazier in the Western Districts of Victoria; and Claude Montgomery (1908-1991), also an officer of the RAF.

BIBLIOGRAPHY

Note: I refer to a number of sources found on the internet. I do not indicate the date of access, for many sites have been viewed on different occasions. All of them, however, have been viewed and checked during calendar year 2017.

Abbott, P D, *Provinces, Pays and Seigneuries of France*, privately printed, Canberra 1981

Ackermann, Rudolf [editor and publisher], *The Microcosm of London* [3 volumes: illustrations by Charles Augustus Pugin and Thomas Rowlandson; text by William Henry Pyne (volumes 1 and 2) and William Combe (volume 3)], London 1808-1810

Agnew, David C A, *Protestant Exiles from France in the Reign of Louis XIV; or, the Huguenot refugees and their descendants in Great Britain and Ireland*, second edition [3 volumes], Reeves and Turner, London 1871-1874 [archive.org]

Allen, Joseph, *Battles of the British Navy* [2 volumes], Bell and Daldy, London 1868

Allport, Douglas, *Collections, illustrative of the Geology, History, Antiquities and associations of Camberwell and the neighbourhood*, privately printed, Camberwell 1841

Anonymous ["A Civilian"], *Trials for Adultery: or, the history of divorces. Being select Trials at Doctors Commons, for adultery, cruelty, fornication, impotence, &c. from the year 1760, to the present time..., Taken in Shorthand, by a Civilian. vol,VII*, S Bladon, London 1780 [Google Books]

Arnold, Thomas [editor], *Henrici archidiaconi huntendunensis Historia Anglorum: the History of the English by Henry, Archdeacon of Huntingdon, from A.C. 35 to A.D. 1154, in eight books* [in Latin], Longman, London 1879

Atlas de France, Editions Géographique de France, Paris 1931-*c*.1960

Bagley, J J, *Historical Interpretation: sources of English medieval history, 1066-1540*, Penguin 1965

Ball, Elaine R, "A History of the Huguenot Family of Champion de Crespigny: a consideration of their life as Huguenot gentry in France and the manner of their integration into British society following their exile," typescript, London 28 May 1973

Barker, Juliet, *Conquest: the English kingdom of France*, Little Brown, London, 2009

Blanch, William Harnett, *Ye Parish of Camerwell: a brief account of the parish of Camberwell, its history and antiquiti*es, E.W. Allan, London 1877

Bouyer, Christian, *Louis XIII: le sceptre et la pourpre 1601-1643*, Tallandier, Paris 2001

Boyd, Percival, *Boyd's London Burial Index 1538-1872*, London 1934; transcription available on the internet.

Brooke, Christopher, *The Saxon and Norman Kings*, Fontana 1967

Brooke-Little, J P, "A Brief Account of the Proceedings in the High Court of Chivalry on 21st December, 1954," in *Coat of Arms* [New Series] 21 [published by The Heraldry Society UK] January 1995

Brown, Jane, *The French Hospital: a short history*, The French Hospital, London *c*. 1980

Bruce, Anthony, *The purchase system in the British Army, 1660-1871*, Royal Historical Society, London 1980

Burke, John (1747-1848), *A General and Heraldic Dictionary of the Peerage and Baronetage of the British Empire*, fourth edition [2 volumes], Colburn and Bentley 1832 [Google Books]: cited as *Peerage and Baronetage*, with references to later editions of the nineteenth and early twentieth century, all from Google Books

—, *A Genealogical and Heraldic History of the Commoners of Great Britain and Ireland, enjoying territorial possessions or high official rank; but uninvested with heritable honours* [4 volumes], Henry Colburn, London 1835 [Google Books]

BIBLIOGRAPHY

Burke, John (1747-1848) and John Bernard (1814-1892), *A Genealogical and Heraldic Dictionary of the Landed Gentry of Great Britain* [2 volumes], Henry Colburn, London 1846-47 [Google Books]

Burke, [John] Bernard (1814-1892), *A Genealogical and Heraldic Dictionary of the Landed Gentry of Great Britain for 1852* [3 volumes], Colburn and Co, London 1852 [Google Books]

—, *A Genealogical and Heraldic Dictionary of the Landed Gentry of Great Britain & Ireland*; fourth edition [2 volumes], Harrison, London 1862-63 [Google Books]

—, *A Genealogical and Heraldic Dictionary of the Landed Gentry of Great Britain & Ireland*, fifth edition [2 volumes], Harrison, London 1871 [Google Books]

—, *Peerage*, Harrison, London 1895 [Google Books]

Burke's Genealogical and Heraldic History of the Landed Gentry [3 Volumes]: vols 1 & 2 edited by Peter Townend, 1965-69; vol. 3, with index to all three volumes, edited by Hugh Montgomery-Massingberd, 1972

Bysshe, Edward, edited by J J Howard, *A Visitation of the County of Essex, begun A.D. MDCLXIIII* [1664], *finished A.D. MDCLXVIII* [1668], Mitchell and Hughes, London 1888

Calendar of Documents preserved in France 918-1206, edited by J Horace Round, H M Stationary Office, London 1907: from *British History Online* http://www.britishhistory.ac.uk/

Calendar of the Patent Rolls preserved in the Public Records Office: Henry VI vol 2, AD 1429-1436, H M Stationery Office, London 1907: cited from Professor G R Boynton and the University of Iowa Libraries Project, at http://sdrc.lib.uiowa.edu/patentrolls/

Calendar of State Papers, Domestic: from *British History Online* http://www.britishhistory.ac.uk/

Calendar of Treasury Books, Volume 29, 1714-1715, edited by William A Shaw and F H Slingsby (London, 1957); includes Warrant Books: from *British History Online* http://www.british-history.ac.uk/cal-treasury-books/vol29

Calmette, Joseph, *Les Grands Ducs de Bourgogne*, Albin Michel, Paris 1949

Cannon, Richard, *Historical Records of the British Army: comprising the history of every regiment in Her Majesty's service: The Fourth, or King's Own, Regiment of Foot, containing an account of the formation of the regiment in 1680, and of its subsequent services to 1839*, Longman, London 1839 [archive.org]

Carter, Thomas [editor], *Historical Record of the Thirteenth, First Somersetshire or Prince Albert's Regiment of Light Infantry*, W O Mitchell, London 1867 [Google Books]

Cassini de Thury, César-François and family, *Carte générale de la France*, Paris 1744-1760

Castries, Duc de, *La du Barry*, Albin Michel, Paris 1986

Chambers, William and Robert, *Chambers' Edinburgh Journal* III, Orr and Smith, London 1845 [Google Books]

Champion de Crespigny, Claude, *Memoirs of Sir Claude Champion de Crespigny Bart*, edited by George A B Dewar, with a preface and notes by the Duke of Beaufort, K G, Lawrence and Bullen, London 1896; third edition [on the spine as *Sporting Memoirs of Sir Claude de Crespigny*], 1897

—, *Forty Years of a Sportsman's Life: with two additional chapters covering the period 1910-1924*, new and revised edition, Mills and Boon, London 1925

Champion de Crespigny, Richard Rafe, *Champions in Normandy: being some remarks on the early history of the Champion de Crespigny family*, privately published Canberra and Ararat 1988

Champion de Crespigny, Stephen, "Pedigree of the Champion de Crespignys," 3 sheets, 1965 with subsequent amendments; and a further edition by David CdeC, Melbourne 1991

—, "Bookplates and Family Trees," *The Bookplate Society Newsletter*, II.20, 1977, 92-97

—, "Huguenot Bookplates," *The Bookplate Society Newsletter*, V.3, London 1983, 27-29

Chamillart, Guy, *Généralité de Caen. Recherche de la noblesse, faite par ordre du roi, en 1666 et années suivantes* [originally in manuscript copies, but later edited by Amédée-Casimir du Buisson de Courson], H Delesques, Caen 1887

Chandler, David "The Siege of Alicante, 1708-9," in *History Today* 19.7 (July 1969), 475-485

Chant, Christopher, *The Handbook of British Regiments*, Routledge, Abingdon 2013

Chapman, Hester W, *Privileged Persons: four seventeenth-century studies*, Jonathan Cape, London 1966

Chibnall, Margaret [translator and editor], *The Ecclesiastical History of Orderic Vitalis* [6 volumes], Oxford UP 1968-1980

Childs, John, *The British Army of William III, 1689-1702*, Manchester UP 1987

Clamageran, Jean-Jules, *Histoire de l'impôt en France* [3 volumes]. Guillaumin, Paris 1867-76

Clodd, Harold Parker, *Aldeburgh: the history of an ancient borough*, Adlard, London 1959

Cobban, Alfred, *A History of Modern France, volume one: old régime and revolution*, Penguin 1957

Colart, L.-Sam, *Histoire de France méthodique et comparée, avec texts, tableaux synopotique et 75 gravures etc*, Truchy 1834 and subsequent editions [Google Books]

Cook, Hartley Kemball, *The Free and Independent: the trials, temptations and triumphs of the parliamentary elector*, George Allen and Unwin, London 1949

Coventry, P J, [editor], *France in Crisis*, Macmillan, London 1977

Cowie, L W, "The Savoy; palace and hospital," in *History Today* 24.3 (March 1974), 173-179

Dalton, C, *English Army Lists and Commissions Registers 1661-1714* [4 volumes], first published London 1892-1904; cited from http://openlibrary.org

—, *George the First's Army 1714-1727*, [2 volumes], Eyre and Spottiswood, London 1910-1912 [Hathi Trust Digital Library]

Davies, Norman, *The Isles: a history*, Macmillan, London 2000

d'Anisy, Léchaudé [compiler], *Extrait des Chartes, et autres Actes Normands ou Anglo-Normands, qui se trouve dans les archives du Calvados* [2 volumes], Caen and London 1835 [Google Books]

de Grèce, Michel, *Louis XIV: l'envers du soleil*, Pocket, Paris 2002

de Freville, Ernest, "Des grandes compagnies au quatorzième siècle. I. Leurs commencements. — Prise de Vire en 1368," in *Bibliothèque de l'école des chartes* 3.1 (1842), 258-281

Deyon, P, "The French Nobility and Absolute Monarchy in the First Half of the Seventeenth Century," in Coventry, *France in Crisis*, 231-246

Debrett's Peerage, Baronetage, Knightage and Companionage, Dean and Son, London 1885 [edited by Robert H Mair] and 1904

Delafontenelle, Jacky, *Les protestants du Bocage normand: l'histoire, de l'origine à nos jours*, Conde-sur-Noireau 2007

D'Hozier, Charles René, *Armorial générale de France*, 1696-1700 [BnF (Bibliothèque nationale de France) Gallica]

Dictionnaire de biographie française volume 8, edited by M. Prévost and Roman d'Amat, Letouzey et Ané, Paris 1959

Dunan-Page, Anne [editor], *The Religious Culture of the Huguenots, 1660-1750*, Ashgate Publishing/Routledge, Farnham 2013

BIBLIOGRAPHY

Edwards, Edward [editor], *Liber monasterii de Hyda, comprising a chronicle of the affairs of England, from the settlement of the Saxons to the reign of King Cnut; and a Chartulary of the Abbey of Hyde, in Hampshire A.D.455 – 1023*, Longmans, Green, Reader, and Dyer, London 1866

Elton, G R, *England under the Tudors*, Methuen, London 1956

Ergang, Robert, *Europe From the Renaissance to Waterloo*, Heath, Boston, 1954

Escott, Margaret M, "Profiles of Relief: Royal Bounty grants to Huguenot refugees, 1686-1709," in *HSP* XXV (1989-1993), 257-278

The Fontana Economic History of Europe, general editor Carlo M. Cipolla,
    volume 1 *The Middle Ages*, London 1972
    volume 2 *The Sixteenth and Seventeenth Centuries*, London 1974

Forester, Thomas [translator and editor], *The Chronicle of Henry of Huntingdon, comprising the history of England, from the invasion of Julius Cæsar to the accession of Henry II; also, the acts of Stephen, king of England and duke of Normandy*, Henry G Bohn, London 1853

Fox-Davies, Arthur Charles, *Armorial Families: a directory of gentlemen of coat-armour*, seventh edition [2 volumes], Hurst and Blackett, London 1929 [archive.org]

—, *A Complete Guide to Heraldry* [with revisions by Charles A H Franklyn], Thomas Nelson and Sons, London 1949

Fraser, Antonia, *The Weaker Vessel: woman's lot in seventeenth-century England*, Methuen, London 1984

Fyvie, John, *Wits, Beaux and Beauties of the Georgian Era*, The Bodley Head (John Lane), London 1909

Galland, J A, *Essai sur l'Histoire du protestantisme à Caen et en Basse Normandie, de l'Edit de Nantes à la Révolution 1598- 1791*, Grassart, Paris 1898 [Google Books]

The Gentleman's Magazine, London 1731-1922 (first published by Edward Cave as *The Gentleman's Magazine or Trader's Monthly Intelligencer*, from 1736 to 1833 it was styled *The Gentleman's Magazine and* Historical Chronicle) [Google Books]

Glozier, Matthew, *Huguenot Soldiers of William of Orange and the Glorious Revolution of 1688: the lions of Judah*, Sussex Academic Press 2002

Grayden, Bernard C [writing anonymously], *The Champion de Crespigny Chronicle*, ring-bound photocopies, Melbourne 1984 [digitised at https://dcms.lds.org]

Green, John, *The Vicissitudes of a Soldier's Life. or a series of occurrences from 1806 to 1815 ... containing ... a concise account of the War in the Peninsula ...*, privately printed Louth 1827

Green, Richard Firth, *A Crisis of Truth: literature and law in Ricardian England*, Pennsylvania UP 2002

Greenway, Diana E [translator and editor], Historia Anglorum*: the history of the English people by Henry, Archdeacon of Huntingdon*, Oxford UP 1996

Grego, Joseph, *A History of Parliamentary Elections and Electioneering from the Stuarts to Queen Victoria*, Chatto and Windus, London 1892

Goubert, Pierre, translated by Anne Carter, *Louis XIV and Twenty Million Frenchmen*, Penguin, London, 1970

Guide Hachette France, 1984

Guillim, John, and Sir George Mackenzie, *A Display of Heraldry: the sixth edition, improv'd with large additions of many hundred coats of arms*, London 1724 [Hathi Trust]

Gwynn, Robin D, "The Arrival of Huguenot Refugees in England 1680- 1705," in *HSP* XXI (1965-70), 366-73

—, *Huguenot Heritage: The history and contribution of the Huguenots in Britain*, Routledge and Kegan Paul, London, 1985

—, "England's 'First Refugees," in *History Today* 35.5 (May 1985), 22-28

Haag, Eugène and Emile, *La France protestante, ou vies des protestants français qui se sont fait un nom dans l'histoire depuis les premiers temps de la réformation jusqu'à la reconnaissance du principe de la liberté des cultes par l'Assemblée nationale; ouvrage précédé d'une notice historique sur le protestantisme en France; suivi des pièces justificatives et rédigé sur des documents en grande partie inédits* [10 volumes], first published Cherbuliez, Paris 1846-1859 [BnF (Bibliothèque nationale de France) Gallica]; second edition Sandoz et Fischbacher, Paris 1881 [Google Books]

Haldane, Charlotte, *Madame de Maintenon: uncrowned queen of France*, Bobbs-Merrill, Indianapolis 1970

Hanson, Paul, *Historical Dictionary of the French Revolution*, second edition, London 2015

Hardy, Thomas Duffus [editor], *Rotuli Normanniae in Turri Londinensi asservati: Johanne et Henrico quinto Angliae regibus*, Public Record Office, London 1835 [Google Books]

Hérelle, Georges, *Documents inédits sur le protestantisme à Vitry-le François, Epense, Heiltz-le-Maurupt, Nettancourt et Vassy depuis la fin des guerres de réligion jusqu'à la Révolution française*, Picard, Paris 1903-08

The Historians' History of the World, edited by Henry Smith Williams [25 volumes], *The Times*, London 1908

Howard, Joseph Jackson [Maltravers Herald Extraordinary] and Frederick Arthur Crisp [editors], *Visitation at England and Wales; notes volume 13*, privately printed 1919: facsimile reprint by Heritage Books, Bowie Maryland 1998 [Google Books]

HSP: *Proceedings of the Huguenot Society of London*

http://www.historyofparliamentonline.org [website]

Huet, Odette, "Champions of the Dukes of Normandy," photocopy of a paper presented 5 December 1970, with supplementary genealogical table of the Vierville/Wierville family prepared by G A Ibbetson

Jacques, Tony, *Dictionary of Battles and Sieges: a guide to 8,500 battles from antiquity to the twenty-first century, volume 1: A-E*, Greenwood Press, Westwood CO, 2007

Jeffares, Neil, *Dictionary of Pastellists before 1800*, Unicorn Press, Norwich 2006 [online as *Pastels and Pastellists* at http://www.pastellists.com]

Keen, M H, *The Laws of War in the Late Middle Ages*, Rutledge and Kegan Paul, London 1965

Kidson, Alex, *George Romney: a complete catalogue of his paintings* [3 volumes], Yale UP 2015

Kirby, John, and others, *The Suffolk Traveller* [second edition] 1764 [Google Books]

Lart, Charles E[dmund], *Huguenot Pedigrees* [2 volumes], Genealogical Pub Co, Baltimore 1967; reprint of original, London 1924-1928

Lawson, Cecil C P, *A History of the Uniforms of the British Army: from the beginnings to 1760* [3 volumes], Norman Military Publications, London 1940, 1941, 1961

Le Roy Ladurie, Emmanuel, translated by Mary Feeney, *Carnival in Romans: a people's uprising at Romans 1579-1580*, Penguin 1981

Lefroy, E H, "Some Huguenot Wills; a communication," in *HSP* XI (1915-1917), 129-137

Lincs to the past [https://www.lincstothepast.com], compiled by Lincolnshire County Council (GB)

Lublinskaya, A D, translated by Brian Pearce, *French Absolutism: the crucial phase, 1620-1629*, Cambridge UP, 1968

Manchée, W H, "Marylebone and its Huguenot Associations," in *HSP* XI (1915-1917), 58-128, with supplement at 249-255; the article was reprinted as a pamphlet by Spottiswoode, London 1916; *HSP* XI has been digitised by *The Internet Archive* in 2015

—, "Huguenot Soldiers and their Conditions of Service in the English Army," in *HSP* XVI (1937-1941), 248-265

—, "The Huguenot Regiments (Supplemental Notes)," in *HSP* XIII (1923-1929), 393-400

Marks, Stephen, "The de Crespigny Family in Camberwell," Supplement to *The Camberwell Society Newsletter* 38 (July 1977), 1-6

Mattingly, Garrett, *The Defeat of the Spanish Armada*, Jonathan Cape, London 1959

Michelin, *France: atlas routier et touristique*, Paris 2003

Minet, William, [writing anonymously], "A Note on Daumont de Crespigny," in *HSP* XIV (1929-1933), 253-256

—, and Susan Minet, *Livre des conversions et reconnaisances faites à l'église françoise de la Savoye 1684-1702*, transcribed and edited, Huguenot Society of London Publications XXII, 1914 [archive.org]

Müller [anonymous], papers on the Family of Le Champion-Marmion and von Mollerus/ Moller/Moller-Le Champion, photocopies, n.d. (*c.*1860?)

Murdoch, Tessa [compiler], *The Quiet Conquest: the Huguenots 1685-1985*, Museum of London 1985

—, "The Quiet Conquest: the Huguenots 1685-1985," in *History Today* 35.5 (May 1985), 29-33

—, and Randolph Vigne, *The French Hospital in England: its Huguenot history and collections*, John Adamson, London 2009

Namier, Sir Lewis and John Brooke, *The History of Parliament: the House of Commons, 1754-1790* [3 volumes], Oxford UP for the History of Parliament Trust 1964

Neilson, George, *Trial by Combat*, William Hodge, Glasgow 1890

Nicholas, Thomas, *Annals and Antiquities of the Counties and County Families of Wales*, [2 volumes], Longmans, Green, Reader and Co, London 1872 [Google Books]

Nicholls, John Bowyer [editor], *Illustrations of the Literary History of the Eighteenth Century consisting of authentic memoirs and original letters of eminent persons and intended as a sequel of* Literary Anecdotes, Volume IV, Nicholls, London 1822

Notes and Queries: a medium of inter-communication for literary men, general readers, etc, Third Series, Volume Eleventh, London January-June 1867

O'Day, Rosemary, *The Professions in Early Modern England, 1450-1800: servants of the commonweal*, Routledge, Oxford 2014

O'Gorman, Frank, *Voters, Patrons, and Parties: the unreformed electoral system of Hanoverian England 1734-1832*, Oxford UP 1989

The Oxford Companion to French Literature, compiled and edited by Sir Paul Harvey and J E Heseltine, Oxford UP 1969

The Oxford Dictionary of the Christian Church, edited by F L Cross, Oxford UP 1958

The Penny Cyclopædia of the Society for the Diffusion of Useful Knowledge XIX [Primaticcio-Richardson], Charles Knight, London 1841 [Google Books]

Perroy, Edouard, translated by W B Wells, *The Hundred Years War*, Capricorn, New York 1965 [first published Paris 1945]

—, "Social Mobility among the French Noblesse in the Later Middle Ages," in *Past and Present*, 21-23 (1962), 25-38

Phillips, John A, *Electoral Behaviour in Unreformed England: plumpers, splitters and straights*, Princeton UP 2014

Playfair, William, *British Baronetage: illustrative of the origin and progress of the rank, honours, and personal merit, of the baronets of the United Kingdom, accompanied with an elegant set of chronological charts*, Thomas Reynolds and Harvey Grace, London 1809-11

Potier de Courcy, Pol Louis, *Nobiliaire et armorial de Bretagne* I, Plihon et Hervé, Rennes 1890 [archive.org]

Reifenscheid, Richard, *Die Hapsburger in Lebensbildern: von Rudolph I bis Karl I*, Styria, Graz 1982

Reulos, Michel, "'Anobli aux francs fiefs:' origine et portée de l'expression [summary]" in *Annales de Normandie* 46ᵉ année, n°5, 1996: first published by the Société d'Ancien Régime: Journée d'Histoire du Droit 1995. 741-742 [www.persee.fr]; original full text in *Recueil d'Études normands offerts en homage à Michel Nortier*, Cahiers Léopold Delisle XLIV, Paris 1996, 80-87

Robson, Thomas, *The British Herald; or, cabinet of armorial bearings of the nobility and gentry of Great Britain and Ireland, from the earliest to the present time ...* [3 volumes], Sunderland 1830 [Hathi Trust]

Roche, O J A, *The Days of the Upright: the story of the Huguenots*, Potter, New York 1965

Round, John Horace, edited by W Page, *Family Origins and Other Studies*, Woburn Books, London 1930; includes "A Huguenot House," at 109-120

—, *Calendar of Documents preserved in France 918-1206* [editor] *q.v. supra*

Scouller, R E, *The Armies of Queen Anne*, Oxford UP 1966

Sévillia, Jean, *Historiquement correct: pour en finir avec le passé unique*, Perrin, Paris 2006

Shaw, William A, *Letters of Denization and Acts of Naturalization for Aliens in England and Ireland 1603-1700*, Huguenot Society of London Publications XVIII, 1911 [archive.org]

—, *Letters of Denization and Acts of Naturalization for Aliens in England and Ireland 1701-1800*, Huguenot Society of London Publications XXVII, 1923 [archive.org]

Shorter, Edward, *The Making of the Modern Family*, Fontana, Glasgow 1977

Smiles, Samuel, *The Huguenots: Their Settlements, Churches and Industries in England and Ireland* [also known as *The History of the Huguenots in England*], first published London 1867; New York edition, *with an Appendix relating to the Huguenots in America*, 1868

Smyth, B, *A History of the Lancashire Fusiliers (formerly XX Regiment; volume I 1688-1821*, Sackville Press, Dublin 1903

Sperling, John G, *The South Sea Company: an historical essay and bibliographical finding list*, Harvard UP 1962

Squibb, G D, *High Court of Chivalry: a study of the civil law in England*, Clarendon Press, Oxford 1959

Stapleton, Thomas, *Magni Rotuli Scaccarii Normanniæ sub Regibus Angliæ* (including "Observations on the Great Rolls of the Exchequer of Normandy" [2 volumes], Society of Antiquaries, London 1841-44 [Google Books]

Statt, Daniel, "The Birthright of an Englishman: the practice of naturalization and denization of immigrants under the later Stuarts and early Hanoverians," in *HSP* XXV (1989-1993), 61-74

Stewart, John Hall, *A Documentary History of the French Revolution*, Macmillan, New York 1951

Stone, Lawrence, *The Family, Sex and Marriage in England 1500-1800*, Penguin, London 1979

—, *Road to Divorce: England 1530-1987*, Oxford UP 1990

Strayer, Joseph Reese, *The Administration of Normandy under Saint Louis*, Medieval Academy of America/Kraus Reprint, New York 1970

Strickland, Matthew, "Henry I and the Battle of the Two Kings," in *Normandy and its Neighbours, 900—1250: essays for David Bates*, edited by David Crouch and Kathleen Thompson, Turnhout, Belgium 2011, 77-116

BIBLIOGRAPHY

Sumption, Jonathan, *The Hundred Years War*, Faber and Faber, London
    I   *Trial by Battle*, 1990
    II *Trial by Fire* 1999
    III *Divided Houses*, 2009
    IV *Cursed Kings*, 2015

Tapié, Victor-L, translated and edited by D McN Lockie, *France in the Age of Louis XIII and Richelieu*, Macmillan, London 1974

Taylor, Charles [editor and publisher], *The Literary Panorama and Annual Register* [variant titles], London 1807- [Google Books]

The Times Atlas of the World, Mid-Century Edition (Volume III: Northern Europe), London 1955

Trévières, Société historique du canton de, *Notes historiques sur Le Bessin: tome I: Trévières, Bernesq, Blagny, La Quièze, Baynes, Cerisy-la-Forêt, Le Molay, Le Breuil, Saon, Ste Honorine des Pertes, Villiers sur Port, Colleville, Engranville* , Caen 1922, reprinted 2007

Trimen, Richard, *An Historical Memoir of the 35th Royal Sussex Regiment of Foot*, Southampton Times [UK] 1873

Tuchman, Barbara, *A Distant Mirror: the calamitous 14th century*, Penguin 1979

Vane, Hon W L, *The Durham Light Infantry: the united red and white rose*, Andrews UK, Luton 2012

Venn, John, and John Archibald Venn [editors], *Alumni Cantabrigienses: A Biographical List of All Known Students, Graduates and Holders of Office at the University of Cambridge, from the Earliest Times to 1900* [ten volumes], Cambridge UP 1922-1953; internet edition 2011

Vieuille, Pierre, *Nouveau traité des Élections, contenant l'origine de la taille, aides, gabelles, octrois, et autres impositions*, Huart, Paris 1739

Vierville-sur-Mer, Commune (14710), http://vierville.free.fr/ [official internet site]

Vigne, Randolph, "Testaments of Faith: wills of Huguenot refugees in England as a window on their past," in David J B Trim [editor], *The Huguenots: history and memory in transnational context: essays in honour and memory of Walter C. Utt*, Brill, Leiden 2011, 263-284

Waddington, Francis, *Le protestantisme en Normandie depuis la révocation de l'Edit de Nantes jusqu'à la fin du dix-huitiéme siécle (1685-1797)*, Dumoulin, Paris 1862

Wagner, Henry, "Notes in Connection with the Montresor Pedigree," *HSP* XI (1915-1917), 293-300, with an *excursus* on the Pierrepont family at 299

—, "Pedigrees of Huguenot Families and Materials compiled and collected," in *HSP* XIII (1923-1929), 287-295

Walford, Edward, *Old and New London: a narrative of its history, its people, and its places; Volume 6: the southern suburbs*, Cassell & Company, London 1878 [from *British History Online* http://www.britishhistory.ac.uk/ and archive.org]

Ward, Stephen George Peregrine, *Faithful: the story of the Durham Light Infantry*, Durham Light Infantry 1963

Wedgewood, C V, *The Thirty Years War*, Penguin, London 1957

White, Jerry, *A Great and Monstrous Thing: London in the eighteenth century*, Harvard UP 2013 [first published Bodley Head, London 2012]

Whitelock, Dorothy, David C Douglas and Susie I Tucker [editors], *The Anglo-Saxon Chronicle: a revised edition*, London 1965

Wilmot, Chester, *The Struggle for Europe*, Fontana 1959

Winstanley, Denys Arthur, *The University of Cambridge in the Eighteenth Century* [4 volumes], Cambridge UP 1922 [Google Books]

INDEX

Abot, Guillaume, 53
Abot, Jean, 55
Abot, Jeanne, wife of Hebert Champion, 37, 53, 55, Table I, Table II
Act of Toleration [British], 105
Admiralty, High Court, 139, 147; Marshal, 139, 153; Supernumerary Proctor, 139, 153; Admiralty Proctor, 139, 153; King's Proctor, 167; Receiver of the Rights and Perquisites/Receiver of the Droits, 137, 139, 163-164, *and see* Court of Admiralty
see also Royal Navy
Agincourt (battle 1415), 8, 36, 43, 47, 56
Aigues Mortes in France, 67, 70
Aix-en-Provence, 75, Archbishop, 74-75
Aldeburgh in Suffolk, 162, 172, 174, 175, *Map Eighteen*; parliamentary borough, 139-140, 154, 162, 171-173, 174
Aldgate in London, 113, 125
Alençon in France, 120, 125, *Map One*
Algeciras in Spain, 128
Alicante in Spain, 111, 122, 129, 162, *Map Fifteen*; siege (1708-1709), 122, 130
Allix, Daniel, 125
Allix, Gilbert, husband of Jane/Jeanne CdeC (1700-1776), 19, 124-125, 152, 154, Table III, Table VII
Allix, Reverend Pierre, 125
Almansa in Spain (battle 1707), 111, 122, 130, *Map Fifteen*
Amboise Conspiracy (1545), 37, 79
American Revolution/War of American Independence (1775-1783), 139, 141, 177
Amiens, treaty (1802-1803), 140, 177
Amsterdam in Holland, 114, 116, 142
Amyand, Dr Claudius/Claude, 149-150
The Ancestor journal, 69-70
Les Andelys in France, 58
Anglicanism, *see* Church of England
Anglo-Saxon Chronicle, 59
Anjou [province in France], *Map Two*
apprentice/indenture *or* articled clerk, 111, 124, 134, 147, 153, 167
Ararat in Victoria, Australia, 179
archery, 164, *and see* Royal Toxophilite Society

Arches Court of Canterbury, *see* Court of Arches
articled clerk, *see* apprenticeship/indenture
Asiento [trading permit], 141-142
Aubonne in Switzerland, 115, *and see* d'Aubonne
Augsburg, Peace of (1545), 37, 78-79; *see also* War of the League of Augsburg
Aunay [*also as* Aulnay] in France, 6, 30, 38, 80, *Map Three*, *Map Ten*
Australia, 137, 157, 162, 173, 177, 178-179
Avranches in France, 82

Bailleul family of Vierville-sur-Mer, 88
Ballarat in Victoria, Australia, 163
Bank of England, 140
Bank of Victoria, 179
Barbery in France, 71, *Map Six*; Abbey of St Marie, 71, *and see* Saint Barberie
Barcelona in Spain, 129-131, *Map Fifteen*; Fort Monjuïc, 130-131
Barking in Essex, 133-134; St Margaret's Church, 134
Barlow, Hugh Owen MP, husband of Anne CdeC (1768-1844), 177
baronetcy, 75, 110, 140, 165
Barron, Oswald, modern scholar, 69-70
Barrymore, Earl, his Regiment [13th Foot], 133, *and see* Somerset Light Infantry
Basnage, Samuel, Huguenot pastor, 100
Bath in Somerset, 125, 132-133, 145, 147, 162, 174-175
Bath, Order of the, 178
Baxter, Stafford Squire, 175
Bayeux in France, 39, 44, 82, 84, 96, 97, 99, *Map One*, *Map Twelve*; *élection* [tax district], 91
Beach, Thomas, portrait painter, 158, 165
Beggs, Francis, husband of Helen Rosalie [Rose] CdeC (1858-1937), 179
Beggs, Sophia Montgomery Grattan, second wife of Philip CdeC (1850-1927), 179
Belgium, *see* Flanders
Belfast in Ireland, 128, 132
Belle-esze/Belleeze, 62, 67

INDEX

Bellis, Francis William, adulterer, 168
Benezet, James, Table VI
Bennett, Captain John, 132, 135
Berlin in Germany, 116
Bern in Switzerland, 116
Berry [province in France], *Map Two*
Bertram family, 70
Bessin in France, 38, 96
Betton Strange in Shropshire, 170
Black Death (fourteenth century plague), 36, 42, 44, 57
Black Prince [Edward, son of King Edward III of England], 42, 60
Blenheim (battle 1704), 132
Blois [province in France], *Map Two*; city in France, 80
Board of General Officers, 111, 128, 130-132
Boehm, Anne, wife of Claude Fonnereau (1677-1740), Table VI, Table VII
Bordeaux in France, 47; Archbishop, 74-75
Borradale, Reverend George, first husband of Betsy Hodges nee Handley, 168-169
Borradale, George Arris Tilden, son of George Borradale and Betsy Hodges nee Handley, 169
Boulogne in France, 179
Bourbon, Duke [future Louis XVIII of France], 74-75
Bounty, Royal/Queen's, 104
Bowles, Colonel Phineas, 131
Bowyer/Bowyer-Smijth family, 28, *and see* Smijth
Boyne (battle 1690), 97, 103
Branthwayt, Arthur, stepfather of Eliza Julia Trent, 178
Breconshire/Brecknock, Wales, 174-175; High Sheriff, 174
Brenneville/Brémule, skirmish at (1119), 36, 58-60
Bréville-les-Monts in France, 46
Brigadier-General, 129
[Great] Britain, *see also* England, Ireland, Scotland *and* Wales
    kings and queens
        Queen Anne, 123, 128, 130
        George I, 115, 128, 148
        George II, accession 109, 148-149

Britain: kings and queens [continued]
    George III, 162, 177;
        his Queen Charlotte, 161
    George IV [as Prince of Wales], 140, 164-165
    James II [deposed in the Glorious Revolution 1678], 78, 97, 102, 103, 105, 110, 115, 119, 120, 132, 140;
        his son the Old Pretender, 132;
        Jacobites, 119, 132
    William III [William of Orange], 78, 97, 102, 105, 110, 115, 120, 128;
        his wife and co-ruler Queen Mary, 78, 110
    Queen Victoria, 115
Britain, religious tolerance, 105
Brittany/Bretagne [province in France], 36, 37, 40, 41, 43, 47, 65, 67, 72, *Map Two*
Broadstreet Ward, London, 125
Bromley in Kent, 176
Bron *miswriting for* Bruz *q.v.*
Brooke, Clarissa Sarah, third wife of Philip CdeC (1738-1803), 139, **169-170,** 173, 174, Table V; portrait, 169
Brooke, Hester, mother of Clarissa Sarah, 169
Brooke, James, father of Clarissa Sarah, 169-170
Broughton Hall near Stowmarket, Suffolk, 154
Bruges in Flanders, 46, 111, 120
Bruz in Brittany, 22, 41, 72-73
Bryn-y-Gwyn near Dolgelley in Wales, 161
Bunbury, Anne, wife of Claude Fonnereau (1701-1784), Table VI, Table VII
Buonaparte, Napoleon, *see* Napoleon Buonaparte
Bureau, Elizabeth, wife of Claude Fonnereau (1677-1740), 149-152, Table VI
Burke, works on *Peerage, Baronetage* and *Landed Gentry*, 58, 60-65, **66-70**, 71, 90
Burgundy/Bourgogne [province in France], *Map Two*
Burgundy, Duke John, 43
Burgundy, Duke Philip, 44
Burnet, Gilbert, Bishop of Salisbury, 125

Burwood House near Walton on Thames, Surrey, 174
Busnel, Jean, 40, 50, Table I
Busnel, the Demoiselle, wife of Maheas Champion, 19, 36, 40, 51, Table I
Bute, Earl [John Stuart], Prime Minister, 169

Cadiz in Spain, 129, 130, 131, *Map Fifteen*
Caen in France, 39, 42, 64, 67, 82, 83, 114, *Map One*, *Map Two*; Bailiff, 82; *Généralité*, 40, 90-93; Intendant, 90, *and see* Chamillart
Calvados, modern department in France, 6, 7, 8, 13, 15, 38, 79, 83, 88, *Map Twelve*
Calvin, Jean, 37; Calvinism/Calvinists, 79, 105, 115
Camberwell, London, 125, 139, 147, 153, 162, 162-163, *Map Seventeen*; Grove House Tavern, 154; Camberwell Club, 154-155; Camberwell Volunteers, 165
Cambridge University, 109, 124, 125, 139, 147, 162, 166, 176; Chancellor, 162
Cambridgeshire, 168, 176
Canivet, Marie-Therese, 89
Canterbury in Kent, 177
Canterbury, Archbishop/archdiocese, *see* Court of Arches *and* Lambeth Palace
Captain [military rank], 110, 111, 119, 122, 123, 124, 127, 128, 130, 131, 133, 177
Captain [naval rank], 133, 135, 160, 167
Captain-Lieutenant [military rank], 110, 119, 122, 127
Cardross, Lord [Henry Erskine], 119, his Regiment, 105, 110, 119, 126, 128, *and see* Cunningham's Regiment
Carmarthenshire, Wales, 166
Cartault, Jean, Huguenot pastor at Trevières, 29, 99
  his wife, 30
Cathedine in Breconshire, Wales, 176
Catholic League, 79-80, 83, *and see* Roman Catholicism/Catholics
Caulfeild, Thomas, 111, 131-132
Caulfeild, William, *see* Viscount Charlemont
Caya in Spain (battle 1709), 133, *Map Fifteen*
Chambers families, heraldry, 2

Chamillart, Guy, Intendant of the *généralité* de Caen in Lower Normandy, 24, 40, 47, 51, 78, 81, 90-95; his *Recherche de Noblesse en la Généralité de Caen*, 24, 40, 66, 78, **90-95**
Champagne [province in France], *Map Two*
Champion surname, origin, 1
champion [occupation], 1, 4-5
Champion [office], of the King of England, 5, 70; of the Duke of Normandy, 5, 64, 66, 69, 70
Champion family of Normandy, later Champion de Crespigny *q.v.*, 37; arms/shield of, 2-3, 44
Champion [*and see* le Champion *below*]:
  Antoine (*fl.*1490), 37, 52, 53, 55, 56, 91, 95-96, Table II
    his wife, *see* Catherine Marye
  Claude, *see* Claude Champion de Crespigny (1620-1695)
  Gabriel (*fl.*1440), 48, 53, Table I, Table II
  Giles (*fl.*1545, son of Martin?), 53, Table II
  Hebert (*fl.*1440), 22, 24, 27, 32, 37, 41, 42, 48, 50-53, 56, 61, Table I, Table II
    his wife, *see* Jeanne Abot
  Jacques (d.1613), 53, 54, 56, 56, 77, Table II
  Jean (*fl.*1415), 22, 24, 36, 37, 41, 47-49, 51-52, 61, 73-74, 90, Table I, *and see* Champion de Cicé
  Jean (*fl.*1490, son of Hebert), 53, 56, Table II
  Jean (*fl.*1545, son of Martin?), 53, Table II
  Jean (d.1622, son of Raoul), 22, 24, 36, 37, 52, 53, 54, 77, 81, Table II
    his wife, *see* Marthe du Bourget
  Magdelaine [married Guillaume Vaillant], 52, 55, Table II
  Maheas (*fl.*1340), 13, 19, 22, 32, 36, 37, 40-42, 44-47, 49, 50-52, 60, 61, 66, 68, 69, 71-72, 90, Table I
    his wife, *see* Demoiselle Busnel
  Marie [married Pierre Thomas], 54, 77, Table II

INDEX

Champion [*continued*]:
    Martin (*fl*.1490), 52, 53, 55, Table II
    Michel (*fl*.1415), 22, 24, 32, 36-37, 41, 47-50, 51-52, 61-62, 74, 91, 94, Table I, Table II
      his wife, *see* Jeanne de la Rivière
    Nicolas (d.1563), 37, 53, 55, 56, Table II
    Oliver/Olivier, 61; shield, 61
    Philippe (*fl*.1473), 48
    Pierre (*fl*.1440), 48, 53, Table I, Table II
    Raoul (*fl*.1540), 37, 55, 56, 91, 95-96, Table II [*see also* Rioul *below*]
      his wife, *see* Jeanne la Forestier
    Ricard le Champion, 36
    Richard (*fl*.1390), 19, 22, 32, 36, 41, 45-47, 49, 51, 61, 66, 71-72, Table I
      his wife, *see* Demoiselle Mensant
    Richard (*c*.1580-1659), 19, 22, 54, 56, 74, 77, 78, **81-84**, 90-92, Table II, Table III; portrait, 83
      his wife, *see* Marguerite Richard
    Rioul [*also as* Roul *and* Raul] (*fl*.1440), 42, 48, 53, Table I, Table II
Champion de Caimbie family, 62, 73; shield, 61, 73
Champion de Chartres family, 41, 73-74; shield, 73-74
Champion de Cicé family, 41, 47, 62, 66, 71, 73-74; shield, 47-48, 73-74
    Champion de Cicé, Jean, 47, 61, 73-74, *and see* Jean Champion (*fl*.1415)
    Champion de Cicé, Jérôme-Marie, 74-75
Champion de Crespigny surname [often shortened to Crespigny], 5-6, 90, 164; arms/shield, 2-4, 61, 87-88, 108; *see also* Champion
[*frequently abbreviated in this work as* CdeC]
Champion de Crespigny *or* Crespigny:
    Ada Isadora Charlotte (1848-1927), 6, 179, Table V
    Albert (1824-1873), 15

Champion de Crespigny/Crespigny [*continued*]:
    Anne (1739-1797) [married Bonouvrier Glover and later James Vernon], 13, 19, 25, 147, **157-162**, Table V, Table VII; portrait, 158
    Anne (1768-1844), 162, 168, **177**
    Augusta Anne (1799-1892), 176
    Augustus James (1791-1825), 14, 18, 28, 33, **167**
      his wife, *see* Caroline Smijth
    Charles (*c*.1679-1723), 25, 32, 118, 126-127, **133-134**, 135, Table III, Table IV
    Charles (1772-1764), 169, 177
    Charles [James] Fox (1785-1875), 18, 28, 137-139, 162, 170, 173, **178**, 179, Table V
      his wife, *see* Eliza Julia Trent
    Charles John (1814-1880), 178
    Clarissa/Clara (1775-1836), 162, 169, **177**; portrait, 169
    Claude (1620-1695) [*also surnamed* Champion], 3, 4, 5, 8, 13, 14, 19, 23, 26-27, 29; 31, 37, 56, 69, 77, 78, 82, **84-93**, 95-96, 97, 100-105, 107, 109, 137, 178-179, Table II, Table III; military career, 82, 84-85, 96, 104-106; portrait, 88
      his wife, *see* Marie de Vierville
    Claude (1701-1703), 121, 123, Table III
    Claude (1706-1782), of South Sea House, 18, 20, 21, 25, 28, 31, 32, 106, 111, 112, 113, 116-117, 118, 121, 123, 124, 125, 134-135, 139, **140-147**, 154, 156, 162, 163, 179, Table III, Table V, Table VII; portrait, 145; *see also* South Sea Book
    Claude (1734-1818), first baronet, 3, 13, 16, 19, 21, 25, 28, 32, 69, 75, 110, 125-126, 137-140, 147, 155-156, 157, **162-165**, 167, 173, 174, 176, Table V, Table VII; portrait, 165
      his wife, *see* Mary Clark

Champion de Crespigny/Crespigny [*continued*]:
- Claude (1787–1813), 14, 28
- Claude (1847–1935), fourth baronet, 4, 17, 19, 25, 28, 33, 58, 66, 68-69, 167; *Memoirs*, 69, *Forty Years of a Sportsman's Life*, 69
- Claude Montgomery (1908-1991), 179
- Claude William (1818-1865) third baronet, 3, 14-16, 18, 23, 25, 26, 28, 29, 32, 33, 68, 165, 167; travel to Normandy, 23, 33, 50, 86
  - his wife, *see* Marie Tyrrell
- Constantine Pulteney Trent (1851-1883), 179
- Constantine Trent (1882-1952), 179
- Daumont, *see* Pierre *and Daumont Letters*
- Dorothea (1800-1800), 170, 178
- Eliza (1784-1831), 139-140, 162, 170, **178**
- Eliza Constantia Frances (1825-1898), 178
- Elizabeth (*c*.1683-*c*.1735), 25, 32, 113, 118, 126-127, **134**, Table III, Table IV
- Eyre Nicholas (1822-1895), 14-15, 25, 33, 87
- Fanny (1779-1865), 162, 169, **177**
- Francis George Travers (1892-1968), 179
- Frederick (1822-1887), 15, 23, 33, 50, 86
- Gabriel (1666-1723), 19, 23, 24, 25, 32, 51, 78, 84, 100-101, 103-104, 106, 110, 110, 111, 113, 119, 122, **126-133**, 134-135, 137, 178, Table III, Table IV
  - his wife, *see* Elizabeth Glasscock
- George (1783-1813), 139-140, 162, 170, **177**
- George Blick[e] (1815-1893), 18, 25, 28, 178
- Guillaume, *see* William (1698-1721)
- Harry (1777-infant), 169, **177**
- Heaton (1796-1858), 14, 163
- Helen Rosalie [Rose] (1858-1937) [married Francis Beggs], 179
- Henry (1882-1946), sixth baronet, 15, 25

Champion de Crespigny/Crespigny [*continued*]:
- Henry Other (1820-1883), 15, 25
- Herbert Joseph (1805-1881), 14, 18, 21, 25, 33
  - his wife, *see* Caroline Smijth
- Hugh Vivian (1897-1969), 179
- Isabella, 126-127, *and see* Elizabeth nee Glasscock
- Jeanne, *see* Jeanne/Jane (1668-1748) *or* Jane/Jeanne (1700-1776)
- Jeanne/Jane/Joan (1668-1748) [married Geronimo de Lamberty], 77, 101, 103-105, 106, 110-110, 111, 113, **114-118**, 135, Table III, Table VII
- Jane/Jeanne (1700-1776) [married Gilbert Allix], 13, 17, 113, 121, 123, **125-126**, 135, 156, Table III, Table VII
- Jane (1733-1734), 113, 162, Table V, Table VII
- Jane (1742-1829) [married Henry Reveley], 13, 17, 19, 21, 23, 25, 32, 125, 147, **162**, Table V
- Jane (1766-1785), 168, **177**
- Julia Eliza (1819-1848), 177
- Marguerite/Margaret (1654-1741) [married Stephen de Borde/Debordes], 77, 100, 103-104, 113, 125, 135, Table III, Table VII
- Maria (1776-1858), 162, 169, **177**; portrait, 169
- Marie/Mary (1655-1756) [married Georges Goslin and later Jacques Fiellet], 78, 100, 103-104, **113**, 114, 135, Table III
- Marie (1699-1700), 120-121, 123, Table III
- Mary (1688-1692), 126-127, Table III, Table IV
- Philip (1738-1803), 3-4, 13, 18, 21, 110, 137-140, 145, 147, 157, 162, **167-176**, 179, Table V; portrait, 170
  - his wives, *see* Sarah Cocksedge, Betsy Hodges Handley, Clarissa Sarah Brooke *and* Dorothy Scott

INDEX

Champion de Crespigny/Crespigny [*continued*]:
  Philip (1765-1851), 139-140, 162, 168, **177**
    his wife, *see* Emilia Wade
  Philip (1850-1927), 6, 179, Table V
    his wives, *see* Annie Frances Chauncy *and* Sophia Montgomery Grattan Beggs
  Philip (1879-1918), 179
  Philip Robert (1817-1889), 6, 28, 178-179, Table V
    his wife, *see* Charlotte Frances Dana
  Pierre/Peter *alias* Daumont (1653-1729), 4, 5, 13, 19, 23, 24, 25, 29-31, 32, 51, 77, 78, 85, 89-90, 97-101, 103-104, 106, 108, 109, 110, **111-112**, 113, 116, 125, 126, 134-135, 140, 145, 148, 153, 178-179, Table III, Table VII; *see also Daumont Letters*
  Renée (1667-1744) [married Pierre Hemet], 78, 100, 103-104, 111, 113, **114**, 117, 135, Table III
  Royalieu Dana [Roy] (1905-1985), 179
  Susanna (1735-1766) [married Richard Sutton], 13, 25, 113, **157-158,** Table V, Table VII; portrait, 158
  Susanne/Suzanne/Sussanna (1656-1726) [married Pierre Gaudy], 77, 100, 103-104, 111, **113-114**, 135, Table III
  Thomas (1664-1712), 14, 17, 19, 23, 24, 25, 27, 32, 33, 51, 78, 84, 100-101, 103-104, 105-106, 107, 110-110, 111, 113, 114, **118-123**, 124-125, 126, 129, 135, 137, 140, 141, 153, 157, 178, Table III, Table V
    his wife, *see* Magdalen/Magdelaine Granger
  Thomas (1753-1799), 139, 162, 168, 172, **176**
    his wife, *see* Augusta Charlotte Thellusson
  Viola Julia Constantia (1855-1929), 6, 179

Champion de Crespigny/Crespigny [*continued*]:
  Vivian Tyrrell (1907-1952), 14, 28, 110, 167, Table IV
  William/Guillaume (1698-1721), 17, 19, 106, 111, 120-121, 123-125, 134, 137, 140, 147, Table III
  William (1765-1829), second baronet, 3, 14, 18, 19, 25, 32, 74-75, 126, 139-140, 162-163, **166-167,** Table V
    his wife, *see* Sarah Windsor
  William Other Robert (1789-1816), 14, 28, 161

le Champion [*and see* Moller/Champion]:
  Bertrand (*fl.*1408) [*as* le Champyon *or as* le Champion-Marmion], 37, 64-65, 67, 69
  Elizabeth, 61
  Guillaume, 67
  Jacques, 61, 65, 66, 67
  Jean, 67
  Pierre, 62, 67
  Raoul, 67
  Ricard I, 62, 67
  Ricard II, 62

Champion Lodge near Maldon in Essex, 68

Champion Lodge, Camberwell, 14, 17, 18, 29, 32, 74-75, 125, 139, 140, 145, 147, 153-154, 156, 162, 165-166, *Map Seventeen*; *fête champètre* (1804), 164-164; sale and demolition, 165-166; dispersal of the library, 14, 18, 21, 25, 29, 33, 165

Championière in France, 23, 50

Champyon, *see* Bertrand le Champion above

Chancellor of the Exchequer, 143

Charing Cross in London, 113, 148

Charlemont, Viscount [William Caulfeild], 130-131; his Regiment [36th Foot], 130-131

Charles the Bad, King of Navarre and Count of Evreux, 43, 45

Chartres-de-Bretagne in France, 22, 72

Chateigner, Marguerite, wife of Zacharie Fonnereau, 151, Table VI

Chauncy, Annie Frances, first wife of Philip CdeC (1850-1927), 179

Chauncy, Philip LaMothe Snell, father of Annie Frances, 179
Cherbourg in France, 44, *Map One*
China, Jesuit mission, 154
Christ Church, Oxford, 147
Christchurch near Ipswich in Suffolk, 154, 171
Christian V, King of Denmark, 61
Christoph von Bayern, King of Sweden, Denmark and Norway, 61
Church of England, 105, *and see* Anglicanism *and* French Church of the Savoy
churches in England [Anglican unless otherwise indicated]:
    Hungerford Market chapel, 113
    Independent Meeting House of St George in the East at Stepney [non-conformist], 162-163
    St Benet's Paul's Wharf[e], 149, 156, *Map Sixteen*
    St Botolph's Church, Aldgate, London, 113
    St George's Hanover Square, London, 160, 176, 178
    St Giles' Church in Camberwell, 156, 157, 162, 165, 169, *Map Seventeen*
    St Margaret's Church in Barking, Essex, 133
    St Martin Orgar, London, 125
    St Martin-in-the-Fields, 156
    St Mary Magdalene at Old Fish Street, London, 120
    St Marylebone, *see* Marylebone
    St Paul's Cathedral, 149, 152, 154, *Map Sixteen*; Dean and Chapter, 153
    St Peter and St Paul in Aldeburgh, Suffolk, 176
    St Peter and St Paul in Bromley, Kent, 176
    St Stephen's Walbrook, London, 151
    St Swithin's at Walcot near Bath, 125
Cicé in France, 22, 47, 72, 74
Clark, Joseph, father of Mary, 162
Clark, Mary, wife of Claude CdeC (1747-1813), 19, 139-140, 162-165, Table V; portrait, 165; *The Pavillion*, 164; *Letters of Advice from a Mother to her Son*, 164
Clark, Mary nee Wilkes, mother of Mary, 162, *and see* Isaac Heaton
Cocksedge, Lydia, mother of Sarah, 167
Cocksedge, Sarah, first wife of Philip CdeC (1738-1803), 139, 162, 167-168, 169, 172, 173, Table V
Cocksedge, Thomas Henry, father of Sarah, 168
College of Arms [*or* Herald's College], 25, 26, 27, 31, 32, 33, 78, 93, 106, 149, *Map Sixteen*; Certificate/statement, 5, 13, 19, 23, 24, 26, 27, 32, 33, 51, 78, 93, 106, 111, 117; Bluemantle Pursuivant, 19; Windsor Herald, 19; York Herald, 27; High Courts of Chivalry, 153
College of Doctors of Law *exercent* in the Ecclesiastical and Admiralty Courts/College of Civilians, *see* Doctors' Commons
Colleville-sur-Mer in France, 89
Collingwood, Admiral Cuthbert, 167
Colonel [military rank], 82, 85, 104, 105-106, 119, 121, *and see by regiment*
Commander [naval rank], 159
Commissioner of Excise, 161
Committee of French Churches in London, 31
Common Law courts, 147
Condé-sur-Noireau, 38, 54, 81, *Map One*, *Map Ten*, *Map Thirteen*; Huguenot congregation, 81, 83-84, 99
Condé-sur-Vire, 47, 73-74
Consolations Book, 14, **17-18**, 31, 32, 33, 106, 113, 121-122, 126, 154, 156-157
Copenhagen in Denmark, 116
Cornelison, Henry, 154
Cornet [military rank], 119, 122, 126, 131
Cornu, Richard, 54
Cornwallis, General Charles, 139, 159
Cornwallis, Admiral William, 159
Cotentin peninsula/region in France, 38, 42, 43, 44, 46, 52, 88, *Map One*, *Map Twelve*
Council of State [French royal], 78, 98-99, 102; President [Duke of Villeroy], 99
Court of Aides of Normandy, 77-78, 81, 92-93; decision of 1591: 37, 77, 81, 91-92. 94; decision of 1622: 77, 81, 91-93, 94; decision of 1674: [13], 15,

INDEX

Court of Aides of Normandy, decision of 1674 [*continued*]: 19, 24, 32, 51-52, 78, 88, 90-93, 95-96, *and see Extract from the Register of the Court of Aides*

Court of Arches/Arches Court of Canterbury, London, 111, 124, 137-139, 140, 147, 168-169, 178; Advocate, 147-148, 155, 162-163, 176; Proctor, 139, 147-148, 149, 153, 167, 177; Procurator-General, 155, *and see* Admiralty *and* divorce

Court of Probate Act 1857, 147

Courts of Chivalry, 153; Proctor, *and see* College of Arms

Coutras (battle 1588), 36, 80

Creville, *Map Twelve*

Crécy (battle 1346), 36, 42

Crepigny, C, 133, *and see* Charles CdeC (*c*.1679-1723) *and* Cripiny [*sic* ?]

Crespigny surname: *individuals are listed under* Champion de Crespigny

Crespigny/Crépigny in Calvados 14670, 6-7, 10, 19, 30-31, 38, 54, 60, 69, 77-78, 81-84, 85, 89-90, 92, 94, 98, 107, 111, *Map One, Map Three, Map Six*

Crespigny House at Aldeburgh in Suffolk, 162

Crespigny/Crépigny House at Vierville-sur-Mer, Calvados 14610, 8, 14, 16, 86-87, *Map Four, Map Five, Map Twelve*

Crespigny and Greene [proctors in partnership], 147 *and see* Philip CdeC (1738-1803)

Crespin, Daniel, merchant, 125

Cripiny [*sic* ?], Captain, of Barking, Essex, 133, *and see* Charles CdeC (*c*.1679-1723) and Crepigny

Crispin and Crispianus, saints, 7-8

Cross, Jane, second [common-law] wife of John Horsley, 177

crusades and crusading ancestors, 61, 66, 67, 69, 71, 73

Cunningham, Sir Richard, 119-120, his Regiment, 110, 119, 128, *and see* Cardross's Regiment of Dragoons *and* Jedburgh's Dragoons

D-Day landings (1944), 8, 88-89

d'Amphernet family, 46

d'Amphernet, Jehan I, 46

d'Amphernet, Jehan II, 46

d'Amphernet, Richard, 46

d'Amphernet, Guillaume, 46

Dana, Charlotte Frances, wife of Philip Robert CdeC, 6, 179, Table V

Danvou-la-Ferrière, 7, *Map Three*

d'Aubonne, Charles, 115, 117, Table III; his mother Madame d'Aubonne, 115-116

d'Aubonne, Victoria Aimée, 110, 117, Table III

d'Auquetonville, Raoul, 46

Daumont de Crespigny *i.e.* Pierre CdeC, 5, 98

Daumont Letters, 5, **28-31**, 32, 89, **97-100**

Dauphiné, county in France, 39; Dauphin [royal heir of France], 39, [future King Charles VII] 43, 48

Dauteuil/d'Auteuil/d'Auteville surname, 124

Dauteuil, André/Andrew, 124, 156, Table VI, Table VII

Dauteuil, Fleurand I, father of Fleurand II, 124

Dauteuil, Fleurand II, 124

Dauteuil, Martha Susanna, 124; *as* Susanna Hemet, 156

Davies, Thomas Henry Hastings, first husband of Augusta Anne CdeC, 176

Davis, Dudley Loftus, 67

Davis, Ellise, 67

Davis, Jacques Loftus, 67-68

Davis, Marie, 67

de Borde[s]/Debordes, Etienne/Stephen, husband of Marguerite/Margaret CdeC (1654-1741), 103, 113, Table III

de Crespigny [surname], *see* Crespigny *and* Champion de Crespigny

de Crespigny, William, 36

de Lamberty, Abraham, 116, 118, Table III

de Lamberty, Esther, 116, Table III

de Lamberty, Geronimo, husband of Jeanne/Jane/Joan CdeC (1668-1748) 104, 113-115, 117, 134, Table III; *Mémoires pour servir à l'histoire du XVIIIe siècle*, 116

de Lamberty, Judith [married Charles d'Aubonne], 110, 115-117, Table III

de Launay, Madelaine, 67
de Maintenon, Marquise [Françoise d'Aubigné], 97, 101
de Marguerye, Gilles, 88
de Meausse Dauteville/d'Auteville, Fleurand, *see* Dauteuil, Fleurand I
Debrett, *Peerage, Baronetage, Knightage and Companionage*, 4, 28, 58, 66, 69, 90, 93-94
Declaration of the Rights of Man and Citizen (1789), 107
denization in England, 78, 103, 106, 110
Denmark, 61
Denmark Hill in Camberwell, London, 139, 153, 165
Dewar, George Albemarle Bertle, 69
divorce, 168-168; legal proceedings, 147, 168-169, *and see* Court of Arches *and* Matrimonial Causes Act
Doctors Commons, London, 19, 117, 147-149, 162, 165, 167, *Map Sixteen*
Dolgelley in Wales, 161
Domfront in France, 44, 82, *Map One*; Huguenot congregation, 83
Donegall, Earl [Arthur Chichester], 128-129, 131; his Regiment [35th Foot], 111, 122, 126, 128-129, *and see* Gorges' Regiment
d'Oüssé, adoptive surname of Hector Mensant
dragonnades, 78, 100
dragoons, 118-119, 120, 122, 133, *and see by regiment*
Drelincourt, Charles, 17, *and see Consolations Book*
Dresden in Germany, 116
Drysdale, John, of the London Hotel, 168
du Barry, Jean-Baptiste, 94
du Barry, Jeanne nee Bécu, comtesse, 94
du Bourget, Marthe, wife of Jean Champion (d.1622), 37, 54, 56, 80, Table II; portrait, 83
du Guesclin, Bertrand, Constable of France, 36, 43, 46
Dublin in Ireland, 134
Ducarel, Dr Andrew Coltée, 154-155
Dumfries in Scotland, 120
Durant, Huguenot pastor, 120-121
Durham Light Infantry [68th Foot], 177
Dymoke, Sir John, 70

East Anglia, 161, 162, 167, 174, *and see* Norfolk, Suffolk *and* Cambridgeshire
[British] East India Company, 141
Eleanor of Aquitaine, wife of King Henry II of England, 39, 106
Edgeworth, the Abbé, 89
Edict of Alès (1629), 80, 97
Edict of Fontainbleau, *see* Edict of Nantes, Revocation
Edict of Nantes (1588), 37, 80, 97-98; Revocation (1685) [by the Edict of Fontainbleau], 13, 37, 78, 85, 86, 90, 96-97, 100, 102, 103, 104, 106, 109, 111, 120, 125
Edict of Versailles (1787), 106
Egerton, William, 133, his Regiment [20th Foot], 133
élection [administrative unit in France], 91, *and see by place-name*; *élu* [official], 91
[parliamentary] elections in England, *see* Parliament
Elijah and ravens insignia, 17-18, 113
England, 97, 101 *et saepe*; Huguenot migration to, 101-104
    kings, 5, *and see* Britain
        Edward II, 43
        Edward III, 42, 43-44
        Henry I, 5, 36, 39, 58-60
        Henry II, 7, 39
        Henry III, 39, 105
        Henry IV, 65, 160
        Henry V, 8, 36-37, 43, 63-65
        Henry VI, 65
        Henry VIII, 61, 67, 105
        John, 36, 39
        Richard I, 39
        William I the Conqueror, 36, 70, 159
        William II Rufus, 155
Ensign [military rank], 131, 133, 177
Essex, 162, 168
Estates-General/*États-Généraux*, 74, 94-95, 141
Eton College, 162, 166, 167
"Eurambeen" near Ararat in Victoria, Australia, 179
Everleigh, John, architect, 174
Evreux in France, 38, 43; Count Charles the Bad, 43, 45

INDEX

Extract from the Register of the Court of Aides [or *Extract*], **26-27**, 32, 33, 41, 51-52, 53, 55, 81-83, 88, 91, 93, 95, 96, *and see* Court of Aides

Fairfax, Betty, cousin of Elizabeth CdeC (*c*.1683-*c*.1735), 134; correspondence with Elizabeth, 134-135
Falaise in France, 38, 39, 44, 63, *Map One*, *Map Six*
Farnham in Essex, 127, 134
Fiellet, Jacques/Jacob, second husband of Marie CdeC (1655-1746), 113, Table III
Flanders, 44, 110, 119-120, 122, 127-128, *Map Two*
Fleet Street, London, 168
La Fleurière, property in France, 23, 50, 53, 69, 81-82, 92, *Map Six*; purchase (1453), 27, 32, 37, 41, 96; sale (1641), 56, 77, 82, 89
Fonnereau family, 149-151, 163, 173, 179, Table VI
Fonnereau:
    Abel, 152, Table VI, Table VII
    Anne, wife of Philip CdeC (1704-1765), 14, 19, 21, 28, 113, 125, 137-139, 149-153, 156, 157, 162, 163, 167, Table III, Table V, Table VI, Table VII
    Claude (1677-1730), 125, 149-153, 154, 171, Table VI
    Claude (1701-1784), 137, Table VI, Table VII; portrait, 150
    Elizabeth, 156, Table VI, Table VII
    Elizabeth-Françoise/Frances, Table VI, Table VII
    John, Table VI
    Marie-Anne/Mary-Anne, Table VI, Table VII
    Martyn, 173, Table VI
    Philip, 172, Table VI, Table VII
    Pierre/Peter, Table VI, Table VII
    Thomas, 139, 171-172, Table VI, Table VII
    Zacharie/Zachary, 149-151, Table VI
    Zachary Philip/Zacharie-Philippe, 171-173, Table VI, Table VII
de Fontenai, Richard, 70

Fontenay-le-Marmion/Fonteneys in France, 37, 64, 65, 66, 67, 68, 69, 70, *Map Six*
de Fonteneys, Ellene, 66
de Fonteneys, Jordan, 66, 71
de Fonteneys, Thomas, 66, 71
1st Foot Guards, 110, 126, 176
13th Foot Regiment, 133, 177, *and see* Earl of Barrymore's Regiment *and* Somereset Light Infantry
le Forestier, Guillaume, 53
la Forestier, Jeanne, wife of Raoul Champion, 37, 53, 55, 56, Table II
le Forestier, Sebastien, father of Jeanne, 53; his widow, 53
Formigny (battle 1450), 44
Foucault, Nicolas-Joseph, 92
Fourey, Nicolas, 53
Fox, Charles James, British politician, 140, 173
francs-fiefs nobility, 47, 73, *and see* noblesse
France, kings and queens, 5
    Catherine de Medici, widow of Henri II then regent Queen-Dowager, 80
    Charles IV, 43
    Charles V, 36, 43, 45; as Dauphin, 43, 48
    Charles VI, 36-37, 43, 60, 64, 67. 69
    Charles VII, 37, 47
    Charles IX, 79
    François/Francis II, 37, 79
    Henri, II, 80
    Henri III, 37, 79, 80
    Henri IV, 37, 77, 80. 83, 97
    John II, 39, 42
    Louis VI le Gros, 58-60
    Louis IX [Saint Louis], 67, 69, 70
    Louis X, 43
    Louis XIII, 77, 80, 82, 84, 94, 97
    Louis XIV, 2, 78, 90, 95, 96-97, 99, 100, 105, 106, 109, 115, 120, 127
    Louis XV, 7, 95, 106
    Louis XVI, 47, 89, 94, 106, 115
    Louis XVIII, 47, 74-75
    Louis XI, 47
    Philip IV, 43
    Philip VI, 43
    Philip Augustus, 36, 39

France, Wars of Religion (sixteenth century), 12, 37; War of the Three Henrys (1587-1589), 37, 80
France, Revolution (eighteenth century), 12, 74, 139, 141
France, Napoleonic empire, 140, *and see* Napoleon Buonaparte
France, nationality legislation, 107
Francis, Duke of Anjou, 80
Freemasons/Freemasonry, 166, 174
French Church of the Savoy, 78, 103, 105, 111, 112
French Churches in London, General Assembly, 111
French Hospital *La Providence*, London, 4, 17, 29, 33, 99, 102, 111-112, 121, 139, 153; Director, 31, 99, 108, 111-112, 145, 150, 153; Secretary, 139, 154
Frênes in France, 40, 50, *Map Six*; putative arms of the baronial family, 44; Huguenot congregation, 83, 99

Garrett, Charles, lawyer at the Court of Arches, 124, 147
Garric, Peter, son of David Garrick, 122
Garrick, David, actor, 122, 169
Gascoin, Judith, wife of Pierre de Vierville, 30-31, 102, Table III
Gaudy, Pierre, husband of Susanne/ Susanna CdeC (1656-1726), 113, Table III
Geelong in Victoria, Australia, 179
généralité [administrative unit], 92, *and see by place-name*
General [military rank], 122, *and see* Board of General Officers *and individual names*
Geneva in Switzerland, 37, 79, 114-116, *Map Fourteen*
Gentleman Usher at Court, 161
Gentleman Volunteer, *see* Volunteer
George of Denmark, Prince, consort of Queen Anne, 131-132
Germany, 3, 14, 37, 67, 77, 78-79, 82, 84, 86, 93-94, 97, 102, *and see* Holy Roman Empire
Ghent in Flanders, 119
Gibraltar, 133-134, 177, *Map Fifteen*; siege (1704-1705), 111, 122, 129; siege (1727), 133

Gladell, James, *see* Vernon, James Gladell
Gladstone, William, Prime Minister, 144
Glasscock/Glascock family, 126-127, 134-135
Glasscock, Elizabeth, wife of Gabriel CdeC and mother of Elizabeth CdeC (*c*.1683-*c*.1735), 19, 24, 110, 126-127, 133, Table III, Table IV
Glasscock, Harry, cousin of Elizabeth CdeC (*c*.1683-*c*.1735), 134-135, Table IV
Glasscock, Ignatius, Table IV
Glasscock, Mary, sister of Elizabeth the wife of Gabriel CdeC, 127, Table IV
Glasscock, William, father of Elizabeth the wife of Gabriel CdeC, 126-127, 134, Table IV
Glasscock, William, brother of Elizabeth the wife of Gabriel CdeC, 127, 134, Table IV
Glasscock, William, cousin of Elizabeth CdeC (*c*.1683-*c*.1735), 134, Table IV
Glorious Revolution, 140, *and see* King James II *sub* [Great] Britain
Gloucestershire, 166; North Gloucestershire militia, 166
Glover, Bonouvrier, first husband of Anne CdeC (1765-1780), 157-160, Table V
Glover, Richard I, father of Bonouvrier, 157
Glover, Richard II, brother of Bonouvrier, 161
Gorges, Richard, Lord, 128-129; his Regiment [35th Foot], 126, 129-131, 133, *and see* Donegall's Regiment
Goslin/Gosselin, Frances, 113
Goslin/Gosselin, Georges, first husband of Marie CdeC (1655-1736), 103-104, 113, Table III
Granger family, 120, 122, 140, 179
Granger:
   Elizabeth, 125
   Israel, father of Magdalen/Magdelaine and of Marthe/Martha, 120, 125
   Israel, father of Paul Desnoës, 120
   Magdalen/Magdelaine, wife of Thomas CdeC (1664-1712), 17, 24, 106, 110, 113-114, 119-121, 123-125, 137-139, 140, 147, 153, Table III, Table V

INDEX

Granger [*continued*]:
    Marie nee Billon, mother of Magdalen/Magdelaine and of Marthe/Martha, 120, 124
    Marthe/Martha, 120, 124, 156
    Paul Desnoës, 120
    Gretna Green in Scotland, 178
Great Company, bandit group, 43
Greencoat School at Camberwell, 154
Grisons in Switzerland, 114
Guards regiments, British army, 122, 135
    Grenadier Guards, *see* 1st Foot Guards
Le Gué, in France, 23; Henri du Gué, 56, 77, 82
Guernsey in the Channel Islands, 120, 127-128, *and see* 1st Foot Guards
Guise family, 79
    Henri, Duke of Guise, 37, 80
Gybbon, Johann, Bluemantle Pursuivant, 19

The Hague in Holland, 116
Hamburg in Germany, 116, 150, 157
Handley, Betsy Hodges, second wife of Philip CdeC (1738-1803), 139, **167-169**, Table V
Handley, Joseph, father of Betsy Hodges, 168
Hanover, 115; Elector, 115
Hanover Square in London, 160; St Georges church, 160, 176, 178
Hapsburg family, 78, 82, 84, *and see* Holy Roman Empire *and* Spain
Hardi, Etienne, 54, 77
Harefield House near Uxbridge, west of London, 177
Harfleur in France, *see* Le Havre
Harley, Robert, Earl of Oxford and Lord Treasurer, 124, 141
Harrison, James, Lieutenant-Colonel, 126
Hartley-Owen, Jane, 161
Hassobury in Essex, 134
Hastings (battle 1066), 39
Le Havre in France, *Map One*
Heaton, Isaac I, 139, 162-163
Heaton, Isaac II, 162-163
Heaton Arms tavern at Peckham, 163
Heaton's Folly at Peckham, 163, *Map Seventeen*
Hebert, Elizabeth, 156

Hebert, Martha Susanna nee Dauteuil, 156, Table VII
Hebert, Thomas, 156
Hemet, Pierre, husband of Renée CdeC (1667-1744), 114, Table III
Henri de Bourbon, King of Navarre and later Henri IV of France *q.v.*, 37, 80
Henry of Huntingdon, *Historia Anglorum*, 59
heraldry, 1-4, 47-48, *and see* Champion *and* Champion de Crespigny, arms/shields
heraldry: heraldic heiress, 87-88
heraldry, recording and regulation of, 1-2, *and see* College of Arms *and* High Court of Chivalry *and* Visitations
Hertfordshire, 168, 174
Heywood, Elizabeth, wife of Abel Fonnereau, Table VI
High Court of Chivalry, 2, 153
Hintlesham Hall near Ipswich in Suffolk, 174-175, 178
Hispaniola in the West Indies, 159
Holland, 115, 127, *and see* United Provinces
Holy Roman Empire, 78, 84, 116
    Emperor Charles V, 61, 67
Honfleur in France, *Map One*
Horsley, John, husband of Maria CdeC (1776-1858), 177
Horsnell, Thomas, of Inner Temple, 134
Hotham, Sir Charles, 123; his Regiment, 111, 122-123, 124
Howe, John, Paymaster General, 124
Huguenots [*also as* Protestants *and as members of the* "Reformed Religion"], 37, 54, 77-107; oppression and emigration, 97-106, 109, 111, 119; in England, 103-107, 135, 147 *et saepe*
Huguenots in the British Army, 106
Hundred Years War (fourteenth and fifteenth centuries), 36, 42, 56, 89
Hungerford Market in London, chapel, 113
Hurien, Baron and Viscount [Richard Champion], 77, 83, 95
Hyde Chronicle, 59

Ile de France [province], 58, *Map Two*
Inner Temple, London, 111, 124, 137, 140, 146, 147

200

Intendant, 91; Intendant of Lower Normandy/Généralité of Caen, 24, 92, *and see* Chamillart

Ipswich in Suffolk, 154, 171, 174, *Map Eighteen*; parliamentary borough, 160

Ireland, 25, 32, 66, 103, 106, 111, 128-130, 132, 133, 134-135; Chancellor, 161

Irish Establishment of the British army, 121

Ipswich in Suffolk, 154, 172, *Map Eighteen*

Isabelle, daughter of King Philip IV of France, 43

Italy, 114

Jamaica in the West Indies, 23, 167

James, John, first husband of Charlotte Frances nee Dana, 6, 179

Jean l'Anglais, 27, 37, 50

Jedburgh in Scotland, 120

Jedburgh, Lord [William Ker/Kerr], 119; his Regiment of Dragoons, 110, 119, 128

Jelf-Reveley family, *see* Reveley

Joan of Arc, 37, 44

Joan, daughter of King Louis X of France, 43

Johnson, Dr Samuel, 169

Katherine, daughter of King Charles VI of France and wife of King Henry V of England, 43

Keane, Sir John, second husband of Dorothea nee Scott, 170-171, 177

Keane, George Michael, son of Dorothea nee Scott, 170

Kelmarsh Hall, Northamptonshire, 10, 18, 54, 60, 104, 158; family portraits, 54, 83, 88, 104, 145, 154, 158, 165, 167, 169, 170

Kelmarsh Book, **16-17**, 33, 84,-85, 86, 89

Kent, 156

Ker/Kerr, William, *i.e.* Lord Jedburgh *and later* Marquess of Lothian *qq.v.*

Knight Rider/Knightriders Street in London, 153

La Gudiña in Spain (battle 1709) *i.e.* battle on the Caya

Lake Llangors in Wales, 176

Lamb, Charles, essayist, 144

Lambeth Palace of the Archbishop of Canterbury, library, 155

Lamotte Blagny *i.e.* Jacob Philippe de Bechevel de la Motte de Blagny, 29, 86, 99

Lancashire, 128, 131

Lancaster, Cecily Valencia, 10, 13, 16, 18, 60

Lancaster Book, 3, **13-16**, 18, 24, 25, 33, 34, 38, 40, 50, 52, 66, 72, 74, 83, 84, 86, 93, 99, 101, 104, 105, 107, 112, 147, 156

La Providence, see French Hospital

La Rochelle in France, 77, 80, 82, 84, 97, 150, *Map Eleven*

Lart, Charles Edmund, modern scholar, 29

Laz in France, 73

Leathes, Cartaret MP, 171

Lensentière in Brittany, 22, 41, 72

Lettres Francoises, see *Daumont Letters*

Leicester Fields in London, 168

Leicester House in London, 148

Lieutenant [military rank], 119, 122, 123, 127, 130, 133

Lieutenant [naval rank], 119, 122, 123, 127, 130, 133

Lieutenant-Colonel [military rank], 127, 166

Lieutenant-General [military rank], 131, 133, 178

Limehouse in London, 156

Lincoln's Inn in London, 162

Lincoln's Inn Fields, London, 165

Lincolnshire, 160

Lisbon in Portugal, *Map Fifteen*

Little Ilford in Essex, 162

Liverpool in Lancashire, 131

Liverpool in New South Wales, Australia, 177

Llangasty Talyllyn near Brecon in Wales, 174, 176

London, *passim*, *Map Two*

London Hotel at Leicester Fields, London, 168

Lorne, Lord [Archibald Campbell], 119; his Regiment of Foot, 119, 127

Lothian, Marquess [William Ker/Kerr], 119, 123; his Regiment, 119-121, 128

Louis de Bourbon, 79

Lovedil, Urban, 117

INDEX

Luther, Martin, 37, 78; Lutheranism/ Lutherans, 78-79, 105, *Map Eleven*

Madrid in Spain, *Map Fifteen*
Magny[-la-Campagne?] in France, 37, 53, 55
maisons de charité/houses of charity [alms-houses], 102, 112
Maitland, Fuller, 14-18, 33
Maine [province in France], *Map Two*
Magistrate, 177, 179
Major [military rank], 19, 165, 177
Maldon in Essex, 68
Malplaquet (battle 1709), 132
Manchester in Lancashire, 131
Marguerye/de Marguerye family, 89
　　Gilles de Marguerye, 89
Marie de Medici, Queen of France, 80
Marlborough, Duke [John Churchill], 132, 133
Marmion family, 61-61; 67, shield, 61-62
Marmion, Robert de, 67, 70
Marmion d'Urvyle family, 62, 68, 69; shield, 62; see also Urvylle
marriage contracts, 52-53, 80-81
Martyn, John, Table VI
Martyn, Margaret, Table VI, Table VII
Marye, Catherine, wife of Antoine Champion, 37, 55, Table II
Marylebone in London, 105; church of St Marylebone, 85, 105, 168; Register, 117, 147; CdeC memorial, 85; burial vault, 105-106, 112, 114, 125, 147, 155, 168, 169, 170
Master of the Horse [royal official], 161
de Matignon, Count Charles de Goyon, *lieutenant-général* of Normandy, 81-82
Matrimonial Causes Act (1857), 147, *and see* Court of Arches *and* divorce
Mauduit, Piers, Windsor Herald, 19
Maulèvrier, Count de, 82
Maximilian, Elector of Bavaria, 127
Melley/Mellé in France, 55
Mensant, Hector [*also surnamed* D'Oüessé], 22, 36, 41, 72, Table I
Mensant, the Demoiselle, wife of Richard Champion (*fl.*1390), 19, 41, 72, Table I
Meredith/Meredyth, General Thomas, 133, his Regiment [20th Foot], 133

Merionethshire, Wales, 21, 147; Deputy Lieutenant, 147; High Sheriff, 147, 161
Merton College, Oxford, 169
Midshipman [naval rank], 160, 167, 177
Mills, Edward, lawyer at Inner Temple, 124
Minet, William, modern scholar, 28-29, 31, 33
Minorca, 132, *Map Fifteen*
Miremont, Marquis [Armand de Bourbon], his Regiment, 120-121
Moller/Champion lineage and legend, **60-65**, 66 *and see* le Champion
　　Andreas von Mollerus, 67
　　Andrew George Moller/Müller, 61
　　Charles Champion le Champion-Mollerus *and similar names*, 61, 66
　　Fra[nci]s Oläus von Mollerus, 67
　　Henricus von Mollerus, 61
　　Henry von Mollerus le Champion/ Henry Le Champion-Möller, 61
　　Joachim von Mollerus, 61
　　Johan von Moller, 61
　　Olaus le Champion Moller, 67
Mont Pinçon in France, 38
Mont-Saint-Michel in France, 38, 62
Montandre, Marquis, his Regiment, 124
Montauban in France, 80
Montpellier in France, 80
Mortain in France, 52, 53, 82

Namur in Flanders, 110, 127
Nantes in France, *Map Eleven, and see* Edict of Nantes *and its* Revocation
Napoleon Buonaparte, 75; his empire, 140; Napoleonic Wars, 140, 141, 163, 167; Peninsula War, 177
naturalisation to England, 78, 102, 103-104, 105, 106, 110, 111, 114, 125
Navarre, kingdom, 43; kings:
　　Charles the Bad, 43
　　Henri de Bourbon, later Henri IV of France, *q.v.*, 37, 80
Nelson, Admiral Horatio, 160, 167
Netherlands, the, 97, 102, 106, 127, 177, *and see* Flanders, Belgium *and* United Provinces
The New Briton, journal, 169-170
New England, American colonies, 131

New Forest, England, 155, 166
New South Wales, Australia, 177
Nimes in France, 80
noblesse/noble status, 24, 39-40, 47, 48-49, 56, 81, 120, 178; and liability to the *taille* tax, 24, 39-40, 81, **90-96**; Chapter of Nobles in a parish, 77, 81, 92; *francs-fiefs* system, 47; purchase, 95-96; law cases, 24, 81, *and see* Court of Aides
Norfolk, 161, 168, 175
Normandy [province in France], 5, 7, 58, 178, *Map Two*, *Map Nine*, *Map Ten*; geography, 37-38; shield, v
    feudal rulers, 38
        Duke Charles, later King Charles V of France, 39
        Duke John, later King John II of France, 39
        Rollo, 38
        Duke Robert I, 5, 36, 38
        Duke Robert II Curthose, 36, 39
        Duke William, 5, 36, *also* King William I of England *q.v.*
    ducal officers, 7;
        Champion, 4-5, 63-65
    English conquest and possession (1407-1450), 36, 47
    royal administration, 38-39; *lieutenant-général*/Lieutenant-Governor, 82
Normandy, Lower [*Basse-Normandie*], 38, 80, *Map One*; Intendant, 39
Normandy, Upper [*Haute-Normandie*], 38
North, Lord [Frederick], Prime Minister, 173
Norway, 61
Nova Scotia, 132; Lieutenant-Governor, 132
Nyon in Switzerland, 116-117, *Map Fourteen*

Old Palace Yard in Westminster, 174
Opie, John, portrait painter, 170
Omaha Beach [D-Day landing-place] (1944), 8, 89
Ordericus Vitalis, *Historia Ecclesiastica*, 59
Orwell Park in Suffolk, 160
Outer Temple in London, 146
Oxford University, 11, 109, 147, 162, 169

Pamplona in Spain, 177
Paris in France, 6, 37, 42, 79, 83, 99, 102, *Map Two*, *Map Eleven*; treaty (1783), 139
parish [administrative unit], 91, *and see by place-name and/or church*
Parliament, British, 109, 171; Houses of Parliament [buildings], 174; House of Commons, 171; House of Lords, 109; Member of Parliament [MP], 137, 139, 157, 161, 176, 177, 178, *and see* constituencies; electoral procedure, 139-140, 171
The Pavillion, novel attributed to Mary CdeC nee Clark, 164
Peckham in London, 163, *Map Seventeen*
Peckham Lodge, *Map Seventeen*
Pedigree Book, 21, **24-25**, 32, 33, 84, 106
Pelham-Holles, Thomas, Duke of Newcastle, 162
Pellot, Monseigneur, First President at Rouen, 30
Peterborough, Lord [Charles Mordaunt], 130-131
Peterloo massacre (1819), 167
Pettit, transcriber of *Daumont Letters*, 29, 33
Phipps, Elizabeth, mother of Eliza Julia Trent, 178
Pierrepont family, 85, 93, 101, 104, 113, 114, 119
    Antoine de Pierrepont, husband of Judith nee de Vierville, 101, Table III
    Antoine/Anthony de Pierrepont, son of Antoine and Judith nee de Vierville, 101, 103-104, Table III
    Etienne/Stephen de Pierrepont, 101, 104, Table III
    Jacques de Pierrepont, 101, Table III
    Judith de Pierrepont, 101, 103, 117, Table III
    Pierre/Peter de Pierrepont, 101, 103, Table III
    Stephen de Pierrepont, *see* Etienne/Stephen
Pitt, William [the Younger], Prime Minister, 173
Plymouth, Earl, 19, 166, *and see* Other Lewis Windsor

INDEX

Poitiers, 100; battle (1356), 36, 42
Poitou [province in France], 100, *Map Two*
Poole in Dorset, 133
Port Royal, Jamaica, 167
Portland Place in Bath, Somerset, 174-175
Portsmouth in Hampshire, 159
Portugal, 128, 130, 133, *Map Fifteen*
Presbyterians, 105
Proctor/procurator, *see* Court of Arches *and* Admiralty Court
Protestants, *see* Huguenots, *also* Calvinists, Lutherans, Presbyterians; non-conformists [in England], 105
Prussia, 166; King Frederick William, 166
purchase of commissions in the British Army, 121-122, 127-128, 132, 135
purchase of noble rank/title in France, 96-97
Pyrenees (battle 1812), 177

Queen's Regiment of Foot, 131

Read, Catherine/Katherine, pastel portraitist, 158
Recherche de Noblesse en la généralité de Caen, *see* Chamillart, Guy
reconnaissance, 78, 103
recruitment for the British army, 130, 132
Reims in France, 37, 44
Rennes in France, 72
Reveley family [later Jelf-Reveley], 21
Reveley, Henry, husband of Jane CdeC (1765-1829), 17, 21, 23, 32, 125, 147, 162, Table V
Reveley, Henry John, 23, 26, 161
Reveley, Hugh, 21, 23, 125, 146, 162, Table V
Reveley Book, 15, **21-23**, 24, 25-26, 32, 33, 40, 50, 52, 53, 55, 66, 71, 74, 83, 84, 112, 162, 173
Réville in France, *Map Twelve*
Richard family, 93
Richard, Adrian, 54, 56, 77, 78, 81, 83
Richard, Marguerite, daughter of Adrian Richard and wife of Richard Champion (d.1659), 31, 54, 56, 77, 78, 81-83, Table II, Table III
Richard de Humeto, 7
Richards, John, Major-General, 122

Richelieu, Cardinal Armand Jean du Plessis, 82, 84, 95
Richmond House at Twickenham, 165
La Rivière, in France, 48
de la Rivière, family, [19-20], 41, 48
    Jeanne de la Rivière, wife of Michel Champion (*fl.*1415), 37, 41, Table I, Table II
Robert of Moulins, 67
Roman Catholicism/Catholics, in France, 78, 79-80, 83, 84, 89, 97, 100-103, *and see* Catholic League; in England, 78, 103, 106
Romney, George, portrait painter, 158, 169, 170
Rouen in France, 13, 30, 39, 44, 78, 82, 92-93, 99, *Map One*, *Map Two*
Round, Horace, modern scholar, 1, 24, 47, 52, 56, 61, 70-71, 90-96
Royal Exchange, London, 148
Royal Horse Guards, 177
Royal Navy, 157, 163, 167, *and see* Admiralty *and* Captain [naval rank]
Royal Navy ships:
    HMS Argo, 159
    HMS Favourite, 158
    HMS Hind, 158
    HMS Janus, 159
    HMS Spartiate, 167
    HMS Tartar, 158
    HMS Unicorn, 158
Royal Society, 150
Royal Toxophilite Society [Society of Royal British Archers], 164
Russell, John Somerset, second husband of Augusta Anne CdeC, 176

Saint Barberie, 67, *and see* Barbery
Saint Bartholemew's Day Massacre (1562), 37, 80
Saint-Germain-en-Laye, 98, 177
Saint Hermies/Hermes, 68
Saint-Jean-le-Blanc, 6, 30-31, 81, 84, 89-93, *Map Three*
Saint Lô in France, 31, 44, 56, 74, *Map One*
Saint Malô in Brittany, 38, 179, *Map One*
Saint-Opportune in France, 38, 53, 55
Saint-Quentin-les-Chardonnets, 50, 54, 53
Salic Law, 43-44, 116

INDEX

Salisbury Cathedral, 125
Salisbury, Marquess [James Cecil], 173
Saumur in France, 80
Savoy, 105 *and see* French Church of the Savoy; Peter of Savoy, 105
Schomberg/Schönberg, Marshal and Duke, 97
Scotland, 97, 111, 118, 119
    Scottish Establishment of the British army, 119, 121
Scott, Dorothy, fourth wife of Philip CdeC (1738-1803), 139, 162, **170,** 174, 176, 179, Table V; portrait, 170
Scott, George, brother of Dorothy, 170
Scott, Elizabeth, mother of Dorothy, 170
Scott, Richard, father of Dorothy, 170
Scott, Richard, brother of Dorothy, 175
Scrivelsby in Lincolnshire, England, 67, 70
Scrope *v.* Grosvenor, heraldic law case, 2
Seize-Quartiers/"Sixteen Quarterings," 28, 68-69
Selwyn, Anne, Table VI, Table VII
Sergeant Surgeon in the royal household, 150
Seven Years War (1756-1763), 139, 159
Seymour, Lieutenant-General William, Colonel of the Queen's Regiment of Foot, 132
Shelburne, Earl [William Petty], Prime Minister, 173
Shiers, Elizabeth, wife of William Glasscock, Table IV
Shipbroke in Cheshire, barony, 159; Earl, 161, *and see* Francis Vernon; Dowager Countess Alice, 161
Shottesbroke/Shottisbroke, Sir Robert, 37, 64-65, 67
Shrewsbury (battle 1403), 160
Shuttleworth, Thomas, embezzler, 139, 142
Silverthorne family, *see* Thorne family
Simpson, Edward, Master of Trinity Hall, 162
slave trade, 142-143
Smijth, Caroline, wife of Augustus James CdeC (1765-1829) and later of Herbert CdeC, 14, 18, 28, 33
Smijth, William, 14, 28
Smith, William MP, 172

Somerset Light Infantry [13th Foot], 177, *and see* Earl of Barrymore's Regiment
Soulet, Mr [advocate], 98-99
South Sea Book, **18-21**, 22, 24, 25, 32, 40, 52, 53, 55, 66, 71, 74, 83, 84
South Sea Company, 114, 124, 139, 140-145, 162, 179; South Sea Bubble (1720), 112, 124, 137, 141; South Sea House, 137, 143-145, *and see* Claude CdeC (1706-1782)
Southampton in Hampshire, 155, 166; parliamentary borough, 166-167
Spain, 80, 84, 97, 111, 115, 122-123, 128-130, 131, 142, 177, *Map Fifteen*
    King Philip II, 80
    Bourbon kings, 130
Spenser, the Honourable John, 146
Spitalfields in London, 102
Spithead naval base, 159
St Albans in Hertfordshire, 168, 169
St Benet Fink parish in London, 125
St James parish in Westminster/London, 19, 120
St Martin-in-the-Fields parish in London, 168, *and see* churches
Stephens, Lieutenant George RN, 159
Stainforth, George, 161
Stockport in Cheshire, 156
Stoke Newington in London, 156
Stowmarket in Suffolk, 154, 172, *Map Eighteen*
Sudbury in Suffolk, 172, *Map Eighteen*; parliamentary borough, 139, 154, 171-172, 174, 176
Suffolk, 139, 156, 161, 162, 168, 171-172, 174, 175, *Map Eighteen*
Surrey, 156, 174
Sutton, Richard, husband of Susanna CdeC (1735-1766), 157-158, 161
Sweden, 61, 115-116
Switzerland, 86, 103, 110, 115-116, 135

taille tax, 24, 32, **90-93**, *and see* noble status; sale of exemption, 95
Talyllynn House near Brecon in Wales, 174
Tamworth in Staffordshire, England, 67, 70; Baron Baldwin de Freville, 70
Tangier, 128
témoignage, 13, 103

INDEX

temple [Huguenot place of worship], 79, 84, 97, 100, 103, *and see by place-name and congregation*
Temple des Isles at Proussy in Calvados, 81
le Tellier, Michel, royal Chancellor, 99-100, 102
Terra Nova fortress at Namur in Flanders, 127
Tessy-sur-Vire in France, *Map Thirteen*
Thellusson, Augusta Charlotte, wife of Thomas CdeC (1763-1799), 176
Thetford in Norfolk, 172, *Map Eighteen*; Recorder, 168
Thirty Years War, 78, 82, 84
Thomas, Pierre, 54, 56, 77, Table II
Thorne family, 126
Thorne, Oliver, 126
Threadneedle Street, London, 125, 143
Tinchebray in France, 38, 40, 46, 50, 53, 54, 84, *Map One, Map Ten, Map Thirteen*; battle (1106), 36, 39, 58, 60
Toker, Edward, husband of Clarissa CdeC (1775-1801), 177
Torigny/Torigni-sur-Vire in France, *Map Thirteen*
Torriano, John Samuel, 125
Touraine [province in France], *Map Two*
Le Tourneur in France, 54
Trafalgar (battle 1805), 167
Trent, Eliza Julia, wife of Charles [James] Fox CdeC (1785-1875), 178
Trent, John, father of Eliza Julia, 178
Trévières in France, 30, *Map One, Map Twelve*; Huguenot congregation, 29, 32, 78, 90, 97-101, 103, 111, *and see Daumont Letters*
trial by combat, 1, 5
Trinity Hall, Cambridge, 139, 161-162, 166; Master, 162; Fellow, 162; Scholar, 162, 176
Troyes, treaty (1410), 37, 43, 48
Turenne, Marshal, 97
Twickenham, London, 165
Tyrrell, Marie, wife of Claude William CdeC (1818-1865), 16
Tyrrell, John Tyson, 16

United Provinces, Dutch, 115, *and see* The Netherlands *and* Holland

Urville in France, 37, 62, 64-65, 67-69, 71, *Map Six*
Urville/Urvylle lineage, *and see* Moller/Champion
Urvylle, Guillaume, 67, 70
Urvylle, Richard, 67, 70; Ricard, 67-68
Urvylle and Bretvyle, Bertrand, 68 [*i.e.* Bertrand le Champion *q.v.*]
Urvylle and Bretvyle, Jean I, 68
Urvylle and Bretvyle, Jean II, 68
Urvylle and Bretvyle, Maheas, 68 [*i.e.* Maheas Champion *q.v.*]
Urvylle and Bretvyle, Oliver, 68
Urvylle and Bretvyle, Roger, 68
Urvylle and Bretvyle, Roland, 68
Urvylle and Moulins, Robert, 67, 70
Uxbridge near London, 177

Va-nu-pieds "Barefooters" rebellion, 82
Vaillant, Guillaume, husband of Magdelaine Champion, 52, 55, Table II
van Loo, Jean-Baptiste, portrait painter, 145, 155
Vassy in Calvados, France, 54, 80, *Map Ten, Map Thirteen*
Vassy/Wassy in Haute-Marne, Massacre (1552), 37, 79
Vauban, Sebastien Le Prestre de Vauban, military engineer, 127
Vaucelles in France, *Map Twelve*; Huguenot congregation, 29-31, 32, 78, 97-100, 111, *and see Daumont Letters*
Verdun in France, 140, 177
Vernon family, 159-160; arms, 160
Vernon, Admiral Edward, 160
Vernon, Francis, Earl of Shipbroke, 160
Vernon, James I, 160
Vernon, James II, 160
Vernon, James Gladell, second husband of Anne CdeC (1739-1797), 159-162, Table V
Versailles, 99
Vexin in France, 38, 58
Vienna in Austria, 116
Vierville in Manche 50840, 38, 89, *Map One, Map Twelve*
Vierville-sur-Mer, Calvados 14610, 8, 10, 13, 14, 38, 77, 84, 86, 89, 93, 96, 99, 126, *Map One, Map Four, Map Five, Map Twelve*; chateau, 89

Vierville/de Vierville family, 85, 94, 96; arms/shield, 87-88, 96
    de Vierville, Judith, wife of Antoine de Pierrepont, 101, 103, Table III
    de Vierville, Judith, wife of Pierre de Vierville, *see* Judith nee Gascoin
    de Vierville, Marie (1628-1708), wife of Claude CdeC (1620-1695), 3, 4, 5, 8, 13, 14, 19, 23, 27, 29, 31, 32, 37, 69, 77, 78, **84-90**, 101-102, 103, 104-105, 106, 109, 110, 111, 114, 137, 178, Table II, Table III; portrait, 88; her title as Countess/*comtesse*, 84, 88
    de Vierville, Pierre (d.1699), 8, 78, 84-85, 88, Table III
Villeroy, Duke, president of the royal Council, 98
Vire in France, 36, 37, 38, 43, 46, 50, 53, 74, 82, 83, *Map One, Map Six, Map Ten, Map Thirteen*; castle, 45; *élection* [tax district] and *élus* [electors], 90-91, 93; Huguenot congregation, 83, 84, 99
Vire, Viscount/viscounty, 36, 40, 45-46, 48, 61-62, 65, 67, 69
Vire River in France, 38, *Map One*
viscounties in Normandy, 39, 46, 62
Visitations. heraldic, 1, 127, 134
Vivian, Richard Hussey, first Baron Vivian, 140, 178
[Gentleman] Volunteer/gentleman ranker [military rank], 111, 119, 122, 123, 126, 133

Wade, Emilia, wife of Philip CdeC (1765-1852), 140, 177
Wagner, Henry, modern scholar, 29
Walcheren in The Netherlands, 177
Wales, 21, 147, 162, 166, 174
Walpole, Robert, Prime Minister, 141, 171
Walton on Thames, Surrey, 174
War of the League of Augsburg [War of the English Succession] (1688-1697), 110
War of the Spanish Succession] (1702-1715), 111, 128, 132, 141, 149

Wardour Street, London, 104, 114
Warner, Dr John, 173
Waterloo (battle 1815), 140, 176
Watts, Sarah, first wife of Isaac Heaton I, 162
Wellington, Duke [Arthur Wellesley], 140, 177, 178
West Indies, 129, 130, *and see* Hispaniola *and* Jamaica; West Indies squadron [Royal Navy], 159
Westminster, 19, 126
Westphalia, Peace of (1648), 82
whaling, 141
Whatley, Joseph, second husband of Augusta Charlotte nee Thellusson, 176
Wigan in Lancashire, 127, 131-132, 135
Wilkes, John, politician, 169-170; *The New Briton*, 169-170
Wilkes, Mary, wife of Joseph Clerk and later of Isaac Heaton I, mother of Mary Clark, 161-162
William Clito, son of Duke Robert II of Normandy, 58
William Crispin, 59-60
William de Crespigny, 58, *and see* William Crispin
William de Mesheudin, lord of Crespigny, 7
Windsor, Other Lewis, Earl of Plymouth, and father of Sarah, 19, 166
Windsor, Lady Sarah, wife of William CdeC (1765-1829), 19, 166
Wine Office Court at Fleet Street, London, 168
Wittenoom and Crespigny [proctors in partnership], 147 *and see* Philip CdeC (1738-1803)
Wivenhoe Hall, Essex, 14, 17
Wolley, Rebecca, of Wine Office Court, 168
Woodbridge, Mr, member of the Camberwell Club, 155

York Herald, 27
Yorkshire, 161
Yorktown, USA (siege 1781), 139, 160, 173

www.ingramcontent.com/pod-product-compliance
Lightning Source LLC
Chambersburg PA
CBHW041714290426
44110CB00025B/2833